"This book will serve as an excellent guide to Taiwan's contemporary and future security risks, offering the reader updated assessments on Taiwan's strategic choices. It is one of those rare gems that all students and practitioners of Taiwan security affairs, Asia-Pacific strategic studies, and foreign policy should own."

Assoc. Prof. Dr Adam Leong Kok Wey, *Senior Lecturer, National Defence University of Malaysia*

The Taiwan Issue

While global attention has been focused on other regional issues, such as China-US tensions and North Korea's nuclear ambitions, little attention has been paid to Taiwan. Yet the so-called Taiwan issue, namely the continued separation of the island from mainland China, remains a major regional security challenge that could potentially spark direct conflict involving the USA, China and Japan, the three largest economies in the world, two of which are nuclear powers. Although Taiwan has continued to find opportunities to maintain the current status quo despite a deteriorating geostrategic environment as a result of the rise of China and the uncertainties of the Trump Administration, its room for manoeuvre continues to narrow. This volume examines the challenges and evaluates the prospects for preventing conflict on the Taiwan Strait by focusing on the political conditions that Taiwan faces internally and externally.

Benjamin Schreer is Professor and Head of the Department of Security Studies and Criminology, Macquarie University, Sydney, Australia. Previous positions include senior analyst for defence strategy at the Australian Strategic Policy Institute; senior lecturer at the Strategic and Defence Studies Centre at the Australian National University; and senior analyst at the German Institute for International and Security Studies (Stiftung Wissenschaft und Politik). He has published widely on international security and defence affairs, including East Asian strategic trends.

Andrew T. H. Tan is Associate Professor in the Department of Security Studies and Criminology, Macquarie University, Sydney, Australia. He was previously Associate Professor at the University of New South Wales and Senior Lecturer at Kings College London, UK. Andrew has published 19 sole authored, edited and co-edited books, and over 60 refereed journal and chapter articles. Some of his latest books include: *Terrorism and Insurgency in Asia* (London: Routledge, 2019), *The United States in Asia* (Cheltenham: Edward Elgar, 2018) and *US–China Relations* (Cheltenham: Edward Elgar, 2016).

Europa Country Perspectives

The *Europa Country Perspectives* series, from Routledge, examines a wide range of contemporary political, economic, developmental and social issues from areas around the world. Complementing the *Europa Regional Surveys of the World series*, *Europa Country Perspectives* is a valuable resource for academics, students, researchers, policymakers, business people and anyone with an interest in current world affairs.

While the *Europa World Year Book* and its associated Regional Surveys inform on and analyse contemporary economic, political and social developments at the national and regional level, Country Perspectives provide in-depth, country-specific volumes written or edited by specialists in their field, delving into a country's particular situation. Volumes in the series are not constrained by any particular template, but may explore a country's recent political, economic, international relations, social, defence, or other issues in order to increase understanding.

Beyond the Drug War in Mexico: Human rights, the public sphere and justice
Wil G. Pansters, Benjamin T. Smith, Peter Watt

Greece in the 21st Century: The Politics and Economics of a Crisis
Edited by Constantine Dimoulas and Vassilis K. Fouskas

The Basque Contention: Ethnicity, Politics, Violence
Ludger Mees

Bolivia: Geopolitics of a Landlocked State
Ronald Bruce St John

The Taiwan Issue: Problems and Prospects
Benjamin Schreer and Andrew T. H. Tan

For more information about this series, please visit: www.routledge.com/Europa-Country-Perspectives/book-series/ECP

The Taiwan Issue
Problems and Prospects

Edited by
Benjamin Schreer and Andrew T. H. Tan

LONDON AND NEW YORK

First published 2020
by Routledge
2 Park Square, Milton Park, Abingdon, Oxon OX14 4RN

and by Routledge
605 Third Avenue, New York, NY 10017

First issued in paperback 2021

Routledge is an imprint of the Taylor & Francis Group, an informa business

© 2020 Benjamin Schreer and Andrew T. H. Tan

The right of Benjamin Schreer and Andrew T. H. Tan to be identified as the authors of the editorial material, and of the authors for their individual chapters, has been asserted in accordance with sections 77 and 78 of the Copyright, Designs and Patents Act 1988.

All rights reserved. No part of this book may be reprinted or reproduced or utilised in any form or by any electronic, mechanical, or other means, now known or hereafter invented, including photocopying and recording, or in any information storage or retrieval system, without permission in writing from the publishers.

Trademark notice: Product or corporate names may be trademarks or registered trademarks, and are used only for identification and explanation without intent to infringe.

Europa Commissioning Editor: Cathy Hartley

Editorial Assistant: Lucy Pritchard

Publisher's Note
The publisher has gone to great lengths to ensure the quality of this reprint but points out that some imperfections in the original copies may be apparent.

British Library Cataloguing in Publication Data
A catalogue record for this book is available from the British Library

Library of Congress Cataloging-in-Publication Data
A catalog record has been requested for this book

Typeset in Times New Roman
by Taylor & Francis Books

ISBN 13: 978-1-03-209116-7 (pbk)
ISBN 13: 978-1-85743-919-9 (hbk)

Contents

List of tables		ix
Acknowledgements		x
List of contributors		xi

1 Reconsidering Taiwan's future in a more contested East Asia   1
  BENJAMIN SCHREER AND ANDREW T. H. TAN

2 The Taiwan issue and small state survival   12
  ANDREW T. H. TAN

3 Taiwan's domestic dynamics and foreign policy   28
  J. MICHAEL COLE

4 Taiwan and the great powers   43
  ANDREA BENVENUTI

5 The Taiwan issue: tracing 70 years of Taiwan-China relations   58
  ROGER LEE HUANG AND ANDREW T. H. TAN

6 Taiwan-China relations: asymmetric trust and Innenpolitik   73
  WEN-TI SUNG

7 Preventing independence, striving for unification: Chinese perspectives on Taiwan   90
  JINGDONG YUAN

8 Taiwan and the United States   107
  ANDREW T. H. TAN

9 New dynamics in Taiwan-Japan relations   123
  BENJAMIN SCHREER AND ANDREW T. H. TAN

10 Taiwan's foreign policy   138
  SHERYN LEE

11 Taiwan's armed forces: development and prospects 156
    SHANG-SU WU

12 Defending Taiwan against China 174
    YVES-HENG LIM

13 Thinking about how to forge lasting peace in the Taiwan Strait 191
    DEREK GROSSMAN

14 Reassessing Taiwan's strategic future 210
    BENJAMIN SCHREER

    Index 227

Tables

2.1	Military power of China and Taiwan (2017)	14
10.1	Key concepts for Taiwan foreign policy	143
11.1	Comparison of combat aircraft owned by the ROCAF and those of its regional counterparts	157
11.2	Comparison of attack helicopters owned by the ROCA and its regional counterparts	159

Acknowledgements

This edited volume aims to better understand the issues and challenges that Taiwan faces in the fast-changing and uncertain geostrategic environment in north-east Asia. This volume would not have been possible without the involvement and contribution of all those whose work appears in this volume.

The editors and contributors are especially grateful to the Chiang Ching Kuo Foundation, Taiwan, which provided a generous grant enabling the contributors of the volume to meet and present their papers at a workshop at Macquarie University, in Sydney, in December 2018. The workshop provided invaluable feedback that enabled the contributors to complete their chapters.

The editors would like to thank Cathy Hartley at Routledge for her support and encouragement for this book project, without which this important and timely volume would not have been possible. The editors are also grateful to the two anonymous referees who evaluated the book proposal for their useful suggestions and comments. Last, but not least, the editors are very grateful to the referee who invested the time and effort to read, comment and offer suggestions on all the final papers in this volume.

Benjamin Schreer and Andrew Tan
Department of Security Studies and Criminology
Macquarie University, Australia

Contributors

Benjamin Schreer is Professor and Head of the Department of Security Studies and Criminology at Macquarie University, Sydney, Australia. Previous positions include senior analyst for defence strategy at the Australian Strategic Policy Institute; senior lecturer at the Strategic and Defence Studies Centre at the Australian National University; and senior analyst at the German Institute for International and Security Studies (Stiftung Wissenschaft und Politik). He has published widely on international security and defence affairs, including East Asian strategic trends.

Andrew T. H. Tan is Associate Professor in the Department of Security Studies and Criminology, Macquarie University, Sydney, Australia. He was previously Associate Professor at the University of New South Wales and Senior Lecturer at Kings College London, UK. Andrew has published 19 sole-authored, edited and co-edited books, and over 60 refereed journal and chapter articles. Some of his latest books include: *Terrorism and Insurgency in Asia* (London: Routledge, 2019), *The United States in Asia* (Cheltenham: Edward Elgar, 2018), *US–China Relations* (Cheltenham: Edward Elgar, 2016), *Security and Conflict in East Asia* (London: Routledge, 2015), *The Arms Race in Asia: Trends, Causes and Implications* (London: Routledge, 2014), *East and Southeast Asia: International Relations and Security Perspectives* (London: Routledge, 2013), *Security Strategies in the Asia-Pacific* (London: Palgrave Macmillan, 2011) and *US Strategy Against Global Terrorism: How It Evolved, Why It Failed and Where It Is Headed* (London: Palgrave Macmillan, 2009).

Andrea Benvenuti is a senior lecturer in International Relations and European Studies at the School of Social Sciences, Faculty of Arts and Social Sciences, University of New South Wales, Australia. Educated at Florence University, Monash University and Oxford University, Benvenuti currently teaches 20th-century international history and European politics at both undergraduate and postgraduate level. His research interest lies in the field of post-1945 international history with a strong focus on the Cold War. He recently published *Cold War and Decolonisation: Australia's Policy towards Britain's End of Empire in Southeast Asia* (Singapore: NUS Press, 2017). He is currently working on a co-authored book on the impact of Western power in shaping the Asian regional system (1900–1989) and on a single-authored book on the Western alliance and the challenge of non-alignment in Asia (1954–61).

J. Michael Cole is a Taipei-based senior non-resident Fellow with the Taiwan Studies Programme at the University of Nottingham, UK, an associate researcher with the French Center for Research on Contemporary China, and a Senior Non-Resident Fellow with the Global Taiwan Institute in Washington, DC, USA. He holds a Master's degree in War Studies from the Royal Military College of Canada and is a former intelligence officer with the Canadian Security Intelligence Service in Ottawa. He is chief editor of *Taiwan Sentinel*. From 2014–16 he was chief editor of *Thinking Taiwan*, a publication of the Thinking Taiwan Foundation founded by Tsai Ing-wen. From 2006–13 he was a deputy news editor and columnist for the *Taipei Times*. His latest book, *Convergence or Conflict in the Taiwan Strait*, was published by Routledge in 2016.

Derek Grossman is a senior defence analyst with RAND Corporation focusing on a range of national security policy and Indo-Pacific security issues. He is particularly interested in China's relationships with Vietnam, India, Pakistan, Taiwan, Japan, and North and South Korea. Grossman has over a decade of experience in the intelligence community, and has served as the daily intelligence briefer to the Director of the Defense Intelligence Agency and the briefer to the Assistant Secretary of Defense for Asian and Pacific Security Affairs at the US Pentagon. Grossman holds an MA from Georgetown University's School of Foreign Service in US National Security Policy and received his BA with honours from the University of Michigan, USA, in Political Science and Asian Studies. He has published articles for the *Australian Strategic Policy Institute, China Brief, Cipher Brief, Defense Dossier, Foreign Policy, Global Taiwan Brief, International Security, Journal of International Security Affairs, Lawfare Blog, Newsweek, PacNet, Studies in Intelligence, The Diplomat, The National Interest*, and *War on the Rocks*.

Yves Heng-Lim is a lecturer in the Department of Security Studies and Criminology, Macquarie University, Sydney, Australia. His work focuses on Asia-Pacific security dynamics and on China's evolving role in the region. He is the author of *China's Naval Power: An Offensive Realist Approach* (Farnham: Ashgate, 2014). His research has been published in the *Journal of Strategic Studies*, the *Journal of Contemporary China*, and *Comparative Strategy*.

Roger Lee Huang is lecturer in Terrorism Studies and Political Violence in the Department of Security Studies and Criminology, Macquarie University, Sydney, Australia. He has previously worked as an associate researcher in the Department of International Affairs, Democratic Progressive Party. He received his PhD from City University of Hong Kong.

List of contributors xiii

Sheryn Lee is a lecturer in the Department of Security Studies and Criminology, Macquarie University, Sydney, Australia. She has a PhD from the Strategic and Defence Studies Centre (SDSC), the Australian National University and was previously a non-resident WSD-Handa Fellow at the Pacific Forum, Center for Strategic and International Studies. She also holds an AM in Political Science from the University of Pennsylvania, where she was a Benjamin Franklin Fellow and Mumford Fellow. She was also a T.B. Millar scholar at the SDSC; and a Robert O'Neill scholar at the International Institute of Strategic Studies (Asia) in Singapore. She has published in *International Security*, the *Texas National Security Review, Survival, Asian Security*, and the *RUSI Journal*.

Shang Su-Wu is a Research Fellow at the S. Rajaratnam School of International Studies, Nanyang Technological University, Singapore. He is attached to the Regional Security Architecture Programme at the school's constituent unit, the Institute of Defence and Strategic Studies. His research specialities include military modernization, Taiwan issues and international relations. His articles, commentaries and op-eds have been published in *Contemporary Southeast Asia, Asian Survey, the Pacific Review, Defence Studies, Naval War College Review*, and *East Asia Forum*, among others. He is also the author of *The Defence Capabilities of Small States: Singapore and Taiwan's Responses to Strategic Desperation* (London: Palgrave Macmillan, 2016).

Wen-Ti Sung is a PhD scholar at Coral Bell School of Asia Pacific Affairs at the Australian National University. He holds a Master of International Affairs from the Columbia University in New York and a BA (Honours Class I) in International Relations from the University of Queensland, Australia.

Jingdong Yuan is Associate Professor of International Security, and Chair of the Department of Government and International Relations at the University of Sydney, Australia. Yuan's research focuses on Indo-Pacific security, Chinese defence and foreign policy, China-India relations, and nuclear arms control and non-proliferation. He has held visiting appointments at the National University of Singapore, the University of Macau, East-West Center, National Cheng-chi University, the Mercator Institute for China Studies, Fudan University, and the WZB Berlin Social Sciences Centre. He is the co-author of *Chinese Cruise Missiles: A Quiet Force-Multiplier* (Washington, DC: National Defense University Press, 2014) and *China and India: Cooperation or Conflict?* (Boulder, CO and London: Lynne Rienner, 2003), and co-editor of *Australia and China at 40* (Sydney: University of New South Wales Press, 2012). He has published in *Asian Survey*, the *Australian Journal of International Affairs, Contemporary Security Policy, International Affairs, International Journal*, the *Journal of Contemporary China*, the *Journal of International Affairs, Nonproliferation Review*, the *Washington Quarterly*, and in many edited volumes. He is currently working on a book manuscript on China-South Asia relations.

1 Reconsidering Taiwan's future in a more contested East Asia

Benjamin Schreer and Andrew T. H. Tan

The strategic situation in the Taiwan Strait is back in the international spotlight given the deteriorating relationship between the People's Republic of China (PRC, or China) and the Republic of China (ROC, or Taiwan), as well as a growing United States–China rivalry. Assessments that cross-Strait rapprochement during the previous Taiwanese Kuomintang (KMT—Nationalist Party)-led government of President Ma Ying-jeou between 2008 and 2016 had made serious conflict rather unlikely (Kastner 2015/16) were too optimistic from the start as China kept upgrading its military posture to threaten Taiwan while Taiwanese voters made it clear that there was no support for a 'one country, two systems' solution akin to Hong Kong or Macau (Lee 2015: 116–18). However, since President Tsai Ing-wen's victory in the 2016 Taiwan general election, Taiwan-China relations have sunk to a new low. Accusing her Democratic Progressive Party (DPP) of promoting Taiwan's *de jure* independence, China's President Xi Jinping put all formal diplomatic exchanges on hold and intensified his threat that the unification issue should not be postponed indefinitely. In a January 2019 address commemorating the 40th anniversary of the 'Message to Compatriots in Taiwan' in 1979, Xi stated that unification was 'inevitable' and made it clear that resort to the use of force remained a serious option for Beijing (SBS News 2019). In a swift rebuke, Tsai categorically rejected the 'one country, two systems' principle as a basis for cross-Strait relations, a position that was overwhelmingly supported by Taiwanese voters (Associated Press 2019).

The Taiwan issue has thus entered a new period of uncertainty in a more contested East Asia. Taiwan is confronted by an increasingly assertive China. While Xi's statements echo previous Chinese pronouncements, there are indicators that the Chinese Communist Party (CCP) has assigned greater urgency to 'solving' the issue of unification with Taiwan sooner rather than later. In the context of China's growing power and influence, Xi at the 19th Party Congress in October 2017 explicitly tied the Taiwan question to his central foreign policy objective of the 'great rejuvenation of the Chinese nation', emphasizing that his country had 'the resolve, the confidence, and the ability to defeat separatist attempts for 'Taiwan independence' in any form' (Xi 2017).

It stands to reason that China's political and military leaders could feel emboldened by their country's growing political, economic and military means to possibly coerce Taiwan into unification. Beijing's remarkable economic growth has turned it into a global economic player. Economically, China now towers over Taiwan. In 2017 Taiwan's gross domestic product (GDP) stood at around US $571 billion, compared to China's $11,900 billion. Indeed, by some measures China has surpassed the United States as the world's largest economy: in 2014 the International Monetary Fund (IMF) reported that China's purchasing power parity (PPP) was higher than America's (IMF 2014). While there is much debate about the real growth of China's economy and the associated risks China has used some of its new wealth to invest in a much more capable People's Liberation Army (PLA) and to incrementally close the gap to America's heretofore undisputed military primacy in the Western Pacific, particularly over the Taiwan Strait. In 2017 China's official defense budget totalled some $150 billion, the second largest in the world after the United States (IISS 2018: 249).

Critically, China has changed the military balance with Taiwan in its favour when it comes to major air and naval platforms. Its growing arsenal of land-based cruise and ballistic missiles, also pose a major threat to Taiwanese airfields, command and control systems, and other critical infrastructure. In contrast, Taiwan's defense budget in 2017 stood at only US $10.4 billion, well below the 3 per cent of GDP promised by successive governments (IISS 2018: 249, 302). Moreover, many of its major air combat aircraft, principal surface warships and submarines face obsolescence, compounded by the challenge of limited access to major arms suppliers due to China's opposition. And Taiwan has faced serious difficulties in adjusting its defense strategy towards an asymmetric approach designed to exploit the PLA's weaknesses. More than ever, Taiwan thus critically relies on the United States to provide military support. Yet, as a 2015 RAND study concluded, the US military might find itself hard-pressed if it had to confront China militarily over the Taiwan Strait. Indeed, the report warned that China's armed forces could, in fact, be able to achieve at least temporary, local superiority that would enable it to achieve limited regional objectives (RAND Corporation 2015). Whether that is true or not, China has displayed greater public confidence in its military options vis-à-vis Taiwan. For instance, in 2018 China's Minister of National Defence Lt-Gen. Wei Fenghe declared that 'if anyone tries to separate Taiwan from China, China's military will take action at all costs' (*Straits Times* 2018), a thinly veiled threat against the United States. In early 2019 US defence officials warned that Chinese military leaders had become increasingly confident in their ability to invade Taiwan (Seligman 2019).

However, while Chinese leaders might think that time is on their side, Beijing's scope for pressuring Taiwan to peacefully accept unification on its terms has actually diminished in recent years. Indeed, often overlooked in current debate about East Asia's political order, Taiwan has undergone a remarkable transformation from an authoritarian regime to a consolidated democracy. It is this fundamental divergence in political systems and way of life – as opposed to Beijing's repeated allegations that the DPP seeks Taiwan's *de jure* independence – which makes a cross-Strait political rapprochement to China's liking increasingly difficult. Successive opinion polls have demonstrated that a majority of Taiwanese voters prefer the status quo, perceive themselves as 'solely Taiwanese' and reject China's 'one party, two systems' mantra. However, they are also opposed to *de jure* independence, knowing that this might well lead to a devastating war with China (Election Study Centre 2018a, 2018b).

Consequently, current President Tsai Ing-wen has steered clear of pro-independence statements and policies, in contrast to her DPP predecessor Chen Shui-bian (2000–08) who moved from a One China narrative to a two sovereign states position (Dittmer 2005: 86), in the process not only annoying Beijing but also complicating Taiwan's relationship with Washington. Tsai is conscious of the need to avoid major provocation of Beijing by adopting a formal pro-independence policy. At the same time, however, any major Taiwanese party has to campaign on a platform that recognizes the country's democratic consolidation and voters' rejection of moving towards China's 'one country, two systems' approach, thereby surrendering Taiwan's sovereignty. This also applies to the KMT, which, under President Ma, concluded a series of political and economic agreements with China, including the Economic Cooperation Framework Agreement in 2010, which was to further smooth the path towards greater integration of both economies. However, in 2014 his policies sparked widespread protests in Taiwan over a proposed services agreement with China, which would have enabled China to penetrate the services sector in Taiwan. This fuelled fears over a Chinese political takeover of Taiwan and served as the catalyst for the grassroots Sunflower Movement led by Taiwanese students and driven by opposition to an erosion of the nation's prospering democracy.

In the process, the KMT suffered a crashing electoral defeat in 2016 and a key lesson learned from this for future KMT leaders is the need to avoid a cross-Strait policy which is regarded by a majority of voters as trading away Taiwan's way of life. Importantly, developments in Hong Kong and Macau, where Chinese authoritarianism has hollowed out any promise of their special provincial status, have been closely watched in Taiwan, further reducing the attractiveness of the 'China model'. However, these socio-political dynamics in Taiwan have not gone unnoticed by China which fears that the island is on its way to permanent de facto independence. The CCP's hopes for a peaceful unification on its terms are fading. China's response has been to increase pressure on Taiwan. This included the suspension of official communications with Taipei in June 2016 and unofficial economic sanctions in the form of reduced Chinese tourist numbers. Beijing also stepped up efforts to convince the small and dwindling number of states that recognize Taipei to switch recognition over to China, thereby further narrowing Taipei's formal diplomatic space. Indeed, since 2016 Taiwan has lost five diplomatic allies, thus reducing its total number at the start of 2019 to only 16 countries plus the Vatican.

China also blocked Taiwan from participating in a number of international organizations that it had previously attended as an observer, such as the International Civil Aviation Organization, the World Health Assembly and the International Labour Conference, thus obstructing Taiwan from carrying out functional cooperation with the international community. Furthermore, the PLA increased its operations in the vicinity of Taiwan, including sailing its warships close to Taiwanese shores, and flying bombers to circle the island. China also opened new civil air corridors along China's east coast without first consulting with Taiwan (Denmark 2018). Moreover, China's Civil Aviation Agency demanded that foreign airlines remove from their websites any reference to Taiwan as a country. Disturbingly, most airlines complied with China's demands, with some even offering up abject apologies (Chan 2018).

Nevertheless, Taiwan has remained firm in the face of China's pressure. Part of its strategy to maintain its de facto independence and to broaden its breathing space is to intensify its political, economic and strategic ties with key regional players. This includes enhancing links with Japan, India and the Association of Southeast Asian Nations (ASEAN). Of particular importance for its survival is to maintain close relations with the USA, its informal security ally. Ever since the US Congress passed the Taiwan Relations Act (TRA) in 1979, which commits Washington to maintaining the capacity 'to resist any resort to force or other forms of coercion that would jeopardize the security, or the social or economic system, of the people on Taiwan' (Taiwan Relations Act 1979), successive US governments have made it clear to both Beijing and Taipei that they prefer to maintain the status quo in the Strait. 'Strategic ambiguity' of whether the USA would defend Taiwan militarily in the event of a Chinese attack became the guiding principle for Washington's policy towards Taiwan. Washington has also supplied Taiwan with 'defensive arms', though it has not provided the island with much needed replacements for some major combat systems, such as advanced combat aircraft.

Still, the TRA does not constitute a formal military alliance between the USA and Taiwan, and China has lobbied extensively in recent years with a view to weakening congressional support for Taiwan's status (Mitchell 2017).There is no guarantee for Taiwan that the USA would come to its support in the event of major hostilities with China. A central issue for Taipei and future cross-Strait stability is therefore whether US commitment to the status quo increases or weakens in the context of China's growing ability to put US forces at risk. Much will depend on Taiwan's value for the USA in the context of its emerging strategic competition with China. Taiwan has resurfaced as a major issue in US-China relations with the arrival of the Trump presidency. Supported by a bipartisan consensus in Washington about the need to push back against China, the Trump administration appears to have embarked on a more competitive course of action (Shambaugh 2018; Sutter 2018). Owing to Taiwan's geostrategic location and its importance as a liberal democracy in East Asia, US support for Taiwan could therefore intensify in a prolonged era of US-Chinese rivalry.

Yet at present this scenario is far from assured. Trump's Asia 'strategy' during his first two years has been full of inconsistencies and unpredictability, and the implications for US-Taiwan relations remain unclear. On the one hand, the USA has provided stronger official support for Taiwan's position. This included the passing of the Taiwan Travel Act in 2018, enabling senior US officials to visit Taiwan, the opening of a new unofficial US embassy in Taipei, and increased passage of US warships through the Taiwan Strait, prompting angry protests from China (*Straits Times* 2018). The US Congress also appeared to assume a more active role as a driving force behind strong US-Taiwan ties. On the other hand, however, President Trump has proven erratic and unpredictable in his dealings with Asia-Pacific allies, partners and potential adversaries alike. This has included flip-flopping on the Taiwan issue, alternating between publicly questioning America's One China policy while seemingly providing China with a veto over closer US-Taiwan relations (Huxley and Schreer 2017). Indeed, Trump reportedly has questioned the benefits of closer ties to Taiwan for the USA and appears critical of any security commitment to the island's defence, a stance that is in keeping with his general distaste for US alliances (Bush 2019). While the Trump administration appears to be broadly supportive of Taiwan, its transactional 'America first' approach holds dangers for Taiwan as well, since it might eventually end up as an expendable bargaining chip for Washington in its dealings with Beijing.

Objectives of volume

It is therefore timely to revisit the Taiwan issue in the context of Taiwan's evolving domestic and external dynamics. While Taiwan could indeed succeed in navigating a more contested regional strategic environment, thereby maintaining its de facto independence from mainland China, its room for manoeuvre could also narrow in future. Over the coming years, cross-Strait affairs will thus re-emerge as one of the Asia-Pacific 'flashpoints' with potentially serious consequences for regional stability and security. Yet it is important to analyse Taiwan's future not simply as the result of strategic choices made in Beijing or Washington but rather to consider Taiwan as an independent foreign policy actor in its own right, influenced by domestic and external factors.

This book therefore seeks to advance our understanding as scholars and practitioners of the contemporary challenges facing Taiwan's future and cross-Strait stability. The main focus is on evaluating the prospects for enhancing Taiwan's resilience against attempts to undermine and ultimately dissolve its democratic system, not least given that President Tsai has identified 'resilience' as the key attribute to describing her country (Office of the President 2018). Consequently, the book predominantly focuses on the political conditions that Taiwan under President Tsai faces internally and externally, asking how the country seeks to respond effectively to a much more uncertain environment. Specifically, it analyses the challenges and prospects of Taiwan's relationships with the key regional powers, particularly China, Japan and the USA; Taiwan's foreign and defence policy constraints and opportunities; its options in the face of China's threat to use military force; and an assessment of Taiwan's future prospects as well as possible strategies to ensure stability in the Taiwan Strait. Importantly, the book puts forward divergent perspectives on Taiwan's future with a view to enriching the contemporary debate on this important issue for East Asia stability.

Structure of the volume

This chapter sets the stage for the following 12 chapters that provide an in-depth discussion of various aspects of the Taiwan issue. Chapter 2, Andrew Tan's review of Taiwan as a case study for 'small state survival', provides a useful conceptual lens. It builds on frameworks developed by Efraim Inbar and Gabriel Sheffer in *The National Security of Small States in a Changing World* (London: Frank Cass, 1997) and by Michael Handel in *Weak States in the International System* (London: Frank Cass, 1990) to examine how the Cold War and post-Cold War literature concerning small state survival might hold lessons for Taiwan. Tan concludes that on balance, given the odds against it, Taiwan's viability as a small state is questionable. It may be that Taiwan can only hope to muster the strengths and strategies of small state survival in order to achieve the limited objective of deterring open war and buying enough time to somehow arrive at a peaceful accommodation with an increasingly powerful and assertive China, one that would at least preserve its internal autonomy, political system and way of life. Indeed, if open war and resort to large-scale violence could be avoided, this might be the least bad outcome for Taiwan.

Chapter 3 by J. Michael Cole examines Taiwan's domestic dynamics and the implications for its foreign policy behaviour. It details the evolution of Taiwan's domestic politics and shows how domestic political as well as sociocultural dynamics have influenced Taiwan's foreign policy towards China, the USA and the rest of the world. It also explains why support for de facto independence has grown but also why reform in some areas that are key to Taiwan's long-term survival has been slow. It analyses the constraints imposed by such domestic dynamics as well as the opportunities and prospects. Finally, it looks at the changing geopolitical environment since 2016 and how this has affected Taiwan's ability to interact with the international community.

Chapter 4 by Andrea Benvenuti provides a historical overview of Taiwan's ties with great powers since 1949. It focuses on its relationship with the USA, China, Japan and Europe, and assesses how Taiwan has managed its uncertain status in the face of decreasing options and an increasingly hostile diplomatic and strategic environment. For obvious reasons, it focuses specifically on Taiwan's relations with the USA and the PRC. However, it also draws attention to how Taiwanese policymakers have dealt with a very hostile politico-strategic environment. Taiwan has come a long way since 1949, and this is due to the perseverance of its political elite. Indeed, if Taiwan is to prevent Chinese hostility from turning violent, this will be in no small measure thanks to its government's decision not to upset the status quo and to make a decisive and open claim to independence.

Chapter 5 by Roger Huang and Andrew Tan provides a broad overview of how Taiwan-China relations have changed over the years from an official ban on engagement to the acceleration of socio-economic exchange. In particular, this chapter examines the changing dynamics of Taiwan-China relations following Taiwan's democratic transition, which has led to the emergence of the pro-Taiwan independence movement. Following Taiwan's democratization, political resolution of the so-called Taiwan issue has become increasingly complicated and difficult.

In Chapter 6, Wen-ti Sung argues that the contours of cross-Strait relations are often shaped by three important factors: first, a long-term incentive structure based on an evolving external Washington-Beijing-Taipei trilateral power balance depending also on domestic public opinion in Taiwan; second, the political insecurity of Taiwan's leaders, and to a lesser extent, of those in China, which in turn shapes their penchant for diversionary cross-Strait policy; and third, the people of China and Taiwan have placed their 'asymmetry trust' in Taiwan's two main political parties, which has caused many missed opportunities for cross-Strait engagement. It remains to be seen whether Xi Jinping will become more proactive in the matter of cross-Strait unification, or whether he will demonstrate more patience and a preference for greater stability in cross-Strait relations. On the other hand, it remains to be seen whether the DPP, facing electoral adversity, will point its cross-Strait platform in a more Beijing-friendly direction, or whether escalating US-Chinese rivalry will lead to greater expectations of US and Western support and thus embolden the DPP to hold fast to its Taiwanese nationalist platform.

Chapter 7 by Yuan Jingdong provides a much needed analysis of China's perceptions of the Taiwan issue. It examines the Chinese elite, media and popular perceptions of Taiwan, a highly charged, emotional and nationalistic issue in China. This chapter also examines how this issue has become China's top foreign policy priority, and assesses the constraints and opportunities facing China's leaders in dealing with the Taiwan issue.

Chapter 8 by Andrew Tan examines Taiwan's contemporary relationship with the USA, focusing on how the relatively stable status quo in the Taiwan Strait has become increasingly volatile in recent years as a result of a number of factors, including the rise of a nationalistic and assertive China, the uncertainty of US congressional sentiments regarding Taiwan, and the fact that Taiwan has increasingly become trapped in the strategic rivalry between the USA and China. The chapter also examines the impact of and implications for bilateral relations as a result of recent political and social developments in Taiwan as well as possible policy changes by the Trump Administration. Tan concludes that in order to sustain the Taiwan-US relationship, Taiwan must not become a dangerous liability to the USA either by pushing for independence, thereby sparking a serious crisis in US-China relations, or by failing to invest sufficiently in its own defence to deter the use of force by China.

Chapter 9 by Andrew Tan and Benjamin Schreer examines Taiwan's key relationship with Japan which retains significant cultural, historical and unofficial ties with its former colony. With the exception of the USA, Japan is Taiwan's most important strategic partnership in East Asia. This chapter examines the continued influence of Japan on Taiwan, mutual perceptions of each other, and assesses the constraints, opportunities and dangers, in Japan's relationship with the island. It argues that despite remaining obstacles to the forging of much closer official Japan-Taiwan political ties due to Tokyo's concerns over Chinese reactions, both sides have intensified their interactions below the political radar.

Chapter 10 by Sheryn Lee examines the recent evolution of Taiwan's foreign policy. Since the ROC forces fled to Taiwan at the end of the Chinese civil war in 1949, Taiwan's foreign policy objective has remained the same: to ensure its survival as a separate entity from mainland China. After the ending of martial law in 1987 and the enactment of a series of democratic reforms, its consolidation as a two-party system has facilitated the development of an electorate that identifies as Taiwanese and which also has a vested interest in remaining an independent democratic polity. Consequently, Taiwan's foreign policy objective has evolved to maintain the cross-Strait status quo in order to sustain the ROC's de facto independence. In the face of increasing geoeconomic and geostrategic pressure from mainland China, both the KMT and the DPP support this goal of de facto independence, and to this end both parties have adopted in three approaches. First, to ensure the US government's unofficial security guarantee via the 'Six Assurances' and the Taiwan Relations Act; second, to strengthen its unofficial ties with ideologically like-minded partners such as Japan; and third, to utilize its development assistance programme to ensure its regional integration.

Chapter 11 by Shang-su Wu focuses on the development of Taiwan's armed forces and its prospects. Wu concludes that despite some advantages, Taiwan's armed forces face dual challenges from China's PLA, as well as other non-China related factors. The PLA's improving capabilities have comprehensively undermined Taipei's strategy for defending the islands. In addition, the three services of Taiwan's armed forces have a number of vulnerabilities stemming from strategy, funding and conscription, which have constrained the development of Taiwan's armed forces. Thus, while Taipei continues to make efforts to strengthen its military, it is less likely that structural constraints would be overcome, unless and until there is political consensus in Taiwan on the need to defend itself against external attack.

Chapter 12 by Yves-Heng Lim also examines Taiwan's defence policy with a specific focus on its military response to China's growing threat. According to Lim, the degradation of cross-Strait relations since the mid-2010s has rekindled fears that Beijing could conclude that the time has come for China to impose a definitive solution to the Taiwan question. While the possibility of war is hardly a new feature of cross-Strait relations, Taipei today faces daunting challenges as the PLA reaps the benefits of a decades-long military modernization process. Confronted by a much stronger adversary, Taiwan has started to explore what official documents term 'asymmetric' and 'innovative' alternatives designed to guarantee its security. Lim explores Taiwan's response to an evolving Chinese threat and the options that still remain available to Taipei. He argues that while Taipei has taken a significant step towards a strategy of denial, it is still far from having developed the type of forces that would optimally support such a strategy.

Chapter 13 by Derek Grossman explores the prospects for lasting peace in the Taiwan Strait. He takes a fresh look at what might be required for Beijing and Taipei to sign a formal and sustainable peace accord, or, at a minimum, to find ways to forge constructive dialogue on the political question. The stakes are simply too high, and the chance of armed conflict too real, to be complacent about the future. Disappointingly, this chapter's research strongly suggests that Chinese President Xi Jinping's decision to 'move the goalposts' on cross-Strait relations makes it highly likely that neither any sort of peace accord nor even some confidence-building measures towards initiating political negotiations are possible in the Strait. Xi's decision to discard or at least downplay former Chinese President Hu Jintao's emphasis on preventing Taiwanese independence and deferring reunification into the indefinite future, and instead to emphasize former paramount leader Deng Xiaoping's 'one country, two systems' framework that envisions only one China, but with different governments, is simply a non-starter with Taiwan. Likewise, Taiwan's President Tsai Ing-wen's refusal to recognize the 1992 Consensus in its exact wording and with the exact meaning that Xi desires will only prolong the political stand-off. Nevertheless, there are elements of a peace deal that could significantly bolster the peaceful status quo and avoid potential calamity. However, maintaining the peace will probably require some compromise on both sides as well as the use of confidence-building measures to work up to political talks that have been deferred to another day.

The concluding chapter by Benjamin Schreer re-assesses Taiwan's strategic future, and ends the volume on a positive note. In the face of increasing Chinese political, diplomatic, economic and military pressure, Taiwan's future appears ever more uncertain. For some observers, its eventual unification with Mainland China is all but inevitable. In contrast, Schreer argues that Taiwan's strategic future might be much brighter than often assumed because of three interrelated factors: China's limited power to compel Taiwan into giving up its de facto independence; Taiwan's societal, political, economic and military resilience; and the growing importance of Taiwan for the USA, its informal security ally, and other critical powers in the context of growing major power competition in East Asia. In a more uncertain East Asia, Taiwan's chances of survival as a thriving democracy have therefore not diminished, although the risks are higher.

References

BBC News (2010) 'Historic Taiwan–China Trade Deal Takes Effect', 12 September. Available at www.bbc.com/news/world-asia-pacific-11275274 (accessed 31 October 2018).

Bush, Richard C. (2019) 'An Open Letter to Mr. Kuo Pei-hung and His Colleagues', Washington, DC: Brookings Institution, 11 February. Available at www.brookings.edu/blog/order-from-chaos/2019/02/11/an-open-letter-to-mr-kuo-pei-hung-and-his-colleagues/ (accessed 13 February 2019).

Chan, Tara Francis (2018) 'China Wants to Dictate How Foreign Companies Refer to Taiwan: This Is How Every Major Airline Is Responding', *Business Insider Australia*, 5 May. Available at www.businessinsider.com.au/what-do-airlines-call-taiwan-china-2018-5?r=US&IR=T (accessed 31 October 2018).

China Daily (2017) 'Xi: Two Sides of Taiwan Straits Share One Destiny', 24 May. Available at www.chinadaily.com.cn/china/2017-05/24/content_29484806.htm (accessed 31 October 2018).

China Morning Post (2019) Xi's Tough Talk on Taiwan Backfired, as Tsai Support Surges', 31 January. Available at www.scmp.com/news/china/politics/article/2184474/xi-jinpings-tough-talk-taiwan-unification-backfires-tsai-ing (accessed 2 February 2019).

CNBC (2018) 'Trump Signs U.S.-Taiwan Travel Bill, Angering China', 17 March. Available at www.cnbc.com/2018/03/17/trump-signs-u-s-taiwan-travel-bill-angering-china.html (accessed 1 November 2018).

Denmark, Abraham (2018) 'China's Increasing Pressure on Taiwan', Wilson Center Blog, 30 January. Available at www.wilsoncenter.org/blog-post/chinas-increasing-pressure-taiwan (accessed 31 October 2018).

Dittmer, Lowell (2005) 'Taiwan's Aim-Inhibited Quest for Identity and the China Factor', *Journal of Asian and African Studies* 40(1–2).

Election Study Centre (2018a) *Changes in the Taiwanese/Chinese Identity of Taiwanese as Tracked in Surveys by the Election Study Centre, NCUU (1992~2018.06)*, Taipei: National Chengchi University, 2 August. Available at https://esc.nccu.edu.tw/course/news.php?Sn=166 (accessed 12 January 2019).

Election Study Centre (2018b) *Taiwan Independence vs. Unification with the Mainland (1992/06~2018/06)*, Taipei: National Chengchi University, 2 August. Available at https://esc.nccu.edu.tw/course/news.php?Sn=167 (accessed 12 January 2019).

Farley, Robert (2018) 'Could This New Chinese Destroyer 'Sink' the U.S. Navy?' *National Interest*, 11 September. Available at https://nationalinterest.org/blog/buzz/could-new-chinese-destroyer-sink-us-navy-31037 (accessed 31 October 2018).

Huxley, Tim and Benjamin Schreer (2017) 'Trump's Missing Asia Strategy', *Survival* 59(3).

International Institute for Strategic Studies (IISS) (2018) *The Military Balance 2018*, London: IISS.

International Monetary Fund (IMF) (2014) *World Economic Outlook Database*, Washington, DC, IMF, October. Available at www.imf.org/external/pubs/ft/weo/2014/02/weodata/index.aspx (accessed 31 October 2018).

Kastner, Scott L. (2015/16) 'Is the Taiwan Strait Still a Flash Point? Rethinking the Prospects for Armed Conflict between China and Taiwan', *International Security* 40(3).

Lee, Sheryn (2015) 'China's Strategy towards Taiwan', in Andrew T. H. Tan (ed.) *Security and Conflict in East Asia*, Routledge: London and New York.

Mitchell, Martin (2017) 'Taiwan and China: A Geostrategic Reassessment of U.S. Policy', *Comparative Strategy* 36(5).

Office of the President, Republic of China (2018) 'President Tsai Interviewed by AFP', 25 June. Available at https://english.president.gov.tw/News/5436 (accessed 10 January 2019).

RAND Corporation (2015) *The U.S.-China Military Scorecard: Forces, Geography, and the Evolving Balance of Power, 1996–2017*, Santa Monica, CA: RAND Corporation. Available at www.rand.org/content/dam/rand/pubs/research_reports/RR300/RR392/RAND_RR392.pdf (accessed 13 February 2019).

SBS News (2019) 'China Says Military Force an Option as It Pushes for Taiwan Reunification', 3 January. Available at www.sbs.com.au/news/china-says-military-force-an-option-as-its-pushes-for-taiwan-reunification (accessed 5 January 2019).

Seligman, Lara, (2019) 'U.S. Increasingly Concerned About a Chinese Attack on Taiwan', *Foreign Policy*, 16 January. Available at https://foreignpolicy.com/2019/01/16/u-s-increasingly-concerned-about-a-chinese-attack-on-taiwan/ (accessed 18 January 2019).

Shambaugh, David (2018) 'The New American Bipartisan Consensus on China Policy', *China-US Focus*, 21 September. Available at www.chinausfocus.com/foreign-policy/the-new-american-bipartisan-consensus-on-china-policy (accessed 13 January 2019).

South China Morning Post (2017) 'Most Taiwanese Consider Taiwan, China Separate Countries, Poll Suggests', 21 June. Available at www.scmp.com/news/china/policies-politics/article/2099286/most-taiwanese-consider-taiwan-china-separate-countries (accessed 31 October 2018).

Straits Times (2018) 'China Calls Any Challenge on Taiwan 'Extremely Dangerous'', 25 October. Available at www.straitstimes.com/asia/east-asia/chinas-defence-minister-vows-never-to-cede-any-territory-including-taiwan (accessed 26 October 2018).

Sutter, Robert (2018) 'Pushback: America's New China Strategy', *The Diplomat*, 2 November. Available at https://thediplomat.com/2018/11/pushback-americas-new-china-strategy/ (accessed 15 November 2018).

Taiwan Relations Act (1979). Available at www.ait.org.tw/our-relationship/policy-history/key-u-s-foreign-policy-documents-region/taiwan-relations-act/ (accessed 13 February 2019).

World Bank (2013) 'GDP Growth Average Annual Growth 2000–2011', *World Development Indicators 2013*, Washington, DC: World Bank, pp. 68, 72. Available at http://data.worldbank.org/sites/default/files/wdi-2013-ch4.pdf (accessed 31 October 2018).

Xi, Jinping (2017) Speech delivered at the 19th National Congress of the Communist Party of China, 18 October. Available at www.xinhuanet.com/english/download/Xi_Jinping's_report_at_19th_CPC_National_Congress.pdf (accessed 31 October 2018).

2 The Taiwan issue and small state survival

Andrew T. H. Tan

Small state survival in the international system

The study of small states in the international system has been an interesting area of scholarly enquiry, particularly as small states emerged and even thrived in the international system following the Peace of Westphalia in 1648. According to Michael Handel, small or weak states are characterized by their lack of power, the result being a continuous preoccupation with the question of survival (1981: 10). While Handel prefers to refer to such states as 'weak states' rather than 'small states' since countries of considerable area could also be weak and vulnerable, the literature as a whole has focused on small states (Vital 1971; Rothstein 1968; Aron 1967).

What, then, is a 'small' (or 'weak') state? Many definitions based on quantifiable criteria have revolved around a state's population. However, the problem is deciding the size of population that would qualify a state as 'small'. This has ranged from up to 1 million to 15 million as the cut-off; however, this method has been acknowledged to be arbitrary (Maass 2009: 75–76). Recognizing that setting objective criteria is problematic, some scholars have thus defined such states in relative terms. One approach is to define the small state in contrast to other, larger, states. Only great and middle powers matter to each other, and small states are those states that are of no importance to larger states (Vital 1971: 9). Furthermore, such states are, according to Martin Wright, small 'relative to the international society they belong to' (1978: 61). Handel also observed that when one speaks of the ability of a weak state to defend itself, one must ask 'against whom?' (1981: 37).

More usefully, small states have limited involvement in international relations, are strong advocates of international law, refrain from the use of military force and also have limited foreign policy priorities (Evans and Newnham 1998: 500–01). In addition, Robert Rothstein has described a small power (or state) as one 'that recognizes that it cannot obtain security primarily by use of its own capabilities, and that it must rely fundamentally on the aid of other states, institutions, processes, or developments to do so' (1968: 29).

The case of Taiwan (Republic of China, or ROC) is an interesting one of small state survival in the face of the existential threat to its de facto independence by a much larger and capable state, namely the People's Republic of China (PRC, or China). The question of whether Taiwan is even a state is dealt with in the following discussion. Assuming that it is a state, Taiwan does in fact possess a number of strengths, such as a fairly large population of 23.6 million in 2018, a developed economy, and considerable technological capabilities, such as its advanced semi-conductor and electronics industries. However, its adversary is China, which in 2017 was the world's second largest economy (World Bank 2017).

This chapter examines the concept of Taiwan as a small state, particularly in relation to China, and the challenges it faces in maintaining its separate de facto independence from China. It also briefly examines how the Taiwan problem or issue came about, and concludes with an assessment of the key challenges in small state survival faced by Taiwan. Ultimately, it must be asked whether Taiwan as a small state is even viable, and what prospects it has.

Taiwan as a small state

Taiwan is an interesting and unique case study of a small state and its survival in the international system. This proposition is somewhat daring on account of the fact that Taiwan is not in fact recognized as a state by much of the international community. Indeed, China has been vociferous in asserting that Taiwan is a province of China, and that reunification must somehow occur in the not-too-distant future as a national priority of the PRC.

The language of China's Anti-Secession Law in 2005, promulgated as a warning to pro-independence forces then ascendant in Taiwan, makes this clear. As Article 2 states, there is 'only one China in the world ... both the mainland and Taiwan belong to one China ... China's sovereignty and territorial integrity brook no division'. Furthermore, Article 4 declares that 'accomplishing the great task of reunifying the motherland is the sacred duty of *all* Chinese people, the Taiwan compatriots included' (emphasis added). To reiterate China's resolute opposition to any separate statehood by Taiwan, Article 8 declares that China 'shall employ non-peaceful means and other necessary measures to protect China's sovereignty and territorial integrity' should Taiwan make any move towards independence (Anti-Secession Law 2005). In other words, China would use force if so required in order to prevent this from happening. This was reiterated in 2018 by China's Minister of National Defence, Lt-Gen. Wei Fenghe, who, in responding to symbolic shows of support for Taiwan by the United States in the context of intensifying US-China tensions, stated that 'Taiwan is China's core interest' and 'if anyone tries to separate Taiwan from China, China's military will take action at all costs' (*Straits Times* 2018).

China's rise in recent times as a regional and global power has led to Taiwan's increasing isolation on the international stage. The ROC was humiliatingly ejected from the United Nations (UN) in 1971 just prior to the normalization of relations between the United States and China, and its seat on the UN Security Council as one of the Permanent Five with the power of veto replaced by its adversary, the PRC (*New York Times* 1971). Taiwan was the price that the United States paid in order to effect the normalization of relations with the PRC that would change the Cold War balance of power against the Soviet Union in Asia.

Since then, Taiwan has been on a losing streak, as China has used generous aid as well as retaliatory gestures to force states to withdraw their recognition of the ROC (*New York Times* 2016b). In 2017 Taiwan had formal diplomatic relations with just 21 states, mostly micro- states such as the Marshall Islands, Nauru and Palau. In addition, since 1971 Taiwan has not been a member of any UN body, since statehood is required and the UN recognizes the PRC as the only legitimate representative of China.

Taiwan's growing international isolation coincided with the startling economic and military rise of the PRC. In 2017 China's gross domestic product (GDP), or the size of its economy, stood at US $11,900 billion, compared to Taiwan's $571 billion. China's population was also 1,387 million in 2017, compared to Taiwan's 23.5 million. In terms of defence expenditure, China's defence budget in that year was $150 billion, compared to $10.4 billion for Taiwan (IISS 2018: 249, 302).

In addition, there has been a huge, and growing, asymmetry in military power between China and Taiwan. Table 2.1 demonstrates this asymmetry, using selected indicators such as military manpower, and the number of main battle tanks, combat aircraft, principal surface warships and submarines.

Taiwan's increasingly obsolescent armed forces have accentuated the huge military imbalance on the Taiwan Strait. Starved of modern weapons systems due to Taiwan's international isolation and the refusal of most states to sell arms to it on account of China's objections, Taiwan's armed forces deploy outdated weaponry which is outdated compared to that of increasingly sophisticated Chinese armed forces. Taiwan's army, for instance, continues to deploy M60A3 tanks from the 1970s, while its M48 tanks are of 1950s vintage. Its air force, comprising Mirage 2000, F5E Tiger, F16A/B and Ching-kuo combat aircraft, are typical of 1980s technology. The navy's principal surface warships are refurbished US navy ships, and its submarine fleet consists of two vessels dating from World War Two and two vessels procured in the 1980s from the Netherlands. In contrast, China's armed forces deploy state-of-the-art weapons systems such as

Table 2.1 Military power of China and Taiwan (2017)

	Military manpower	Main battle tanks	Combat aircraft	Principal surface warships	Submarines
China	2,035,000	6,740	2,397	83	62
Taiwan	215,000	565	481	24	4

Source: IISS (2018) *The Military Balance 2018*, London: IISS, pp. 249–59, 302–05.

modern tanks, frigates and nuclear submarines. Its air force also deploys clearly superior combat aircraft, such as the Su30 MKK Flanker, the Su-27, the J10 and the J11. It is also developing the J20 and the J31 fifth-generation stealth combat aircraft (Tan 2014: 46–48).

By 2018 China's navy had emerged as a particularly significant force for long-range military projection, as its second aircraft carrier began sea trials amid reports of its ambition to field between six and ten aircraft carriers (*Newsweek* 2018). China has also been building large 13,000-ton Type 055 guided-missile destroyers, the largest and most capable warships in the world next to the latest US navy's Zumwalt-class vessels, as well as amphibious assault ships which are the size of small aircraft carriers (CNN 2018). The emergence of a large and efficient blue-water naval fleet means that it increasingly has the capability to put pressure on Taiwan, an island dependent on sea-lines of communications for its commerce and economic survival. In contrast, Taiwan's navy is small and outdated, and its air force is expected to face bloc obsolescence in the coming years with little prospect of replacing its fighter squadrons.

In every conceivable measure of power, such as size of economy, population and military capability, Taiwan has therefore been dwarfed by the PRC, with the asymmetry growing greater with time. In addition, unlike many other small states, Taiwan is diplomatically isolated and does not therefore enjoy the legitimacy and normative protection that comes with the status of a sovereign state. As it is not even a member of the UN, having been expelled in 1971, it does not enjoy the protections afforded by the UN Charter to sovereign states – the right of self-defence under Article 51, for instance. Regardless of what constitutes a small state, Taiwan is therefore, in relation to its key security referent, the PRC, indeed small and vulnerable in every respect.

Yet despite Taiwan's international diplomatic isolation, it does have most of the necessary attributes of statehood. According to Max Weber, a state has the following characteristics or attributes:

a   the monopoly of the legitimate use of physical force within a given territory;
b   centralization of the material and the ideal means of rule;
c   a rational constitution;
d   an administrative and legal order which claim binding authority over all actions taking place within its area of jurisdiction;
e   subjection to change of this order through legislation;
f   organized activities oriented to the enforcement and realization of this order; and
g   regulation of the competition for political offices and selection of the bearers of ruler-ship according to established rules. (1968: 56)

Taiwan clearly fits the Weberian definition of a state. It possesses its own armed forces and police, and does have a monopoly of the use of force over its own defined territory. It has a functioning government, is governed by its own Constitution, and has jurisdiction over its own territory and citizens. On top of all these factors, it is today also a functioning democracy, with regulated rules governing the political process, including free and fair elections. Despite strenuous attempts by China to deny Taiwan the legitimacy of a state, it does in fact function like a sovereign state.

However, both the UN and even its most important ally, the USA, do not recognize Taiwan as a state. In 2007 the UN issued a declaration over Taiwan, stating that it considered the island 'for all purposes to be an integral part of the People's Republic of China' (Tkacik 2008). The US Department of State's position is that the USA recognizes the PRC as 'the sole legal government of China', and that 'Taiwan is part of China'. In addition, 'the United States does not support Taiwan's independence'. In other words, the USA does not recognize Taiwan as a state. Yet, at the same time, 'the 1979 Taiwan Relations Act provides the legal basis for the unofficial relationship between the United States and Taiwan, and enshrines the U.S. commitment to assist Taiwan in maintaining its defensive capability'. The USA also 'insists on the peaceful resolution of cross-Strait differences, opposes unilateral changes to the status quo by either side, and encourages both sides to continue their constructive dialogue on the basis of dignity and respect' (US Department of State 2016).

Thus, while not recognizing Taiwan as a sovereign state, the USA has nonetheless justified its unofficial relations and military support for Taiwan on the grounds that the Taiwan issue (see below) was left 'unsettled' at the end of the Second World War in 1945, and that the issue must be resolved with the assent of the people of Taiwan (Tkacik 2008). Under the 'Six Assurances' given to Taiwan by the Reagan Administration in July 1982, the USA undertook that it 'would not formally recognize Chinese sovereignty over Taiwan' (Six Assurances 1982). Thus, according to the convoluted US position, Taiwan is neither a sovereign state nor has its status been settled. This legal contortion has enabled the USA to justify its One China policy while at the same time providing political and security support to enable Taiwan to maintain its de facto independence. This suits the interests of the USA just fine, as it is able to overcome the Taiwan issue in China-US relations to conduct political and substantial economic interactions with China, yet is able to continue to offer support to Taiwan in order to sustain the status quo on the Taiwan Strait. This status quo, to all intents and purposes, is in fact the continued de facto independence of Taiwan.

Taiwan as a 'problem' or 'issue'

The Taiwan problem or issue in East Asian security resulted from the Chinese civil war between the then ruling Kuomintang (KMT – Nationalist Party) and the Communist Party of China (CPC) which raged from 1945–49 after Japan's surrender at the conclusion of the Second World War. The problem was that Japan's invasion of China in 1937 and the subsequent war had sapped the strength of the KMT. By the time of Japan's surrender in 1945, the KMT was gravely weakened. Inflation was rampant, and the middle and upper classes had been impoverished by the long and bitter struggle against Japan. Worse still, the KMT was riven by corruption and nepotism, to the extent that the United States, the KMT's ally in the war against Japan, lost faith in the party as well as in the leadership of its leader, Chiang Kai-shek (Teon 2018).

After a series of devastating military defeats at the hands of the communists, the KMT withdrew to Taiwan for its last heroic stand, with the United States washing its hands of Chiang (Acheson 1949). However, the outbreak of the Korean War in June 1950 changed US perceptions of Taiwan, which now assumed frontline status in the Cold War containment against communist expansionism. The United States intervened in the Chinese civil war to prevent a communist invasion and takeover of Taiwan by sending its navy to protect the island. From then onwards, the United States gradually deepened its involvement in the Chinese civil war by underwriting Taiwan's defence. Following China's artillery shelling of outlying islands occupied by Taiwan in 1954, the United States concluded a Mutual Defene Treaty with Taiwan in November 1954 (MDT 1954).

This was the origin of the Taiwan problem or issue, namely the continued separation of Taiwan from mainland China. Both the CPC and the KMT claimed to be the legitimate government of China, and both asserted then, as now, that Taiwan is part of China. However, recent political developments in Taiwan, namely the rise of pro-independence sentiments, have complicated the picture. There is no doubt that the KMT would have suffered its final defeat over the Taiwan issue had not the United States intervened in the Chinese civil war in 1950.

From the Chinese perspective, Taiwan remains an unresolved issue of considerable national importance. As Article 3 of China's Anti-Secession Law of 2005 made explicit, 'the Taiwan question is one that is left over from China's civil war of the late 1940s', adding that 'solving the Taiwan question and achieving national reunification is China's internal affair, which subjects to no interference by any outside forces' (Anti-Secession Law 2005). China's perspective on Taiwan is elaborated in greater detail in its White Paper on 'the Taiwan Question and Reunification of China':

> The modern history of China was a record of subjection to aggression, dismemberment and humiliation by foreign powers. It was also a chronicle of the Chinese people's valiant struggles for national independence and in defense of their state sovereignty, territorial integrity and national dignity. The origin and evolution of the Taiwan question are closely linked with that period of history. For various reasons Taiwan is still separated from the mainland. Unless and until this state of affairs is brought to an end, the trauma on the Chinese nation will not be healed and the Chinese people's struggle for national reunification and territorial integrity will continue.
> (State Council 1993)

From China's perspective, therefore, Taiwan is a national priority in that it is unfinished business resulting from the Chinese civil war. China has maintained that the cause of the Taiwan problem lies squarely with the United States. As the White Paper asserted, reunification would have been achieved in 1950 had it not intervened. Thus, the 'erroneous policy of the U.S. government of continued interference in China's internal affairs led to prolonged and intense confrontation in the Taiwan Strait area and henceforth the Taiwan question became a major dispute between China and the United States' (State Council 1993).

President Nixon's ground-breaking visit to China in 1972 was accompanied by the Shanghai Communiqué, in which the United States acknowledged that 'there is but one China', and that 'Taiwan is a part of China' (Shanghai Communiqué 1972).

However, even as the United States stripped Taiwan of its status as a state as the price for the normalization of relations with China, the US Congress passed the Taiwan Relations Act on 1 January 1979, reserving for the United States the right to provide Taiwan with 'defensive arms' and to 'maintain the capacity of the United States to resist any resort to force or other forms of coercion that would jeopardize the security, or the social or economic system, of the people on Taiwan' (TRA 1979). Although the United States had abrogated the Mutual Defense Treaty with Taiwan in January 1980, the Taiwan Relations Act made it clear that 'any effort to determine the future of Taiwan by other than peaceful means, including by boycotts or embargoes, [is] a threat to the peace and security of the Western Pacific area and of grave concern to the United States' (ibid.). Thus, instead of the explicit security guarantee under the previous Mutual Defense Treaty, the strategic ambiguity of how the United States might react if China used force against Taiwan became the principal deterrent against an attack by China.

The Taiwan problem or issue has become an increasingly serious potential flashpoint following the rise of pro-independence sentiments and political forces in Taiwan. This began with the presidency of Lee Teng-hui of the KMT in 1988. Lee was emblematic of the rise of native Taiwanese in local politics, namely those who felt little connection with mainland China, with some having actually fought alongside Japanese troops during the Second World War when Taiwan was a Japanese colony. Indeed, Lee himself served as an officer in the Japanese Imperial Army during the war (*Taipei Times* 2015). Lee was instrumental in fostering democracy as well as the then nascent pro-independence movement. During the new era of democracy pro-independence sentiments representing the aspirations of local Taiwanese as opposed to those who had roots in mainland China began to come to the fore. However, Lee's political reign was marked by tensions with China, culminating in the Taiwan Strait crisis in 1995–96. This was sparked by his unofficial visit to the United States, reversing a self-imposed US government ban that since 1979 had vetoed visits by high-level Taiwan officials. On his visit to his alma mater, Cornell University, Lee gave a speech in which he stated that we sincerely hope that all nations can treat us fairly and reasonably, and not overlook the significance, value and functions we represent ... some say that it is impossible for us to break out of the diplomatic isolation we face, but we will do our utmost to demand the impossible.

(*New York Times* 1995)

Predictably, China strongly opposed the rise of pro-independence sentiments on Taiwan, referring in its 1933 White Paper on 'the Taiwan Question and Reunification of China' to '"Taiwan independence" protagonists who trumpet "independence" but vilely rely on foreign patronage in a vain attempt to detach Taiwan from China, which runs against the fundamental interests of the entire Chinese people including Taiwan compatriots' (State Council 1993).

The presidency of Chen Shui-bian of the pro-independence Democratic Progressive Party (DPP) from 2000–08 was thus marked by moves perceived by China to be aimed at achieving independence. Yet, despite his overt stance on independence, most Taiwanese people understood that *de jure* independence would not occur since it would be inconceivable that the international community would turn away from the PRC to recognize a Taiwanese republic. Indeed, surveys carried out in 2004 and in 2012 demonstrate that most Taiwanese were against any immediate declaration of independence, preferring the status quo (Niou 2004; Wendall 2012). Instead, Chen embarked on the more realistic agenda of advancing an explicit Taiwanese, as opposed to Chinese, national identity. Chen focused on a deliberate nation-building effort, marked by de-Sinification and the promotion of Taiwanization. The implications of this, however, was not lost on China, which feared that this would lead to the normalization of Taiwan's de facto independence from China (Sullivan and Lowe 2010: 623–24). Indeed, as Lowell Dittmer noted regarding political developments in Taiwan, 'the overall pattern of political movement, whether public opinion or macro political narratives, is from one China to a two sovereign states position' (2005: 86).

Recognizing the implications of this, China's defence White Paper in 2002 declared that 'the Taiwan separatist force is the biggest threat to peace and stability in the Taiwan Straits', and went on to state that one of the key tasks of China's armed forces was to 'stop separation and realize complete reunification of the motherland' (State Council 2002).

The subsequent return to power by the KMT following the 2008 election led to a period of calm in cross-Strait relations as President Ma Ying-jeou sought to reduce tensions with China through his reaffirmation of the 1992 Consensus under which both sides recognized that there is only one China, though each could have its own interpretation of what that meant. Ma also pursued a policy of 'no unification, no independence and no use of force', which reassured China. Ma enhanced economic ties with China, signing the Economic Cooperation Framework Agreement in 2010, which led to the growing integration of both economies (BBC News 2010b). Indeed, by 2010 40 per cent of Taiwan's exports went to China and bilateral trade totalled US

$100 billion. Many companies and factories in Taiwan relocated to China in order to take advantage of its cheap labour as well as the vast and growing market there (ibid. 2010a).

However, the proposed services agreement with China in 2014 was met with widespread protests by what has been dubbed the Sunflower Movement, during which student demonstrators occupied parliament to prevent the ratification of the services agreement with China (Reuters 2014). The strength of opposition to further integration with China reflected a fundamental shift in popular attitudes towards China as well as the growing strength of a Taiwanese national identity. Indeed, the Sunflower Movement was dominated by young Taiwanese who felt little identification with China, feared domination by China and opposed reunification.

These fundamental shifts in attitudes towards China were reflected in the landslide victory of the pro-independence DPP in the 2016 election, when it captured both the presidency and the legislature, the first time this had occurred (ABC News 2016). The run-up to the election, however, was marked by a trivial incident that had a major political impact. This involved Chou Tzu-yu, a 16-year-old singer with TWICE, a South Korean girl band that was popular in China, who waved a Taiwanese flag while appearing on a television show in the Republic of Korea. This seemingly innocuous act caused a huge wave of netizen anger in China, fired up by intense emotional nationalist feelings over this purported show of support for Taiwanese independence. The result was an abject video apology by the shaken singer, in which she repeated the PRC line that 'there is only one China ... the two sides of the Strait are one' (Chou 2016). In China, the popular tabloid, the *Global Times*, lauded China's internet users for their 'patriotic-mindedness' and proclaimed Chou's apology to be a victory over Taiwanese independence. However, the video went viral in Taiwan on election day itself, and many Taiwanese expressed deep anger at the lack of respect for Taiwan. The incident was deemed so significant that incoming President, Tsai Ing-wen, addressed it in her first press conference (*New York Times* 2016a). Indeed, the video had a huge political impact as it also prompted all political parties in Taiwan, including the KMT, to rally behind the President, the Taiwanese flag and the official name of Taiwan as the 'Republic of China' (*South China Morning Post* 2016). Outgoing President Ma Ying-jeou declared that she need not apologize as she had not done anything wrong. Furthermore, Ma stated that 'I believe this is not right ... it's something we cannot accept', a sentiment widely shared by many Taiwanese (Ma 2016).

More telling have been surveys of changing Taiwanese attitudes towards China and perceptions of their own identity. In 2016 72 per cent of Taiwanese people felt that Taiwan was already an independent country under the name 'Republic of China'. In 2014 only 3 per cent of Taiwanese people identified themselves as Chinese, with 60 per cent identifying themselves as Taiwanese. Moreover, as an indication of future trends, an overwhelming 78 per cent of those aged 29 years and younger identified themselves as Taiwanese. Surveys have also shown that about three-quarters of all Taiwanese people would support Taiwanese independence if it could be guaranteed that it would not lead to a direct attack on Taiwan by the PRC. More interestingly, 43 per cent of people under the age of 40 years supported independence even if an attack by China would therefore be inevitable (*Washington Post* 2017).

Thus, the Taiwan problem (or issue or question, depending on who frames it), has now arguably become an even more serious potential flashpoint that could spark conflict in the Taiwan Strait, given the political trajectory on Taiwan, and the absolute insistence by China, backed by an increasingly nationalistic population, that Taiwan must be reunified with the mainland. As China's President, Xi Jinping stated in May 2017, both sides across the Taiwan Strait represent a community of shared destiny that cannot be prised apart (*China Daily* 2017). Given the huge and growing asymmetry in power between the PRC and Taiwan, the United States is the only power in a position to hinder reunification. Without US support, Taiwan's de facto independence would not be viable. The problem is that while tensions that have emerged in recent times between the United States and China owing to the two countries' growing strategic rivalry have enhanced Taiwan's strategic value to the United States, the fact is that the United States nevertheless has always put its national interests first, not Taiwan's. The election of Donald Trump as US president in late 2016 also holds dangers for Taiwan, given his Administration's subsequent incoherence on US policy in Asia and his transactional approach to foreign policy based on 'America first'. Therefore Taiwan could conceivably become an expendable bargaining chip in the negotiation of some kind of regional understanding with China, notwithstanding tensions from 2018 between the United States and China due to the outbreak of their mutual trade war.

Taiwan: challenges of small state survival

The question of small state survival in the international system was addressed by the Commonwealth Secretariat, which issued its seminal report entitled *Vulnerability: Small States in the Globalised Society* in 1985, a report that remains relevant today. This is particularly so in the increasingly realist geostrategic environment after the ending of the Cold War, especially in Asia, where the US-China strategic rivalry has intensified in recent years on account of China's dramatic rise. According to the report, there are three major categories of threats to security. The first category involves threats to territorial security as a result of military and non-military incursions. The second involves threats to political security, including actions intended to influence a threatened state's national policies. The third involves actions that could undermine a state's economic welfare (Commonwealth Secretariat 1985: 23).

Taiwan must confront these threats to its security – all of which emanate from China. China has always maintained its intention to use force against Taiwan if necessary (see, for instance, its 2005 Anti-Secession Law). The massive military expansion and modernization of the PLA in recent years has also provided China with military options that it did not previously possess, such as A2AD (anti-access, area denial) capabilities that could prevent the United States from responding to any regional crisis right from the outset, thus giving China freedom of action. In such a scenario, it could overwhelm Taiwan's defences and present the United States with a fait accompli which America could well accept given the potential cost of escalation. The second has been the expansion of China's economic and social influence over Taiwan, through the deep economic linkages between the two and the presence of Chinese cultural products that are popular in Taiwan, such as books and television programmes. According to Shang Su-wu, this enables China to gain influence 'by means of its easy access to sponsorship of certain activities, groups and even politicians'. The deep economic linkages also mean that 'taking economic measures against Taipei is even more feasible for Beijing than in previous decades' (2016: 127–28).

The Commonwealth report recommended the following measures to reduce small state vulnerability. These include the strengthening of national defence capabilities; entering into defence agreements with other states; underpinning security through economic growth; promoting internal cohesion; and adopting sound diplomatic policies at both bilateral and multilateral level (Commonwealth Secretariat 1985: 23). While Taiwan could make attempts to strengthen its defence capabilities, it is not able to carry out effective diplomacy at state level. The problem with most studies on small state security is that Taiwan is a unique case, given that it is a de facto state without recognized sovereign rights. While Maniruzzaman asserts that either a collective security system or a balance of power could ensure small state survival, the reality is that Taiwan does not enjoy the normative or legal protections of the international system since it is not even recognized by the UN as a state (1982: 37–39). While analysts have approvingly explored the adroit foreign policy strategies adopted by small states such as Azerbaijan, these are, however, not available to Taiwan (Mehdiyeva 2011). Shunned by much of the international community as well as most great powers including its own former colonial master, Japan, Taiwan has not been able to play the traditional balance of power game that has historically enabled small states to survive in an anarchic and Hobbesian international system. As Shang noted in his comparative study of Taiwan and Singapore, 'Taiwan does not have the opportunity to conduct proper foreign policies, as Singapore does, in order to ensure its survival in the face of the second strongest power in the world' (2016: 193). Pessimistically, Shang concludes that 'unless serious unexpected events occurred in China, such as a Soviet style collapse, it is evident that Taiwan will either be substantially merged with China or formally annexed by it, either of these events being only a matter of time' (ibid.: 137).

However, according to Michael Handel, 'weak states are not entirely weak', since they 'have important internal sources of strengths which they have learned to use to their advantage ... they have also learned to manipulate the strength of the great powers on their behalf and to draw on this external source of strength to further their own interests' (1981: 51). Small or weak states do possess strengths which enable them to manoeuvre in the anarchic international system and which enhance their chances of survival.

In the case of unequal conflicts between weak states and great powers, Handel asserted that even under unfavourable conditions 'it still makes sense for a weak state to fight back, either to hold out until external help arrives, or to inflict such heavy damage on the attacking side that the attack proves unprofitable'. Thus, it is 'logical for a weak state to maintain large enough forces to deter a possible attack by a great power'. The objective would not be victory against the great power but 'to successfully deter or evade war' in order to survive. The development of weak states' own military power can enable them, under certain conditions, to improve their bargaining position (1981: 103–04, 258). Conventional deterrent capabilities may also be supplemented by inexpensive counter-value weapons that could inflict damage on important military and civilian targets, and by weapons of mass destruction as a form of ultimate deterrence. Strategists have also argued the case for hybrid warfare because 'modern hybrid war that simultaneously combines conventional, irregular, and terrorist components is a complex challenge that requires an adaptable and versatile military to overcome' (Deep 2015). As Shang has noted, for instance, Taiwan does in fact possess missile capabilities capable of deterrence by punishment (2016: 131).

Furthermore, Handel has also argued that weak states must learn to draw on the strength of other states by manipulating and committing the strength of such states. He recommended that a weak state could try to appeal to and cultivate public opinion in the states whose support it wants to secure. This could be aided by the weak state's symbolic value, for instance, as a bastion of democracy (1981: 120–27). Therefore, Taiwan does have strengths, since as a result of its historical lobbying efforts it still retains support in the US Congress and is seen as a bastion of democracy and an old Cold War ally among some elites in the United States.

Other clues to small state survival can be found in case studies on Qatar and Singapore. In the case of Qatar, its economic and political resilience has enabled it to punch above its weight diplomatically (Cooper and Momani 2011). This diplomacy could be focused on the exercise of soft power, as in the case of Singapore, which has utilized its soft power in political economy potential and as a model of good governance, thus 'converting [its base] of anomalous power into instruments for virtual enlargement' (Chong 2010: 386). Moreover, nationalism based on a strong national identity could also play a crucial role in deterring strong states, since this would translate into the will to resist any subjugation (Walker 1968: 67). This suggests that there are steps that Taiwan could take on its own, such as improving its soft power diplomacy and finding ways of utilizing the growing Taiwanese identity to bolster deterrence.

Handel's key observation that 'no state is all powerful and no state is completely weak' (1981: 257) provides grounds for some optimism for Taiwan, at least in the short term. In the final analysis, however, Taiwan's case is unusual in that it is not recognized by most countries as a state. In fact, in the face of overwhelming odds and the existential threat from China, Shang Su-wu's pessimism is well justified. On balance, given the odds against it, Taiwan's viability as a small state is questionable. While it is strategically significant to the United States in the context of rising US-China tensions, there is no guarantee that US support will last. The reality is that Taiwan as a small state may well be living on borrowed time. Indeed, it may be that all Taiwan can really do is to utilize all the strengths and strategies of small state survival that it can muster in order to achieve the limited objective of deterring open war and to buy enough time to somehow arrive at a peaceful accommodation with an increasingly powerful and assertive China, one that would at least preserve its internal autonomy, political system and way of life. If open war and resort to large-scale violence can be avoided, this might be the least poor outcome for Taiwan.

References

ABC News (2016) 'Taiwan Election: First Female President Tsai Ing-wen Elected After Landslide Victory Against Ruling Kuomintang', 17 January. Available at www.abc.net.au/news/2016-01-16/taiwan-elects-first-female-president-tsai-ing-wen/7093338 (accessed 26 August 2018).

Acheson, Dean (1949) *Letter of Transmittal, The China White Paper: United States Relations with Special Reference to the Period 1944–1949*, Washington, DC: US Department of State. Available at https://archive.org/stream/VanSlykeLymanTheChinaWhitePaper1949/Van%20Slyke,%20Lyman%20-%20The%20China%20White%20Paper%201949_djvu.txt (accessed 25 August 2018).

Anti-Secession Law (2005) 14 March. Available at www.china.org.cn/china/LegislationsForm2001-2010/2011-02/11/content_21898679.htm (accessed 23 August 2018).

Aron, Raymond (1967) *Peace and War*, New York: Praeger.

BBC News (2010a) 'China-Taiwan Trade Pact Sparks Street Protest in Taipei', 26 June. Available at www.bbc.com/news/10423409 (accessed 26 August 2018).

BBC News (2010b) 'Historic Taiwan–China Trade Deal Takes Effect', 12 September. Available at www.bbc.com/news/world-asia-pacific-11275274 (accessed 25 August 2018).

China Daily (2017) 'Xi: Two Sides of Taiwan Straits Share One Destiny', 24 May. Available at www.chinadaily.com.cn/china/2017-05/24/content_29484806.htm (accessed 26 August 2018).

China Post (2011) 'Ma Reaffirms 1992 Consensus and 3 Nos', 29 August. Available at www.chinapost.com.tw/taiwan/china-taiwan-relations/2011/08/29/314938/Ma-reaffirms.htm (accessed 25 August 2018).

Chong, Alan (2010) 'Small Power Soft Power Strategies: Virtual Enlargement in the Cases of the Vatican City State and Singapore', *Cambridge Review of International Affairs* 23(3).

Chou, Tzu-yu (2016) '16-Year-Old Taiwanese K-Pop Singer Chou Tzu-yu Apologizes for Waving Own Country's Flag on TV', Youtube, 16 January. Available at www.youtube.com/watch?v=SsZmxqnwDXo (accessed 26 August 2018).

CNN (2018) 'China's New Destroyers: Power, Prestige and Majesty', 14 July. Available at https://edition.cnn.com/2018/07/13/asia/china-new-destroyers-intl/index.html (accessed 26 October 2018).

Commonwealth Secretariat (1985) *Vulnerability: Small States in the Globalised Society*, London: Commonwealth Secretariat.

Cooper, Andrew F. and Bessma Momani (2011) 'Qatar and Expanded Contours of Small State Diplomacy', *International Spectator* 46(3).

Deep, Alex (2015) 'Hybrid War: Old Concept, New Techniques', *Small Wars Journal*, 2 March. Available at http://smallwarsjournal.com/jrnl/art/hybrid-war-old-concept-new-techniques (accessed 26 August 2018).

Dittmer, Lowell (2005) 'Taiwan's Aim-Inhibited Quest for Identity and the China Factor', *Journal of Asian and African Studies* 40(1–2).

Evans, Graham and Jeffrey Newnham (1998) *The Penguin Dictionary of International Relations*, London: Penguin Books.

Handel, Michael (1981) *Weak States in the International System*, London: Frank Cass.

International Institute of Strategic Studies (IISS) (2018) *The Military Balance 2018*, London: IISS.

International Monetary Fund (IMF) (2017) *World Economic Outlook Database*, Washington DC:IMF, April. Available at www.imf.org/external/pubs/ft/weo/2017/01/weodata/weoselgr.aspx (accessed 23 August 2018).

Ma Ying-jeou (2016) 'Taiwanese President Ma Ying-jeou Says Tzuyu Does Not Need to Apologize', Youtube, 16 January. Available at www.youtube.com/watch?v=DD-HYcHXzk0 (accessed 26 August 2018).

Maass, Matthias (2009) 'The Elusive Definition of the Small State', *International Politics* 46(1).

Maniruzzaman, Talukder (1982) *The Security of Small States in the Third World*, Canberra: Australian National University.

Mehdiyeva, Nazrin (2011) *Power Game in the Caucasus*, New York: Palgrave Macmillan.

Minnick, Wendell (2012) 'China Tries to Expand Control as Taiwan Resists: Report', *Defense News*, 28 August. Available at www.defensenews.com/article/20120828/DEFREG03/308280011/China-Tries-Expand-Control-Taiwan-Resists-Report (accessed 26 August 2018).

Mutual Defense Treaty (MDT) (1954) *Mutual Defense Treaty between the United States and the Republic of China*, December 2. Available at http://avalon.law.yale.edu/20th_century/chin001.asp (accessed 27 August 2018).

New York Times (1971) 'UN Admits Red China: Nationalists Ousted', 25 October. Available at www.archives.nd.edu/Observer/1971-10-26_v06_033.pdf (accessed 25 August 2018).

New York Times (1995) 'Taiwan's President Tiptoes Around Politics at Cornell', 10 June. Available at www.nytimes.com/1995/06/10/world/taiwan-s-president-tiptoes-around-politics-at-cornell.html (accessed 25 August 2018).

New York Times (2016a) 'Sidelined at the UN, a Frustrated Taiwan Presses On', 23 September. Available at www.nytimes.com/2016/09/23/world/asia/taiwan-china-united-nations-un.html?_r=0 (accessed 23 August 2018).

New York Times (2016b) 'Singer's Apology for Waving Taiwan Flag Stirs Backlash of Its Own', *17 January*. Available at www.nytimes.com/2016/01/17/world/asia/taiwan-china-singer-chou-tzu-yu.html?_r=0 (accessed 25 August 2018).

Newsweek (2018) 'How Does China's Navy Compare to America's?' 23 April. Available at www.newsweek.com/how-does-chinas-navy-compare-us-897209 (accessed 26 October 2018).

Niou, Emerson (2004) 'Understanding Taiwan Independence and its Policy Implications', *Asian Survey* 44(4).

Reuters (2014) 'Over 100,000 Protest in Taiwan Over China Trade Deal', 30 March. Available at www.reuters.com/article/us-taiwan-protests-idUSBREA2T07H20140330 (accessed 25 August 2018).

Rothstein, Robert L. (1968) *Alliances and Small Powers*, New York: Columbia University Press.

Shang, Su-wu (2016) *The Defence Capabilities of Small States: Singapore and Taiwan's Responses to Strategic Desperation*, London: Palgrave Macmillan.

Shanghai Communiqué (1972) 28 February. Available at www.taiwandocuments.org/communique01.htm (accessed 25 August 2018).

Six Assurances (1982) *Six Assurances*, July. Available at www.taiwandocuments.org/assurances.htm (accessed 24 August 2018).

South China Morning Post (2016) 'Mainland China Needs a New Approach to Taiwan, Experts Say, after Flag Controversy Sparks Huge Support for Victorious Pro-independence DPP', 28 January. Available at www.scmp.com/news/china/policies-politics/article/1906527/mainland-china-needs-new-approach-taiwan-experts-say (accessed 25 August 2018).

State Council (1993) *White Paper: The Taiwan Question and Reunification of China*, Beijing: State Council. Available at www.china-embassy.org/eng/zt/twwt/White%20Papers/t36704.htm (accessed 25 August 2018).

State Council (2002) *China's National Defence in 2000*, Beijing: State Council, 9 December. Available at http://fas.org/nuke/guide/china/doctrine/natdef2002.html (accessed 25 May 2017).

Straits Times (2018) 'China Calls any Challenge on Taiwan "Extremely Dangerous"', 25 October. Available at www.straitstimes.com/asia/east-asia/chinas-defence-minister-vows-never-to-cede-any-territory-including-taiwan (accessed 26 October 2018).

Sullivan, Jonathan and Will Lowe (2010) 'Chen Shui-bian: On Independence', *China Quarterly*, 203.

Taipei Times (2015) 'Lee Teng-hui Brushes Off KMT Barbs as Politicking', 23 August. Available at www.taipeitimes.com/News/front/archives/2015/08/23/2003625968 (accessed 25 August 2018).

Taiwan Relations Act (TRA) (1979) Taiwan Relations Act, 1 January. Available at www.ait.org.tw/en/taiwan-relations-act.html (accessed 25 August 2018).

Tan, Andrew T. H. (2014) 'The Implications of Taiwan's Declining Defense', *Asia-Pacific Review* 21(1).

Teon, Aris (2018) 'Why Did Chiang Kai-shek Lose China? The Guomindang Regime and the Victory of the Chinese Communist Party', *Greater China Journal*, 26 February. Available at https://china-journal.org/2018/02/26/why-did-chiang-kai-shek-lose-china-the-guomindang-regime-and-the-victory-of-the-chinese-communist-party/ (accessed 19 February 2019).

Tkacik, John (2008) 'Taiwan's "Unsettled" International Status: Preserving U.S. Options in the Pacific', Washington, DC: The Heritage Foundation, 19 June. Available at www.heritage.org/asia/report/taiwans-unsettled-international-status-preserving-us-options-the-pacific (accessed 24 August 2018).

US Department of State (2016) *U.S. Relations with Taiwan: Fact Sheet*, Washington, DC: Department of State, 13 September. Available at www.state.gov/r/pa/ei/bgn/35855.htm (accessed 24 August 2018).

Vital, David (1971) *The Survival of Small States: Studies in Small/Great Power Conflict*, London: Oxford University Press.

Walker, Connor (1968) 'Ethnology and the Peace of South Asia', *World Politics* 22(1).

Washington Post (2017) 'The Taiwanese See Themselves as Taiwanese, Not as Chinese', 2 January. Available at www.washingtonpost.com/news/monkey-cage/wp/2017/01/02/yes-taiwan-wants-one-china-but-which-china-does-it-want/?utm_term=.36a3fc538b67 (accessed 26 August 2018).

Weber, Max (1968) *Economy and Society*, ed. Guenther Roth and Claus Wittich, New York: Bedminster.

World Bank (2017) *China: Overview*, Washington, DC: World Bank, 28 March. Available at www.worldbank.org/en/country/china/overview (accessed 23 August 2018).

Wright, Martin (1978) *Power Politics*, Leicester: Leicester University Press.

3 Taiwan's domestic dynamics and foreign policy

J. Michael Cole

Introduction

Since the loss of its seat at the United Nations (UN) and de-recognition by most players within the international community starting in the 1970s, the Republic of China (ROC, or Taiwan) has been forced to conjugate with a difficult, and arguably unique, external environment. Taiwan has existed in an uncomfortable limbo, its official status challenged by the People's Republic of China (PRC, or China), which claims to be a successor state to the ROC after the latter's defeat in the Chinese civil war that ended in 1949 with the retreat of Chiang Kai-shek, the leader of the Kuomintang (KMT – Nationalist Party), across the Taiwan Strait. As diplomatic allies switched allegiance from Taipei to Beijing, Taiwan nevertheless continued to prosper, developing a vibrant economy and, from the 1980s onwards, starting on the road to liberalization and eventually democratization. Political developments in Taiwan provided a powerful contrast with the kind of authoritarianism that continued to prevail in China, even more so after the Tiananmen Square massacre in June 1989. As the Taiwanese embraced democracy, that choice played a crucial role in bolstering Taiwan's legitimacy and de facto independence, and this despite the increasingly small number of states that officially recognized the island.

Despite the extraordinary achievements of its people, Taiwan continues to suffer from the legacy of its troubled history. This, above all, is characterized by a highly politicized divide between 'greens' and 'blues' that continues to undermine unity. In turn, this has exacerbated the mixed signals that Taiwan has broadcast to the international community on the 'China question' – i.e. on whether the Taiwanese are amenable to eventual political unification with the PRC, whose regime maintains that Taiwan is an inalienable part of China.

Much misunderstanding has surrounded the political divide in Taiwan, and without an intimate understanding of the key political players and the many factions involved in both camps, it is easy to see why governments and analysts outside Taiwan might struggle to understand what Taiwan wants, and the extent to which its people are committed to preserving their way of life as well as independence from China. It is also essential to look at the generational shift that has occurred in recent years now that the aspirations of the generation that came from China with the KMT after its defeat in 1949 fade into memory. Despite the rift that continues to characterize the boisterous politics in Taiwan, and even though they may be framing this differently, the overlapping values and interests of the majority of voters and politicians in both camps are, without doubt, much greater than that which divides them. Nevertheless, the highly politicized divisions, often exacerbated for short-term electoral gain, has proven confusing to international actors and, more dangerously, have often created openings which the Communist Party of China (CPC) has been able to exploit.

Still, pragmatism and a tacit consensus among the Taiwanese has allowed the island-nation to prosper and to weather the vagaries of a tough international environment. Its appeal as a democracy, and its location in an increasingly important corner of the geopolitical puzzle, have also contributed to its continued status as a de facto sovereign state, even when everything seemed to indicate that abandonment by major international players, the United States chief among them, seemed imminent. By restraining its many domestic contradictions and finding ways to engage the international community – and this despite its reduced status in the community of nations as China became a major economic and military power in its own right – Taiwan successfully hedged against Beijing, at times through deepened engagement, as it did during the Ma Ying-jeou era (2008–16), while at others by putting a premium on diversification and deepening relationships with key democracies, a top priority of the current Tsai Ing-wen administration (2016–). A more permissive international environment since 2016, in large part the result of an attitudinal change in the West after it became clear that decades of engagement with China had not yielded a more liberal, let alone democratic, China, has also provided an unprecedented opportunity for Taiwan to strengthen its ties with the international community, albeit often at the unofficial level. Even here, however, domestic politics in Taiwan have at times undermined efforts by the Tsai administration to fully exploit that opening.

This chapter first discusses some of the key unresolved issues which continue to divide the Taiwanese body politics and to hamper development of a unified foreign policy. It then explores the generational change that has occurred in Taiwanese society and how this has gradually, albeit imperfectly, mitigated that long-standing political rift and could hold the key to future resolution. Finally, it discusses the intersection of domestic politics and foreign policy under the Tsai administration in a rapidly changing global context as international players increasingly recognize the value of Taiwan amid efforts to push back against an aggressive China under President Xi Jinping.

Structural weaknesses, ghosts from the past

The single most important contributor to Taiwan's political divisions is the island-nation's history itself. The seeds of that rift were sown at the end of the Second World War, when a defeated Japan was forced to cede control of

Taiwan, over which it had ruled since 1895. Tragically, no sooner had China, then still under KMT rule, replaced the Japanese on the island than troubles arose. At first welcome as liberators, the KMT was poorly equipped to govern an island which Japan had treated as a model colony. Shell-shocked after years of war with Japan and civil war with Mao Zedong's communists, the new rulers of Taiwan reacted with violence when the local population rose up against inefficiency and corruption. Instability led to bouts of savagery, such as the '228 Massacre' that began in February 1947, and the imposition of martial law known as the 'White Terror,' during which tens of thousands of critics of the Chiang regime were silenced, disappeared or killed.

Those series of incidents became the basis for a decades-long rift between the *waishengren* ('mainlanders') who came to Taiwan with the KMT after the end of the Second World War and the *benshengren* who were regarded as 'natives' of Taiwan (while native Taiwanese were the primary targets of KMT repression, mainlanders, as well as Hakka and indigenous minorities were also victims). Betrayed by the Nationalists, the sentiment grew among the native population that the ROC was a new colonizer, an illegitimate regime in exile. That view persisted even after the KMT leadership, first Chiang Kai-shek and then his son, Chiang Ching-kuo, came to realize the futility of their hopes of retaking the 'mainland.' After decades of unfinished civil war, the KMT and the ROC it had implanted in Taiwan, was, for better or worse, here to stay. From the 1950s onwards, the Chiang regime sought to re-Sinicize the Taiwanese population through tight controls on education, language, the creative industry and, of course, the political sphere. The civil service, too, was marked by over-representation of 'mainlanders', particularly at the senior level and overwhelmingly so in institutions such as the Ministry of National Defence, the Ministry of Foreign Affairs and the Ministry of Education. The Ministry of National Defence, especially its Garrison Command, as well as law enforcement and intelligence agencies, were complicit in the repression of the Taiwanese, who often were accused (unjustly, as it would be proven many years later) of being collaborators with the communists.

Up until the 1980s the government did not permit the existence of opposition parties, which gave rise to the *dangwai* ('outside') movement that called for the lifting of martial law and the democratization of Taiwan. Many of the future leaders of the Democratic Progressive Party (DPP), which won the presidential elections in 2000, were former members of the *dangwai* movement. The severance of diplomatic relations between Taipei and Washington in 1979, as well as mounting pressure on the government to relax its grip on Taiwanese society, compelled the government to gradually open up the political space (Tucker 2009: 125). Whether this was instrumental or heartfelt, the decision to liberalize contributed (Tien 1989), years later, to the lifting of martial law, the registering of opposition parties, a freer media, and eventually full democratization, with free and direct presidential elections occurring in 1996.

Despite these impressive developments, which came to be regarded as part of the 'Third Wave' of democratization (Huntington 1991), the structural imbalances that were created during authoritarian rule still existed. Among other things, and despite the gradual inclusion (often with the aim of co-optation) of Taiwanese in government (including that of Lee Teng-hui, a Taiwan native who succeeded Chiang Ching-kuo to the presidency), the civil service, as well as the corporate sector, education, the military and the entertainment industry, remained firmly under the control of the 'mainlanders' and the KMT. The ideology that was cultivated during martial law, along with the power structure within government, survived democratization but did not disappear altogether. In fact, the legacy of authoritarian rule still exists today, and many of the people who joined the civil service during that period now occupy senior positions. Pressures for promotion have also encouraged the perpetuation of many of the practices that were first implemented during that era. Additionally, the KMT continued to benefit from the riches it had amassed, often illegally, during the authoritarian era, giving it an unfair advantage, as its critics saw it, even in the democratic era.

Above all, mistrust was the most corrosive legacy of authoritarian rule. It pitted the 'blue camp' – the KMT and smaller parties, such as the New Party – against the 'green camp' – the DPP and smaller ideological allies such as the Taiwan Solidarity Union, which often engaged in zero-sum politics in the nation's parliament, the Legislative Yuan. On critical issues such as national defence, high polarization (Fell 2011: 75–97) meant that opposition parties used their seats in the legislature, or, as the KMT did during the Chen Shui-bian presidency (2000–08), their majority, to repeatedly block important bills. This scorched-earth style of politics not only cost Taiwan years of defence modernization, for example, but also contributed to foreign perceptions, especially in the United States, Taiwan's principal security guarantor, that Taiwan could not get its act together and was 'freeloading' on defence. It also remains a source of friction within Taiwanese society, whereby *waishengren*, or descendants of former KMT civil servants, continue to be regarded with suspicion regardless of their ideology and commitment to Taiwan.

Also related to defence, long-standing perceptions of the military and intelligence establishments as instruments of the KMT and tools of repression under martial law have undermined the appeal of, and trust in, the very institutions that are now mandated with defending Taiwan against the existential threat posed by China. Fledging efforts at transitional justice, added to the fact that a number of generals are holdovers from the previous era (many of them having being born in China), have exacerbated the view that such institutions cannot be trusted. This has translated into difficulties in recruiting young men and women to join the military amid efforts to phase out conscription, and a derisive view of the armed forces among the Taiwanese public, views that have been exacerbated by highly critical, though not always accurate, reports in the media as well as by aggressive Chinese espionage and propaganda. Such handicaps, in turn, have undermined morale among the troops and fuelled unfavourable perceptions of the Taiwanese military abroad.

Over the years, the KMT has also positioned itself as the party which can best negotiate with the CPC in Beijing to ensure stability in the Taiwan Strait. Due to its supposed ability to defuse conflict, it has, furthermore, convinced a large segment of the corporate sector that the KMT is better equipped to ensure continuity of trade and business across the Taiwan Strait. As many as one million Taiwanese, known as *taishang*, work in China. Their early contributions to the Chinese economic miracle have mostly gone unrecognized, and their willingness to work in China has often led to accusations that they are 'pro-unification' and would unhesitatingly sell Taiwan out if it meant further enrichment (the reality is in fact much more complex). Given this, the KMT has often been described as 'pro-Beijing' and therefore 'pro-unification'. Conversely, the more Taiwan-centric DPP has been seen as 'anti-Beijing' and 'pro-independence'. As a result, at times when the international community has prioritized stability in the Asia-Pacific, such as in the wake of the 11 September 2001 terrorist attacks perpetrated on the US mainland, the DPP was often regarded as a risk factor and potential source of conflict in the region, and thus was treated with high scepticism. Meanwhile, Beijing, which presented itself as the responsible actor in the relationship, encouraged the view that the DPP was a 'troublemaker'.

Far too often, the zero-sum battles that the 'green' and 'blue' camps were waging at home were also exported abroad. These, too, contributed to confusion among foreign governments, which grew impatient with Taiwan. One salient example of this is in Washington, where Taiwan is represented by the Taipei Economic and Cultural Representative Office (TECRO), its de facto embassy in the absence of official diplomatic ties. Moreover, both the KMT and the DPP have offices in the capital, and a lobby group, the Formosan Association for Public Affairs, is also engaged in representation. Depending on which party is in power in Taipei, officials have on occasion bypassed TECRO officials and instead have dealt directly with party offices, a violation of which undoubtedly harms Taiwan's ability to present a coherent foreign policy and represents a failure of separation of powers.

> These conflicting inputs make it difficult for Taiwan as a whole to communicate a unified message. As Taiwan's political-economic challenges in asserting a distinct identity in Northeast Asia continue to deepen, its problems of coherent representation in Washington do so as well.
>
> (Calder 2014: 168)

Taiwan's democracy also ensured plurality of opinion at academic conferences and meetings abroad, which contrasted sharply with the unified – and seemingly coherent – position espoused by their Chinese counterparts.

The political divide was brought to those settings, which Taiwanese participants often used to disparage their domestic opponents and, in doing so, undermine the notion that the two main camps in Taiwanese politics could ever see eye-to-eye on anything, let alone collaborate. Some public events abroad, organized by institutions with undisclosed ties to the Chinese military and United Front apparatus (Cole 2015), also used various occasions to invite Taiwanese academics, former officials and retired generals who harboured pro-unification views, which compounded the confusion among their foreign counterparts and greatly misrepresent popular support for such an outcome with the Taiwanese public.[1] According to the latest poll by the most credible source (NCCU Elections Studies Center 2018), only 3 per cent of Taiwanese support unification with China as soon as possible, while 12.5 per cent favour maintaining the status quo and moving towards unification at a later date; 23.7 per cent support maintaining the status quo indefinitely, 33.4 per cent for the status quo now and deciding later, while 15.5 per cent favour the status quo now and moving towards independence later; and 4.8 per cent want independence as soon as possible.

Finding itself at a disadvantage, and with signs that Washington was no longer willing to help to defend Taiwan, the DPP government under President Chen began to fear that it would be abandoned by its long-standing ally, which, under the Taiwan Relations Act of 1979, had some obligation to help Taiwan to ward off pressure from China. Fears of abandonment, in turn, were recycled in domestic politics, whereby the KMT accused the DPP of creating instability that, in turn, was harming a fragile economy that had been largely stagnant since the Asian Financial Crisis of 1997–98. Embattled, the DPP administration felt that it needed to demonstrate its accomplishments in foreign policy, which often meant advertising bilateral achievements that foreign partners, fearful of angering Beijing, had hoped would remain secret. As a result, the kind of pragmatism that allowed Taiwan to strengthen ties with important allies gave way to publicity, which alienated many governments from the DPP. It would take a decade for the DPP to rebuild its reputation with foreign governments.

Additionally, seeking re-election for a second term and aiming to boost the party's appeal in nationwide local elections, the Chen administration began to flirt with referenda and constitutional changes, political tactics that caused great alarm in Washington and elsewhere. Although there is certainly a case for changing a constitution that was drafted in China in 1947, or even for changing the ROC's official name to Taiwan, the instrumental use of plebiscites for political gain – which is largely how the move was perceived – threatened instability in the Taiwan Strait at a time when the United States was struggling with two difficult wars in Iraq and Afghanistan. Thus, while there was nothing fundamentally wrong with holding a referendum on such issues (after all, self-determination is perfectly legitimate under international law and under the UN charter), the timing was wrong, and the Chen administration failed to appreciate the context in which it sought to implement those policies.[2] This, therefore, was a clear example of primarily domestic politics causing great harm to Taiwan's foreign policy and ability to engage its partners abroad.

The KMT, for its part, saw rapprochement with Beijing as a better way to reinvigorate Taiwan's economy and reduce tensions in the Taiwan Strait. This more 'responsible' approach largely contributed to the election, by a wide margin, of Ma Ying-jeou in 2008. The 'correction course' was welcomed in most international circles, which feared instability and continued to hope that China was on the way to reform, and was certainly so in Beijing, which saw this as an opportunity to drag Taiwan ever closer into its sphere of influence. Various agreements, including a landmark Economic Cooperation Framework Agreement, were signed during the eight-year Ma presidency; cross-Strait tourism boomed, and exchanges in education, culture and other sectors were routinized. The amplification of cross-Strait détente during the Ma era was such that Taiwan went from being seen as a potential source of conflict which could spark major hostilities between Beijing and Washington – in other words, an object of interest to journalists and academics – to a problem that had largely been resolved. Vowing, during his election and re-election campaigns, to repair ties with Beijing and thereby revive Taiwan's economy, Ma won handsome praise abroad and the KMT seemed unstoppable. The fact that Taiwanese voters had given Ma a second mandate in 2012 also was proof, foreign observers claimed, that Taiwan was indeed amenable to eventual unification with China.

Domestic developments, however, would prove that all of this was wrong and would send foreign analysts scrambling for answers. The first act was the emergence of, and wide popular support for, the Sunflower Movement, which in March and April 2014 occupied the chambers of the Legislative Yuan in Taipei over the controversial Cross-Strait Services Trade Agreement, a pact which many regarded as imperilling Taiwan's freedoms and to have been negotiated without sufficient government transparency (Hsu 2017: 134–53). The Movement precipitated a decline of Ma's fortunes, from which he, and his party, never recuperated, not even when Ma made history by meeting Xi during a summit in Singapore in late 2015. The 16 January 2016 general elections, in which the DPP regained control of the presidency and, for the first time in the nation's democratic history, won a majority of seats in the legislature, constituted further proof that Taiwanese voters did not want a continuation of Ma's 'pro-Beijing' policies. In fact, the KMT dropped its initial candidate, Hung Hsiu-chu, over the low appeal that her policies, which sought an even closer relationship with China, had among 'blue' voters. Within eight years, Taiwanese voters, and an activist civil society, had discredited all notions that the Taiwanese did not care about the sovereignty of their nation. With that, the international community once again had a problem on its hands: rather than go away, as many had hoped, the Taiwan issue was back – with a vengeance.

Changing societal attitudes

With the exception of small, electorally unviable political parties that favour immediate unification,[3] Taiwan's main political parties, in both the 'blue' and 'green' camps, have internalized the democratic rules of the game. Even though their observance of the rules are occasionally breached (e.g. vote buying), nevertheless there is recognition that political legitimacy is now contingent upon adhesion to the democratic principles that have been consolidating since the late 1980s. As noted earlier, the need to respect the democratic wishes of Taiwanese voters compelled the KMT in 2015 to replace its initial candidate for the 2016 elections due to the low appeal of her proposed China policies. The democratic requirement has, in turn, determined the kind of foreign policy that Taiwan is capable of engaging in.

Much of this is the result of a generational change in Taiwan, which increasingly has defined citizenship along the lines of 'civic values' (i.e. democracy, civility) and away from the traditional – and often immutable – 'blue' versus 'green' (political affiliation) or 'ethnic' (e.g. *waishengren* versus *benshengren*) categories. Self-identification is increasingly shaped by being born in Taiwan and the democratic experience, which for the generations born after 1990 is the only experience they know. This 'civic nationalism' is therefore multicultural, conferring citizenship upon anyone, regardless of ethnic origin, as long as he or she respects the democratic norms that now define the nation. The number of Taiwanese who self-identify as 'Chinese' has also dropped steadily over the years, and even among those who regard themselves as Chinese or 'Chinese and Taiwanese', there is no contradiction in this: for them, it is possible to be both of 'Chinese' ethnic or cultural origin (*huaren*) and Taiwanese in one's nationality or citizenship, a view that aligns with that of multicultural societies in the West but which clashes with China's civilizational and ethnic concept of statehood. This also explains why it is possible to argue that Beijing is facing not one but rather two independence movements in Taiwan – the Taiwanese independence movement (*taidu*) that is associated with the 'green' camp, and those who continue to regard the ROC – now transformed through an often ad hoc process of indigenization and democratization – as a legitimate political entity which now exists solely in Taiwan and its outlying islands, and whose ideology remains fixedly anti-communist (Lin 2016). This movement, *huadu*, has more traction among the elderly segment of *waishengren* society, but nevertheless overlaps with the traditional *taidu* movement in its opposition to communist rule over Taiwan (Cole 2016a). It also explains why a group such as the Blue Sky Alliance, a 'deep blue' political movement that is highly critical of the Tsai government and which is openly opposed to *taidu*, nevertheless physically clashed with pro-unification members of the China Unification Promotion Party during a protest in 2017 over the large number of PRC flags that the CUPP were flying at the event. Many of the members of the Alliance were retired ROC soldiers who had fought the communists in the Chinese civil war.

This departure from hitherto fixed political affiliations has also translated into wider criticism of any party which is seen to be violating democratic rules, thus giving the KMT and the DPP equal status and responsibilities (Cole 2016b: 104–34). As the Sunflower Movement and many before it demonstrated, young Taiwanese were now willing to break with family rules on political affiliation, which in many cases caused frictions with their elders that, over time, came to be reconciled. This, in turn, has empowered 'swing voters', who are increasingly important in determining electoral outcomes. The decisive victory of Tsai Ing-wen and her DPP in the 2016 general elections was in large part attributable to swing voters and 'light blues' who crossed over the divide and voted for the DPP rather than for the KMT, as they normally would have done.

A recent opinion poll of young Taiwanese shows that despite dissatisfaction (58.2 per cent) with the state of Taiwan's democracy, 94 per cent of respondents declared that living in a democratic society is 'important', and 65.8 percent stated that it is 'very important'. Meanwhile, almost 70 per cent agreed with the statement that 'there exist some problems in democracy, but it is still the best political system' (Taiwan Foundation for Democracy 2018).

While increasingly important as an element of Taiwanese self-identity, the impact of a more homogenous nationalism nevertheless should not be overstated. That is largely because the transformation of nationalism and self-identification within Taiwanese society has outpaced the ability of the Taiwanese institutions to adjust accordingly. As we saw earlier, Taiwan's government institutions remain conservative and have retained many elements of the past. This has undermined reform, added friction to the policymaking process, and caused frustration among an impatient public that expected rapid change (Shih 2018). This explains why, despite Taiwan's much vaunted democracy, some Taiwanese representatives posted abroad have not hesitated to lament Taiwan as 'too free' and 'too democratic', statements that, for good reason, have befuddled foreign counterparts who regard Taiwan's impressive democratic achievements as one of its main assets.

Besides the slow pace of reform that is alienating a segment of society, foreign policy imperatives have also fuelled impatience within the 'deep green' camp – those who, following the Tsai election in 2016, expected a fundamental shift in the government's handling of its relationship with China and the international community. Many of Tsai's critics have accused her of being too cautious with regard to China and unwilling to challenge it even amid an international context that, for the time being, appears to be more favourable to Taiwan.[4] The Tsai administration, however, has understood the careful balance it must strike between defending Taiwan's sovereignty amid intensifying efforts by Beijing to erode Taiwan's international space on the one hand, and reassuring its partners abroad that Taiwan is not about to embark on brinksmanship that is bound to increase tensions with China and heighten the risks of war. Much of her administration's success abroad since 2016 can arguably be attributed to this careful and pragmatic approach. Still, that requirement for careful policymaking, added to Tsai's decision to abide by the status quo in the Taiwan Strait, has been a source of discontent among traditional members of her party and more extreme factions within the 'green' camp. This has led to efforts to hold a referendum on rectification of the country's name, as well as to highly invidious accusations that Tsai is a 'Nationalist at heart' and therefore a 'traitor' to the cause of Taiwan independence. Some of those voices have even called for another candidate to lead the DPP in the 2020 general elections.

Although the Tsai administration has so far withstood popular pressure from below to adopt a more confrontational policy, thus avoiding the mistake committed by Chen Shui-bian, her ability to hold the line will be contingent on the level of her popular support as the next elections approach. Pressure within the party, especially of the electoral prospects do not appear promising, as well as external pressure from the 'deep green' civil society, such as the Formosa Alliance (Ihara 2018), could compel the leadership to assuage that segment to ensure voter turnout in its favour. As a result, the Taiwanese leadership could adopt policies that, on the external front, may appear to be irrational and self-defeating, and which in turn could cost Taiwan some important relationships.

Foreign policy under Tsai Ing-wen

Almost immediately after Tsai's inauguration on 20 May 2016, Beijing embarked on a highly punitive strategy against Taiwan to bring the new government to heel. Among other things, the Chinese regime resumed its efforts, put on hold during the Ma presidency, to lure Taiwan's official diplomatic allies, which by the end of 2018 numbered only 16. It ramped up its pressure to deny Taiwan participation at multilateral organizations, such as the World Health Assembly, Interpol and the International Civil Aviation Organization that require statehood. And it launched a campaign that targeted foreign private companies, among them major airlines, forcing them to remove all references to Taiwan on their websites and apps. Beijing also ramped up its military activity around Taiwan, and intensified its political warfare, propaganda, cyber and disinformation efforts against the island.

All these efforts compelled the Tsai administration to double down on its campaign promise to reduce Taiwan's economic dependence on China through diversification. Rather than cow the Taiwanese public as Beijing hoped, this increased belligerence bolstered the appeal of such measures with the Taiwanese public. A major component of that effort was the New Southbound Policy, which seeks to engage 18 targeted countries in South and South-East Asia at the economic, social, educational and cultural level. Soon enough, the measures taken by the government to deepen interactions with its southern neighbours began paying dividends, such as by making up for the substantial decrease in the number of Chinese tourism arrivals, much of it dictated by Beijing, that had occurred since Tsai's election in the 16 January 2016 elections.[5] As a result, initial protests by players in the tourism industry which had been most affected by the reduction in the number of Chinese tourists due largely to over-reliance developed during the Ma era, fizzled out and failed to generate the kind of public support that could have forced the Tsai administration to change its policy towards China (e.g. by recognizing the '1992 consensus').

Meanwhile, geopolitical developments, mainly in the form of a readjustment by several Western countries to their China policy, created unprecedented avenues for engagement with Taiwan. A long overdue recognition among advanced democracies that China was not on the way to democratization, and furthermore that its growing influence was having a detrimental effect on their democratic institutions, engendered a newfound desire to engage Taiwan and to learn from its vast experience of dealing with China. Relying mostly on Track 1.5 and Track 2, bilateral and multilateral exchanges with major democratic countries reached unprecedented levels and were made possible by the growing confidence in foreign capitals that the Tsai administration would not burn them by drawing too much attention to these developments.

The major shift in the United States' perceptions of China and, accordingly, in its recognition of the value of its Taiwan partnership, also led to a marked increase in bilateral exchanges, as well as the passage of various bills in the United States that facilitated contact at high levels of government and between their respective military establishments, and deepened the American commitment to the preservation of Taiwan's security and democracy. Key bills include the Taiwan Travel Act, the John S. McCain National Defense Authorization Act for Fiscal Year 2019, and the Taipei Act (US Congress 2017, 2018a, 2018b). The latter, introduced in reaction to Beijing's capture of Taiwan's remaining official diplomatic allies, had, in 2019, yet to become law. More than ever, the Department of State, the Department of Defense, the Congress and other agencies were keen on engaging their counterparts in Taiwan. Just as importantly, support for greater contact with Taiwan was bipartisan, a reflection of the institutional change that had taken place across the US government and the academic establishment in recent years, much of it in reaction to China's alarming behaviour under Xi Jinping.

One of the most high-profile endeavours involving Taiwan and the United States has been the Global Cooperation and Training Framework (GCTF), which has seen a total of 13 rounds of engagement since 2015, when the initiative was launched (American Institute in Taiwan 2018). Among other things, the GCTF has brought American officials and experts to Taiwan for high-level meetings on media literacy, transnational crime and forensic science, disease control, disaster relief and e-commerce. In October 2018 Deputy Assistant Secretary of State Scott Busby travelled to Taiwan to take part in a GCTF workshop. The success of the GCTF has also generated interest among other democracies, including Japan and Australia, to participate in, or to emulate, this mechanism for exchange with Taiwan. Several delegations have also met since 2016 to elaborate strategies to counter Chinese cyber espionage, and Taiwan is increasingly regarded as a reliable partner in efforts to keep Pacific Islands, many of them official diplomatic allies of Taiwan, on the side of the democratic community amid growing efforts by China to increase its influence in the region and displace the United States as the military hegemon in the Indo-Pacific.

In the aggregate, this deepening and multifaceted engagement with important international actors has help to mitigate the impact of China's punitive strategy against Taiwan since 2016. While segments of the 'deep green' camp and prospective KMT candidates in the 2020 elections have attempted to portray Beijing's successes against Taiwan as a result of 'weak' or 'dangerous' leadership on Tsai's part, those voices have remained a minority and therefore have failed to translate into the kind of pressure from below that would compel the administration to make major adjustments to its foreign policy. Thus, while support rates for the Tsai government have dropped since 2016, much of it has been the result of its handling of domestic issues (e.g. reform, pensions, land, transitional justice, labour, judiciary), rather than unfavourable perceptions of the government's handling of China and foreign relations.

Views of China among ordinary Taiwanese people have also been affected by developments there in recent years. Although the general public does not obsess about China (something that may be difficult for foreign observers to understand), there is sufficient awareness among the Taiwanese of the current trends in China, of the hardening authoritarian controls on every aspect of society, for them to understand that the two societies are incompatible. This should not, however, be regarded as a denial of the existence or of the legitimacy of the PRC. But it is a stark reminder that this is not what they want for their country – for older Taiwanese, this brings back painful memories of the authoritarian era; for the younger generations whose only experience is that of living in a liberal democracy, it is downright alien. China may be a land of opportunities, and indeed many young Taiwanese have considered going to China to work or study. But despite many attempts by Beijing to turn the attractiveness of its economy into a political tool, such as the '31 incentives programme' unveiled by China's Taiwan Affairs Office in early 2018 (Huang 2018), such efforts have not succeeded in altering the balance of desire in the Taiwan Strait. The troubled experience of Hong Kong under 'one country, two systems' – the same 'offer' made to Taiwan for unification – has above all else shaped Taiwanese views on Beijing's respect for local views under 'one China'. For the Taiwanese, Hong Kong is the canary in the mine shaft, and this *prise de conscience* has in turn translated into pressure on the government, at the polls and within civil society, to ensure that a similar fate does not await Taiwan.[6]

China and its proxies in Taiwan, meanwhile, have intensified their political warfare and disinformation operations against the island, with the aim of undermining the central government, democratic practices and institutions, and to widen domestic contradictions by turning various camps and factions against each other. Taiwanese law enforcement authorities revealed in late 2018 that Beijing was using various means, some of them learned from similar Russian activities, to interfere with year-end nationwide elections by providing financing and other types of assistance to pro-Beijing candidates (Lin 2018). According to intelligence sources, Beijing was using local elections as a 'trial run' for similar, ramped-up efforts ahead of the 2020 presidential elections. The long-term effects of such operations, should they succeed, on Taiwan's foreign policy can only be guessed at this point.

Conclusions

Taiwan's troubled and incompletely addressed authoritarian past, added to its idiosyncratic position within the international community resulting from China's sovereignty claims, have polarized the domestic political environment and generated various pressures on decision makers which can influence the government's foreign policy. Any administration in Taipei must not only strike a balance between the 'pro-China' and 'pro-independence' camps, but also reassure allies like the United States that it will not spark major hostilities in the Taiwan Strait. This art of balance has therefore compelled governments to ignore, or to redirect, extremist public sentiment which, if turned into policy, could quickly derail a carefully crafted foreign policy. Taiwan's foreign policy also occurs under the shadow of China, which, through intimidation and the flexing of its considerable power, often has succeeded in limiting Taiwan's ability to practise a normal foreign policy, which in turn can engender frustration among Taiwanese voters who regard their leadership's inaction as a sign of weakness. As this chapter has demonstrated, the scope of Taiwan's foreign policy is also largely contingent upon the vagaries of the international system, which at times can be permissive and at others frustratingly restrictive, especially given the island-nation's rather unusual status as a de facto state without membership at the UN. This has compelled the leadership to engage in creative foreign policymaking with willing partners who nevertheless must maintain good relations with the world's second-largest economy and an increasingly influential country in international affairs.

Notes

1 One such organization is the China Energy Fund Committee (CEFC), which has organized a number of conferences and trilaterals in the United States in recent years. At the time of writing, the CEFC is currently under investigation in China and the United States, and its representative to the United States, Patrick Ho, is facing various charges of bribery and conspiracy in a New York court. See *United States of America v. Chi Ping Patrick Ho*, available at www.justice.gov/opa/press-release/file/1012531/download.
2 Author interview with Paul Wolfowitz, former US Deputy Secretary of Defense.
3 Among those are the triad-linked China Unification Promotion Party (CUPP) of Chang An-le and, increasingly, the New Party.
4 Taiwanese human rights non-governmental organizations severely reprimanded the Tsai administration over its 'failure' to strike back at China following the kidnapping, and eventual sentencing, of Lee Ming-che, a human rights activist, in March 2017. Rather than publicly disparage the Chinese regime, the Tsai government used back channels to obtain information about Lee's whereabouts, and to secure visits by members of his family at a time when official mechanisms, the State Council's Taiwan Affairs Office and its counterpart, the Mainland Affairs Council, had been suspended by Beijing in retaliation for the Tsai government's refusal to abide by the so-called 1992 Consensus, a prerequisite by Beijing for the resumption of regular cross-Strait talks. This was a clear instance of the Tsai government holding firm to a pragmatic cross-Strait policy despite being under severe pressure domestically to escalate. Given the environment in China, it is difficult to see how a firmer stance

by Taipei could have helped to secure Lee's release or reduce his sentence. Lee received five years' imprisonment for subversion.
5 From a historical high of 4.1 million Chinese tourists in 2015. The number of tourists from Association of Southeast Asian Nations countries rose by 16 per cent in 2016 and continued to rise in 2017.
6 Very few groups, such as the pro-unification CUPP, continue to argue that 'one country, two systems' is a viable formula for Taiwan. The CUPP's own political manifesto makes the case for implementing that system after unification.

References

American Institute in Taiwan (2018) 'Global Cooperation and Training Framework'. Available at www.ait.org.tw/tag/gctf/.
Calder, Kent E. (2014) *Asia in Washington: Exploring the Penumbra of Transnational Power*, Washington, DC: Brookings Institution Press.
Cole, J. Michael (2011) 'Interview: Wolfowitz Praises Taiwan's Democratic Legacy', *Taipei Times*, 24 October. Available at www.taipeitimes.com/News/taiwan/archives/2011/10/24/2003516558 (accessed 22 January 2019).
Cole, J. Michael (2015) 'Chinese Propaganda: Coming Soon to a Conference Near You', *The Diplomat*, 23 September. Available at https://thediplomat.com/2015/09/chinese-propaganda-coming-soon-to-a-conference-near-you/ (accessed 22 January 2019).
Cole, J. Michael (2016a) 'China Faces Not One but Two Forces for Independence in Taiwan', *Asia Dialogue*, 22 March. Available at http://theasiadialogue.com/2016/03/22/90972/ (accessed 22 January 2019).
Cole, J. Michael (2016b) *Convergence or Conflict in the Taiwan Strait: The Illusion of Peace?* Abingdon: Routledge.
Fell, Dafydd (2011) 'The Polarization of Taiwan's Party Competition in the DPP Era', in Robert Ash, John W. Garver and Penelope B. Prime (eds) *Taiwan's Democracy: Economic and Political Challenges*, Abingdon: Routledge.
Hsu Szu-chien (2017) 'The China Factor and Taiwan's Civil Society Organizations in the Sunflower Movement: The Case of the Democratic Front against the Cross-Strait Service Trade Agreement', in Dafydd Fell (ed.) *Taiwan's Social Movements under Ma Ying-jeou: From the Wild Strawberries to the Sunflowers*, Abingdon: Routledge.
Huang, Kristin (2018) 'Taiwanese Given 'Equal Status' on China's Mainland, but Is Beijing Just Trying to Buy Their Support?' *South China Morning Post*, 1 March. Available at www.scmp.com/news/china/policies-politics/article/2135291/taiwanese-given-equal-status-chinas-mainland-beijing (accessed 22 January 2018).
Huntington, Samuel (1991) *The Third Wave: Democratization in the Late Twentieth Century*, Norman: University of Oklahoma Press.
Ihara, Kensaku (2018) 'Pro-Independence Forces in Taiwan Align to Push Referendum', *Nikkei Asian Review*, 9 April. Available at https://asia.nikkei.com/Politics/Pro-independence-forces-in-Taiwan-align-to-push-referendum (accessed 22 January 2018).
Lau, Mimi (2017) 'Rights Activist Lee Ming-Cheh First Taiwanese to be Jailed for Subversion on Mainland China', *South China Morning Post*, 28 November. Available at www.scmp.com/news/china/policies-politics/article/2121882/taiwanese-rights-activist-jailed-five-years-china (accessed 22 January 2018).
Lin, Hsiao-ting (2016) *Accidental State: Chiang Kai-shek, the United States, and the Making of Taiwan*, Cambridge, MA: Harvard University Press.

Lin, Qingchuan (2018) 'There Are Funds to Support Specific Candidates', *Liberty Times*, 22 October. Available at https://news.ltn.com.tw/news/focus/paper/1241193 (accessed 13 February 2019).

NCCU Elections Studies Center (2018) *Taiwan Independence vs. Unification with the Mainland Trend Distribution in Taiwan (1992/06–2018/06)*, NCCU Elections Studies Center, 2 August. Available at https://esc.nccu.edu.tw/course/news.php?Sn=167# (accessed 22 January 2018).

Shih, Hsiu-chuan (2018) 'Survey Finds Dissatisfaction with Tsai's Reform Agenda', *Focus Taiwan*, 20 May. Available at http://focustaiwan.tw/news/aipl/201805200013.aspx (accessed 22 January 2018).

Taiwan Foundation for Democracy (2018) 'A Political Profile of Taiwan's Youth: Democratic Support, Natural independence, and Commitment to Defense', 3 April. Available at www.tfd.org.tw/export/sites/tfd/files/download/democracy_in_Taiwan_20180323_rev_Hsu3_04032018-1.pdf (accessed 22 January 2018).

Tien, Hung-mao (1989) *The Great Transition: Political and Social Change in the Republic of China*, Taipei: SMC Publishing.

Tucker, Nancy Bernkopf (2009) *Strait Talk: United States-Taiwan Relations and the Crisis with China*, Cambridge, MA: Harvard University Press.

US Congress (2017) H.R.535 – Taiwan Travel Act. Available at www.congress.gov/bill/115th-congress/house-bill/535/text.

US Congress (2018a) H.R.5515 – John S. McCain National Defense Authorization Act for Fiscal Year 2019. Available at www.congress.gov/bill/115th-congress/house-bill/5515/text.

US Congress (2018b) S.3406 –Taiwan Allies International Protection and Enhancement Initiative (TAIPEI) Act of 2018. Available at www.congress.gov/bill/115th-congress/senate-bill/3406/text?q=%7B%22search%22%3A%5B%22taiwan%22%5D%7D&r=1.

4 Taiwan and the great powers

Andrea Benvenuti

Introduction

Since the Chinese Kuomintang (KMT, or Nationalist Party) government's final retreat from the mainland to Taiwan in 1949, two overriding objectives have characterized the foreign policy of the Republic of China (ROC, or Taiwan): securing its survival in a very challenging politico-strategic environment, and boosting its legitimacy internationally in competition with the People's Republic of China (PRC, or China). Although for many years one of the ROC's stated foreign policy goals was the restoration of its authority over the whole of China, this was never a realistic proposition. Given the disparity of forces between the two Chinas, the only sensible course of action for successive ROC governments was to build a viable and prosperous nation, and to garner enough international support to ensure its continued existence. Born out of inauspicious beginnings, the ROC immediately had to take stock of its inherent weaknesses and vulnerability. As one historian recently noted, the emergence of Taiwan as a separate state was very much the result of the growing tensions between the United States and the PRC (Lin 2016a). As Washington's containment policy and Beijing's support for revolutionary movements across Asia, along with its enduring hostility towards the Chinese Nationalists, had crystallized to produce enduring regional divisions, the key factors shaping Taiwan's future as well as its foreign policy were already very much in place.

It is against this backdrop that this chapter will approach the theme of Taiwan's relations with the great powers. In doing so, it will focus on the ROC's relations with the United States and China. The reason for doing so is simple. Not only did the United States play a crucial role in ensuring the country's survival, but it also significantly shaped its political outlook. Given the ROC's dependence on the United States, its foreign policy options could not but be profoundly influenced by the very nature of this patron-client relationship. While Taiwan's overwhelming reliance on the United States undoubtedly played a large part in setting the contours of its foreign policy, these were also shaped, to a significant degree, by the ROC's chequered relationship with the PRC. Beijing's unrelenting opposition to Taiwanese independence has also been a defining factor in Taipei's foreign policy.

Taiwan and the great powers during the early Cold War (1949–69)

Despite growing American concerns about deepening Cold War tensions, Washington's initial policy towards the KMT government was far from reassuring for President Chiang Kai-shek (1949–75). Until the outbreak of hostilities in Korea in mid-1950, the Truman Administration had displayed a remarkable distrust of the KMT. Nor had it shown any willingness to endorse Chiang's plans for a regional anti-communist (and North Atlantic Treaty Organization (NATO)-like) Pacific Pact in 1949 (Mabon 1988: 151). Not only had 'the fundamental corruptness of the KMT and its unpopularity on the island … fueled American distaste for Taiwan', but broader American strategic concerns had militated against closer US-Taiwan ties (Cha 2016). On this count, Washington had hoped to induce the Chinese communists to follow a deviationist path similar to the one pursued by Yugoslavia's Josip Broz Tito in an attempt to prevent them from aligning with the USSR. With this in mind, it had downplayed Taiwan's significance to American regional interests and had been careful to distance itself from the Nationalist government (ibid.; Accinelli 1996: 6). The State Department, in particular, was concerned that even limited military assistance to Chiang might not only frustrate Western efforts to drive a wedge between Beijing and Moscow, but it might also bind the US close to the KMT regime, and commit American power to the seemingly futile goal of preventing a probable communist takeover of Taiwan (ibid.: 12). In this context, it was significant that in a January 1950 address to the National Press Club Secretary of State Dean Acheson failed to mention Taiwan as part of the US offshore defence perimeter in the Western Pacific (Cohen 1993: 63).

The attitude of Washington's key ally, Britain, was no more reassuring for Chiang. In London, Clement Attlee's Labour government had shown a similar distaste for the KMT regime and appeared reconciled with the prospect of a communist takeover of Taiwan (Accinelli 1996: 10). More significantly, in January 1950 London had granted recognition to the PRC, thus plainly revealing its accommodationist attitude towards the mainland. For a KMT regime that had completed its final retreat to Taiwan only a few months earlier and remained under the threat of a communist takeover (Roy 2003: 111), the attitude of the two key Western powers boded ill for its survival. No less discouraging was the behaviour of major Asian powers, such as India, Burma and Indonesia, all of whom recognized the PRC. India, in particular, after having established diplomatic ties with the Nationalist government in 1948, switched recognition to the PRC in December 1949 (Heimsath and Mansingh 1971: 186).

North Korea's surprise attack on the South in June 1950 and the PRC's subsequent intervention in the Korean conflict were to change Washington's approach to Taiwan dramatically (Lin 2016a). The combination of these two events proved to be a veritable lifesaver for Chiang's regime, not least because the despatch of the US Seventh Fleet to the Taiwan Strait averted an impending communist takeover (Tsang 1993: 50–52; Roy 2003: 112). Having previously deemed Taiwan expendable, the Truman Administration now concluded that the island was vital to the protection of the southern flank of American military operations in Korea and, thus, was worth defending (Accinelli 1996: 31). Accordingly, it ceased to keep the KMT government at arm's length and moved to inject new life into its political relationship with it (ibid.: x-xi).

Convinced that the USSR's expansionist designs lay behind the North Korean attack, Truman was determined to stand firm against further Soviet encroachments in East Asia. As the Administration's NSC 48–5 memorandum revealingly put it in 1951, Soviet tactics aimed to bring 'the mainland of Eastern Asia and eventually Japan and the other principal off-shore islands in the Western Pacific under Soviet control, primarily through Soviet exploitation of the resources of communist China'. Such an outcome, however, was 'an unacceptable threat to the security of the United States' for, by 'securing [its] eastern flank', Moscow would be able 'to concentrate its offensive power in other areas, particularly Europe'. Hence, the Administration viewed, as its key tasks, the denial of 'Formosa to any Chinese regime aligned with or dominated by the USSR' and 'the strengthening of [its] defense capabilities'. Furthermore, it thought it essential to 'encourage political change in the Nationalist regime' so as to increase 'its prestige and influence in China proper' (FRUS 1977: doc 12). In so doing, the Administration hoped that a reformed Nationalist regime might one day provide an attractive political alternative for disaffected mainlanders as well as gaining the loyalty of Chinese people overseas. Incidentally, winning the latter's hearts and minds was not an exclusively American goal. Quite the opposite: it was also an important factor in the foreign policies of both Chinese states since Chinese people living overseas 'represented remittances, investment and a source of foreign exchange' (Oyen 2010: 60).

With this in mind, the Truman Administration soon began to provide sizeable military and economic assistance to Taiwan, and to use its territory and manpower to wage limited covert operations against the mainland (Accinelli 1996: 254). For Chiang and his loyalists, American political, military and economic support was to prove crucial to the regime's survival and 'to the realisation of both [its] internal and external aspirations' (CIA 1974a: 20). In this context, it is not surprising that the ROC government was to make the maintenance of close relations with the United States the cornerstone of its foreign policy. The upshot of it all, however, was that Taiwan's external relations were to develop within the strict confines imposed by a profoundly asymmetrical relationship with the United States. This, of course, is not to say that Chiang's Taiwan was to become a malleable and subservient ally of the United States (Accinelli 1996: 264; Lin 2016a). On the contrary, the Generalissimo proved, at times, to be more than capable of deflecting American pressure and exploiting Taiwan's dependent status 'to extract the maximum benefit' (Accinelli 1996: 264).

For its part, the Truman Administration, despite its change of heart, was in no mood to give Chiang a blank cheque and its support was to remain highly conditional. Although both Washington and Taipei deeply mistrusted the communist leadership in Beijing, they often found themselves at odds on how best to deal with it (Roy 2003: 113). Truman settled for the containment of Red China. By contrast, Chiang – who had never given up the idea of reconquering the mainland (Tsang 1993: 48–72) – favoured rolling back communism. He argued that the United States ought to challenge the PRC head on before it became too strong (Roy 2003: 114). In his view, the Communist Party of China (CPC) was unpopular domestically. Hence, the conditions existed for a successful landing of ROC troops on the mainland, which would trigger an anti-communist uprising (ibid.: 113). To Chiang's chagrin, however, Truman was not prepared to go that far. Fears of entrapment pushed the Administration to 'systematically restrain Chiang' and caution him against behaving recklessly lest American aid dry up (Cha 2016). Significantly, it also shunned Chiang's offers to provide troops for the US-led war effort in Korea for fear that Taiwan's military involvement might lead to an all-out confrontation with the PRC. Washington did, however, provide covert support to the Chinese Nationalists' cross-border guerrilla operations along the Chinese-Burmese border in an attempt to distract the Chinese communists and undermine their military efforts in Korea (ibid.). Following the PRC's successful efforts in 1950 to drive KMT forces out of Yunnan, nearly 50,000 Nationalist troops had taken shelter in Burma (ibid.). Only after the armistice in Korea in 1953 did the United States exert strong pressure on Chiang to withdraw them (ibid.). By then, they had 'become a liability in the fragile [Korean] ceasefire' and complicated US relations with Burma – a country whose friendship the United States was keen to cultivate for the sake of preventing further communist inroads in Asia (ibid.). Despite intense pressure from Washington, the KMT government would budge only very reluctantly and only after it sent forces from Burma into China one more time during the 1958 Taiwan Strait Crisis. They were finally withdrawn in 1961 (ibid.).

Washington's complicated balancing act in Taiwan was to continue under Truman's successor, Dwight Eisenhower. As a National Intelligence Estimate (NIE) for the new Republican Administration pointed out in September 1954, the PRC was expected to continue to threaten Taiwan's 'security and international standing'. For its part, the KMT leadership would 'almost certainly not become reconciled to an insular future, nor will it concentrate principally on the development of Taiwan' (CIA 1954). However, as long as the United States did 'not reduce materially its present commitment to Taiwan', the PRC would not dare to attack Taiwan and the latter would not 'undertake major military or diplomatic moves without US endorsement' (ibid.). Yet, as the NIE implied, Taiwan would not cease to be a major headache for US policymakers. One problem was its vulnerability to Chinese 'propaganda, diplomatic effort, threats and military demonstrations'. A further complication was the limited international support it enjoyed, which prompted it to demand – despite Washington's sheer determination to avoid being drawn into quarrels of Taipei's own making – membership of 'any regional security system organised by the US in the Far East' (ibid.). On the other hand, as the NIE noted, the United States needed to be aware that Taiwan 'retain[ed] a considerable capability for independent action' and that any reduction in American support might drive Taipei to take inconsiderate steps 'in the hope of involving the US and communist China in full-scale war' (ibid.).

In the event, it was the PRC, not Taiwan, that took inconsiderate steps. Viewing the island as 'a strategic threat' and 'a highly embarrassing piece of unfinished business', in July 1954 Chairman Mao Zedong instructed the Chinese military to develop plans to invade Taiwan (Hitchcock 2018: 506). Less than two months later, the PRC's artillery began shelling the island of Quemoy, thus raising the question in Washington whether Beijing was gearing up to invade or was only testing American support for Chiang (ibid.: 507). Faced with this dilemma (and fearing that inaction would hurt American prestige and infuriate sections of his party), Eisenhower decided to offer Chiang a treaty committing the United States to the defence of Taiwan (ibid.: 509). Under the US-Taiwan Mutual Defence Treaty, a 'significant amount of assistance' was to flow into Taiwan (Cha 2016). The effect of such a windfall was to transform the island into the largest recipient of US military aid in Asia and make its prosperity largely dependent 'on American investments and capital inflows (ibid.). Furthermore, by bolstering the ROC's defence, the Mutual Defence Treaty provided an effective deterrent against future Chinese encroachments. That said, it also restricted the ROC's freedom of action and ability to launch an attack against the mainland (Lin 2016a; Tsang 1993: 53–54). In this regard, the Eisenhower Administration was also careful to ensure that its military aid programme was restricted to defensive equipment (DAFP 2002: doc. 120; Tsang 1993: 64). Faced with these limitations, it is no surprise that Chiang would complain that the treaty was 'binding the Republic of China by "hand and foot"' (Cha 2016).

Yet, for all his grumbling, Chiang could hardly afford to alienate his American backers. Therefore he temporarily shelved his plans to retake the mainland (Tsang 1993: 48), focusing instead on 'cultivating Taiwan's cultural, social, economic, and educational assets' (Lin 2016a). In so doing, he hoped to be able, one day, to 'recover the mainland by political means' – that is, by turning the ROC 'into a model for appealing to the Chinese' living under communist rule (ibid.; Tsang 1993: 55). With the PRC also unable to turn its aggressive plans into deeds, the two Chinas became inevitably locked into a mutual 'zero-sum game of competitive legitimation and delegitimation' (Kim 1994: 148). In this context, the KMT government saw both economic development and diplomatic recognition as a means of achieving such legitimation. Believing that economic growth would help to create a resilient and viable Taiwan, it began to lay 'the groundwork for the foreign investment and export-led growth that was to become a trademark of Taiwan's development in later years' (Sutter 1994: 3). At the same time, it sought to gain recognition as the legal government representing the whole of China by 'entering into more international agreements' (Lin 2016a). In both regards, American support was critical. The United States was instrumental in pushing Taiwan to open up and prosper economically. It also continued to support the island as the only legitimate government of China and the rightful holder of the Chinese seat in the United Nations Security Council (Sutter 1994: 2–3).

Washington's diplomatic support was, therefore, crucial in reducing Taiwan's international isolation. If the Soviet bloc were to recognize the PRC, Washington's Western European allies, except for Britain, would follow Washington's lead (Wacker 2016: 515). However, despite diplomatic recognition, Western European support remained qualified and Taiwan's ability to build strong relationships with Western Europe would continue to be limited. Not only did the interest of Western European nations in the world beyond Suez decline over the years, but their support was always bound to be contingent upon other foreign policy considerations. The French recognition of the PRC in 1964 was a case in point. As President de Gaulle sought to reassert France's freedom of manoeuvre within the Atlantic alliance and pursued his version of détente, he pushed towards a rapprochement with the PRC at the expense of Taiwan. In 1963 France even blocked Taipei's attempts to establish official ties with the European Economic Community lest support for such a move jeopardize Paris's opening to China (ibid.). Needless to say, France was not alone in making support for Taiwan dependent upon other political considerations. In the early 1950s America's European allies had expressed concern at US attempts to build Taiwan's military capacity for fear that it might reduce US resources for other theatres of war and provoke a general conflict in East Asia (FRUS 1985: doc. 150). In truth, similar concerns existed in East Asia, too. Tokyo, for instance, was apprehensive that Taiwan's military build-up might hamper US ability to defend Japan (ibid.). However, these worries notwithstanding, Japan maintained close relations with Taiwan throughout the early Cold War (Wang 2000: 353). Initially, Japan had contemplated establishing formal ties with the PRC, but, under pressure from Washington, Shigeru Yoshida's government ended up recognizing the ROC by signing a peace treaty with that country in 1951 (ibid.: 354–55). Japan aside, Taipei was also able to establish friendly relations with non-communist Asian countries such as South Korea, Thailand, the Philippines and South Vietnam (CIA 1974a).

Throughout the 1960s, as his hostility towards the PRC continued unabated, Chiang remained on the lookout for opportunities to undermine the CPC's grip on the mainland. One such opportunity presented itself with the unravelling of the Chinese-Soviet alliance. Between the late 1960s and early 1970s the deepening ideological rift between the PRC and the USSR provided the impetus for secret contacts between Taipei and Moscow. Although nothing tangible would emerge from them, both governments appeared willing, at least for a while, to explore ways of wrecking Mao's rule (Zhai and Xiao 2015: 533–56). And, while toppling Mao remained uppermost in Chiang's mind, collaboration with the USSR also threw up other intriguing opportunities for the Generalissimo, including the prospect of enlisting Soviet support to destroy the PRC's nascent nuclear deterrent as well as to counterbalance American attempts to improve relations with Beijing (ibid.: 550–51, 54).[1]

During the 1960s Chiang's hostility towards the mainland manifested itself in other ways too. Keen to limit Red China's influence in East Asia, he provided help to Ngo Dinh Diem's beleaguered South Vietnamese government by sending a Taiwanese Army's psychological warfare team to Saigon to train local officers on how to run a 'hearts and minds' campaign (Zhai 2010: 51; Lin 2016b). He also provided South Vietnam with ammunition and matériel, and secretly despatched special forces 'to work with South Vietnamese paramilitary groups, including one involved in sabotage raids into the North' (ibid.; Taylor 2009: 527; Tucker 1994: 97). Incidentally, Cambodia, too, was to receive similar help in the wake of General Lon Nol's March 1970 coup against Cambodian ruler Norodom Sihanouk (Lin 2016b). More importantly, the ROC acted as a crucial rear-base and staging area for American military operations in Vietnam (Taylor 2009: 527; Tucker 1994: 97). Finally, Chiang urged the United States to stand firm in Vietnam and to provide 'effective aid to [Asian] nations involved in [the] struggle against communism' (FRUS 1996: doc. 26; (Moyar 2006: 141–42). In 1964 he went so far as to tell Lyndon Johnson's Administration that Taiwan would be willing to commit troops to an attack on North Vietnam if the United States were to provide support (ibid., 384). Whenever the issue of Vietnam came up with the Americans, he could be heard, now and again, reiterating his readiness to make troop contributions to the American war effort there (Taylor 2009: 526). Apprehensive, however, that the deployment of Taiwanese troops to Vietnam might bring the PRC into the war, Johnson never took up Chiang's offer (ibid.; Moyar 2006: 384, 412).

To be sure, Johnson had another good reason to treat Chiang's advances with circumspection given that the Generalissimo's support for Washington's involvement in Vietnam hid a more ambitious goal – that of seeing an escalation take place in Vietnam. He viewed such an escalation as his best chance of mounting an attack against the mainland with American help (Jones 2001: 177). In this, he was to be sorely disappointed for the Johnson Administration had no intention of widening the conflict to China (ibid.: 178). Yet, despite Washington's best efforts to throw cold water on such an idea, Chiang was reluctant to let it go. In June 1966 Australian Minister of Foreign Affairs Paul Hasluck gathered that much, when, in talks with Chiang, he was told that political developments in China (then in the throes of the Cultural Revolution) had given the ROC 'new hope of making a successful landing on the mainland' and that 'there could be no permanent security in Asia until the Communists had been overthrown and the legitimate government of China restored'. Revealingly, the Generalissimo added that the United States 'could not itself contain Communist China' and only the ROC forces 'could deal with the problem'. He was confident that if the ROC attacked, the USSR would not merely refrain from invoking the 1950 Chinese-Soviet treaty, but would in fact 'welcome the destruction of the Peking regime'. Hence, all the ROC needed 'was material help to the extent of about one-tenth of what the Americans were at present providing in South Vietnam' (DAFT 2002: doc. 117). Regrettably for Chiang, his clarion call for action was to fall on deaf ears, once again.

Taiwan and the great powers during the late Cold War (1969–89)

Taiwan's foreign policy approach remained virtually unchanged until the late 1960s when President Richard Nixon's efforts to extricate the United States from Vietnam and cut American commitments in Asia, along with Mao's less radical foreign policy, raised significant challenges for Taipei. Predictably enough, Nixon's reappraisal of America's role in Asia sparked concerns in Taipei about the reliability of American support and caused Chiang and his entourage to question Washington's resolve to remain engaged in Asia (CIA 1970). As for the PRC, its shrill radicalism, coupled with the havoc that the Cultural Revolution wreaked on the country, had reinforced Asian perceptions of the Chinese threat and led to Beijing's increasing international isolation. In the late 1960s, however, Mao's steps to rein in the excesses of the Cultural Revolution gradually eased regional concerns and helped to restore the PRC's respectability internationally. In 1970 both Canada and Italy granted diplomatic recognition to the PRC while support in the United Nations (UN) for its admission also gathered pace. From then on, as an American intelligence report noted at the time, Taiwan's 'international position rapidly deteriorated' (ibid. 1974a). In the early 1970s a growing number of nations recognized the PRC and simultaneously withdrew diplomatic recognition from Taipei. In mid-1969 only 45 countries had diplomatic relations with Beijing compared with the 66 nations that still recognized Taipei as the legitimate government of China. However, by 1973 the tables had turned dramatically: now 86 countries entertained formal relations with Beijing and only 38 with Taipei (ibid.).[2] Significantly, key regional partners such as Japan, Australia and New Zealand switched diplomatic recognition to the PRC in 1972 (ibid.).

In the early 1970s two further developments intervened to make things worse for the ROC. In November 1971 the PRC was admitted to the UN while Taiwan was expelled. More importantly, in mid-1971 Nixon announced his historic decision to visit Beijing in 1972 in an attempt to normalize relations with the PRC and to exploit the ensuing thaw with Beijing to score important foreign policy goals, including the withdrawal of US troops from Vietnam and the reduction of the American military burden in Asia (Benvenuti 2016: 55–56). Nixon's successful to trip to China in February 1972 boded ill for Taiwan as it paved the way for a gradual improvement in US-PRC relations. In the late 1970s, keen to set the seal on the long-drawn-out normalization process initiated by Nixon, the Carter Administration recognized Beijing as the sole legal government of China and ended all formal relations with Taiwan, including the 1954 Mutual Defence Treaty (Roy 2003: 138–39;

Sutter: 1994: 4). It also reduced America's military presence on the island although it agreed to continue arms sales to the ROC under the Taiwan Relations Act passed by Congress in 1979 (Roy 2003: 141–42).[3] Predictably, as the United States moved to downplay its commitment to Taiwan, the PRC was quick to exploit the ROC's growing isolation to push Taipei to agree to formal negotiations on reunification (Sutter 1994: 4). For the remainder of the Cold War, Beijing's policy appeared to rest on the assumption that the PRC's growing military and economic power would inexorably force its small neighbour to accept Beijing's sovereignty (Pike 2011: 685).

As Sutter has rightly noted (1994: 5), these events were to pose 'the most serious challenge' for Taiwan's nationalist administration since its final flight from the mainland in 1949. Such a remarkable reversal of political fortunes inevitably pushed the ROC to reassess its policy options and to pursue a new course in foreign policy. Forced to make the best of a dire situation, it began to show growing flexibility by dropping its claim to be the sole legitimate government of China in favour of a de facto two-China policy (Sutter 1994: 8; CIA 1974b). For a brief moment, it toyed, once again, with the idea of improving relations with the USSR in an attempt to prevent too close a rapprochement between Washington and Beijing (Roy 2003: 136–37). It also strove to 'build up a greater measure of economic and military self-sufficiency' (CIA 1974b). In this context, between the mid-1970s and the early 1980s, Taipei worked to foster secret military and intelligence cooperation with almost every anti-communist nation in South-East Asia (Lin 2016b). Furthermore, it endeavoured to maintain ties with the countries now recognizing Beijing through economic, technological, scientific, cultural and sports exchanges (Kim 1994: 150; CIA 1974a).

This strategy failed to reverse Taiwan's isolation (Kim 1994: 150), but it was not without results. Despite Taipei's vigorous complaints that Carter's recognition of the PRC in 1979 threatened its survival, Taipei's relations with Washington remained both close and extensive (Sutter 1994: 8; Pike 2011: 685–86). Moreover, Taipei was able to retain strong informal ties with Japan – still its second largest trading partner (Sutter 1994: 8; CIA 1974a). Furthermore, it managed to maintain economic and informal political ties with various European governments (ibid.). During the 1980s Taiwan not only established liaison offices in different Western European countries, it also tried to go one step further by upgrading its unofficial links with them. By the early 1990s these liaison offices had been turned into de facto consulates – a move reciprocated by European countries (Wacker 2016: 516–17). European cabinet ministers also visited Taiwan (ibid.: 517).[4] In the 1980s it also strengthened its economic ties with that region (ibid.: 522–52). Finally, Taipei sought to use its increasing economic power to broaden its links with developing countries (Sutter 1994: 8–9; Kim 1994: 152). In 1988 President Lee Teng-hui (1988–2000) created the so-called International Economic Cooperation Development Fund to assist 'friendly' nations with their developmental efforts (Sutter 1994: 10).

The ROC's new foreign policy course went hand in hand with political and economic reforms domestically. Under the presidency of Chiang's son, Chiang Ching-kuo (1978–1988), the KMT government fostered greater political liberalization, encouraged greater representation of the native Taiwanese in both the KMT and the national government, and sought to boost the country's economic development and modernization (Sutter 1994: 6; Pike 2011: 688–89 and 690; CIA 1974b). By the end of the Cold War, a predominantly agrarian country had been transformed into a prosperous economy with a gross national product per head far outstripping that of Southern European countries such as Greece and Portugal (Pike 2011: 690; Kim 1994: 145–46). Growing democratization and faster economic growth were seen in Taipei as essential to strengthening the KMT regime's domestic legitimacy and to boosting its international credentials (Sutter 1994: 9). With this in mind, the KMT government continued to be against reunification talks with the PRC. Its approach remained centred on its 'three noes' policy – namely no contact, no negotiations and no compromise (Roy 2003: 148). Taipei's view was that Beijing might try not only to coerce the ROC into accepting its own terms, it might also exploit the talks in order to weaken American and international support for Taiwan as a de facto state (Sutter 1994: 9). Of concern was also the fact that any attempt to reach an understanding with the PRC on the matter of reunification might be seen domestically by the locally born Taiwanese as a sell-out to Beijing (ibid.: 5). However, as was to become increasingly clear after the ending of the Cold War, the island's increasing prosperity and political liberalization, coupled with China's economic rise, would put the ROC government under increasing domestic pressure to allow for greater economic and cultural exchanges with the mainland (ibid.: 6–7). Notwithstanding initial concerns that increasing cross-Strait social and economic contacts might undermine Taiwan's security, the KMT government eventually came around to the view that such interactions might instead work in its favour by making the Taiwanese people (as well as the mainland Chinese) aware of Taiwan's social and economic achievements (Roy 2003: 148–50).

Taiwan and the great powers after the end of the Cold War

In the early 1990s, therefore, the KMT sought to meet growing popular demands for increased cultural and economic ties with the mainland by trying to control the extent of such contacts and by pursuing a policy of official exchanges under the principle of 'one country-two governments' or 'one country-two areas' (Sutter 1994: 7). By the end of the decade, such policies had produced a marked increase in cross-Strait economic interactions, with total trade averaging US $20 billion between 1993–98 (NIC 1999). The early 1990s also witnessed an attempt to kick-start a political dialogue between the PRC and the ROC. In 1992 they conducted a round of talks in which they accepted the principle of One China but disagreed on its definition (*The Economist* 2000d). Predictably enough, the CPC leadership insisted that it represented the legitimate government of China, thus implying that it still considered Taiwan a rebel province. All that Beijing was prepared to countenance under its 'one country, two systems' formula was no more than a limited degree of autonomy for Taiwan (NIC 1999). For its part, the KMT government refused, quite understandably, to make concessions on issues of political autonomy and sovereignty.

How precarious its policy of accommodation with the PRC was became evident in 1995 when President Lee Teng-hui's (1988–2000) unofficial visit to the United States triggered an exceedingly harsh response from Beijing. The PRC's missile tests in the Taiwan Strait in March 1996 were perceived internationally as an attempt by Beijing to intimidate the ROC and prevent the principle of 'one country-two governments' from gaining traction. The PRC's heavy-handed tactics, however, elicited strong international support for the ROC. In the United States, the Clinton Administration despatched the US Seventh Fleet to the waters close to Taiwan as a warning against Beijing's bullying (*The* Economist 2000a). In Japan, Ryutaro Hashimoto's government pledged to provide logistic support to the United States in the event of military operations in the Taiwan Strait (Wang 2000: 353). Regrettably, Beijing's bullying tactics did not stop with the 1996 missile tests (*The* Economist 2000a). In 1999 Lee's calls for bilateral relations to be conducted on a 'special state-to-state' footing drew another angry response from Beijing, which also entailed small-scale military moves across the Taiwan Strait (ibid. 2000b; NIC 1999).

Beijing's heavy-handed tactics would also resurface, now and then, in the early years of the new century. The election to the presidency of former Democratic Progressive Party (DPP) mayor of Taipei Chen Shui-bian in 2000 and DPP chairwoman Tsai Ing-wen in 2016 provoked more angry responses from Beijing. Fears that the pro-independence DPP might upset the status quo and assert Taiwan's independent political identity pushed the CPC leadership to increase its political and military pressure on Taiwan. In the run-up to the 2000 presidential election, Beijing threatened to attack Taiwan if the latter continued to hold off talks on reunification and also made clear that it viewed Chen Shui-bian as no suitable candidate (*The* Economist 2000b, 2000c). In 2001 the PRC responded provocatively to Chen's visit to the United States and Latin America by carrying out one of its most extensive military exercises in the Taiwan Strait (ibid. 2001a). More Chinese sabre-rattling – with its usual mix of angry rebukes, military exercises and missile deployments – was to follow during the remainder of Chen's two terms in office (ibid. 2003a, 2003b, 2004c, 2000d, 2005). More recently, Chen's successor, Tsai Ing-wen, has been at the receiving end of Beijing's bullying tactics as well as its persistent efforts to undermine Taiwan's international standing by competing for international recognition and opposing its membership of international organizations (Chen 2017; Mazza 2018; Lynch 2018).

For its part, Taiwan's response has been both cautious and, in the main, sensible. In spite of increasing domestic support for an independent Taiwan, both Chen and Tsai have generally (but not always) refrained from taking steps that might antagonize Beijing (Mazza 2018; Lynch 2018). Notwithstanding his refusal to accept the One China principle (Campbell and Mitchell 2001, 2002), Chen Shui-bian enabled Taiwanese companies to invest on the mainland and facilitated direct cross-Strait travel (*The* Economist 2001b). He also called for a resumption of bilateral talks provided that Beijing refrained from demanding Tapei's acceptance of the One China principle as a precondition for such talks (ibid. 2000d). In his inauguration speech in May 2000, Chen also promised not to seek independence if the PRC did not attack Taiwan (ibid.). True, later in his presidency, he made a few separatist noises and failed to comply with the dictates of Beijing's political *bon ton*, but these were made for domestic political reasons and not as a display of a separatist intent (although he also carefully sought to strengthen Taiwan's political identity) (ibid. 2002, 2003a, 2003b, 2004a, 2004b). Like Chen, Tsai steered well clear of making a unilateral change to Taiwan's status quo while refusing to accept the KMT's more accommodationist formula that both the PRC and ROC belong to One China and that each country is free to interpret what One China means in practice (Babones 2016; Lynch 2018). Whether such a moderate attitude will satisfy Beijing is most unlikely. However, one thing is clear: For all its bullying, the PRC has made no progress towards unification. Nor has it managed to stifle Taiwan's desire for greater international status – a desire that has grown hand in hand with its rising international profile as a vibrant democracy and the world's 22nd largest economy in real gross domestic product terms (CIA 2018). Hence, while no CPC leader can appear to be soft on Taiwan, Beijing knows that it will never win any Taiwanese government over to its views on unification and, hence, its goal must be to prevent a formal declaration of independence. For, thanks to continuing American politico-military backing (notwithstanding Washington's well-known policy of 'strategic ambiguity' which has allowed successive administrations to avoid clarifying what they would do if the PRC or the ROC sought to change the status quo), resilient statecraft and, not least, growing popular support for an autonomous Taiwan, the latter's claim to independent statehood has never been more realistic – which is something any leadership in Beijing will find it hard to disregard.

Conclusion

As was the case in 1949, the future of Taiwan very much rests on two fundamental factors: a continuing US politico-military commitment to the island's de facto independence and the PRC's opposition to it. While there is no doubt that over the past seven decades Taiwan has managed to transform itself from a seemingly non-viable rump state into a functional and prosperous democracy, now as then, its continued existence is significantly contingent upon the policies of the region's major powers. As this chapter has emphasized, as long as the United States is willing to stand by its small Asian ally, the ROC government can remain reassured that the PRC's hostility can be held at bay. It can also be hopeful that the mutual rivalry between the two Chinas can be effectively confined to the diplomatic level and contained to what Kim has described as the 'legitimation-delegitimation' game. But if this chapter has indeed told the story of how two major powers have shaped (and still shape) Taiwan's future, it has also drawn attention to the ROC government's relentless quest for security and its desire to ward off Beijing's attempts to isolate it. In other words, the chapter has tried to show how Taiwanese policymakers have dealt with a remarkably hostile politico-strategic environment. For all the ROC's vulnerability and weakness, Taiwanese 'agency' has been far from representing a negligible factor in the unfolding of the story recounted in this chapter. If Taiwan has come a long way from where it stood in 1949, this is in no small part thanks to the perseverance of its political elite. In a similar vein, if Taiwan is to prevent Chinese hostility from turning violent, this will be in no small measure thanks to its government's decision not to upset the status quo and to make a decisive and open claim to independence.

Notes

1 For the PRC's nuclear deterrent see Jones (2001: 182–83).
2 Kim (1994: 151) provides slightly different figures. By 1975 112 nations had recognized the PRC while 26 still entertained relations with the ROC (Roy 2003: 132).
3 However, neither Carter nor his successor, Ronald Reagan, were as generous as their predecessors in providing military assistance to Taiwan.
4 They, however, did not include prime ministers or ministers of foreign affairs or of defence.

References

Accinelli, Robert (1996) *Crisis and Commitment: United States Policy toward Taiwan 1950–1955*, Chapel Hill: University of North Carolina Press.
Babones, Salvatore (2016) 'One China, One Taiwan', *Foreign Affairs*, 12 January. Available at www.foreignaffairs.com/articles/taiwan/2016-01-12/one-china-one-taiwan (accessed on 12 December 2018).
Benvenuti, Andrea (2016) 'US Relations with the PRC during the Cold War', in Andrew T. H. Tan (ed.) *Handbook of US-China Relations*, Cheltenham: Edward Elgar.
Campbell, Kurt M. and Mitchell, Derek J. (2001) 'Crisis in the Taiwan Strait?' *Foreign Affairs*, 80(4).
Campbell, Kurt M. and Mitchell, Derek J. (2002) 'Postscript: Crisis in the Taiwan Strait', *Foreign Affairs*, 1 August. Available at www.foreignaffairs.com/articles/asia/2002-08-01/crisis-taiwan-strait (accessed on 18 December 2018).
Central Intelligence Agency (CIA) (1954) 'Probable Developments in Taiwan through Mid-1956': National Intelligence Estimate 43–54(1954)', 14 September, CIA-RDP79R01012A004400010001–3. Available at www.cia.gov/library/readingroom/.
Central Intelligence Agency (CIA) (1970) 'Taipei and the Nixon Doctrine', Intelligence Memorandum, 17 April, CIA-RDP85T00875R01100090020–5. Available at www.cia.gov/library/readingroom/.

Central Intelligence Agency (CIA) (1974a) 'Nationalist China', National Intelligence Survey, April, CIA-RDP01–00707R000200080025–0. Available at www.cia.gov/library/readingroom/.
Central Intelligence Agency (CIA) (1974b) 'Nationalist China Revisited', Weekly Summary Report, no. 0026/74A, 28 June, CIA-RDP85T00875R001500060012–3. Available at www.cia.gov/library/readingroom/.
Central Intelligence Agency (CIA) (1985) 'China-Taiwan: Strategies for Reunification', May, CIA-RDP87T00495R000900940021–6. Available at www.cia.gov/library/readingroom/.
Central Intelligence Agency (CIA) (2018) *The World Factbook*. Available at www.cia.gov/library/publications/the-world-factbook/geos/tw.html (accessed on 20 December 2018). Available at www.cia.gov/library/readingroom/.
Cha, V. D. (2016) *Powerplay: The Origins of the American Alliance System in Asia*, Princeton, NJ: Princeton University Press.
Chen, Charles I. (2017) 'How Beijing Could Squeeze Taiwan', *Foreign Affairs*, 13 April. Available at www.foreignaffairs.com/articles/taiwan/2017-04-13/how-beijing-could-squeeze-taiwan (accessed on 18 December 2018).
Cohen, Warren I. (1993), *The Cambridge History of American Foreign Relations*, vol. IV, *America in the Age of Soviet Power, 1945–1991*, Cambridge: Cambridge University Press.
Documents on Australian Foreign Policy (DAFP) (2002) *Australia and Recognition of the People's Republic of China 1949–1972*, Canberra: Department of Foreign Affairs and Trade.
Foreign Relations of the United States (FRUS) (1977) *1951, Asia and the Pacific*, vol. 6, part 1, Washington, DC: US Government Printing Office.
Foreign Relations of the United States (FRUS) (1985) *1952–54, China and Japan*, vol. 16, part 1, Washington, DC: US Government Printing Office.
Foreign Relations of the United States (FRUS) (1996) *1961–1963, Northeast Asia*, vol. 22, Washington, DC: US Government Printing Office.
Foreign Relations of the United States (FRUS) (1998) *1964–1968, China*, vol. 30, Washington, DC: US Government Printing Office.
Heimsath, Charles H. and Surjit Mansingh (1971) *A Diplomatic History of Modern India*, Bombay: Allied Publishers.
Hitchcock, William (2018) *The Age of Eisenhower: American and the World in the 1950s*, New York: Simon and Schuster.
Jones, Matthew (2001) '"Groping toward Coexistence": US-China Policy during the Johnson Years', *Diplomacy & Statecraft*, 12(3).
Kim, Samuel S. (1994) 'Taiwan and the International System: The Challenge of Legitimation', in Robert G. Sutter and William R. Johnson (eds) *Taiwan in World Affairs*, Boulder, CO: Westview Press.
Lin, Hsiao-ting (2016a) *Accidental State: Chiang Kai-shek, the United States, and the Making of Taiwan*, Cambridge, MA: Harvard University Press.
Lin, Hsiao-ting (2016b) 'Taiwan's Cold War in Southeast Asia', CWIHP e-Dossier no. 70. Available at www.wilsoncenter.org/publication/taiwans-cold-war-southeast-asia (accessed on 1 January 2017).
Lynch, Daniel (2018) 'Playing the Taiwan Card', *Foreign Affairs*, 19 March. Available at www.foreignaffairs.com/articles/china/2018-03-19/playing-taiwan-card (accessed on 12 December 2018).
Mabon, David W. (1988) 'Elusive Agreements: The Pacific Pact Proposals of 1949–1951', *Pacific Historical Review*, 57(2).

Mazza, Michael (2018) 'Is a Storm Brewing in the Taiwan Strait?', *Foreign Affairs*, 27 July. Available at www.foreignaffairs.com/articles/asia/2018-07-27/storm-brewing-taiwan-strait (accessed on 12 December 2018).

Moyar, Mark (2006) *Triumph Forsaken: The Vietnam War, 1954–65*, Cambridge: Cambridge University Press.

National Intelligence Council (NIC) (1999) 'China-Taiwan. Prospects for Cross-Strait Relations', National Intelligence Estimate 99–13, September, no. 0005526243. Available at www.cia.gov/library/readingroom/.

Oyen, Meredith (2010) 'Communism, Containment and the Chinese Overseas', in Yangwen Zheng, Hong Liu and Michael Szonyi (eds) *The Cold War in Asia: The Battle for Hearts and Minds*, Leiden: Brill.

Pike, Francis (2011) *Empires at War: A Short History of Modern Asia since World War II*, London: I. B. Tauris.

Roy, Denny (2003) *Taiwan: A Political History*, Ithaca, NY: Cornell University Press.

Sutter, Robert G. (1994) 'Taiwan's Role in World Affairs: Background, Status, and Prospects', in Robert G. Sutter and William R. Johnson (eds) *Taiwan in World Affairs*, Boulder, CO: Westview Press.

Taylor, Jay (2009) *The Generalissimo: Chiang Kai-shek and the Struggle for Modern China*, Cambridge, MA: Harvard University Press.

The Economist (2000a) 'Taiwan Stands Up', 25 March.

The Economist (2000b) 'Taiwan's China Dare', 25 March.

The Economist (2000c) 'Taiwan Stands Up', 27 May.

The Economist (2000d) 'Time for a Chat About Taiwan', 5 August.

The Economist (2001a) 'More Sound Than Fury', 9 June.

The Economist (2001b) 'Kuomintangled', 8 December.

The Economist (2002) 'Strait Talk', 10 August.

The Economist (2003a) 'Ripple Effect', 9 August.

The Economist (2003b) 'Trouble on the Fringes', 29 November.

The Economist (2004a) 'Riling China, and America Too', 21 February.

The Economist (2004b) 'The Strait Widens', 27 March.

The Economist (2004c) 'Chen Redux', 22 May.

The Economist (2004d) 'Dangerous Games', 17 July.

The Economist (2005) 'Own Goal', 2 April.

Tsang, Steve (1993) 'Chiang Kai-shek and the Kuomintang's Policy to Reconquer the Chinese Mainland, 1949–1958', in Steve Tsang (ed.) *In the Shadow of China: Political Developments in Taiwan since 1949*, Hong Kong: Hong Kong University.

Tucker, Nancy Bernkopf (1994) *Taiwan, Hong Kong, and the United States, 1945–1992: Uncertain Friendship*, New York: Twayne Publishers.

Wacker, Gudrun (2016) 'European–Taiwan Relations', in Gunter Schubert (ed.) *Routledge Handbook of Contemporary Taiwan*, Abingdon: Routledge.

Wang Qingxin Ken (2000) 'Taiwan in Japan's Relations with China and the United States after the Cold War', *Pacific Affairs*, 73(3).

Zhai Qiang (2010) 'A One-sided Picture of the Chinese-Vietnamese Ties during the Vietnam War', in Andrew Wiest and Michael Doidge (eds) *Triumph Revisited: Historians Battle for the Vietnam War*, New York: Routledge.

Zhai Xiang and Xiao Ruping (2015) 'Shifting Political Calculation: The Secret Taiwan-Soviet Talks, 1963–1971', *Cold War Studies*, 15(4).

5 The Taiwan issue: tracing 70 years of Taiwan-China relations

Roger Lee Huang and Andrew T. H. Tan

Introduction

Taiwan-China relations lie at the heart of the so-called Taiwan issue, namely the continued separation of Taiwan from China. Taiwan's expected unification with the mainland after the conclusion of the Chinese civil war in 1949 was interrupted by the emergence of the Cold War. Since then, the People's Republic of China (PRC, or China) has never wavered in claiming Taiwan as part of its sovereign territory. Taiwan's political space has gradually shrunk, with the Republic of China (ROC, or Taiwan) ejected from the United Nations in 1971 and de-recognized by much of the international community. Yet, despite this, Taiwan has continued to enjoy de facto independence with all the trappings of a sovereign state. As Chapter 2 in this volume has observed, Taiwan possesses all the necessary Weberian attributes of statehood, such as its own military and police, a monopoly of the use of force over its own defined territory, a functioning government, a Constitution and jurisdiction over its own territory and citizens (Weber 1968: 56).

From the PRC's perspective, Taiwan's unification with China remains a principal national objective. According to China's leader Hu Jintao, the Taiwan issue is a legacy of the Chinese civil war, and that 'to return to unity is not a recreation of sovereignty or territory but an end to political antagonism' (Hu 2008). Indeed, Chinese national identity has been consciously constructed to include Taiwan, as well as Tibet and Xinjiang, as integral parts of China's national sovereignty and territorial integrity, over which China would never compromise (Lin and Wu 2017: 76).

This chapter examines and assesses the development of relations between the two protagonists on either side of the Taiwan Strait. It begins with an analysis of the historical antecedents of the relationship between China and Taiwan. It then examines key events and developments during the Cold War and the changes in cross-Strait relations that followed the ending of the dominance of the Chiang family (i.e. Chiang Kai-shek and his son, Chiang Ching-kuo) in Taiwan. The chapter concludes with an analysis of the future prospects for cross-Strait relations in the current era marked by a rising and increasingly nationalistic China under the leadership of Xi Jinping.

China and Taiwan: early antecedents

In 1683 Taiwan was formally incorporated as part of the Qing dynasty after the Manchurians captured the island that was used by Ming dynasty 'Han' rebels as a military base (Charney and Prescott 2000: 454–56). However, the massacre of Japanese sailors in Taiwan by indigenous peoples led to Japan dispatching a military expedition to Taiwan in 1874, the first foreign excursion under the modernizing Japan following the 1868 Meiji Restoration. Japan, as an emerging regional power, quickly recognized that Taiwan was part of its strategic backyard, and this resulted in the Japanese annexation of Taiwan two decades later, in 1895, following the First Sino-Japanese War (Fraleigh 2010: 43).

As Fraleigh observed, Taiwan subsequently 'became configured as a part of the Japanese territory, one that held the prospect of developing in such a way as to be particularly beneficial to the metropole' (2010: 62). Under the Japanese, the colonisers implemented a Japanization policy, and gradually transformed Taiwanese residents into 'loyal imperial subjects' who were familiar with the Japanese language and customs (Ching 2001: 91–93). Following Japan's defeat in the Second World War, Taiwan reverted to China's orbit, as the ROC took over control of the island. However just four years later, Taiwan once again became a separate political entity to China when the Kuomintang (KMT – Nationalist Party) under Chiang Kai-shek fled to Taiwan, after its defeat in 1949 by the Communist Party of China (CPC). The outbreak of the Korean War in 1950, however, thwarted China's plan to annex Taiwan. Taiwan now suddenly assumed new strategic significance for the United States with the emergence of the Cold War.

In Taiwan, the KMT, under the Chiang family, maintained a repressive rule over the island and consoled itself with the illusion that it could one day reclaim the mainland. The KMT's use of brutal and repressive tactics to suppress the local Taiwanese was epitomized by the February 28 Incident of 1947, in which a minor incident led to an anti-government uprising that resulted in the deaths of an estimated 28,000 people, possibly more (Wang 2017; Philips 1999: 293–99). The repression and domination of power by the *waishengren* ('mainlanders') who had arrived with the KMT alienated political dissidents and much of the local populace. The White Terror campaign under the KMT laid the foundation for the later rise of pro-democracy and pro-independence forces that rejected the KMT's One China position as well as the notion of Chinese unification.

China and Taiwan during the Cold War

During the civil war the CPC established a 'working committee' on Taiwan as early as 1946, and initially focused on 'liberating' the island from the KMT. In the First Taiwan Strait Crisis (1954), China bombarded Taiwan's offshore islands of Kinmen, Matsu and Dachen. The signing of the China-US Mutual

Defense Treaty in 1955 meant that Taiwan was now under the protection of the US military (Office of the Historian n.d.). This led to a series of peace initiatives by China in 1955–56, with Premier Chou Enlai inviting Chiang Kai-Shek to visit the mainland and proposing an official bilateral meeting, both of which were rejected by Chiang (Chao 1990: 126). In 1958 a Second Taiwan Strait Crisis occurred when China returned to militancy and initiated an intensive bombardment campaign of the Kinmen islands. However, Taiwan was not a priority in the 1960s when China became preoccupied with the growing rift with the Soviet Union as well as internal convulsions during the Cultural Revolution (ibid.). Although several secret and informal bilateral communication channels functioned during this period, which continued even after the death of Chiang Kai-shek in 1975, nothing came of these discussions (Sheng 1998: 66–68).

The normalization of relations between the United States and China in 1979, and the abrogation of the Mutual Defense Treaty between the United States and Taiwan in 1980, marked a new phase in China's approach to Taiwan. With US troops no longer on the island, China now embarked on a strategy of advancing the notion of 'peaceful reunification' instead of the previous belligerent objective of 'liberation'. In 1979, on the day that formal US-China relations were established, China's National People's Congress (NPC) issued a 'Message to Compatriots in Taiwan', which urged the establishment of direct trade, postal and transportation links (the 'three links'), as well as exchanges in the fields of academe, culture, sports and the arts (the 'four exchanges'). China also announced that it would stop shelling Matsu and Kinmen (Chao 1990: 127).

In 1981 Ye Jianying, Chairman of the Standing Committee of the NPC, proposed his 'nine points' for the peaceful 'reunification' of Taiwan with China. This proposal promised that Taiwan would be able to retain its own armed forces, and that it would have a high degree of autonomy as a special administrative region of the PRC. Ye also promised that 'the national government will not intervene in the local affairs of Taiwan', and that 'Taiwan's current social and economic systems will remain unchanged, its way of life will not change, and its economic and cultural ties with foreign countries will not change'. This was followed by Deng Xiaoping's 'one country, two systems' proposal in 1982, with similar provisions for Taiwan to have administrative autonomy and its own army, but under PRC sovereignty (Ministry of Foreign Affairs, n.d.).

However, these proposals amounted to Taiwan becoming a Chinese province under the authority of the PRC, albeit one with a special status. Not surprisingly, Chiang Ching-kuo rejected all of these overtures with his 'three noes' policy of 'no contact, no compromise and no negotiation' (Chang 1993 :202). However, in 1986 he agreed to negotiations for the release of a hijacked Taiwan-owned China Airlines cargo aircraft that had landed in China.

Rapid political changes in the latter half of the 1980s saw an increased opening up of Taiwan-China relations. Anti-KMT dissidents founded the pro-democracy and independence-leaning Democratic Progressive Party (DPP) to contest the 1986 supplementary legislative elections. One year later, the KMT government lifted the 38-year martial law imposed on Taiwan. In November 1987 Chiang liberalized cross-Strait exchanges by allowing Taiwanese residents to visit China for family reunions (Chao 1990: 128). The lifting of the travel ban sparked a 'China fever' and by July 1988 more than 100,000 Taiwanese had taken the opportunity to visit their relatives. In 1988 Taiwan lifted the ban on investments in China, thereby allowing indirect investments via third countries. Taiwan also legalized two-way trade with China through Hong Kong and other third countries, and approved a list of importable commodities from China (Lee 1989: 135–36). The establishment of trade ties led to a tremendous boom in trade. By 1991 trade between China and Taiwan had increased to US $7 billion, with China becoming Taiwan's fifth largest trading partner, and Taiwan becoming China's sixth largest trading partner (Chang 1993: 199).

China and Taiwan after the Chiangs

After Chiang Ching-kuo's death in 1988, Lee Teng-hui, selected by Chiang Ching-kuo as his successor, became president. Lee's ascension to power was significant as this was the first time that a *benshengren* (native Taiwanese) had risen to the highest office in Taiwan. Initially, relations with China actually improved, with the two sides agreeing in 1990 to establish a forum for unofficial discussions. In 1991 Taiwan proclaimed that the state of war with China, which had existed since 1949, was over. This allowed Taiwan and China to establish the semi-official Straits Exchange Foundation (SEF) and the Association for Relations Across the Taiwan Straits (ARATS), respectively, in order to conduct cross-Strait negotiations.

In 1992 representatives from both sides met in Hong Kong to discuss postal exchanges, among other topics. The KMT would claim that both sides reached a 'consensus' during this meeting. According to the KMT, the so-called 1992 Consensus meant that both sides accepted the principle of One China, although they differed on their respective interpretations of the meaning of China. In 1993 the Hong Kong meeting paved way for Taiwan and China to hold their first direct, official talks in Singapore.

China, however, became increasingly alarmed at Lee Teng-hui's apparent advocacy for Taiwanese independence, culminating in the suspension of high-level talks in 1995. That year, Lee visited his US alma mater, Cornell University, where, in a speech, he decried the ending of communism and his hope for a unified China under democracy (UPI 1995). This was the first visit by a top Taiwanese official to the United States since 1979. To China, this was an egregious breach of the one-China principle, and it responded with a series of military exercises and missile tests near Taiwan, prompting the outbreak of the Third Taiwan Strait Crisis in 1996. The United States reacted by despatching an aircraft carrier battle group to the vicinity of the Taiwan Strait in order to deter any further moves by China. China's attempt at coercion backfired, as Lee was re-elected with a clear majority in Taiwan's first direct presidential election.

In 1999 China's fears about Lee Teng-hui were realized when Lee announced that Taiwan and China now enjoyed a special state-to-state relationship. At the time, Lee feared that Taiwan's legal status would be undermined during negotiations with China if the United States accepted China's definition of One China. Therefore he launched his 'two-state' formulation in 1999 to defend Taiwan's bottom line, namely the principle of parity in cross-Strait negotiations (Lin 2011: 229). China responded to the new 'two state theory,' by suspending all talks with Taiwan (ibid.: 179). Lee was in fact instrumental in encouraging the emergence of pro-independence forces in Taiwan, which led to his expulsion from the KMT in 2001, after his term as president ended. Indeed, in 2000, the KMT lost power for the first time when DPP's Chen Shui-bian won the presidential election.

The Anti-Secession Law and the Chen Shui-bian era

Conventional wisdom considered the two terms under President Chen Shui-bian as a low point for Taiwan-China relations. In popular accounts, the Taiwanese president was a reckless, revisionist leader, who was personally responsible for escalating Taiwan-China tensions (Ross 2006: 455; Sullivan and Lowe, 2010: 619; Wang 2005: 271). Chen's refusal to renounce the option of a future independent Taiwan, and China's insistence on the acceptance of the One China principle meant that there was no common ground to restart suspended political discussions. This key divergence in position meant eight years of political deadlock, although paradoxically Taiwan-China trade and cultural ties actually blossomed during the Chen Shui-bian era.

At the beginning of Chen's presidency, leaders from both sides were initially cautious. Just days after the election, China's President Jiang Zemin stated that:

> [W]hoever is in power in Taiwan is welcome to the mainland for talks. Meanwhile, we may also go to Taiwan. But there must be a basis, i.e. the One China Principle must be recognized. Under this prerequisite, we can talk about anything.
>
> (Sheng 2001: 132)

President Chen's conciliatory response in his 2000 inaugural speech referred to the possibility that 'the leaders on both sides possess enough wisdom and creativity to jointly deal with the question of a future "one China"' (Cheng 2006: 596). Chen offered an olive branch by vowing not to unilaterally change the status quo during his term in office. Dubbed as the 'four noes and one without' pledge, Chen promised that he would not enact policies that would lead to a de jure independent Taiwan, as long as the CPC was able to demonstrate that it had no intention of using military force against Taiwan.

Although Chen could not accept the One China principle, he did refer to the 'spirit' of the 1992 Hong Kong talks instead of the 1992 Consensus, and appeared positive about the doctrine of 'one China, respective interpretations'

(Su 2009: 131). During his administration the KMT-controlled legislature passed the three 'mini-links', allowing for the first time since 1949 direct postal, transport and trade exchanges between designated Chinese cities and the offshore islands of Kinmen, Matsu and, later, Penghu. Special charter flights between Taiwan and Shanghai were launched during the 2003 Spring Festival, which allowed Taiwanese airlines to fly to China, albeit indirectly after transiting via Hong Kong or Macau (Clough 2003: 242).

One year into his presidency, Chen abandoned Lee Teng-hui's 'no haste, be patient' policy, and, lifted restrictions on direct Taiwanese investments in China. Following the policy change, China became Taiwan's largest export market, with Taiwanese exports to China (including Hong Kong) reaching US $40.8 billion in 2002, a 28 per cent increase from the previous year. By 2003, in addition to the accelerated economic exchange, more than 148,000 Chinese spouses were living in Taiwan, and at least half a million Taiwanese expatriates were residing in China (Clough 2003: 242–43). When Ma Ying-jeou took office in 2008, China (including Hong Kong) had already become Taiwan's largest trading partner and the home of Taiwan's largest expatriate community.

China, however, did not view Chen and the DPP government as reliable stakeholders, and refused to restore the suspended SEF-ARATS talks. Probably frustrated at the lack of goodwill from China, Chen, in a 2002 telecast, commented that there is 'one country on each side' of the Taiwan Strait. Chen's comment did not reinvent the wheel but merely repackaged the 'two state theory' articulated by President Lee Teng-hui in 1999. As Sullivan and Lowe have observed, Chen's telecasted words were in all likelihood 'playing to the crowd' as a calculated move designed to appease his supporters, although China was unsurprisingly quick to condemn Chen, and even the United States felt compelled to criticize the Taiwanese president (Sullivan and Lowe 2010: 627–28). Furthermore, Chen's attempt to redress past injustices under KMT authoritarianism included an active nativization campaign, which encouraged the growth of 'civic nationalism' in Taiwan that was perceived by critics as an attempt to de-Sinicize and separate Taiwan from the Chinese political community (Hughes 2011: 51–52).

The lack of formal dialogue between the two sides was further complicated when Taiwan held its first referendum on the same day as the 2004 presidential election, which Chen won by a slim margin, one day after an assassination attempt on his life. In Chen's inaugural address, he reaffirmed his commitment to the status quo, but also spoke about a wide range of possibilities for future Taiwan-China political relations based on 'peaceful development and freedom of choice', but only with the consent of the Taiwanese populace (Chen 2004: 8).

Antagonistic exchanges between the two governments thus became the norm throughout the remainder of the Chen presidency. As far as China was concerned, talks could only resume if the Taiwanese accepted the One China principle and the 1992 Consensus, a prerequisite that was untenable for the

DPP government. China's growing impatience with the Chen administration translated into a hardened strategy intended to further isolate Taiwan on the international stage. By the end of the Chen presidency, China had poached six more states from among Taiwan's dwindling number of diplomatic allies, meaning that it now had official recognition from only 23 countries.

On the military front, China began an aggressive build-up of its coercive abilities, with more than 1,000 ballistic missiles directed at Taiwan (US Department of Defense 2009: viii). Under President Hu Jintao, China passed the 2005 Anti-Secession Law to deter Taiwan from declaring *de jure* independence (Wang 2005: 266). The Anti-Secession Law was hardly a departure from China's long-held unification policy of 'military coercion and peaceful offence'; however, it expanded the scope for the permissible use of force which now included the ambiguously worded condition 'when all possibilities for a peaceful reunification should be completely exhausted' (People's Daily Online 2005; Zhao 1999: 495). A year later, Chen responded to the passage of the Anti-Secession Law and broke one of his pledges by announcing that the National Reunification Council and the National Reunification Guidelines were now defunct, therefore making it impossible for any form of formal rapprochement to take place between the two governments during Chen's remaining time in office.

Beside the stick, China also offered carrots to Taiwan by employing 'opposition party diplomacy' whereby China directly courted key opposition leaders such as KMT Chairman Lien Chan (Wang 2005: 271). The divide and rule strategy led to the institutionalization of the KMT-CPC forum whereby China would offer some economic concessions to Taiwan and engage in political discussions with the pro-China (or 'pan-blue') camp, which had control of the legislature (ibid.: 271–72). At the first crucial KMT-CPC forum, just one month after China's passage of the Anti-Secession Law, KMT Chairman Lien released a joint statement with China's President Hu Jintao, effectively rebuking President Chen for refusing to accept the 1992 Consensus, while confirming a new KMT-CPC alliance against the Taiwanese independence movement (Beckershoff 2014: 235). As a result, although the deterioration of the political relationship between Taiwan and China did not reflect the realities of enhanced bilateral socio-economic ties, the KMT and its allies were able maintain that the DPP had 'closed Taiwan's door' to the Chinese market.

A myriad of political scandals, including allegations of corruption by President Chen and his family, plagued the second half of Chen's presidency. Building on Chen's low approval ratings, and positioning itself as the most reliable party to navigate the complex channels of cross-Strait relations, the KMT, under the leadership of Ma Ying-jeou, defeated the DPP in the January and March 2008 legislative and presidential elections.

Return of the 1992 Consensus: détente during the Ma Ying-jeou era

At his first inaugural speech in 2008, President Ma Ying-jeou declared that he would maintain the status quo with a new 'three noes' policy, in which he promised that there would be no unification, no independence, and no use of force. In reality, the advent of the new KMT government almost immediately led to a paradigm shift in Taiwan-China relations. Citing the ROC Constitution, Ma openly rejected Taiwanese independence as an option for Taiwan's future, and staunchly embraced the 1992 Consensus, which facilitated the revival of the long-suspended SEF-ARATS platform. Ma also explicitly rebuked the 'two state theory' developed under the successive presidencies of Lee and Chen, and declared that although there was a special relationship between Taiwan and China, it was 'not a state-to-state relationship' (Shih 2013: 49). Ma further clarified his position during his second presidential term, describing relations between Taiwan and China as 'one Republic of China, two areas' (Chen 2013: 24). In short, although maintaining the constitutionality of the ROC, the Ma administration adopted a series of positions which converged with Beijing's agenda, namely the implicit long-term goal of eventual unification. Under the new KMT regime, the old policy of 'no contact, no compromise and no negotiation' was reversed. This was particularly evident after President Ma floated the idea of signing a peace accord with China, and following the 2015 meeting between Ma and China's President Xi Jinping in Singapore.

The most significant development during the Ma presidency was the rapid deepening of economic integration and regular official communication between Taiwan and China. Within months of his presidency, the long-proposed 'three links' became a reality as direct flights, shipping and postal services between Taiwan and China became normalized. Cross-Strait relations also expanded into other arenas of cooperation, for example the signing of the Cross-Strait Agreement on Joint Crime-fighting and Judicial Mutual Assistance in May 2009 (Mainland Affairs Council 2009).

Linking Taiwan's economic future with its dependence on the Chinese market, in 2010 the KMT administration signed the Economic Cooperation Framework Agreement (ECFA) with China, a bilateral agreement that aimed to develop China and Taiwan into a common market (Lai 2011: 173). Most remaining restrictions governing cross-Strait contact were relaxed yet further, such as allowing Chinese tourists to visit Taiwan for the first time, as well as the enrolment of Chinese students in Taiwanese universities. Chinese tourists soon comprised the largest number of foreign visitors to Taiwan, while more than 140,000 Chinese had studied at Taiwan's universities by the end of the Ma presidency in 2016 (Rowen 2014: 64, Mainland Affairs Council, n.d.). The Ma government promoted these breakthroughs purely as great commercial successes, and Taiwan's economy certainly benefited from these agreements (Cabestan 2010: 24). However, these concessions were always of political significance and were evidently part of China's grand strategy to promote its unification agenda (Huang 2012: 87; Rowen 2014; Matsuda 2015).

Détente between Taiwan and China allowed some flexibility in Taiwan's international relations. Ma's diplomatic truce had the tacit approval of the upper echelon of the CPC (Matsuda 2015: 9). During Ma's tenure Gambia was the only state to switch its diplomatic recognition to the PRC, and this occurred during Ma's lame duck presidency, after the KMT's Eric Chu lost his bid for the presidency (Ramzy 2016). In fact, prior to the DPP's 2016 presidential electoral success, Beijing had refused to accept official diplomatic recognition from the Dominican Republic, Panama and Paraguay, in order to prevent any backlash to cross-Strait rapprochement (Atkinson 2014: 418). One of Ma's greatest diplomatic achievements was when Taiwan attended, for the first time, the World Health Assembly (WHA), as an observer under the 'Chinese Taipei' moniker in 2009. With China's approval, Taiwan also participated in a number of international organizations, such as the International Civil Aviation Organization (ICAO), and continued to receive annual observer status invitations to attend the WHA proceedings for the remainder of Ma's presidential tenure (Chen 2013: 32).

Cross-Strait rapprochement, however, did not lead to a relaxation of China's military coercion of Taiwan. As a gesture of goodwill, Ma instructed Taiwan's military to reduce the frequency of the Han Kuang war games, a routine military exercise aimed at countering a stimulated invasion from China (Zhang 2011: 274). Although Ma had proposed military-to-military confidence-building measures between Taiwan and China, there was little progress in this regard (National Defense Report Editing Committee 2015: 77). China also ignored Ma's calls for the PRC to moderate its military presence, and to decrease, or remove, its missiles targeting Taiwan. The People's Liberation Army (PLA) has continued to consider Taiwan a main 'strategic direction', namely a core interest of the CPC, and therefore China's military has contingency plans for a hostile takeover of Taiwan (US Department of Defense 2016: 43, 86–93). The ambitious modernization of the PLA has led to an asymmetrical balance of military power in China's favour. Despite warming ties, it was a 'highly militarised détente' as China continued to build up its stockpile of missiles at the rate of over 100 a year, directly targeting Taiwan (Cabestan 2010: 25).

Although Ma's initial economic policies with China were popular, segments of the Taiwanese populace remained suspicious of the KMT, concerned that the government was eroding Taiwan's sovereignty. Public distrust and resentment of the government manifested itself into routine mass protests against the Ma government, most significantly leading to the development of the 2008 Wild Strawberries Movement, with many of the 'strawberry' veterans later becoming leaders of the more successful Sunflower Movement in 2014 (Fell 2017: 5–6). The 'sunflower' leaders were able to mobilize popular support by appealing to the public to defend Taiwan's democracy (ibid.: 2). The 23-day occupation of the Legislative Yuan was the largest setback for the Ma administration, as the protest successfully lobbied the suspension of the bilateral Cross-Strait Service Trade Agreement (CSSTA), which would have integrated Taiwan and China's economies yet further.

At the end of the Ma administration, his cross-Strait legacy had a mixed reputation. On the one hand, the intensified socio-economic engagement, and the token goodwill from China saw a cessation of dollar diplomacy, while

Taiwan was also able to participate, albeit on an ad hoc basis, in a number of international organizations. Closer trade ties and economic growth did not lead to a more equitable sharing of profits, and there was a popular perception that a small group of cronies, well connected in cross-Strait affairs, were monopolizing rents from their cross-Strait links, which was a key factor that swayed public support against the unratified CSSTA (Matsuda 2015: 32; Wang 2017). However, the KMT's acceptance of the 1992 Consensus, Ma's methodological rollback of the 'two state theory,' the 2015 Ma-Xi summit, and even the floating of the idea of a peace accord, had pushed Taiwan's position 'closer to Beijing than it had ever been since the end of the Cold War' (Lim 2018: 326).

The Tsai administration under the curse of the 1992 Consensus

The return of the DPP administration to power in 2016 was a historic moment in Taiwan's electoral history. For the first time, a non-KMT party was able to take control of both the executive and legislative branches of government. At her inauguration, President Tsai Ing-wen was initially cautious in her message to China. Working within the constitutional framework of the ROC, she discussed the 'historical fact' of the 1992 meeting, when the SEF and the ARATS were able to reach 'joint acknowledgements and understandings … in a spirit of mutual understanding and a political attitude of seeking common ground while setting aside differences' (Office of the President, Republic of China (Taiwan) 2016). Tsai's cordial overture and moderate position intended to alleviate Chinese concerns about Taiwanese independence were rebuked as insufficient by China, as Ma's rapprochement had left a paradoxical legacy that further shifted China's reference point in cross-Strait dynamics (Lim 2018: 331; Romberg 2016: 7). China has continued to insist on the mantra of the 1992 Consensus, which calls for Taiwan's subordination to the One China principle for the ultimate goal of unification. President Xi Jinping made this explicitly clear in his speech on 4 January 2019 to celebrate the 40th anniversary of the 'Message to Taiwan Compatriots' that the only possible framework for Taiwan's 'peaceful unification' with China is under the principle of 'one country, two systems' (China Daily 2019). This narrow 'interpretation' effectively rejected the 'two states theory' of previous years, and made it politically impossible for the DPP administration to assent to the 1992 Consensus.

China's greater economic and political influence also translated into a more assertive posture in its foreign policy (Chang Liao 2018). The temporary détente during the Ma era quickly became obsolete, as China immediately punished Taiwan following the DPP's electoral success. After Tsai came into office, the PRC cut off all official communications and revived a series of punitive sanctions against Taiwan. China's tactics included the poaching of Taiwan's diplomatic allies, the systematic isolation of Taiwan in the international community, and the curtailing of the number of Chinese tourists and students to Taiwan, all backed by a series of coercive military exercises 'tailored for Taiwan separatists' (Johnson 2018; Rowen 2017: 32). The CPC has a long history of developing a complex network of state and non-state actors to do the party's bidding via the coordination of the United Front Work Department (UFWD) (Brady 2018; Wang and Groot 2018: 571–72). President Xi Jinping has referred to the UFWD as a 'magic weapon', and some analysts have asserted that there is evidence that the CPC has utilized non-state actors including Taiwanese businesspeople, journalists, pro-China politicians, fringe nationalist groups, and even Taiwan-based gangsters to undertake clandestine operations to promote China's political agenda, thereby effectively undermining Taiwan's democracy and the independence movement (Lee 2018; Garnaut 2014).

In 2018 Taiwan was once again blocked from participating in the WHA and ICAO, while the first East Asian Youth Games planned in Taiwan was cancelled. China's plan to reduce Taiwan's international space also expanded into the private sector. The 'politics of erasing Taiwan' led to international companies submitting to China's pressure, and forced businesses with interests in the Chinese market to label Taiwan as a part of China on their website content (Huong and Yang 2018). By 2019 Taiwan had lost five diplomatic allies since President Tsai came into office, leaving Taiwan with only 17 official diplomatic ties (Goh 2018).

The downturn in Taiwan-China relations under Tsai and the tightening of Taiwan's official diplomatic space did not align with the DPP's moderate international success elsewhere. Under Tsai, the DPP administration began to develop a 'new southbound policy' in order to enhance 'economic and trade collaboration, people-to-people exchanges, resource sharing and regional connectivity' between Taiwan and 18 countries in South and South-East Asia, and Oceania (Executive Yuan, n.d.). This has led to modest success, so that in 2018 more than 2.3 million visitors from 'new southbound policy' countries visited Taiwan, a 15 per cent increase from the previous year (Chung 2018). Anecdotal evidence suggests that some Taiwanese manufacturers are making contingency plans to relocate their factories from China to South-East Asia, as a precaution to mitigate US President Donald Trump's trade war with China (Cheng and Ihara 2018).

In the opinion of Huong and Yang (2018), China's assertive attitude towards Taiwan may have led to a backlash by liberal democratic states against China. For example, the White House has described China's measures against Taiwan as 'Orwellian nonsense' (Buckley 2018). Furthermore, bipartisan support for Taiwan in the United States has resurged, best exemplified by the passage of the Asia Reassurance Initiative Act of 2018. As part of the United States's broader strategic interest in the Indo-Pacific Region, the Act referred to Taiwan as one of America's 'economic, political and security partners' (US Congress 2018). Section 209 of the Act entitled 'Commitment to Taiwan' stipulates a series of US government commitments to Taiwan, including direct references to the Taiwan Relations Act of 1979, support for a peaceful resolution acceptable to countries on both sides of the Taiwan Strait, and the continued sale of arms to maintain Taiwan's capacity to defend itself against the PRC. The Act also directly refers to the 2018 Taiwan Travel Act, which encourages top US officials to visit Taiwan.

China: friend or foe: Taiwan's 2020 presidential elections and beyond

At the time of writing, Tsai is facing a difficult re-election year, as her support rate has plummeted following the DPP's defeat in the 2018 local elections. Undoubtedly, the worsening of cross-Strait relations played a role in the 2018 elections; however, more nuanced observations suggest that domestic factors, such as Tsai's broad reform agenda including pension reforms for civil servants and military veterans, and a mobilized conservative constituency against same-sex marriage have damaged DPP's electoral appeal (Templeman 2018). Nevertheless, the fact that the victorious KMT mayors quickly declared their acceptance of the 1992 Consensus, in direct contradiction of the central government's policy, suggest that Taiwan-China relations remain the most salient issue in Taiwan's polarized political environment.

Since the founding of the PRC in 1949, and the parallel development of a de facto Taiwan state under the formal title of the ROC, there has been cycles of ebb-and-flow in Taiwan-China relations. From the total ban that prevented families from reuniting, to the accelerated blossoming of socio-economic relations today, China has consistently played a critical role in influencing the direction of Taiwan's political economy. Pro-China political leaders from both Taiwan and China continue to emphasize their common ancestral ties to promote the ultimate goal of eventual unification. On the other hand, pro-Taiwan actors and defenders of liberal democracy see China as the greatest threat to Taiwan's democracy and de facto independence. Although popular accounts generally portray the Taiwanese electorate as pragmatic voters who consistently chose the status quo, that is neither independence nor unification in the near future. The reality is that 70 years of cross-Strait relations has seen various shifts in the meaning of this status quo. Nevertheless, irrespective of whichever party wins Taiwan's 2020 elections, China will remain an ally for some actors, yet an adversary for others.

References

Atkinson, Joel (2014) 'Aid in Taiwan's Foreign Policy: Putting Ma Ying-Jeou's Aid Reforms in Historical Perspective', *Pacific Review*, 27(3).

Beckershoff, André (2014) 'The KMT–CCP Forum: Securing Consent for Cross-Strait Rapprochement', *Journal of Current Chinese Affairs*, 43(1).

Brady, Anne-Marie (2018) 'New Zealand and the CCP'S "Magic Weapons"', *Journal of Democracy*, 29(2).

Buckley, Chris (2018) '"Orwellian Nonsense"? China Says That's the Price of Doing Business', *New York Times*, 6 May.

Cabestan, Jean Pierre (2010) 'The New Détente in the Taiwan Strait and Its Impact on Taiwan's Security and Future: More Questions than Answers', *China Perspectives*, 3.
Chang, Jaw-ling Joanne (2010) 'Taiwan's Participation in the World Health Organization: The U.S. "Facilitator" Role', *American Foreign Policy Interests*, 32(3).
Chang, Liao Nien-chung (2018) 'Winds of Change: Assessing China's Assertive Turn in Foreign Policy', *Journal of Asian and African Studies*, 53(6).
Chang, Maria Hsia (1993) 'The Future of Taiwan-Mainland Relations', in Lin Bih-Jaw (ed.) *Contemporary China and the Changing International Community*, Taipei: National Chengchi University.
Chao Chien-min (1990) 'China's Policy Towards Taiwan', *Pacific Review*, 3(2).
Charney, Jonathan I. and R. J. V. Prescott (2000) 'Resolving Cross-Strait Relations Between China and Taiwan', *American Journal of International Law*, 94(3).
Chen, Dean P. (2013) 'The Strategic Implications of Ma Ying-jeou's "One ROC, Two Areas" Policy on Cross-Strait Relations', *American Journal of Chinese Studies*, 20(1).
Chen, Shui-bian (2004) 'Full Text of Inaugural Speech: Paving the Way for a Sustainable Taiwan', *Taipei Times*, 21 May.
Cheng, Maria (2006) 'Constructing a New Political Spectacle: Tactics of Chen Shui-bian's 2000 and 2004 Inaugural Speech', *Discourse & Society*, 17(5).
Cheng, Ting-fang and Ihara Kensaku (2018) 'Trade War Fuels Taiwanese Producers' Withdrawal from China', *Nikkei Asian Review*, 16 August. Available at https://asia.nikkei.com/Business/Business-trends/Trade-war-fuels-Taiwanese-producers-withdrawal-from-China (accessed 26 February 2019).
China Daily (2019) 'Highlights of Xi's Speech at Taiwan Message Anniversary Event', 2 January.
Chinese Ministry of Foreign Affairs (n.d.) *A Policy of 'One Country, Two Systems' on Taiwan*. Available at www.fmprc.gov.cn/mfa_eng/ziliao_665539/3602_665543/3604_665547/t18027.shtml (accessed 19 February 2019).
Ching, Leo T. S. (2001) *Becoming "Japanese": Colonial Taiwan and the Politics of Identity Formation*, Berkeley: University of California Press.
Chung, Lawrence (2018) 'Tourists Flock to Taiwan in Record Numbers Despite Drop from Mainland China', *South China Morning Post*, 31 December.
Clough, Ralph N. (2003) 'Progress and Problems in Taiwan's Cross-Strait Relations', *American Foreign Policy Interests*, 25.
Executive Yuan (n.d.) 'New Southbound Policy Promotion Plan '. Available at https://english.ey.gov.tw/News_Hot_Topic.aspx?n=D61190201622DA50&sms=B5449820D7077391 (accessed 25 February 2019).
Fell, Dafydd (2017) 'Social Movements in Taiwan after 2008: From the Strawberries to the Sunflowers and Beyond', in Dafydd Fell (ed.) *Taiwan's Social Movements under Ma Ying-jeou: From the Wild Strawberries to the Sunflowers*, Abingdon andNew York: Routledge.
Fraleigh, Matthew (2010) 'Japan's First War Reporter: Kishida Ginko and the Taiwan Expedition', *Japanese Studies*, 30(1).
Lin Gang, and Wu Weixu (2017) 'Chinese National Identity under Reconstruction', in Lowell Dittmer (ed.) *Taiwan and China: Fitful Embrace*, Oakland: University of California Press.
Garnaut, John (2014) 'China's Rulers Team Up with Notorious "White Wolf" of Taiwan', *Sydney Morning Herald*, 11 July.
Goh Sui Noi (2018) 'Taiwan Loses Third Diplomatic Ally This Year after El Salvador Breaks Ties', *Strait Times*, 21 August.

Hu Jintao (2008) 'Let Us Join Hands to Promote the Peaceful Development of Cross-Straits Relations and Strive with a United Resolve for the Great Rejuvenation of the Chinese Nation', 31 December. Available at https://china.usc.edu/hu-jintao-let-us-join-hands-promote-peaceful-development-cross-straits-relations-and-strive-united (accessed 19 February 2019).

Huang Jie (2012) 'TPP versus ECFA: Similarities, Differences, and China's Strategies', *China Review*, 12(2).

Hughes, Christopher (2011) 'Negotiating National Identity in Taiwan: Between Nativisation and Desinicisation', in Robert Ash, John W. Garver and Penelope Prime (eds) *Taiwan's Democracy: Economic and Political Challenges*, London: Routledge.

Huong Le Thu and Alan H. Yang (2018) 'The Politics of Erasing Taiwan', *Taiwan Insight*, 14 August. Available at https://taiwaninsight.org/2018/08/14/the-politics-of-erasing-taiwan (accessed 25 February 2019).

Johnson, Jesse (2018) 'China to Begin Large-Scale Military Exercise "Tailored for Taiwan Separatists" in East China Sea,' *Japan Times*, 18 July.

Lai, Yen-Hsueh (2011) 'Interpreting the ECFA: A New Common Market for Taiwan and Mainland China Regional Focus and Controversies: Cross-Strait Economic Cooperation', *Journal of East Asia & International Law*, 4.

Lee, Lai To (1989) 'Taiwan and the Reunification of China', *Pacific Review*, 2(2).

Lee, Lynn (2018) 'Taiwan: Spies, Lies and Cross-straits Ties', *Al Jazeera*, 6 September. Available at www.aljazeera.com/programmes/peopleandpower/2018/09/taiwan-spies-lies-cross-straits-ties-180906054720310.html (accessed 25 February 2019).

Lin, Neng-Shan (2011) 'Lee Teng-hui's "Two-State" Theory: Perceptions and Policy Change', *Soochow Political Journal*, 29(4).

Low, Stephanie (2001) 'KMT Breaks It Off with Lee Teng-hui', *Taipei Times*, 22 September.

Mainland Affairs Council (2009) 'Cross-Strait Joint Crime-Fighting and Judicial Mutual Assistance Agreement', 29 May. Available at www.mac.gov.tw/en/cp.aspx?n=FD37619195CF6DA5&s=CED288DC9B1EC576 (accessed 24 February 2019).

Mainland Affairs Council (n.d.) 'Statistics on Mainland Students Researching and Studying for Degrees in Taiwan'. Available at www.mac.gov.tw/en/News_Content.aspx?n=CA7B5FA9C0EC7005&sms=D645444CA321A4FA&s=54D121541C911FB1 (accessed 24 February 2019).

Matsuda, Yasuhiro (2015) 'Cross-Strait Relations under the Ma Ying-jeou Administration: From Economic to Political Dependence?' *Journal of Contemporary East Asia Studies*, 4(2).

National Defence Report Editing Committee (2015) *2015 National Defence Report, the Republic of China*, Taipei: Ministry of National Defence.

Office of the Historian (n.d.) *The Taiwan Straits Crisis: 1954–1955 and 1958*. Available at https://history.state.gov/milestones/1953-1960/taiwan-strait-crises (accessed 19 February 2019).

Office of the President, ROC, (2016) 'Inaugural Ceremony of the 14th-Term President and Vice President of the Republic of China (Taiwan)', 20 May. Available at https://english.president.gov.tw/Page/252 (accessed 25 February 2019).

People's Daily Online (2005) 'Full Text of Anti-Secession Law', 14 March. Available at http://en.people.cn/200503/14/eng20050314_176746.html (accessed 22 February 2019).

Philips, Steven (1999) 'Between Assimilation and Independence: Taiwanese Political Aspirations under Nationalist Chinese Rule, 1945–1948', in Murray A. Rubinstein (ed.) *Taiwan: A New History*, New York: M. E. Sharpe.

Ramzy, Austin (2016) 'China Resumes Diplomatic Relations with Gambia, Shutting Out Taiwan', *New York Times*, March 18.
Romberg, Alan (2016) 'Tsai Ing-wen Takes Office: A New Era in Cross-Strait Relations', *China Leadership Monitor*, 50: 1–13.
Ross, Robert (2006) 'Explaining Taiwan's Revisionist Diplomacy', *Journal of Contemporary China*, 15(48).
Rowen, Ian (2014) 'Tourism as a Territorial Strategy: The Case of China and Taiwan', *Annals of Tourism Research*, 46.
Rowen, Ian (2017) 'Touring in Heterotopia: Travel, Sovereignty, and Exceptional Spaces in Taiwan and China', *Asian Anthropology*, 16(1).
Sheng, Lijun (1998) 'China Eyes Taiwan: Why Is a Breakthrough so Difficult', *Journal of Strategic Studies*, 21(1).
Sheng, Lijun (2001) 'Chen Shui-bian and Cross-Strait Relations', *Contemporary Southeast Asia*, 23(4).
Shih Cheng-feng (2013) 'China Policy of the Ma Ying-jeou Administration', *Taiwan International Studies Quarterly*, 9(2).
Su, Chi (2009) *Taiwan's Relations with Mainland China: A Tail Wagging Two Dogs*, London: Routledge.
Sullivan, John and Lowe, Will (2010) 'Chen Shui-bian: On Independence', *China Quarterly*, 203.
Templeman, Kharis (2018) '2018 Taiwan Local Elections: What Happened?' *Global Taiwan Brief*, 3(23). Available at https://globaltaiwan.org/2018/11/vol-3-issue-23/#KharisTempleman11282018 (accessed 25 February 2019).
United Press International (1995) 'Taiwan's Lee Speaks at Cornell', 9 June. Available at www.upi.com/Archives/1995/06/09/Taiwans-Lee-speaks-at-Cornell/4706802670400/ (accessed 20 February 2019).
US Congress (2018) *S.2736 - Asia Reassurance Initiative Act of 2018*, Washington, DC: US Congress.
US Department of Defense (2009) *Annual Report to Congress: Military Power of the People's Republic of China 2009*, Washington DC: Office of the Secretary of Defense.
US Department of Defense (2016) *Annual Report to Congress: Military and Security Developments Involving the People's Republic of China 2016*, Washington DC: Office of the Secretary of Defense.
Wang, Amy (2017) 'For Decades, No One Spoke of Taiwan's Hidden Massacre: A New Generation Is Breaking the Silence', *Washington Post*, 28 February.
Wang, Chih-ming (2017) 'The Future That Belongs to Us': Affective Politics, Neoliberalism and the Sunflower Movement', *International Journal of Cultural Studies*, 20(2).
Wang, Jianwei (2005) 'Seize the Moment-Cross Strait Relations after the Antisecession Law', *American Foreign Policy Interests*, 27(4).
Wang, Ray and Gerry Groot (2018) 'Who Represents? Xi Jinping's Grand United Front Work, Legitimation, Participation and Consultative Democracy', *Journal of Contemporary China*, 27(112).
Weber, Max (1968) *Economy and Society*, ed. Guenther Roth and Claus Wittich New York: Bedminster.
Zhang, Baohui (2011) 'Taiwan's New Grand Strategy', *Journal of Contemporary China*, 20(69).
Zhao, Suisheng (1999) 'Military Coercion and Peaceful Offence: Beijing's Strategy of National Reunification with Taiwan', *Pacific Affairs*, 72(4).

6 Taiwan-China relations: asymmetric trust and Innenpolitik

Wen-ti Sung

Introduction

The so-called Taiwan issue emerged towards the end of the Chinese civil war in 1949, which saw the creation of two separate self-governing governments on each side of the Taiwan Strait. At its core, the cross-Strait rivalry is a competition of duelling national narratives: on the one hand, the ruling Communist Party of China (CPC) which governs the People's Republic of China (PRC, or China), as well as the Kuomintang (KMT – Nationalist Party) in Taiwan, both uphold a historical vision of Chinese history, of which Taiwan is a subsidiary and indivisible part; therefore they see the current political separation between China and Taiwan as but a remnant of the Chinese civil war and their eventual reunification is viewed as being essential for the great rejuvenation of the Chinese nation and for bringing to an end the 'century of humiliation'. On the other hand, the ruling Democratic Progressive Party (DPP) in Taiwan and increasingly mainstream Taiwanese society maintain a national narrative that sees Taiwan as a separate nation in its own right, especially since its democratization in the 1990s. They increasingly see the Chinese nation as a close civilizational cousin with whom Taiwan shares a significant common history and culture, of which Taiwan is no longer necessarily a part (DPP 1999).

These contrasting national narratives have led to fundamental differences in their preferences on the future of cross-Strait relations. The CPC insists that unification is the only acceptable end-state, according to its One China principle, although it has exhibited various degrees of flexibility over time on the exact timing and means of achieving unification, from military liberation to peaceful unification under various formulae of 'one country, two systems'. Meanwhile, Taiwanese society is divided on the issue of a preferred cross-Strait end-state. Of Taiwan's two main political parties, the unification-seeking KMT believes that people living in Taiwan are both Chinese and Taiwanese and is committed to seeking some form of eventual unification with mainland China at an unspecified point in the future. Conversely, the independence-seeking DPP considers the people to be entirely Taiwanese and seeks to preserve Taiwan's current status as a de facto independent state, although it is also open to future changes to Taiwan's sovereignty status – be that towards de jure independence from, or unification with, China – so long as it is determined by the will of the Taiwanese people.

Beyond the actors' preferences, the contours of cross-Strait relations are often shaped by three important factors: first, a long-term incentive structure based on an evolving external Washington-Beijing-Taipei trilateral power balance as well as domestic public opinion in Taiwan; second, the political insecurity of Taiwanese, and to a lesser extent, Chinese leaders, which in turn shapes their penchant for diversionary cross-Strait policy; and third, both Chinese and Taiwanese society's 'asymmetry trust' in Taiwan's two main political parties, causing many missed opportunities for cross-Strait engagement.

Let us briefly address these three factors in order. First, cross-Strait relations are often caught up in the broader Cold War strategic triangle of Washington-Beijing-Taipei relations, as the United States acts as a balancer whose latent extended deterrence dissuades both Beijing and Taipei from launching an all-out military offensive against each other. Taiwan's public opinion has consistently demonstrated a preference for the status quo (de facto independence) and an aversion to either de jure independence or immediate unification, and this limits Taiwanese leaders, regardless of their political affiliation, from pursuing either option unreservedly. Second, the Taiwanese mainstream national identity trend is, however, evolving in an ever more 'Taiwanese' direction at the expense of 'Chinese', thus incentivizing Taiwanese politicians to entertain independence-friendly cross-Strait platforms in exchange for nationalistic legitimacy, especially during periods of political insecurity and heightened perceptions of external threat.

Third, particularly since the 1990s Beijing has maintained a strategy of 'asymmetric engagement' in Taiwan's two main political parties (Lin 2016: 9–11). It is more likely to trust the KMT's long-term unificationist intentions and to accept the KMT's pro-status quo proposals than similar proposals from the DPP. Meanwhile, Taiwanese society also views the two parties asymmetrically: it is relatively more likely to trust the independence-seeking DPP as having Taiwan's best interests at heart in cross-Strait affairs – even if some observers occasionally question the DPP's efficacy at managing them. These asymmetries have resulted in a dilemma whereby the KMT is historically more effective at striking agreements with Beijing, but experiences a weaker mandate during their ratification and implementation back home, while the DPP, despite its relatively stronger domestic mandate, is ineffective at confidence building with Beijing. This dilemma then results in a chronic impasse and volatility in the Taiwan Strait.

This chapter will apply this framework to analyse modern Taiwan-China relations since 1949. It divides the relationship into three broad eras: the 'military liberation' era (1949–66); the 'peaceful unification' era marked by ideological rather than military rivalry (1966–96); and finally the era of Taiwanese nationalism and its responses (1996–present day). This chapter will focus particularly on the third era, during which Taiwan's democratization and the emergence of Taiwanese nationalism as a major factor has continued to shape much of cross-Strait relations today.

The military liberation era, 1949–66

Following the ending of the Second World War, Taiwan reverted to Chinese sovereignty under the auspices of the Republic of China (ROC, or Taiwan). The Chinese civil war soon broke out between the ruling KMT-led government and the insurgent CPC. As the latter achieved decisive victories and gradually took control of most of mainland China by 1949, it established a new state known as the People's Republic of China (PRC or China). Consequently, the CPC claimed that the ROC had ceased to exist, implying that Taiwan constituted little more than a renegade Chinese province. Meanwhile, the defeated KMT fled to Taiwan, insisting that the ROC still existed (albeit that its territory had been reduced so that it comprised just Taiwan and its surrounding islands), and continued to assert sovereignty over all of China.

Both states adhered to a version of the One China principle, insisted on the indivisibility of Chinese sovereignty, shared almost completely overlapping sovereign claims, and proclaimed that they alone were the only one true legitimate government of all of China, including Taiwan. This battle over the 'mandate of heaven' (*fatong*) dominated cross-Strait relations early on.

Internally, the KMT government was caught between the dual realities of its minority rule status within Taiwan and its need to claim to represent all of China and to leverage local resources to that effect. The KMT resorted to declaring a constant state of emergency, which mainly included a 38-year-long period of martial law (1949–87), which witnessed violations of human rights and the rule of law, and the freezing of most elections at the central level, so that the ROC's electorate could remain part of China rather than being 'Taiwanized'. This had the convenient side-effect that the KMT could remain permanently in power without having to hold elections or express the views of those it governed. Both of these authoritarian legacies would later become fertile breeding grounds for anti-KMT and anti-Chinese sentiment, as well as in a tragic sense the 'background to the Taiwanese independence movement.

Futile military adventures

While the PRC continued to assert its ambition to 'militarily liberate' Taiwan, the ROC's KMT-led government also never fully relinquished its claim that it would retake the whole of China by force. Practically, however, neither party was able to take over the other side by force, mainly due to the stabilizing American security posture in East Asia.

While initially hesitant, the onset of the Korean War and the formation of the Chinese-Soviet alignment in 1950 led the United States to commit to continue its recognition of the ROC. With the signing of the China-US Mutual Defense Treaty in 1955, Washington unmistakably extended its security umbrella to cover Taiwan, thereby precluding Beijing's 'military liberation' of Taiwan as a serious possibility. Several such attempts nonetheless still occurred, such as the 1949 Guningtou amphibious offensive, and Beijing's bombardment of Taiwan's offshore islands Quemoy and Matsu in 1954 and again in 1958–79, during what became known as the First and Second Taiwan Strait Crises.

Meanwhile, Taiwan's KMT-led government continued to flirt with the possibility of retaking China from two fronts: by pursuing guerilla warfare via China's south-western interior, and by launching a naval offensive against its eastern seaboard (Yeh 2016). By the 1960s the KMT's chances of retaking China by force had been severely diminished, however, after the PRC conducted its first successful atomic bomb test in 1964. By 1965 the KMT was engaged in a final attempt at reversing its declining military fortunes following the launching of two naval offensives, both of which ended disastrously. Soon afterwards, the KMT cut back on its 'Guoguang Project' ('National Recovery Project') Office, the inter-agency organization responsible for coordinating military projects to retake China, and by 1972 the office had been completely disbanded.

Ideological rivalry and peaceful unification era, 1966–96

As military measures proved futile for both sides, the main undertone of cross-Strait rivalry gradually shifted from military competition to ideological rivalry, implying that henceforth unification would occur through peaceful negotiations.

For China, it was both a matter of diminished capability and reduced will. Internationally, heightened external threats such as China's intense border clashes with its former Soviet patron in 1969 left China isolated strategically, creating an opening for the China-US rapprochement that took place in 1971–72 during the Nixon Administration (Wu 2001). Reflecting on the CPC's shifting priorities, Mao Zedong announced to the then US Secretary of State Henry Kissinger that China could do without Taiwan for the time being, though 'a hundred years hence we will want it' (Kissinger 2011: 307).

Second, internally, the destruction and dysfunction of the Cultural Revolution from 1966 to 1976 devastated the economy, leaving scant resources for waging military adventures. Following the end of the Revolution, Deng Xiaoping and the second generation of leadership, presided over the reprioritization of China's grand strategy objectives: the historic 1978 Third Plenum of the 11th CPC Central Committee ushered in an era of 'reform and opening' (*gaigekaifang*) and noted a fundamental shift from class struggle to economic development as well as the removal of all references to the liberation of Taiwan (Beijing Review 2019). The watershed 1979 fifth 'Letter to Taiwanese Compatriots' solidified this approach to peaceful unification, primarily along the one country, two systems lines, coupled with strategic patience.

Likewise, as the military option was clearly untenable, under KMT rule Taiwan moved towards ideological rivalry, as its slogan changed from *fangong fuguo* ('defeat communism and recover the nation') to *sanmin zhuyi tongyi zhongguo* ('unify China with three principles of the people'). In a case of international-domestic linkage, the United States' decision to realign with

Beijing increased Taiwan's fear of abandonment, incentivizing the ruling KMT to win back US support through a series of liberalization initiatives that eventually created enough space for the formation in 1986 of Taiwan's first opposition party, the DPP, followed by the lifting of martial law in 1987.

These culminated in Taiwan's first direct legislative elections in 1992 and the first direct presidential election in 1996, thus marking a symbolic redrawing of the boundaries of the ROC's national 'imagined community' (Anderson 1983). As only residents of Taiwan were enfranchised to vote in these purported 'national' elections, henceforth the ROC's electorate no longer included mainland China, and in practical terms the ROC became synonymous with Taiwan and its surrounding islands. In the 1996 presidential election, three-quarters of the votes went to two candidates that Beijing considered as either overt or covert 'Taiwan independentists'. Meanwhile, Taiwan's 1994 White Paper on Relations across the Taiwan Strait declared that Taipei 'would no longer compete with Beijing for the right to represent China in the international arena', thereby further cementing the notion of Taiwan and China as two separate nations (Dickson and Chao 2002: 225).

The speed of the 'Taiwanization' of the ROC alarmed Beijing. No longer convinced that time was inevitably on the side of eventual unification, Beijing moved from passively shelving cross-Strait relations to actively opposing Taiwan's so-called creeping independence by the mid-1990s, culminating in the 1995–96 Taiwan Strait Crisis.

Rise of Taiwanese nationalism and its responses (1996–)

Following Taiwan's first direct presidential election, the boundaries of Taiwan's 'imagined community' were unmistakably drawn, and henceforth the notion of Taiwan (rather than China) became the pre-eminent basis for the Taiwanese voters' sense of 'community of shared destiny'. A commitment to uphold de facto, if not necessarily *de jure*, Taiwanese statehood, thus became the new orthodoxy in Taiwan. Furthermore, by 1998, in order to boost the electoral prospects of the KMT's mayoral candidate in Taipei, the KMT's Chairman and President Lee Teng-Hui introduced his candidate Ma Ying-jeou, who was of *waishengren* ('mainlander') descent, as a 'New Taiwanese'. The episode revealed a new consensus that failure to identify as Taiwanese (or at least as both Taiwanese and Chinese) would henceforth be considered politically disadvantageous, if not disqualifying, for future aspirants to marquee public offices.

Cross-Strait relations worsened when Taiwanese President Lee Teng-hui them as a 'special state-to-state relationship' in an interview in July 1999, and especially when the opposition DPP presidential candidate Chen Shui-bian narrowly won the presidency in March 2000. Desperate to prevent Chen's election, Beijing issued a February 2000 White Paper entitled the 'One-China Principle and the Taiwan Issue'. In this Beijing had added a new condition that would warrant a Chinese invasion 'if the Taiwan authorities refuse, *sine die*, the peaceful settlement of cross-Strait reunification through negotiations'; ultimately, it was to no avail (Chen 2012: 327).

The Chen era (2000–08): primacy of Innenpolitik

Contrary to conventional wisdom, Chen Shui-bian was not an ideologue bent on the pursuit of independence at all costs during his presidency. Rather, Chen belonged to the bloc within the DPP that was more supportive of the notion of opening up economically to Beijing (known as the DPP's 'go West' faction, or *xijinpai*), and openly contemplated signing a cross-Strait interim agreement to lock-in the cross-Strait status quo (i.e. to rule out *de jure* independence, at least for the duration of the agreement). The primary driver of Chen's seemingly erratic fluctuations between moderate and confrontational cross-Strait policies remained domestic politics, namely his own sense of political security.

In the 2000 presidential campaign, Chen ran as a pragmatic candidate, calling his platform the 'Third Way' or 'new centrist path' (*xin zhongjian luxian*). He summed up his platform as 'make money not war, open doors not open fire, compete not conflict' (*daping budazhang, kaifang bukaizhan, jingzheng budouzheng*). Chen downplayed the DPP's traditional commitment to pursuing *de jure* independence and was the most proactive of all three main candidates on opening cross-Strait economic exchanges.

The Chen Shui-bian presidency, which lasted for two terms, was ultimately marked by turbulence in cross-Strait as well Taiwan-US relations. Domestically, Chen was limited by the DPP's permanent minority in the legislature and its struggles during municipal elections, which incentivized him to periodically resort to a populist-nationalist rhetoric to drum up a rallying-around-the-flag effect and to compensate for his weaker institutional power base. Internationally, Chen administration's domestic politics-driven agenda entailed periodic fluctuations between a moderate status quo oriented cross-Strait policy on the one hand, and diversionary foreign policy on the other.

On winning the presidency with a 39.3 per cent plurality, and controlling barely one-third of the legislature, Chen, lacking political capital, was sworn into office in May 2000 and committed to preserve the cross-Strait status quo. He delivered a carefully crafted inaugural speech that was allegedly cleared beforehand by both Washington and Beijing (Copper 2006: 290; The Initium 2004). In his speech, Chen pledged a policy of 'four noes and one without'; namely, so long as Beijing had no intention of using military force against Taiwan, under Chen's administration there would be no declaration of independence, no changes to the nation's official moniker, no push to incorporate the 'special state-to-state relations' doctrine into the Constitution, no push for a referendum to change the status quo in regard to the question of independence or unification, and finally abrogation of the National Unification Council or National Unification Guidelines would be out of the question.

Chen did fall short of accepting Beijing's One China principle in his inaugural address, for fear of antagonizing his DPP power base. But where he could not concede the present, he tried to meet Beijing half-way by committing to China in the past and future tenses. As he said:

> The people across the Taiwan Strait share the same ancestral, cultural, and historical background ... we believe that the leaders on both sides possess enough wisdom and creativity to jointly deal with the question of a future 'one China'.
>
> (Chen 2000)

Chen's pragmatism was initially met with a cold but not outright adversarial reception from Beijing, which claimed that it would 'wait and see' (*tingqiyan guanqixing*) whether Chen's actions matched his words. While the previous freezing of cross-Strait dialogue from the 'special state-to-state relationship' episode remained in place, Beijing refrained from criticizing Chen by name during the first two years and four months after Chen won the presidential election (Tung 2003). Internally, Beijing, too, was in no hurry to escalate tensions, as it was undergoing its own power transition process, as the fourth generation of Chinese leaders spearheaded by Hu Jintao prepared to assume power in 2002.

Periodic shifts between status quo policy and Taiwanese nationalism

Chen would soon develop the view that his pragmatism was a political luxury that he could ill-afford at times of political weakness. While his political weakness initially drew him to moderation, Chen found that moderation would win him no new friends politically. Beijing would not reward Chen for meeting it half-way; internally, Chen was not able to break the KMT-led pan-blue coalition's parliamentary majority, while his DPP still lost ground in the municipal elections and saw only modest gains at the elections held in November 2001. It was clear that his moderate strategy had hit its political ceiling.

To prepare for his re-election, Chen switched gears to a more assertively nationalist strategy and adopted a pro *de jure* independence platform. By August 2002 Chen had announced his 'one country on each side of the Taiwan Strait' doctrine (*yibianyiguo*) in order to rebrand his platform. To shore up nationalist support, Chen established Taiwan's first popular referenda to be held on the same day as the 2004 presidential election. The referenda topics concerned cross-Strait relations, highlighted China as a military threat, and were probably aimed at creating a rally-around-the-flag effect to the benefit of the incumbent leader (Chen) on voting day.

The nationalist platform proved more effective than pragmatism at expanding Chen's political base, at least temporarily, as Chen won a surprise re-election in March 2004, albeit with the narrowest of margins (0.2 per cent).

Missed opportunity following Chen's re-election

Having succeeded in being re-elected to the presidency, Chen swiftly pivoted back to his earlier stance of pragmatism. He reaffirmed commitment to his 'four noes and one without' policy during his second inaugural speech in May 2004. That was followed by a March 2005 video-conference with members of the European Parliament, when Chen acknowledged the practical limits to his earlier Taiwanese nationalist platform during the election, thus arguably indirectly admitting it was diversionary or domestic politics-driven in nature: 'I cannot deceive myself; I cannot deceive others … during my term as president, it will be impossible for me to change our national moniker to 'Republic of Taiwan" (Office of the President, ROC, 2005).

Many senior American policy officials and scholars made numerous ultimately unfruitful calls for a cross-Strait 'interim agreement' or modus vivendi. Chen's nationalist playbook during 2002–04 created an American perception that Chen was being a unilateralist 'trouble-maker' who had destabilized the Washington-Beijing-Taipei trilateral relations, leading then-Secretary of State Colin Powell to go as far as to break with precedence and to state that the United States favoured reunification as an eventual outcome (Kahn 2004).

Under pressure, Chen heeded to these calls. From 2004 to 2005, according to Chen's minister of foreign affairs and later presidential chief of staff, Mark Chen (no relation), Chen Shui-bian openly explored the idea of negotiating a cross-Strait 'interim agreement' with Beijing in early 2005, including holding parliamentary hearings, in an attempt at cross-Strait confidence building (Apple Daily 2004; *Taiwan People News* 2017).

However, due to its inherent lack of trust in the DPP, Beijing was unmoved by Chen's apparent reversion to moderation, and it progressively continued to apply pressure vis-à-vis Taiwan. Internationally, the cross-Strait diplomatic tug-of-war continued as China sought to win over Taiwan's remaining diplomatic allies. Legislatively, China ratified the Anti-Secession Law in March 2005 to shore up deterrence against Taiwanese independence, partly by upwardly managing perceptions of Chinese resolve to use force.

Beijing's efforts at deterrence were in vain, however. Chen would be undeterred by the Anti-Secession Law, and he probably welcomed it. Domestically, it generated short-term patriotic pushbacks in Taiwan that benefited the incumbent President Chen. Taking the longer view, however, the Anti-Secession Law led to a missed window of opportunity, as Chen, riding on the post-Anti-Secession Law anti-Beijing sentiment in Taiwan, could no longer openly entertain serious interim agreements with Beijing. The Anti-Secession Law further provided Chen with a shield from American pressure, as Chen could at least plausibly argue it was no longer him, but Beijing, with its Anti-Secession Law, that was 'rocking the boat'.

Chen's waning electoral fortunes and cross-Strait destabilization

As with Chen's first term, that period of relative stability quickly ended half-way through Chen's second term. Chen's DPP suffered a crushing electoral defeat at the local elections at the end of 2005, partly owing to political scandals and partly because of the Taiwanese electorate's recurring pattern of mid-term popular weariness and pushback against the second-term incumbent.

Facing internal pressure from within his own party, Chen again reverted to diversionary cross-Strait policy. By early 2006 Chen had announced his intention to push for Taiwan to rejoin the United Nations, not under the usual moniker 'Republic of China', but under the name 'Taiwan'. On 28 February 2006 Chen announced that the National Unification Guidelines 'ceased to apply' (*zhongzhi shiyong*) while the National Unification Council 'ceased to function' (*zhongzhi yunzuo*), with immediate effect. The following year, at a speech at the Formosan Association for Public Affairs' banquet, Chen formally broke with his 'four noes and one without' policy by replacing it with a policy of 'four wants and one without', namely 'Taiwan wants independence, wants name rectification, wants a new Constitution, and wants development', and that the fundamental dividing line in Taiwanese politics is not left-versus-right, but independence-versus-unification (*China Post* 2007).

Beijing opted for a relatively muted response, knowing that drastic reactions would either boost Chen's political agenda or risk partaking in action-reaction escalation spirals that might spin out of control. As Jianwei Wang put it, Hu Jintao decided to come up with Beijing's own 'three noes' policy: do not dance to Chen's rhythm; do not be used by Chen, but also do not force Chen [in]to a corner (2007: 27).

As Chen's approval ratings continued to plummet, Beijing was optimistic that it could outwait Chen. A new Taiwanese leader emerged by early 2008. That leader turned out to be KMT Chairman Ma Ying-jeou, who handsomely won the presidency in a landslide and whose pan-blue coalition won a three-quarters' majority in the legislature.

Ma Ying-jeou rapprochement (2008–14)

Ma emerged as a consensus candidate between the KMT's factions. Being a Hong Kong-born *waishengren* ('mainlander') by ethnicity and a former personal secretary of the charismatic President Chiang Ching-kuo, Ma won the support of the KMT's old guard virtually by default. Moreover, Ma came to political prominence during the administration of the more Taiwanese-minded President Lee Teng-Hui, making Ma not unsympathetic to the KMT's more predominantly ethnic *Minnan* local faction's 'Taiwan first' concerns. Yet because Ma was the leader of the KMT, Beijing gave Ma greater benefit of the doubt regarding his cross-Strait intentions than Ma's predecessor Chen ever received.

Thus, Ma's administration was marked by much more amicable cross-Strait political relations and more bi-directional cross-Strait economic relations than those witnessed during Chen's administration.

Ma came to power in 2008 committing to return to a centrist position that was substantively comparable with the moderate version of Chen Shui-bian's early cross-Strait platform (2000–02). Yet in place of Chen's 'no negatives' wording ('four noes and one without'), Ma substituted it for a more positive-sounding formula of 1992 Consensus, which Ma defined as a commitment to 'one China, respective interpretations'.

Intentionally strategically ambiguous, the wording of Ma's One China formula paid just enough respect to Beijing's One China principle, while the 'respective interpretations' left Taiwanese voters confident, at least during his first term, that Ma would preserve Taiwan's de facto independence. Strategically, Ma espoused his new 'three noes', i.e. that during his administration there would be no declaration of independence, no push for unification, and no use of force (war) across the Taiwan Strait (*butong budu buwu*), which again coincided with most of the core elements of the interim agreement proposals that Chen Shui-bian contemplated but eventually abandoned between 2004 and 2005.

In this case the asymmetric trust issue exerts a benign influence. Where Chen's moves failed, Ma's similar overtures were enough to reassure Chinese President Hu Jintao. Hu's 2008 speech commemorating the 30th anniversary of the 'Message to Compatriots in Taiwan' omitted any mention of the 'use of force', probably in an attempt to reinforce the upturn spiral in cross-Strait atmosphere. Ma's acceptance of the 1992 Consensus also brought enough constructive ambiguity to enable formal political talks that had been frozen since 1999 to finally reopen. Protocols gradually upgraded from the Lee Teng-Hui era semi-official talks to Ma's official ministerial level dialogues by 2014. It culminated in the unofficial summit in November 2015, when Taiwanese President Ma Ying-jeou and Chinese President Xi Jinping held a bilateral meeting in Singapore, albeit that they attended in their personal capacity, addressing each other as simply 'Mister Ma' and 'Mister Xi', and avoided reference to their official titles, so as to preserve constructive ambiguity and neither affirm nor deny the existence of two states.

Internationally, Beijing's satisfaction with Ma's 'three noes' led Beijing to reciprocate by conceding greater 'international space' for Taiwan, most significantly in not vetoing Taiwan's gaining of non-permanent observer status at the World Health Assembly and the International Civil Aviation Organization. Beijing's accommodation, in addition to apparent backing from the US government in a breach of protocol, helped Ma to sail through his re-election in 2012 with a reduced but still comfortable margin.

At the same time, cross-Strait economic relations accelerated during Ma's presidency (2008–16). Beijing maintained a neo-functionalist approach modelled on the European Union's experience (Lin 2016: 1–4). Taking an 'economy first, politics later' and 'easy things first, difficult things later' approach, two landmark free trade agreements were signed. The first was the 2010 Economic Cooperation Framework Agreement (ECFA) which reduced trade barriers in the manufacturing sector, and was preceded by a widely anticipated televised debate between President Ma Ying-jeou and the DPP Chairwoman Tsai Ing-wen, and the second was the Cross-Strait Service Trade Agreement (CSSTA), which proved to have an even greater impact.

The Sunflower Movement (2014–18)

By 2014 earlier optimism about the economic windfalls from Ma's conciliatory cross-Dtrait platform had soured into discomfort with the rapid pace of cross-Strait economic integration. The CSSTA stoked fears that its implementation might lead to irreversible Taiwanese economic dependence on China, thereby setting Taiwan on a path of ever-diminishing freedom to choose its own future.

The perceived illegitimacy and opaqueness of the CSSTA's ratification process sparked the emergence of the student Sunflower Movement on 18 March 2014. The Movement saw students and citizens performing acts of civil disobedience and forcibly occupying Taiwan's Legislative Yuan for 23 days in order to protest against and to boycott their elected representatives from ratifying the CSSTA.

The Sunflower Movement became a rallying point for the resurgence of Taiwanese nationalism, especially among Taiwanese civil society and Taiwanese youth. While the cause of Taiwanese nationalism had once become too closely associated with the diversionary foreign policy and the international instability of Chen's unpopular second term, the CSSTA's lack of transparency provided an opportunity to renew popular support for Taiwanese identity, as the percentage of those self-identifying as 'Taiwanese only' surged to a record high of 60.6 per cent in 2014, up from 48.4 per cent in 2008, the year in which Chen stepped down (Election Study Center National Chengchi University 2019).

Politically, as the Sunflower Movement changed the narrative of Taiwanese nationalism, shifting its dominant conceptual association from 'causing instability' to 'preserving autonomy'. Consequently, Taiwanese nationalism once again returned as a winning formula for the DPP. Riding on the coattails of the Sunflower Movement, the DPP achieved hitherto unimaginable electoral victories in local elections in 2014 and again in legislative and presidential elections in early 2016. Overall, the DPP and its allies won 14 out of 22 municipalities (including all but one of the major metropolitan areas), gained a two-thirds' majority in the legislature, and won a convincing 56 per cent of the vote in the presidential election. All of these achievements were historic firsts. Indeed, they would seem even more remarkable when one recalled that the DPP-led pan-green coalition had only ever won a majority in any election at the national level precisely one single time since 1949 (in the razor-thin 2004 presidential election, when it reached 50.1 per cent).

Beijing received the news of the DPP's return to power in 2016 by reverting to the 'wait and see' approach it took during the Chen Shui-bian era. Early on, the new DPP Chairman and President Tsai Ing-wen largely followed Chen's early playbook of strategic ambiguity. Prior to her election, Tsai delivered a speech in May 2015 at the US think tank, the Center for Strategic and International Studies. In a confidence-building exercise with the American audience, Tsai pledged 'no surprises' and committed to working within 'the existing ROC constitutional order' and the cross-Strait status quo. Moreover, should she be elected as president, she promised to 'treasure and secure the accumulated outcomes of *more than twenty years* of negotiations and exchanges' (Tsai 2015, emphasis added). Thus, Tsai intentionally left vague whether she endorsed the 1992 Consensus, which was at once a political taboo to her Taiwanese nationalist electorate by 2014 on the one hand, and a cornerstone of cross-Strait relations for Beijing on the other.

Tsai continued this challenging balancing act in her inaugural presidential address in May 2016. She refrained from explicitly endorsing the 1992 Consensus, but affirmed all the key components of it. She pledged to respect the 'joint acknowledgements and understandings' of 1992 and committed herself to a close cousin of the 1992 Consensus – Taiwan's 1992 Act Governing Relations between the People of the Taiwan Area and the Mainland Area. To be sure, the Act affirms that both Taiwan and mainland China belong to the same nation (China), constitute two functioning political entities of unspecified sovereignty status, and sees eventual 'national unification' as the end goal (Mainland Affairs Council 2019). Besides Tsai, her National Security Advisor (later Minister of Foreign Affairs), Joseph Wu, as well as her eventual Minister of Mainland Affairs, Chen Mintong, both frequently repeated their commitment to the 'spirit of 1992' (*jiuer huitan jingshen*) and the '1992 understanding' (*jiuer liangjie*). Again, it was to communicate to Beijing that Tsai would accept the 1992 Consensus, but she simply needed to use a different language to avoid a domestic backlash.

As the asymmetric (dis)trust thesis would predict, Tsai's concessions were not enough for Beijing. While Tsai endorsed the 1992 Consensus in virtually everything but name, Beijing viewed her piecemeal approach as evasive, and described her speech as a 'incomplete exam paper' (*weiwancheng de dajuan*). Much like Beijing's handling of Chen in 2000, it froze official cross-Strait talks, vetoed the continuation of Taiwan's observer status in international organizations such as WHO, and gradually pursued additional punitive measures such as increasing the number of military exercises in the Taiwan Strait and coercing international airlines to switch from 'Taiwan' to 'Taiwan, China' on their websites in early 2018 (*Foreign Policy* 2018).

Tsai experienced a similar dilemma to that of her DPP successor, Chen. For a DPP president serving at a time when post-Sunflower Movement Taiwanese nationalism had reached a new high, Tsai had already made virtually all her maximum politically viable concessions to Beijing, albeit ones couched in creatively ambiguous language (ironically, creative ambiguity was after all what the 1992 Consensus was intended for, according to its author Su Chi) (United Daily News 2019). Yet in a repeat of 2000–02, it failed to win Tsai any friends in Beijing. Meanwhile, her own power base gradually grew dissatisfied with her deviation from the Taiwanese nationalism orthodoxy. By mid-2018 Tsai faced intra-DPP political challenges from her orthodox independentist faction during the nomination process for the 2018 local elections, which further diminished her hold over the party's flank.

Bleeding on both fronts, Tsai was forced to repeat Chen's trajectory, including the exact timing of when the party ceased to hope that it would receive an olive branch from Beijing. Whereas Chen declared 'one country on each side' by August of his third year in office, Tsai's Minister of Foreign Affairs, Joseph Wu, declared by September of Tsai's third year, that Taiwan was no longer in an ambiguous sovereign relationship with mainland China or seeking a cross-Strait entente. Rather, Wu declared that Taiwan was a separate 'frontline state' caught in the struggle between an increasingly aggressive China and the West. As Wu put it, 'Taiwan is the David to China's Goliath. And we will prevail' (2018). Thus, Tsai completed her shift from strategic ambiguity (to reconcile with Beijing) towards a strategic clarity of cross-Strait rivalry, now supported by 'like-minded countries' presumably from the West (Global Taiwan Institute 2018).

By late 2018 Tsai's mandate had been significantly weakened as a result of constant challenges from her ruling coalition's hardline Taiwanese nationalist wing, as well as from a number of policy setbacks. As a result, the DPP suffered arguably its worst electoral defeat in 30 years during the mid-term municipal elections in November 2018, when it retained only six out of 22 municipalities and alienated key formerly DPP-friendly independent allies. These adverse results further narrowed the DPP's power base.

Beijing might have taken the DPP's unpopularity as evidence of the waning of the Sunflower Movement which had inspired the Taiwanese nationalism surge and the re-emergence of a political space for the 1992 Consensus within Taiwan. Certainly, Beijing could have plausibly deduced the results to mean weakening of the DPP's cohesion, between Tsai's moderate wing and the hardliner Taiwanese nationalist wing, and between the DPP's loyalists and the younger Sunflower Movement generation alienated by the DPP's break with formerly DPP-friendly populist independents such as Taipei's Mayor, Ko Wen-je.

Chinese President Xi Jinping's 2 January 2019 speech on the 40th anniversary of the Message to Compatriots in Taiwan thus signalled an interest in rekindling the drive to promote unification, as the higher urgency issue of opposing independence since 2016 seems to have yielded results as Beijing defined them.

Conclusion: tragedy of asymmetric trust

The different combination of natural internal and cross-Strait trust that Taiwan's two main political parties receive have undergirded the Gordian knot of cross-Strait relations, especially since the 1990s when Taiwanese national identity emerged in the political mainstream. Of the two parties, the DPP holds a primarily 'Taiwanese only' self-identity and enjoys greater default internal trust from Taiwanese society that it would not 'sell out' Taiwan's interests in negotiations with Beijing; conversely, it receives a lower degree of trust from Beijing, which fears that any accommodation of DPP administrations would be used by the latter as a platform to further the cause of Taiwanese independence. Meanwhile, the KMT receives greater natural affinity and benefit of the doubt from Beijing; it can have the same 'no independence, no unification, and no use of force' formula accepted by Beijing (where the DPP failed); yet the KMT receives lower trust internally, as its policies of furthering economic exchanges are perceived within Taiwan as a one-way street towards Taiwan's complete economic dependency on China in the future. Thus, a conciliatory DPP would nonetheless be rejected by Beijing, and suffer deficit to its economic performance legitimacy and diminish its mandate in the long run; while a similarly conciliatory KMT would be acceptable to Beijing but would invite suspicion from within Taiwan. In addition, Ma's 2011 proposal to sign 'peace agreements' with China would be forced to withdraw, while Chen put forth similar proposals (2004–05) and proudly championed it as a positive 'cross-Strait framework for peace, stability, and development' (*liangan hepingwending hudongjiagou*).

It is clear that early on both DPP presidents, Chen and Tsai, attempted to reconcile with Beijing and made significant political concessions, including on the issue of One China. Yet each time they were undermined by the low degree of political trust from the CPC. Questioning the good faith of DPP leaders, Beijing needed extra assurance before it would proceed, and it responded with hardline negotiation tactics in the hope of coercing and extracting further concessions. That coercive diplomacy inevitably undermined the DPP, leaving it with little choice other than to stand up and counter-escalate cross-Strait tensions, so as to prevent being seen as 'spineless' and to repair its political standing with a nationalist rallying-around-the-flag strategy. Thus, we see a recurring pattern of DPP administrations taking reconciliatory cross-Strait positions when they felt politically secure, and switching to more nationalistic stances to protect their political flank when their authority was weakened.

It may be impossible to ascertain whether Beijing simply failed to read the DPP administrations' conciliatory intentions, or whether it simply wished to differentiate its treatment of the DPP and the KMT regardless of their actions, in order to demonstrate that being the Taiwanese equivalent of 'old friends of the (mainland) Chinese people' pays, thereby incentivizing more Taiwanese political parties and other groups to consistently adopt a Beijing-friendly stance.

In other words, Beijing may prioritize long-term united front policy objectives over short-to-medium term cross-Strait stability. If this is true, it would reveal a Chinese assessment that military conflict is never a real possibility, because short-term cross-Strait instability is unlikely to spiral out of control without Chinese escalation or counter-escalation. Beijing in this scenario would believe itself to hold ultimate agency. If 'unification through force' (*wutong*) is neither possible nor desirable, then it follows that Beijing will focus on a 'peaceful unification', which is inevitably a long-term project of changing hearts and minds. That in turn supports an united front work-based strategy that envisages the cultivation of Taiwanese actors who are sympathetic to the CPC as a higher priority than maintaining cross-Strait stability, if that stability would benefit actors like the DPP administrations, who may at times be genuinely conciliatory, but ultimately share different (though not immutable) long-term national imagination.

This view of the primacy of united front-oriented view of Taiwanese affairs is partly reflected in the CPC's leadership structure. Organizationally, the Taiwan affairs portfolio is usually run by the chairman of the National People's Political Consultative Conference, Wang Yang, whose primary responsibility is not Taiwanese affairs, but united front work.

This reading of the primacy of united front on thinking about Taiwanese policy may explain why the Chinese President Xi Jinping reintroduced a key united front concept into his speech commemorating the 40 anniversary of the Message to Compatriots in Taiwan in January 2019. Implicitly borrowing a playbook from the 1940s, Xi invited all political parties and society in general in Taiwan to participate in 'comprehensive and deep democratic consultations' with Beijing in order to develop a 'Taiwan model for one country, two systems'.

Looking forward

As Xi consolidated power from the outset and commanded key military and administrative (personnel appointment) powers long before becoming General Secretary in 2012 (Sung 2014), his tenure experiences less instability born of succession politics and diversionary foreign policy impulses. Yet Xi has also shown greater international ambition than his two predecessors. In his various pronouncements including his signature report to the 19th CPC National Congress, he has repeatedly referred to three distinct phases of PRC history and three corresponding leaders, namely the eras of 'standing up' (Mao Zedong), 'getting rich' (Deng Xiaoping), and 'becoming strong' (Xi Jinping himself).

It remains to be seen whether Xi's oft-cited sense of historical mission and correspondingly heightened expectations will lead to him becoming more proactive towards cross-Strait unification, or whether Xi's apparently solid command of the armed forces and his luxury of policy continuity – having lifted presidential term limits and being the first serving leader to be incorporated into the CPC party Charter and the PRC Constitution since Mao – will condition Xi to exhibit greater patience and prefer greater stability on cross-Strait relations.

Meanwhile, it remains to be seen whether the DPP, in facing electoral adversity, would revise its cross-Strait platform in a more Beijing-friendly direction, as it did during its eight years in opposition (2008–16), when it held multiple rounds of internal meetings dubbed the Huashan Forum to soften its cross-Strait message. On the other hand, perhaps the emergence of China-US proto-bipolarity and escalating rivalry between the two nations will lead to greater expectations of US and Western support and embolden the DPP to hold firm to its Taiwanese nationalist platform.

References

Anderson, Benedict ([1983] 1991) *Imagined Communities: Reflections on the Origin and Spread of Nationalism*, London: Verso.
Apple Daily (2004) 'Luweihui kaolv hetan xinjiagou: Meixuezhe ti 'taiwanbudu zhongguobuwu' ('The MAC Considers Peace Talks about the New Architecture: American Scholars Say 'Taiwan Is Not Alone, China Is Not Martial'). Available at https://tw.appledaily.com/international/daily/20041104/21356072 (accessed 1 March 2019).
Beijing Review (2019) *Communique of the Third Plenary Session of the 11th Central Committee of the Communist Party of China, 29 December 1978*. Available at www.bjreview.com/Special_Reports/2018/40th_Anniversary_of_Reform_and_Opening_up/Timeline/201806/t20180626_800133641.html (accessed 13 February 2019).
Chen, Shui-bian (2000) 'President Chen Shui-bian's Inauguration Speech', 20 May. Available at http://ken_davies.tripod.com/inaugural.html (accessed on 19 February 2019).
Chen, Zhiming (2012) 'The Logic and Strategies of Beijing's Policy Towards Taiwan', in E. Kavalski (ed.) *The Ashgate Research Companion to Chinese Foreign Policy*, Farnham: Ashgate Publishing.
China Post (2007) 'Chen Declares "Four Wants and One Without"', 4 March. Available at https://chinapost.nownews.com/20070304-129958 (accessed 1 March 2019).
Copper, John E. (2017) *Playing with Fire: The Looming War over Taiwan* (Chinese edn), Taipei: Sinobooks.
Democratic Progressive Party (DPP) (1999) 'DPP Resolution on Taiwan's Future', *New Taiwan*. Available at www.taiwandc.org/nws-9920.htm (accessed 1 March 2019).
Dickson, Bruce and Chao Chien-Min (2002) *Assessing the Lee Teng-hui Legacy in Taiwan's Politics: Democratic Consolidation and External Relations*, London: M. E. Sharpe.
Election Study Centre, National Chengchi University (2019) *Taiwanese/Chinese Identity* (1992/06–2018/12). Available at https://esc.nccu.edu.tw/app/news.php?Sn=166# (accessed 1 March 2019).
Financial Times (2011) 'US Concerned about Taiwan Candidate'. Available at www.ft.com/content/f926fd14-df93-11e0-845a-00144feabdc0 (accessed 1 March 2019).
Foreign Policy (2018) 'China Threatens U.S. Airlines over Taiwan References'. Available at https://foreignpolicy.com/2018/04/27/china-threatens-u-s-airlines-over-taiwan-references-united-american-flight-beijing/ (accessed 1 March 2019).
Global Taiwan Institute (2018) 'Recorded Video Remarks by Foreign Minister Joseph Wu for the 2018 GTI Annual Symposium'. Available at www.mofa.gov.tw/Upload/RelFile/662/167619/5494af4e-3370-4e1f-9354-be8cf9a73f36.pdf (accessed 1 March 2019).
Kahn, Joseph (2004) 'China Praises Powell for Warning Taiwan on Independence', *New York Times*. Available at www.nytimes.com/2004/10/27/international/asia/china-praises-powell-for-warning-taiwan-on-independence.html (accessed 1 March 2019).

Kissinger, Henry (2011) *On China*, New York: Penguin Press.
Lin, G. (2016) 'Beijing's New Strategies Toward a Changing Taiwan', *Journal of Contemporary China*, 25(99).
Liu, Chih-Nien (2011) 'Beijing's Strategy towards Taiwan and Its Effect: A Strategic Analysis from a "Coercive Diplomacy" Perspective', *Prospect and Exploration* 9(6).
Mainland Affairs Council (2005) 'Domestic Public Reaction to the Chinese Communist Party's "Anti-Secession Law"'. Available at https://www.mac.gov.tw/News_Content.aspx?n=AD6908DFDDB62656&sms=161DEBC9EACEA333&s=683B5FCD52750C47 (accessed 1 March 2019).
Mainland Affairs Council (2019) 'Act Governing Relations between the People of the Taiwan Area and the Mainland Area', 17 June. Available at https://law.moj.gov.tw/ENG/LawClass/LawAll.aspx?pcode=Q0010001 (accessed 19 February 2019).
Mainland Affairs Council (n.d.) *Act Governing Relations between the People of the Taiwan Area and the Mainland Area*. Available at https://ws.mac.gov.tw/001/Uploa d/OldFile//public/Attachment//910311210303.pdf (accessed 1 March 2019).
Nathan, Andrew J. and Bruce Gilley (2003) *China's New Rulers: The Secret Files* (2nd rev. edn), New York: New York Review of Books.
Office of the President, ROC, (2005) 'President Chen's Videoconference with Members of the European Parliament, March 1, 2005'. Available at https://english.president.gov.tw/NEWS/1892 (accessed 1 March 2019).
People's Daily Online (2003) 'Lien Chan shoucichenglianganwei yibianyiguo' ('For the First Time, Lien Chan Called the Two Sides of the Strait "One Country at a Time"'). Available at http://tw.people.com.cn/BIG5/14812/14875/2258226.html (accessed 1 March 2019).
Sung Wen-Ti (2014) 'Is Xi Jinping a Reformer?' *The Diplomat*. Available at http://thediplomat.com/2014/03/is-xi-jinping-a-reformer/ (accessed 1 March 2019).
Taiwan People News (2017) 'Clinton's Advice: Clinton Told President Chen Shui-Bian That He Opposed Signing a Cross-Strait Peace Agreement'. Available at www.peoplenews.tw/news/c90df491-56d4-4e04-b9d4-b71e4aa08c77 (accessed 1 March 2019).
The Initium (2017) 'Chen Shui-Bian's 20 wanzikoushulishi, tahuipilousheme?' ('Chen Shui-bian's 200,000-Word Oral History, What Will He Disclose?'). Available at https://theinitium.com/article/20170411-taiwan-Chen-shui-bian/ (accessed 1 March 2019).
Tsai Ing-wen (2015) 'Tsai Ing-wen 2016: Taiwan Faces the Future', speech at the Center for Strategic and International Studies, Washington, DC, 3 June. Available at www.csis.org/events/tsai-ing-wen-2016-taiwan-faces-future (accessed 19 February 2019).
Tung Chen-yuan (2003) 'Analysis of CCP's Taiwan Policy after the Sixteenth Party Congress', *Mainland China Studies* 46(2).
United Daily News (2019) 'Su Chi: 1992 Consensus bianxingdewodourenbuchulai' ('Su Qi: I Can't Recognize the Change in the 1992 Consensus'). Available at https://udn.com/news/story/11311/3584631 (accessed 1 March 2019).
Wang, Jianwei (2007) 'Hu Jintao's "New Thinking" on Cross-Strait Relations', *American Foreign Policy Interests*, 29(23–24).
Wu Yu-Shan (2001) 'Does Chen's Election Make Any Difference? Domestic and International Constraints on Taipei, Washington, and Beijing', in Muthiah Alagappa (ed.) *Taiwan's Presidential Politics*, New York: M. E. Sharpe.
Yeh Hui-fen (2016) 'Chiang Kai-shek and the Formulation of the "Strike Back" Policy on Mainland China: A Case Study of the "Wuhan Plan"', *Academia Historica Journal*, 50.

7 Preventing independence, striving for unification: Chinese perspectives on Taiwan

Jingdong Yuan

Introduction

In a speech to mark the 40th anniversary of the issuing of the Message to Compatriots in Taiwan, Chinese President Xi Jinping reiterated that resolving the Taiwan question to realize unification has always been a historic task for the Communist Party of China (CPC) and the Chinese people. Xi emphasized that '[i]t is a historical conclusion drawn over the 70 years of the development of cross-Straits relations, and a must for the great rejuvenation of the Chinese nation in the new era' (*China Daily* 2019). While adhering to the principles of 'peaceful reunification' and 'one country, two systems' as the best approach for realizing national reunification, Xi made no promise to abandon the use of force and issued strong warnings against the interference of external forces and the very small number of 'Taiwan independence' separatists. Xi was emphatic that China must and will be reunited (An 2019). Xi's speech elicited swift and strong rebuttal from Tsai Ing-wen, the president of the Republic of China (ROC, or Taiwan). She dismissed but also erroneously equated the mainland's 1992 Consensus to its 'one country, two systems' principle, vowing that the island would not buckle under any pressure or threats, and that Taiwan's fate would be determined by its people (Reuters 2019).

Cross-Strait relations have stagnated since 2016 after Tsai Ing-wen, the Democratic Progressive Party (DPP) candidate won the Taiwan elections and became the island's first female president. While making assurances that her government would not change the status quo in cross-Strait relations, and would recognize the 'historic fact' of the 1992 discussion between Taiwan's Strait Exchange Foundation (SEF) and the mainland's Association for Relations Across the Taiwan Strait (ARATS) on setting aside differences and seeking dialogue, Tsai has so far refused to acknowledge the so-called 1992 Consensus that Beijing insists should be the guiding principle of cross-Strait relations. At the same time, the mainland considers many of the initiatives undertaken by the Tsai government, such as revisions to high school history and social studies textbooks, as alleged 'de-Sinicification' efforts to further divide the two on either side of the Strait (Glaser 2017).

This stands in sharp contrast to the Ma Ying-jeou era (2008–16) when noticeable progress was made, including the resumption of semi-official dialogues on the basis of the 1992 Consensus, with regular high-level meetings held in both China and Taiwan and, for the first time, direct contacts between the two sides' official offices responsible for cross-Strait relations. Twenty-three agreements were signed that aimed to facilitate cross-Strait trade, investment, tourism, education and public health. Beijing and Taipei stuck to the diplomatic ceasefire they had tacitly agreed to, while Taiwan was able to secure a place at the World Health Assembly as an observer. Of particular significance was the signing of the Economic Cooperation Framework Agreement (ECFA), which would provide free trade area treatment to each other's commodity transactions, and Taiwan would thereby enjoy high growth rates in its exports to the mainland. Bilateral trade reached US $152 billion in 2010, a 39 per cent increase compared with 2009 (Lai 2011: 9). The 'three links' and direct flights across the Taiwan Strait further enhanced the flow of people and business, and gradually led to better mutual understanding between the two sides. By 2017 bilateral trade had grown further to $181.76 billion (China here also includes Macao and Hong Kong), even though Tsai had already been in power for 18 months (Albert 2018; Xinhua 2017a).

Improvements in cross-Strait relations during the Ma Ying-jeou government (2008–16) contributed to regional stability and were welcomed in Washington (Hsiao 2018: 114–15). However, apart from growing economic interactions, the two sides remained apart on fundamental political issues such as the terms of negotiation, the Kuomintang (KMT –Nationalist Party)'s emphasis on 'interpretations' of who represents the One China, and Taiwan's international space. The two sides maintained a diplomatic truce and Beijing in particular discouraged countries that had diplomatic ties with Taipei to switch recognition. Growing cross-Strait contacts remained confined to managing routine bilateral matters rather than paving the way for serious political dialogue. Xi Jinping and Ma held a historical meeting in Singapore in November 2015, but by then Ma's KMT government had become mired in difficulties, having just suffered a landslide defeat in the local elections held in late 2014. At the same time, the growing military imbalance had policymakers in Taipei concerned over their ability to negotiate with Beijing from a position of strength.

By 2019 the Tsai government had already witnessed significant strain in bilateral ties. Beijing had cut off regular official contacts while introducing strong measures aimed at isolating Taiwan yet further. With the sources of conflicts and instability remaining potent, the security environment in the Taiwan Strait continued to deteriorate, with some analysts characterizing it as a 'flash point' in East Asia and predicting a mainland invasion of the island (Taylor 2018; Easton 2017). The United States has played a crucial role in helping to maintain cross-Strait stability over the past four decades, with its policy of strategic ambiguity and through arms sales to Taiwan mandated by the 1979 Taiwan Relations Act. However, Washington faces major challenges of balancing multiple and at times competing foreign policy objectives at a time of growing Chinese economic and military power and relative US decline, further constrained by the two decade-long wars in Afghanistan and Iraq and out-of-control budget deficits. The Trump Administration appears to be embarking on a different track in that Washington is becoming less hesitant and more open in its support of Taiwan – albeit while still upholding its One China policy – through more regular interactions, enhanced defence contacts, and expansion of economic ties. The US Congress is also becoming more involved, with pro-Taiwan provisions and legislation adopted in 2016–18.

Cross-Strait relations during the Ma and Tsai eras

The Ma Ying-jeou administration (2008–16) witnessed stable and improving cross-Strait relations, in sharp contrast to the tumultuous eight years under Chen Shui-bian of the DPP (2000–08). During the presidential campaign candidate Ma promised to reduce tensions between Taiwan and the mainland, to promote cross-Strait relations based on the 1992 Consensus on the concept of One China and respective interpretations thereof, and pledged that his mainland policy would be guided by the 'three noes', namely no unification, no independence and no use of force. Ma reiterated the 'three noes' position in his inaugural speech of May 2008, which ushered in a new period of cross-Strait reconciliation, expansion of ties, and improvement of relations.

Ma's conciliatory gesture had been reciprocated by the Hu Jintao and Xi Jinping administrations, which essentially had shifted the near-term focus of China's Taiwan policy from pursuing unification goals to preventing the island from moving towards independence or separation (Saunders and Kastner 2009: 88). The March 2005 Anti-Secession Law, passed during a period of heightened tension in cross-Strait relations, lays down the legal marker on what Beijing considers – and declares – to be the red line whereby all options must be available to deter any attempts at *de jure* independence. But the law also emphasizes and advocates the promotion of contacts between the two sides and, following Ma's 2008 presidential victory, Beijing was able to put into practice a new Taiwan policy of influencing the Taiwan people towards accepting the long-term prospect of unification. For that purpose, the Hu administration advocated increasing communication and dialogue on economic, political, diplomatic and security issues, with a focus on boosting peaceful developments across the Taiwan Strait (Xin 2010: 525–39).

Ma's mainland policy and Beijing's near-term focus led to the restoration and regularization of high-level semi-official SEF-ARATS dialogues. In addition, bilateral negotiations between agencies in both governments further facilitated the expansion of trade, investment and greater interaction between people living on both sides of the Strait. Direct flights between the two sides increased so that there are now hundreds of flights each week. Over one million Taiwanese live permanently in mainland China while millions of mainland tourists visit Taiwan annually. Trade and investment grew rapidly, with Taiwan enjoying a sizeable surplus. China became Taiwan's largest trading partner and number one export destination. By the late 2000s, 70,000 Taiwanese companies were operating in China. Before 2008 Taiwan's annual approved direct investment in China was below US $10 billion. After Ma came to power, investment grew rapidly and by the end of 2015 Taiwan's overall cumulative investment in China stood at $154.9 billion (Kan and Morrison 2011; Tung 2018). Indeed, Taiwan's growing exports to the mainland benefited the island amid the global economic downturn in the wake of the 2007–08 global financial crisis. Meanwhile, the signing of the ECFA also opened up the possibility for Taipei to conclude similar free trade arrangements with other countries, with New Zealand and Singapore soon signing a free trade agreement with the island (Glaser 2011; Craymer 2013; AFP 2013).

The historic meeting between Ma Ying-jeou and Xi Jinping in Singapore in November 2015 ushered in new possibilities for cross-Strait relations in terms of resolving some of the nagging issues between the two sides, such as venues and protocols whenever officials from China and Taiwan meet – the insistence on equity and respect from Taiwan's side – and the larger question of whether a third way beyond either unification or independence could be found. The reality is that neither is acceptable and indeed could be dangerous, and maintaining the status quo and stability may prove to be the most pragmatic ways of managing cross-Strait relations (Hsiao 2018; Chen 2018).

Despite the growing economic interdependence between the two sides, and indeed Taiwan's increasing dependence on the mainland for its economic prosperity – from exports to tourism – a strong sense of Taiwanese identity has emerged during this period as well. At the same time, the majority of people in Taiwan prefer the status quo; those who are either pro-unification or pro-independence form a small minority. And the mainland's 'peaceful unification' strategy has been eroded by its own coercive and heavy-handed approach to any sign of resistance to Beijing's unification agenda (Cole 2018; Horton 2018a). The risk of cross-Strait conflict is growing as a result of Beijing's disappointment in and frustration about the continuing drift away from unification, a core element of Xi's 'China dream'; impatience coupled with misinformation could fuel an assertive unification agenda resulting in military conflict in the Taiwan Strait (Mazza 2018; Chu and Kastner 2017: 42–60).

Where Taiwan's security was concerned, Ma Ying-jeou's strategy was to assure the mainland that under his administration the status quo (i.e. no unification and no independence) would be maintained and, coupled with efforts to expand bilateral economic ties and institutionalize dialogue, would serve to develop and promote common interests, enhance mutual trust and hence incentives for keeping the peace. This would be a much better way of keeping Taiwan safe than provocation (Chen 2017; Zhang 2011: 269–85). In essence, Ma believed that 'Taiwan could better assure its prosperity, dignity, and security by engaging and reassuring China rather than provoking it' (Bush 2011: 275). Some observers have argued that based on the progress achieved, it might be possible and perhaps desirable for both sides to negotiate a peace agreement. For Taiwan, this could lock in mainland commitment not to use force; for Beijing, such an agreement could constrain future non-KMT governments from trying to achieve independence. At a minimum, the two sides should seriously consider cross-Strait confidence-building measures (Saunders and Kastner 2009: 91; Glaser and Glosserman 2008).

Beijing's strategy of offering economic benefits to Taiwan in order to build up goodwill and even receptivity to unification has had mixed results despite efforts to win the hearts and minds of the Taiwanese people. The Sunflower Movement effectively killed the cross-Strait agreement on services and the 2014 nine-in-one local elections dealt the KMT a severe blow with the DPP candidates winning 13 of the 22 contested municipal seats. This was followed by a landslide victory for Tsai in the 2016 presidential election. This had serious implications for China's strategy for the peaceful development of cross-Strait relations (Lin 2016: 321–35). Since Xi Jinping came to power in late 2012, he has on many occasions emphasized the importance of the unification agenda and the need to show strong resolve in responding to any independence attempts. At the 19th CPC National Congress in October 2017, President Xi declared:

> We have firm will, full confidence, and sufficient capability to defeat any form of Taiwan independence secession plot. We will never allow any person, any organization, or any political party to split any part of Chinese territory from China at any time or in any form.
> (Xinhua 2017b; Bush 2018)

Indeed, some observers have argued that Beijing's policy has shifted from deterring Taiwan from seeking *de jure* independence and maintaining a patient, long-term goal of unification, to a more active push towards unification. Xi once observed to a former high-ranking Taiwanese official attending an event on the mainland that the unification task should not be left to future generations. Furthermore, Xi has adopted a two-pronged approach that involves displaying massive and intimidating military power to deter Taiwan from any attempt at independence while also proposing the concept that the two sides of the Taiwan Strait belong to one family (Huang 2017: 243–46; Romberg 2014; Zheng 2018: 13–17).

Despite the progress made during the Ma period, the fundamental issues that affect long-term cross-Strait peace and stability, and in particular Taiwan's security, have remained unresolved. Beijing's ultimate goal of unification and its steadfast One China principle continue to guide its policy towards Taiwan, including the use of diplomatic, military, as well as economic means (Bush 2011: 277, Wang 2010: 147–68). Not surprisingly, while in opposition the DPP warned that the KMT government was putting Taiwan's long-term security and independence in jeopardy by moving too close and too fast in expanding ties with the mainland. DPP Chairwoman and presidential candidate Tsai Ing-wen charged Ma with pursuing a dangerous policy of 'gambling Taiwan's sovereignty in exchange for short-term economic benefits from China' (Lee 2011; Glaser 2011; Kan and Morrison 2011: 6). Indeed, as pointed out by analysts, just as political tension had not prevented growth in economic interactions across the Strait, even during the 2000–08 Chen Shui-bian presidency, it would be equally simplistic to assume that growing economic contacts between the two sides, in particular Taiwanese businesses' increasing dependence on the mainland, would inevitably give Beijing the political upper hand (Kastner 2009; Keng and Schubert 2010: 287–310).

Meanwhile, the Ma administration's defence transformation had stalled, plagued by Taipei's inability to maintain its pledged level of defence spending at 3 per cent of gross domestic product (GDP), the cost of moving towards a professional military and the non-combatant tasks that the ROC armed forces had to undertake in recent years, and the outlays needed for major weapons procurement programmes. All of these had imposed a significant financial burden and the lack of sufficient resources in turn limited what could be accomplished with regard to the stated defence modernization plans laid out in the Quadrennial Defense Review first published by Taiwan's Ministry of National Defence in 2011 (Mei 2011: 7–9; Huang 2011). Taiwan's defence budget shortfalls stood in contrast to the mainland's growing defence spending and military build-up that significantly enhanced the latter's military capabilities not only vis-à-vis Taiwan but also posed serious threats to the United States' ability to intervene. This had important implications for Taiwan's national security. Some analysts have already pointed to Taiwan's diminishing freedom of action that over time could seriously undermine its sovereignty and autonomy, thus paving the way for the mainland to achieve its ultimate goal – unification on its own terms (Sutter 2011; Lowther 2011).

In came the DPP government in 2016 and cross-Strait relations began to return to a state of mutual suspicion and even growing hostility. Not only has Tsai refused to acknowledge the 1992 Consensus, Beijing suspects that her government is undertaking activities to promote the independence agenda. For instance, Tsai has not publicly reprimanded the remarks by the former head of the Legislative Yuan, William Lai Ching-te, when he claimed that he was a 'political worker who advocates Taiwan independence' (Reuters 2017). She has also been accused by Beijing of engaging in activities aimed at 'splitting' China, such as her high-profile visit to the NASA Houston Space Center during a stopover in the United States after visiting Central and South America. This was the first time a Taiwanese leader had ever visited a US government facility (Jennings 2018).

China's responses have been quite predictable under the circumstances, with a combination of diplomatic isolation, economic coercion, and military intimidation (Chase 2019). Not only has it sought to restrict Taiwan's ability to participate in international organizations where in the past observer status under the name Chinese Taipei was possible, Beijing has also launched diplomatic offensives to chip away at diplomatic recognition of the island by the few remaining states that still do so, thus effectively ending the cross-Strait 'diplomatic truce' that was in place during the Ma Ying-jeou government. A number of countries have since switched recognition from Taipei to Beijing, including Panama and the Dominican Republican, and El Salvador in Central and South America, as well as The Gambia, São Tomé and Príncipe, and Burkina Faso in Africa, often to the surprise and humiliation to the DPP government. Given what Beijing can offer through its attractive economic incentives such as infrastructure investments under the umbrella of the Belt and Road Initiative, Taipei is ill-positioned to compete with its meagre chequebook (USSC 2018: 345–46; Ward 2018). In addition, China has also launched a global campaign demanding that foreign companies and enterprises should use the proper name when referring to Taiwan, i.e. the 'correct' nomenclature' should be 'Taipei, China', rather than 'Taiwan', which is deemed offensive to China's sovereignty and territorial integrity. Most foreign entities have complied, fearing retribution and loss of business opportunities in China (Palmer and Allen-Ebrahimian 2018).

At the same time that Beijing is exerting pressure on the Tsai government through a combination of diplomatic and economic measures such as reducing Taiwan's international space and inflicting punitive measures by restricting the number of mainland tourists allowed to visit the island, it is also reaching out to the KMT, the opposition party, to build a united front of some sort, given that the latter acknowledges the 1992 Consensus, unlike Tsai Ing-wen. There are regular CPC-KMT exchanges, including frequent visits by KMT chairpersons to the mainland, and the high-profile KMT-CPC Forum. One astute observer commented: 'In just two decades, the KMT, once the staunchly anti-communist party of Chiang Kai-shek, has evolved into a deeply pro-Beijing party'. Ma, for instance, has recently revised his 'three noes' – no unification, no independence and no use of force, to include the phrase 'no opposition to unification' (Lian 2018). Beijing is also designing special policies and offering economic incentives to attract skilled personnel, students and workers from Taiwan through the so-called 31 incentives. All this in an effort to isolate DPP to the tune of 'acknowledging the "1992 Consensus", there will be business and economic benefits, or else' (USSC 2018: 355–56).

Cross-Strait military balance and US-Taiwan policy

China's military modernization of the past two decades is steadily changing the military balance across the Taiwan Strait in Beijing's favour even as the two sides are ever more integrated economically, with Taiwan's dependence on China increasing more rapidly (IISS 2018; Chu and Kastner 2017). Granted, not all of the weapons procurement and deployment activities have been driven by the Taiwan factor; China's growing economic interactions with the outside world have expanded and exposed its interests that require protection and hence power projection. In recent years, the Chinese People's Liberation Army (PLA) has gradually built up its inventory in the amphibious assault and sea lift capabilities, continues to deploy ballistic and cruise missiles aimed at Taiwan's military installations, stage military exercises aimed at Taiwan more frequently, and increasingly has exerted pressure on Taiwan with its island-circling flights led by PLA air force bombers. In addition, Beijing has also launched what is called political warfare through disinformation and media infiltration. Some observers accused China of interfering in Taiwan's recent local elections (Easton 2017; Wu 2018; *Asia Times* 2018a, 2018b). However, the fact that the mainland now has an ever growing inventory that it can draw upon in a future Taiwan scenario makes it imperative that Taiwan's defence policy, including force structure and arms procurement, must be informed by the need to protect its political autonomy, resist Chinese coercion, and defend against Chinese assault. Recent analyses increasingly point to the possibility that Beijing may be planning an eventual military assault on Taiwan. This is reflected in its growing defence expenditure, procurement of weapons systems and military training intended for conquering the island, and deterring US intervention in the event that China decides to invade Taiwan. Whether or not Beijing would succeed remains debated by analysts and under US government assessments (You and Hao 2018; Easton 2018; Greer 2018).

Between 2007 and 2018 US arms sales to Taiwan totalled US $25 billion (Albert 2018; Kan 2014). Taipei's arms acquisition efforts are aimed at maintaining the military balance across the Strait, thus ensuring a level of security and stability necessary for Taiwan's continued social and economic well-being. Given that China has succeeded in the past two decades in dissuading previous and potential suppliers from selling arms to Taiwan, the role of the United States has become ever more critical. However, the uneven and sometimes precarious nature of US arms sales policy has raised the larger questions about the interpretation and implementation of the Taiwan Relations Act since its inception in 1979 (Wolff and Simon 1982; Goldstein and Schriver 2001: 147–72).

US-Taiwan defence ties are not confined to US arms sales only. Over the years, the United States and Taiwan have developed close defence cooperation that goes beyond arms sales. These include regular defence consultations, such as the so-called Monterey Talks that were first held in Monterey, California, in 1997, the training of Taiwanese military officers in US military institutions, the participation by US military personnel in Taiwanese military exercises such as the Han Kuang, and training related to the transfer of procured defence equipment. In addition, more frequent interactions between Taiwan and the United States at the functional level have enabled Washington to better understand Taipei's defence planning and procurement processes so that effective coordination during crises can be facilitated. In 2002 the Clinton Administration asked the US Congress to pass legislation to allow active-duty US military personnel to be assigned to Taiwan. Subsequently, in August 2005 a US army colonel began duties in Taipei although he was expected to wear civilian clothes (Chase 2005: 162–185; Kan 2014:5).

Proponents of the cross-Strait balance maintain that only when Taiwan has sufficient defence capabilities can it negotiate with the mainland from a position of strength, and certainly at a minimum would be able to withstand Chinese military assaults long enough so that the United States could come to its assistance. There are deeper reasons as well. Taiwan has become a democracy, and Washington's credibility would be at stake if it were to fail to act in defence of Taiwan should the island come under unprovoked attack. Another concern regarding the military balance has always been that with the mainland continuing to build up its military capabilities, it would be in a position to coerce Taiwan to accept a political settlement on Beijing's terms. This would be considered by Washington as a unilateral change in the status quo across the Taiwan Strait (Greer 2018; Lin and Zhou 2018).

However, sustaining a long-term military balance across the Taiwan Strait would present serious political, resource and military obstacles. To begin with, if such a balance is calculated solely in military terms, it means that Taiwan, with a much smaller economic base and a much lower defence budget will have to raise its level of expenditure even to keep up with China's military modernization programme. In fact, Beijing is capable of spending more basically by keeping its defence budget to a certain percentage of its overall and fast growing GDP, which now is estimated to be anywhere between the official figure of US $175 billion as recently announced by Beijing, to over $220 billion, according to SIPRI. China spends, even using Beijing's official figures, 15 times more than Taiwan on defence. As a result, seeking to maintain a military balance risks an arms race that Taiwan would struggle to keep up with, much less to win. Consequently, this is not an appealing proposition for political reasons, it is hardly sustainable financially, and in the long term, without defining what objectives such a military balance is meant to achieve, continued attempts to maintain parity would only deepen a security dilemma and raise the costs for all involved (Wachman 2009: 25–32; You 2009: 33–39). Taiwan's introduction in 2017 of the so-called Overall Defense Concept places more emphasis on asymmetrical defence strategy, and seeks to prevent amphibious invasion first by targeting the PLA forces in the Taiwan Strait, and annihilating any enemy units landing on Taiwan's coastline (*National Defense Report* 2017). Confronting a more powerful Chinese military, the focus would be on denial rather than control. Targeted procurement of relevant capabilities, including indigenous projects, would be encouraged. US arms transfers remain critical; however, these acquisitions are now directed more towards area defence than to the projection of power (Thompson 2018; Wu 2018: 704–25).

Although cross-Strait relations witnessed significant improvements in economic and diplomatic spheres after President Ma took office in May 2008, Taiwan's security environment and its ability to defend itself vis-à-vis the mainland continued to become eroded as China's military capabilities increased. For instance, Taiwan has been losing its superiority in the air space, and China's growing stock of ballistic and cruise missiles threatens to overwhelm and paralyse the island's inadequate air defence systems (*Defense News* 2010). While Taiwan has a fleet of about 400 combat aircraft the actual number that are operationally viable is far lower as Taiwan's foreign-purchased fighter aircraft lack spare parts and servicing (Fisher 2010; US Economic and Security Review Commission 2010: 143–59; US-Taiwan Business Council 2010; Minnick 2010). In 2019 Taipei was reported to have committed funding of US $5.3 billion to upgrade its fleet of F-16A/B fighter aircraft to include the F-16 *Fighting Falcon Viper* (V) Block 70 multirole combat aircraft. Meanwhile, the Tsai government has pledged to increase defence spending in the face of growing threats from the Chinese mainland (Gady 2018; AFP 2018).

US arms sales to Taiwan over the past four decades have been informed by how they best advance America's key interests in the region – strong alliances, stability and continued US supremacy while avoiding unnecessarily provoking Beijing and without becoming entrapped by inflexible commitments and hence risk being dragged into conflicts with China or other potential adversaries (Chan 2010: 1–27; Ong 2010: 56–75). This policy of strategic ambiguity, which is intended to act as a double deterrence against both China and Taiwan, runs the risk of being misinterpreted by both Beijing and Taipei – and indeed one could argue deliberately so at times (Christensen 2002: 7–21; Pan 2003: 387–407). However, despite calls for greater clarity, on balance, the policy has served US interests well and in general has contributed to cross-Strait stability. In fact, successive US administrations have for all practical purposes enacted policies that span the spectrum of clarity at one end, and ambiguity at the other (Hsu 2010: 139–62; Kastner 2006: 651–69; Bush 2005: 245–65). However, in 2016 the US Congress passed legislation that turned the 'six assurances' – an informal pledge by the Reagan Administration to Taipei on the eve of the signing of the 17 August 1982 joint communiqué with Beijing – into a cornerstone of US-Taiwan relations (the other being the Taiwan Relations Act) (*Taiwan Today* 2016).

In recent years, debates have emerged in the United States on whether it should continue to provide security assistance to Taiwan, especially through the sale of arms, or whether Washington can and should make deals with Beijing to suspend these ties, resulting in greater stability in China-US relations. Opponents of such a move suggest that were the United States to desert Taiwan this could result in China exercising coercive measures against the island, thus heightening the risks of confrontation (Chen *et al*. 2017: 221–38).

Beijing watches intensely for any tell-tale signs by the Trump administration that could be interpreted as elevating US-Taiwan relations while eroding China-US relations. Of particular concern might be any signals that US policy shifts send to Taipei that could encourage independence tendencies. For instance, prior to the grand opening of the newly built American Institute in Taiwan, there were rumours that US Marine Corps personnel would be stationed there to guard the premises, as is usually the case with diplomatic security measures for US diplomatic missions around the world. However, in Taiwan's case this would be a significant departure from Washington's current position – that the US should only maintain non-official ties with the island.

Furthermore, the matter of which American officials would be present at the opening ceremony could also have had serious implications. Ultimately, an assistant secretary of state in charge of culture was sent to attend the ceremony and no Marine Corps personnel were stationed there (Kazer 2018; *Asia Times* 2018c).

Beijing has repeatedly warned the Trump Administration not to interfere in China's internal affairs and to carefully manage its relationship with Taiwan. This stance is in response to activities undertaken by US lawmakers aimed at shoring up US support for Taipei. For instance, pro-Taiwan lawmakers drafted legislation requesting that the US downgrade relations with any country that switches diplomatic recognition from Taipei to Beijing. In 2018 Washington recalled its senior diplomats in three Central American countries in response to those countries' decision not to recognize Taiwan (Gehrke 2018). Meanwhile, a number of former US officials and analysts urged the Trump Administration to enter into negotiations with Taiwan to draw up a free trade agreement to advance US economic and strategic interests. Taiwan is the United States' tenth or 11th largest trading partner and some of Taiwan's technological sectors are important for the production of components for use in defence systems (Tellis 2018; *Asia Times* 2018d).

The Trump Administration has made significant shifts in its Taiwan policy to the point of openly challenging Beijing's bottom line. There have been more official exchanges – although still at the level maintained over the past few decades, and public support has been extended to Taiwan with regard to its participation in international organizations. High-ranking US officials have also publicly emphasized Taiwan's important position in Washington's free and open Indo-Pacific strategy (Fang 2018). The Administration has already approved two batches of arms sales to Taiwan in June 2017 and September 2018 worth US $1.75 billion and could move to more regular rather than bundled or package sales. The emphasis has also shifted toward providing – and encouraging Taiwan to develop – asymmetrical systems and options to enhance its deterrence and defence systems. Taiwan has been encouraged to develop its own indigenous defence systems and the new US envoy, Brent Christensen, emphasized US commitment to come to Taiwan's defence. Meanwhile, the US Congress has passed a number of bills – signed by Trump into law – that contain pro-Taiwan provisions. These include the National Defense Authorization Act, the Taiwan Travel Act, and the Asia Reassurance Initiative Act of 2018, which call for increased US engagement in the Indo-Pacific and greater support, including arms sales, for its allies in the region. They also call for stronger US-Taiwan defence ties, including visits by high-ranking officials, visits by military ships to each other's ports, and participation in each other's military exercises. By the end of 2018 there had been ten visits by Taiwan's ministers to Washington while five US deputy assistant secretaries had visited Taiwan (Tsai 2019; IndraStra 2019; Murray 2014: 61–79; *Asia Times* 2018e; DePetris 2018). Beijing, in addition to making statements of protest, recalled a high-ranking PLA naval officer visiting the United States at the time, and declined to give permission for US naval ships to visit Hong

Kong. However, the fact that the United States announced the sales – mostly inconsequential spare parts for defence systems procured by Taiwan in the past, as a routine transaction, therefore indicating a shift away from the bundling practice, is worrying for Beijing. At the same time, reports that Taiwan has started to contact other potential arms suppliers, including French companies for spare parts for the Mirage fighter aircraft Taiwan purchased in the 1990s, and even that Taiwan is basing its indigenous submarine upgrade on European designs, could become a serious issue for Beijing (Thim 2018).

At the 2018 Xiangshan security forum, Chinese Minister of Defense Gen. Wei Fenghe reiterated that Taiwan is a core interest for China and that the PLA would take action in the event of this core interest being threatened or put at risk. In this context, continued US arms sales to Taiwan, US naval ships sailing through the Taiwan Strait, and growing US-Taiwan security ties are considered as serious impediments to China-US relations (Hille *et al.* 2018). Beijing has become increasingly annoyed about US naval ships sailing through the Taiwan Strait, claiming that they are violating China's sovereignty and territorial integrity (Associated Press 2018). Chinese analysts have pointed out that the Tsai regime is delusional in thinking that by actively positioning itself in the US 'Free and Open Indo-Pacific' strategy, it could be assured of security protection from Washington. Taiwan, it claims, will remain a pawn in Washington's bargaining with Beijing (Wang 2018: 13–16).

Conclusion

Three broad conclusions can be drawn from the above analysis. First, the past decade, especially during the Ma Ying-jeou era, has witnessed significant improvements in cross-Strait relations, chiefly in the field of economics and in people-to-people contacts. The reduction of tensions, the resumption and expansion of bilateral dialogue and the institutionalization of interflows between the two sides ranging from trade, investment and people have, in general, been conducive to peace and stability in the Taiwan Strait, and in turn have contributed to regional security. These developments have been welcomed by Beijing, Taipei and Washington.

Second, despite such progress, many key issues remain unresolved. These concern the divergent interpretations, expectations and long-term goals of Beijing and Taiwan. While the KMT-led government endorses the so-called 1992 Consensus, it has a completely different notion of what the term One China represents to Beijing. At the same time, the gap in perceptions, expectations and policy goals could widen and cracks could become apparent when the sides start to tackle tougher issues ranging from Taiwan's demand for greater international space and a reduction in military threats from the mainland (for instance, the number of missiles deployed in the Strait), to Beijing's interest in seeing its economic largesse yielding political dividends. This was confirmed after the DPP returned to power in 2016. Not only have political interactions been significantly rolled back – largely by Beijing in retaliation to the Tsai government for its refusal to acknowledge the 1992 Consensus – to the extent that they have virtually ceased, the economic ties between the two sides have also been negatively affected. Given the current US-China trade dispute, there is great uncertainty among Taiwan businesspeople about the future prospects for a close mainland-Taiwan relationship (Horton 2018b; Chung 2018).

And finally, the security environment in the Taiwan Strait has deteriorated noticeably. With the PLA steadily exerting pressure on Taiwan through intimidation and other coercive measures, and the United States under the Trump Administration adopting a hardline approach towards Beijing, there are growing concerns that misinformation and miscalculation could trigger a serious military conflict between the two powers. Meanwhile, Taiwan's domestic politics are also very volatile and vulnerable to the mainland's economic allure, political warfare and military threat. China is continuing with its military modernization programme not only with a view to dominating any potential future conflict with the island, but increasingly also to impose significant costs on the United States should it contemplate intervention in a Strait crisis. Taking into consideration China's rise and US needs to enlist Beijing's cooperation on many global and regional issues, Washington could become ever more cautious about fulfilling its security commitments to Taiwan, including the provision of arms requested by Taipei. This leaves Taiwan vulnerable to an ever-assertive China that could make (mis)calculation part of its unification game plan.

Taiwan's ultimate recourse in securing its sovereignty and autonomy lies not so much in its military capabilities – although it needs a strong defence system to withstand and defeat intimidation if not fully fledged military assaults from the mainland, than in a national security strategy that integrates effective soft power diplomacy, its democratic credentials, and its value as an economic partner for the international community, the United States and its regional allies and, ultimately, its nemesis, mainland China. The Overall Defense Concept is an important adjustment to Taiwan's defence strategy, but many challenges remain. From Beijing's perspective, while reunification will remain its ultimate goal, how to accomplish it will require the successful execution of a carefully integrated strategy that combines diplomatic, political and socio-economic factors. Patience, rather than haste, is called for.

References

AFP (2013) 'Taiwan, Singapore Sign Free-Trade Agreement', *South China Morning Post*, 7 November.

AFP (2018) 'Taiwan's President Tsai Ing-wen Seeks US$11 Billion Defence Budget as China Threat Grows', *Straits Times*, 6 August.

Albert, Eleanor (2018) 'China-Taiwan Relations', Council on Foreign Relations, 15 June. Available at www.cfr.org/backgrounder/china-taiwan-relations (accessed 8 December 2018).

An, Baijie (2019) 'Xi Envisions Peaceful Unification', *China Daily*, January 3.

Asia Times (2018a) 'Chinese Destroyer and Frigates Stage Drills Off Taiwan', 28 June.

Asia Times (2018b) 'Cyber War Is on as Taiwan Heads to Polls This Weekend', 22 November.
Asia Times (2018c) 'Plans for US Marines to Guard Taipei Mission Infuriates Beijing', 30 July.
Asia Times (2018d) 'Envoys Push for Taiwan-USA Free Trade Agreement', 3 December.
Asia Times (2018e) 'Taiwan Stresses Self-Defense Amid Rumors of US Arms Sales', 31 October.
Associated Press (2018) 'China Expresses Concerns over 2 US Navy Ships in Taiwan Strait', 29 November.
Bush, Richard C. (2005) *Untying the Knot: Making Peace in the Taiwan Strait*, Washington, DC: Brookings Institution.
Bush, Richard C. (2011) 'Taiwan and East Asian Security', *Orbis* (spring).
Bush, Richard C. (2018) 'What Xi Jinping Said about Taiwan at the 19th Party Congress', Washington, DC: Brookings Institution, 19 October.
Chan, Steve (2010) 'The Taiwan Relations Act Considered from Alternative Perspectives', *Issues & Studies* 46(3).
Chase, Michael S. (2005) 'US-Taiwan Security Cooperation: Enhancing an Unofficial Relationship', in Nancy Bernkopf Tucker (ed.) *Dangerous Strait: The US-Taiwan-China Crisis*, New York: Columbia University Press.
Chase, Michael S. (2019) 'A Rising China's Challenge to Taiwan', in Ashley J. Tellis, Allison Szalwinski and Michael Wills (eds) *Strategic Asia 2019: China's Expanding Strategic Ambitions*, Seattle, WA and Washington, DC: National Bureau of Asian Research.
Chen, Charles I-hsin (2018) 'One Country, Two Interpretations, and the Third Alternative for Taiwan', *The Diplomat*, 6 November.
Chen, Dean P. (2017) *US-China Rivalry and Taiwan's Mainland Policy: Security, Nationalism, and the 1992 Consensus*, Cham: Springer.
Chen, Ping-Kuei, Scott L. Kastner and William L. Reed (2017) 'A Farewell to Arms? US Security Relationship with Taiwan and the Prospects for Stability in the Taiwan Strait', in Lowell Dittmer (ed.) *Taiwan and China: Fitful Embrace*, Berkeley, CA: University of California Press.
China Daily (2019) 'Highlights of Xi's Speech at Taiwan Message Anniversary Event', 2 January. Available at www.chinadaily.com.cn/a/201901/02/WS5c2c1ad2a 310d91214052069_1.html (accessed on 3 January 2019).
Christensen, Thomas J. (2002) 'The Contemporary Security Dilemma: Deterring a Taiwan Conflict', *Washington Quarterly*, 25(4).
Chu, Ming-chin Montique and Scott L. Kastner (eds) (2017) *Globalization and Security Relations across the Taiwan Strait: In the Shadow of China*, London and New York: Routledge.
Chung, Lawrence (2018) 'Trade War: Taiwanese Firms to Flee Mainland China over Donald Trump's Tariffs, Claims Taipei', *South China Morning Post*, 18 September.
Cole, Michael J. (2018) '"Peaceful Unification" Is Dead and Buried', *Taiwan Sentinel*, 9 September.
Craymer, Lucy (2013) 'Taiwan and New Zealand Sign Free-Trade Agreement', *Wall Street Journal*, 10 July.
Defense News (2010) 'Nien-Dzu Yang: Deputy Minister for Defense Policy, Taiwan', 1 February.
DePetris, Daniel R. (2018) 'Is a US-Taiwan Clash Over Taiwan Inevitable?' *National Interest*, 9 November.

Easton, Ian (2017) *The Chinese Invasion Threat: Taiwan's Defense and American Strategy in Asia,* Manchester: Eastbridge Books.
Easton, Ian (2018) 'China's Next Act: Invade Taiwan?' *National Interest,* 8 September.
Fang, Frank (2018) 'Pentagon Top Asia Official Affirms Taiwan's Role in the Indo-Pacific Region', *Epoch Times,* 19 July.
Fisher, Richard Jr (2010) 'The Air Balance on the Taiwan Strait', *International Assessment and Strategic Center,* 21 February.
Gady, Franz-Stefan (2018) 'Taiwan Received First Upgraded F-16 Viper Fighter Jet', *The Diplomat,* 24 October.
Gehrke, Joel (2018) 'China Warns US about Taiwan Diplomacy', *Washington Examiner,* 11 September.
Glaser, Bonnie and Brad Glosserman (2008) *Promoting Confidence Building across the Taiwan Strait,* Washington, DC: Center for Strategic and International Studies.
Glaser, Bonnie S. (2011) 'US-China-Taiwan Relations in the Run-Up to 2012 Elections in Taiwan and the US and Leadership Transition in China', paper presented at the International Conference on 'Facing the Challenges of Cross-Strait Relations in 2012', co-organized by National Chengchi University's Institute of International Relations and the Carnegie Endowment for International Peace, Washington, DC, 7 July.
Glaser, Bonnie S. (2017) 'Managing Cross-Strait Ties in 2017: Recommendations for the Trump Administration', Center for International and Strategic Studies, January 26.
Goldstein, Steven M. and Randall Schriver (2001) 'An Uncertain Relationship: The United States, Taiwan and the Taiwan Relations Act', *China Quarterly,* 165.
Greer, Tanner (2018) 'Taiwan Can Win a War with China', *Foreign Policy,* 25 September.
Hille, Kathrin, Emily Feng and Katrina Manson (2018) 'US-China Military Tension Heightens over Taiwan', *Financial Times,* 1 November.
Horton, Chris (2018a) 'As China Rattles Its Sword, Taiwanese Push for a Separate Identity', *New York Times,* 26 October.
Horton, Chris (2018b) 'Trade War Traps Taiwan between Two Superpowers', *Nikkei Asian Review,* 5 December.
Hsiao Hsu-tsen (2018) *Ma Ying-jeou, Written by Hsiao Hsu-tsen: A Memoir of My Eight-Year Presidency,* Taipei: Commonwealth Publishing Group.
Hsu, Philip S. (2010) 'Reappraising the Debate and Practice of US Strategic Ambiguity/Clarity in Cross-Strait Relations', *Pacific Review,* 23(2).
Huang, Alexander Chieh-cheng (2011) 'A Midterm Assessment of Taiwan's First Quadrennial Defense Review', Washington, DC: Brookings Institution, February.
Huang, Jing (2017) 'Xi Jinping's Taiwan Policy: Boxing Taiwan in with the One-China Framework', in Lowell Dittmer (ed.) *Taiwan and China: Fitful Embrace,* Berkeley, CA: University of California Press.
IndraStra (2019) 'The Summary of Asia Reassurance Initiative Act of 2018', 5 January.
International Institute for Strategic Studies (IISS) (2018) *Military Balance 2018,* London: IISS.
Jennings, Ralph (2018) 'China Rankled by the Taiwanese President's Visit to NASA', *Los Angeles Times,* 20 August.
Kan, Shirley (2014) *Taiwan: Major US Arms Sales to Taiwan since 1990,* Washington, DC: Congressional Research Service, RL30957, 29 August.
Kan, Shirley A. and Wayne M. Morrison (2011) *US-Taiwan Relationship: Overview of Policy Issues,* Congressional Research Service, 4 August.
Kastner, Scott L. (2006) 'Ambiguity, Economic Interdependence, and the US Strategic Dilemma in the Taiwan Strait', *Journal of Contemporary China,* 15(49).

Kastner, Scott L. (2009) *Political Conflict and Economic Interdependence across the Taiwan Strait and Beyond*, Stanford, CA: Stanford University Press.

Kastner, Scott L. (2015) 'Rethinking the Prospects for Conflict in the Taiwan Strait', in Ming-Chin Monique Chu and Scott L. Kastner (eds) *Globalization and Security Relations across the Taiwan Strait: In the Shadow of China*, London andNew York: Routledge.

Kazer, William (2018) 'China Sets "Red Line" for US Ceremony in Taiwan', *Wall Street Journal*, 10 June.

Keng, Shu and Gunter Schubert (2010) 'Agents of Taiwan-China Unification? The Political Roles of Taiwanese Business People in the Process of Cross-Strait Integration', *Asian Survey* 50(2).

Lai Shin-yuan (2011) 'The Republic of China's Mainland Policy: Piloting Cross-Strait Relations to Create a Peaceful Environment for Benign Interaction between the Two Sides of the Taiwan Strait', keynote speech at the international conference on 'Facing the Challenges of Cross-Strait Relations in 2012', co-organized by National Chengchi University's Institute of International Relations and the Carnegie Endowment for International Peace, Washington, DC, 7 July.

Lee, John (2011) 'Why Taiwan Will Fail', *Wall Street Journal*, 31 March.

Lian Yi-Zheng (2018) 'Will Taiwan Be the First Domino to Fall to China?' *New York Times*, 27 November.

Lin, Gang (2016) 'Beijing's New Strategies toward a Changing Taiwan', *Journal of Contemporary China*, 25(99).

Lin, Gang and Wenxing Zhou (2018) 'Does Taiwan Matter to the United States? Policy Debates on Taiwan Abandonment and Beyond', *China Review*, 18(3) (August).

Lowther, William (2011) 'Unification Looms: US Academic', *Taipei Times*, 11 May.

Mazza, Michael (2018) 'Is a Storm Brewing in the Taiwan Strait?' *Foreign Affairs*, 27 July.

Mei, Fu S. (2011) 'Taiwan's Defense Transformation and Challenges under Ma Ying-jeou', *China Brief* 11(7), 22 April.

Minnick, Wendall (2010) 'US Intel Report on Taiwan Air Power Released', *Defense News*, 22 February.

Murray, William S. (2015) 'Asymmetrical Options for Taiwan's Deterrence and Defense', in Ming-chin Monique Chu and Scott L. Kastner, *Globalization and Security Relations across the Taiwan Strait: In the Shadow of China*, London and New York: Routledge.

Ong, Russell (2010) 'Taiwan's Strategic Options and the US', *Asia-Pacific Review*, 17(2).

Palmer, James and Bethany Allen-Ebrahimian (2018) 'China Threatens US Airlines over Taiwan References', *Foreign Policy*, 27 April.

Pan, Zhongqi (2003) 'US-Taiwan Policy of Strategic Ambiguity: A Dilemma of Deterrence', *Journal of Contemporary China*, 12(35).

Reuters (2017) 'Taiwan Leader Affirms Support for Independence', *Straits Times*, 28 September.

Reuters (2019) 'Taiwan's Tsai Rejects Xi Call for "Reunification"', *Asahi Shimbun*, 3 January.

Romberg, Alan D. (2014) 'From Generation to Generation: Advancing Cross-Strait Relations', Hoover Institution, 14 March.

Saunders, Phillip C. and Scott L. Kastner (2009) 'Bridge over Troubled Water? Envisioning a China-Taiwan Peace Agreement', *International Security*, 33(4).

Sutter, Robert (2011) *Taiwan's Future: Narrowing Straits*, NBR Analysis, Seattle, WA: National Bureau of Asian Research, May.

Taiwan Today (2016) 'Taiwan Relations Act, Six Assurances Reaffirmed as US Policy toward Taiwan', 3 May.

Taylor, Brendan (2018) *The Four Flash Points: How Asia Goes to War*, Melbourne: La Trobe University Press.

Tellis, Ashley J. (2018) 'Sign a Free-Trade Deal with Taiwan', *Wall Street Journal*, 2 December.

Thim, Michal (2018) 'Behind the US' Smaller Arms Package to Taiwan Lie Bigger Problems for China', *South China Morning Post*, 3 October.

Thompson, Drew (2018) 'Hope on the Horizon: Taiwan's Radical New Defense Concept', *War on the Rocks*, 2 October.

Tsai Chung-min (2019) 'Taiwan in 2018: A Bitter Campaign and an Uncertain Future', *Asian Survey*, 59(1).

Tung Chen-yuan (2018) 'Opportunities and Pitfalls of Cross-Strait Economic Integration in the Ma Ying-jeou Era: Taiwan after the ECFA', in André Beckershoff and Gunter Schubert (eds) *Assessing the Presidency of Ma Ying-jiu in Taiwan: Hopeful Beginning, Hopeless End?* London: Routledge.

United States Studies Center, University of Sydney (2018) *Annual Report*.

US Economic and Security Review Commission (2010) *2010 Report to Congress*, Washington, DC: US Government Printing Office.

US-Taiwan Business Council (2010) *The Balance of Air Power in the Taiwan Strait*, Arlington, VA: US-Taiwan Business Council, May.

Wachman, Alan M. (2009) 'Thinking about a Healthy Military Balance in the Taiwan Strait', *Asia Policy*, 8.

Wang, Jianwei (2010) 'Is the Honeymoon Over? Progress and Problems in Cross-Strait Relations', *American Foreign Policy Interests*, 32(3).

Wang, Weixing (2018) 'The US Indo-Pacific Strategy and Taiwan's Strategic Choice', *China Review*, 250: 13–16.

Ward, Jarad (2018) 'China Is Luring Away Taiwan's Longtime Partners in Central America and the Caribbean', *World Politics Review*, 8 June.

Wolff, Lester L. and David Simon (eds) (1982) *Legislative History of the Taiwan Relations Act: An Analytic Compilation with Documents on Subsequent Developments*, Jamaica, NY: American Association for Chinese Studies.

Wu, Dee (2018) 'China's Evolving Military Strategy Against Taiwan: An Interview with Bernard D. Cole', *Policy Q&A*, Seattle, WA: National Bureau of Asian Research, 4 June.

Wu, Shang-su (2018) 'Taiwan's Defense under the Tsai Administration', *Asian Survey*, 58(4).

Xin, Qiang (2010) 'Beyond Power Politics: Institution-Building and Mainland China's Taiwan Policy Transition', *Journal of Contemporary China*, 19(65) (June).

Xinhua (2017a) 'Cross-Strait Trade Down 4.5 Pct in 2016', 4 February.

Xinhua (2017b) 'Xi Jinping: Secure a Decisive Victory in Building a Moderately Prosperous Society in All Respects and Strive for the Great Success of Socialism with Chinese Characteristics for a New Era', 27 October.

You, Ji (2009) 'Politics as the Foundation of a Healthy Military Balance', *Asia Policy*, 8.

You, Ji and Yufan Hao (2018) 'The Political and Military Nexus of Beijing-Washington-Taipei: Military Interactions in the Taiwan Strait', *China Review*, 18(3) (August).

Zhang, Baohui (2011) 'Taiwan's New Grand Strategy', *Journal of Contemporary China*, 20(69).

Zheng, Jian (2018) 'Preliminary Analysis of Xi Jinping's Thoughts on Countering "Taiwan Independence"', *China Review*, 251 (November).

8 Taiwan and the United States

Andrew T. H. Tan

Introduction

This chapter examines the evolution of Taiwan's relationship with the United States, starting from the early relations with the Kuomintang (KMT – Nationalist Party), to the contemporary era following Donald Trump's unexpected presidential electoral victory in the United States in late 2016. The chapter also focuses on changing US national interests that have dictated Taiwan-US relations, as well as the implications for bilateral Taiwan-US relations as a result of recent political developments in both countries, namely the ascendency to power of the pro-independence Democratic Progressive Party (DPP) in the Republic of China (ROC, or Taiwan) in 2016 and Donald Trump to the US presidency. This chapter concludes with the assessment that the key factor in determining US-Taiwan relations has always been US national interests, and that despite the obvious sympathy in the US Congress for Taiwan in the context of a growing trade war and tensions between China and the United States, it is in fact ultimately expendable. The question is what Taiwan can do in such circumstances.

Historical antecedents

Taiwan's relations with the United States can be said to have predated 1949, the year when the then ruling KMT regime fled to Taiwan after losing the Chinese civil war to the Communist Party of China (CPC), which then went on to establish the People's Republic of China (PRC, or China) on the mainland. Although Sun Yat-sen, the founder of the KMT, received part of his education in Hawaii, United States, the KMT espoused socialist ideals and received support and training from communist Soviet Union. Nonetheless, the United States established relations with China after the KMT led by Chiang Kai-shek consolidated power in the 1920s, ending the chaos that had engulfed China since the end of the Qing dynasty in 1911. However, the United States kept out of the Chinese-Japanese conflict that began in 1937 with Japan's invasion of China. US neutrality was tested when a US gunboat, the USS *Panay*, was attacked and sunk by Japanese warplanes in the Yangtze

River in December 1937, killing three sailors and wounding 45 others. Three Standard Oil tankers that the gunboat was escorting were also attacked. In the end, immediate war between the United States and Japan was averted when Japan apologized and paid in excess of US $2 million in indemnity (Scherr 2010: 462–64). While the incident hardened US public attitudes towards Japan, the United States remained neutral for a further four years until it was forced to enter the war against Japan due to Japan's pre-emptive attack on the US navy at Pearl Harbor in Hawaii in December 1941.

In China, as recounted by Robert Sutter, relations between the KMT and the United States began to deepen in the prelude to the United States' own entry into the Second World War at the end of 1941. Japan's alliance with Nazi Germany and news of Japanese atrocities in China hardened American attitudes towards Japan. In the United States, there were influential voices, particularly those with a long association with China, which urged the provision of US aid to China. This included Henry Luce (who was born in China and was the son of missionaries there), who used his influential magazines, namely *Time* and *Life*, to promote and support Chiang Kai-shek and his American-educated wife Soong May-ling, as well as the KMT, in the existential struggle against Japan's invasion. Thus, after the Japanese attack on Pearl and the United States' own entry into the war against Japan and Germany, China quickly became an important ally in the course of the Second World War (Sutter 2010: 37–41).

US military aid for the KMT was stepped up, and in 1943 Chiang met with US President Theodore Roosevelt and British Prime Minister Winston Churchill at the Cairo Conference. The joint press conference cemented China's status as one of the four allied great powers (together with Russia) and it was agreed that territories taken from China by Japan, including Manchuria, Taiwan and the Pescadores, would be returned to China following the end of the conflict (US Department of State 1943). Soong Ching-ling also toured the United States in 1943, delivering a speech to the US Congress and wooing American support for the KMT and for China (Soong 1943).

However, despite the wartime alliance, the United States eventually made the decision to abandon the KMT soon after Japan's defeat and surrender in 1945. While China was a useful ally against the Axis powers in the course of the Second World War, its utility diminished as soon as the war with Japan ended in 1945. As then US Secretary of State Dean Acheson's China White Paper in 1949 explained, the deep corruption, dysfunction and failures of the KMT government, and the consequent loss of its legitimacy meant that the only way to support the ruling KMT in the Chinese civil war that broke out between the KMT and the Chinese Communist Party after 1945 would be

> full-scale intervention on behalf of a Government which had lost the confidence of its own troops and its own people. Such intervention would have required the expenditure of even greater sums than have been fruitlessly spent thus far, the command of Nationalist armies by American

officers, and the probable participation of American armed forces ... in the resulting war. Intervention of such a scope and magnitude would have been resented by the mass of the Chinese people.

(Acheson 1949)

Indeed, the disillusionment with the KMT and with Chiang was so complete that President Truman himself commented in a hand-written note, in reference to Chiang's KMT regime, that 'we picked a bad horse' (Casey 2010: 47). Abandoned by its American ally after a series of devastating defeats on the mainland to the communists, the rump KMT was thus forced to evacuate to Taiwan island for what was expected to be its last stand. The United States ruled out supporting the KMT on Taiwan even as the communists were preparing to attack the island. In NSC 48/2 issued in December 1949, the United States' loss of confidence in the KMT was reflected by the National Security Council recommendation that

> The United States should continue the policies of avoiding military and political support of any non-Communist elements in China unless such elements are willing actively to resist Communism with or without United States aid and unless such support would mean reasonable resistance to the Communists and contribute to the over-all national interests of the United States.
>
> (NSC 1949)

Thus, the United States had concluded at the time that it was not in its interests to continue supporting its wartime ally, the KMT, and that events in China should be allowed to run their natural course. This would have meant the eventual annihilation of the KMT and the unification of Taiwan, which was previously a colony of Japan, with the mainland. However, the outbreak of the Korean War in June 1950, fierce debates in the United States over who 'lost' China and rising fears over communism epitomized by McCarthyism in domestic US politics, led to a reversal of US policy towards the KMT and Taiwan. The United States now enacted a policy of containment against communism as the fear of monolithic communist expansionism and the Cold War between itself and the Soviet bloc deepened (Tucker 2009: 13). In Asia, the containment strategy involved the building of a 'hub and spokes' system of alliances, under which the United States would constitute the hub and regional allies the spokes, in the fight against the spread of communism. In the Cold War context, particularly given the evidence of communist expansionism as a result of the Korean War, Taiwan now assumed strategic significance. Reversing its earlier policy, the United States now perceived that defending Taiwan and preventing a communist takeover would be in its national interests. The United States now moved to shore up the KMT in Taiwan and to prevent the reunification of the island with mainland China by announcing that the US navy would prevent a communist attack on Taiwan (Roy n.d.). With US support, the rump ROC under the KMT retained its seat at the United Nations (UN) Security Council as one of the Permanent Five great powers with the power of veto. However, as Denny Roy observed, the alliance was rocky, as Chiang Kai-shek made continual efforts to prepare his forces to retake the mainland, while the United States insisted this was not realistic and that he should concentrate on defending Taiwan (ibid.).

Chiang's insistence at holding offshore islands such as Kinman (or Quemoy) and Matsu in preparation for a KMT reinvasion of China led to serious incidences as the PRC shelled the islands using artillery in 1954 and 1958. However, these incidences had the effect of consolidating US support for Taiwan, epitomized by the signing of the Mutual Defense Treaty between the United States and the ROC in November 1954 and the establishment of a US Military Assistance Advisory Group in Taiwan (MDT 1954). As Nancy Tucker observed, 'between 1949 and 1969, Taipei and Washington found each other useful in their shared opposition to communism in China' (2009: 26). Indeed, Taiwan dominated the tense and hostile relations between the United States and China during that time.

China-US rapprochement and Taiwan

The Chinese-Soviet split in the 1960s occurred as a result of differences between China and the Soviet Union over ideology, divergences in national interests, territorial disputes and the personality clash between their respective leaders, namely Mao Tse-tung and Nikita Khrushchev (Luthi 2008: 345–50). Mutual suspicions and tensions led to border clashes in 1967–69, culminating in fears of a Soviet nuclear attack on China (ibid.: 340–42). These developments had important consequences for the hitherto hostile US-China relationship. As Andrew Nathan and Robert Ross explained,

> the Sino-Soviet border crisis revealed China's strategic vulnerability to Soviet power and suggested that Chinese leaders might be interested in reducing Sino-US friction ... by 1969, the Nixon administration had perceived an opportunity to improve relations with China to contain the spread of Soviet power.
>
> (1997: 65)

The realization that it was in the strategic interests of both China and the United States to work together to counter the Soviet Union led to a rapprochement between the two countries in 1972, when US President Richard Nixon made a groundbreaking visit to China, where he met Chairman Mao. The main obstacle to a Chinese-US rapprochement was the question of Taiwan, the unfinished problem of the Chinese civil war, over which China has been consistent as well as insistent that Taiwan must eventually be reunified with the mainland. However, the Nixon Administration was prepared, for the sake of greater strategic objectives that would serve US national interests, to sacrifice Taiwan. In the run-up to the landmark Nixon visit to China, Taiwan was not only ousted from the UN Security Council and replaced by the PRC as the sole representative of China, it was even voted out of the UN altogether in October 1971 (*New York Times* 1971).

In the joint US-China Shanghai Communiqué in February 1972, Beijing asserted that Taiwan 'is the crucial question obstructing the normalization of relations between China and the United States'. Furthermore, Beijing stated that

> The Government of the People's Republic of China is the sole legal government of China; Taiwan is a province of China which has long been returned to the motherland; the liberation of Taiwan is China's internal affair in which no other country has the right to interfere; and all U.S. forces and military installations must be withdrawn from Taiwan.
> (Shanghai Communiqué 1972)

For its part, the United States conceded that there is one China, that Taiwan is a part of China and that America would not challenge that position. In addition, the United States stated that 'it reaffirms its interest in a peaceful settlement of the Taiwan question by the Chinese themselves', and that 'it affirms the ultimate objective of the withdrawal of all U.S. forces and military installations from Taiwan'. The United States would also 'progressively reduce its forces and military installations on Taiwan as the tension in the area diminishes' (Shanghai Communiqué 1972). Thus, the United States, while sacrificing Taiwan, also insisted on a peaceful settlement of the Taiwan issue, and while it would withdraw its forces, no timetable was set and such a withdrawal would be contingent upon a reduction of tensions in the Taiwan Strait. In other words, Taiwan was sacrificed, but not entirely, as the United States also wanted to maintain its security relationship with it. After all, the Cold War was still in progress and China, while a useful strategic partner, had been in the past a communist foe.

Yet the US military withdrawal from Taiwan did in fact occur fairly quickly. Nixon's visit in 1972 was followed by the full normalization of relations between China and the United States in January 1979 under the Carter Administration. This was announced in a joint communiqué with China, which referred to the Taiwan question by stating that 'the United States of America recognizes the Government of the People's Republic of China as the sole legal Government of China', although 'within this context, the people of the United States will maintain cultural, commercial, and other unofficial relations with the people of Taiwan' (Joint Communiqué 1971). The United States, having recognized one China, namely the PRC, now downgraded its relations with Taiwan to unofficial relations. The United States also abrogated the Mutual Defense Treaty in January 1980 (*People's Daily* n.d.).

Fortunately for Taiwan, however, strong support for it existed in the US Congress, as a result of the efforts of the Taiwan lobby, which comprised missionaries, businessmen, military leaders and members of Congress, especially Republicans, who sought to build support in the executive and legislative branches of the US government for Taiwan (Star 2007). Thus, from 1972 to 1979, despite the momentous changes in US-China relations that seemed to point to Taiwan being abandoned, there remained strong support in the US Congress for an old Cold War ally. Indeed, the US Congress enacted the Taiwan Relations Act on 1 January 1979 even as the United States seemingly abandoned Taiwan when it normalized relations with the PRC. The Act declared that it is the policy of the United States

> to make clear that the United States' decision to establish diplomatic relations with the People's Republic of China rests upon the expectation that the future of Taiwan will be determined by peaceful means; to consider any effort to determine the future of Taiwan by other than peaceful means, including by boycotts or embargoes, a threat to the peace and security of the Western Pacific area and of grave concern to the United States; to provide Taiwan with arms of a defensive character; and to maintain the capacity of the United States to resist any resort to force or other forms of coercion that would jeopardize the security, or the social or economic system, of the people on Taiwan.
>
> (TRA 1979)

Furthermore, despite the loss of recognition as a state, the Act also provided for the establishment of the American Institute in Taiwan, which would carry out diplomatic and consular functions and thus serve as the de facto US embassy in Taiwan. The wording of the Act also marked the adoption of strategic ambiguity on the part of the United States over how it would actually react should the PRC attack Taiwan, on the assumption that this would complicate China's calculations and thus deter it from using force.

China predictably saw the Act as a direct challenge to the normalization agreement and threatened to downgrade bilateral relations with the United States. This led to intense negotiations that led to the 17 August 1982 US-China Communiqué on Arms Sales to Taiwan. However, both sides had their own interpretation of what the communiqué meant. US officials focused on the correlation between the reduction of arms sales to Taiwan and the PRC's peaceful policy towards the island, while PRC officials focused on US pledges to gradually reduce arms sales to Taiwan (Office of the Historian 1982). The Reagan Administration also quietly provided to Taiwan, one month before the communiqué was signed, what became known as the Six Assurances. These included the promise that the United States would not set a date for the termination of arms sales to Taiwan. Significantly, the United States also promised that it would not pressure Taiwan to enter into negotiations with China, nor would it recognize China's sovereignty over it (Six Assurances 1982).

The Taiwan Relations Act and the Six Assurances provided the basis for continued US ties with Taiwan, in particular, the preservation of the security relationship through a firm commitment that the United States would continue to sell arms to Taiwan to enable it to defend itself and thus maintain the status quo in the Taiwan Strait. The two instruments that preserved US support for Taiwan came about as a result of strong Republican support in both the Congress and the new Reagan Administration which took office in early 1981.

The end of the Cold War and Taiwan

The end of the Cold War following the fall of the Berlin Wall in 1989 also coincided with pro-democracy protests in Tiananmen Square, Beijing, and their violent suppression by the CPC. The end of the Cold War removed the rationale for the strategic alignment between the PRC and the United States since the Soviet threat no longer existed. The Tiananmen incident shocked the Western world as it was broadcast around the world on live television, leading to revulsion in the United States as well as to the imposition of limited sanctions on China. The breakdown in China-US relations benefited Taiwan in the 1990s, at a time when democratization emerged on the island and pro-independence sentiments could now be openly expressed. This was the backdrop to the massive arms sale in 1992 to Taiwan by the Administration of George H. W. Bush, who came to office in 1989. The arms deal involved up to 150 F16 combat aircraft to Taiwan, worth over US $5 billion (*Los Angeles Times* 1992).

The Taiwan Strait crisis that broke out in the mid-1990s was sparked by the unofficial visit of Taiwan's President Lee Teng-hui to Cornell University, his alma mater, in the United States. Pro-Taiwan Republicans in the US Congress pressed for the visit and President Bill Clinton agreed to allow it to proceed despite China's strong protests (Sutter 2010: 106). China reacted by conducting large military exercises as well as missile tests in close proximity to Taiwan during the period July 1995 to March 1996. In response, the United States dispatched two aircraft carrier battlegroups to waters near Taiwan in a strong show of support for the island. However, as Hickey pointed out, at no time during the crisis had US officials clearly promised to defend Taiwan with military force if China attacked it (1998: 406–08). The policy of strategic ambiguity had not changed.

The emergence of pro-independence sentiments in Taiwan, epitomized by the victory in the presidential election by the DPP's Chen Shui-bian in 2000, led to increased tensions between Taiwan and China (Shirk 2007: 201–04). To deter any move by Taiwan to declare independence, China enacted the Anti-Secession Law in March 2005, under which China reserved the right to resort to military force should Taiwan declare independence (*People's Daily* 2005). In April 2001, in an indication of early support for Taiwan after a presidential campaign marked by anti-China sentiments, US President George Bush approved a large arms sales package to Taiwan, consisting of 12 P-3C Orion anti-submarine warfare aircraft, four refurbished Kidd-class destroyers, anti-ship missiles, mine-sweeping helicopters and artillery. The approval also included the possibility of eight diesel-powered submarines (Kan 2002: 3).

However, Chen's open push for independence raised fears in the United States that this would upset the status quo in the Taiwan Strait that the United States was committed to maintaining. Worse, this could spark conflict with China that would involve the United States. The US preoccupation with its wars in Iraq and Afghanistan following the terrorist attacks perpetrated on the US mainland on 11 September 2001 also meant that it could not afford to be distracted by another crisis in East Asia. The Bush Administration therefore made every effort to dampen moves by Chen towards independence. Thus President Bush, in the presence of China's Premier Wen Jiabao, affirmed the United States' opposition to Taiwanese independence at a press conference in Washington in December 2003, stating that

> we oppose any unilateral decision by either China or Taiwan to change the status quo ... the comments and actions made by the leader of Taiwan indicate that he may be willing to make decisions unilaterally to change the status quo, which we oppose.
>
> (White House 2003)

This was followed by the unusually strong assertion by then US Secretary of State Colin Powell in October 2004 that 'there is only one China', and that 'Taiwan is not independent ... it does not enjoy sovereignty as a nation, and that remains ... our firm policy'. This led to a strong reaction in Taiwan, with President Chen Shui-bian angrily declaring that 'Taiwan is absolutely a sovereign, independent nation. It's a great nation, and it absolutely does not belong to the People's Republic of China. That is the present situation, that is the reality' (NBC News 2004).

The Chen presidency was thus marked by a deterioration in relations with the United States. Chen pursued his pro-independence agenda domestically by dissolving the National Unification Council over the objections of the United States, and attempted to develop a national Taiwanese identity through changes in national education and in the country's Constitution. Externally, his administration made approaches to the UN and its agencies, and sought international recognition of Taiwan as a country that was separate from China (Sutter 2010: 227).

However, the disapproval of the United States had the desired effect, and Taiwan's independence movement began to falter as it became obvious that there was little international support for it. Domestically, the DPP lost support owing to corruption scandals as well as rising tensions with China. Thus, Chen's national referendum on Taiwan's application for UN membership in 2008 was ruled invalid due to a low turnout (*Taipei Times* 2008).

Ma Ying-jeou and Barack Obama in power

The electoral victory of the KMT led by Ma Ying-jeou in 2008 was welcomed by both the United States and China, as Ma was committed to restoring stability to cross-Strait relations with China, and the KMT was also committed to the principle of One China. Indeed, Ma took steps to increase economic cooperation with China, eventually signing the Economic Cooperation Framework Agreement, which cut tariffs on 539 Taiwanese exports to China and 267 Chinese products entering Taiwan (BBC 2010). The thaw in cross-Strait tensions was evident in the approval of China for Taiwan's participation in the World Health Assembly meeting in May 2009 under the name 'Chinese Taipei' (DeLisle 2009).

Ma's election coincided with the election of Barack Obama as president of the United States. Obama's visit to China in November 2009 raised hopes of a future cooperative US-China relationship. In the joint press statement issued during the visit, the United States acknowledged the importance of the Taiwan issue in US-China relations and reaffirmed its policy of One China. The United States, evidently relieved at the departure of Chen and the restoration of stability in the Taiwan Strait, also stated that it welcomed 'the peaceful development of relations across the Taiwan Strait', and looked forward to 'efforts by both sides to increase dialogues and interactions in economic, political, and other fields, and develop more positive and stable cross-Strait relations' (White House 2009).

The improved Taiwan-US relationship under Ma and Obama was the context that underpinned the sale of arms valued at US $6.4 billion by the United States to Taiwan in 2010, consisting of 60 *Black Hawk* helicopters, 114 *Patriot* air defence missiles, two *Osprey* mine-hunting ships, and advanced communications systems. Significantly, the sale did not include the advanced F16 combat aircraft that Taiwan had requested earlier (CNN 2010).

By then, however, US-China relations had deteriorated as China continued its spectacular economic rise despite the Global Financial Crisis in 2008, sustained its military modernization and expansion, and began to assert its claims over disputed maritime territory in the South and East China Seas. The open challenge to the United States' dominant position in Asia could not be ignored. This was the context that underscored Obama's seminal 'pivot to Asia' speech delivered in Australia in November 2011, in which he stated that he had 'made a deliberate and strategic decision ... [as] a Pacific nation, the United States will play a larger and long-term role in shaping the region and its future' (Obama 2011). While the speech did not mention China, it was clear that the United States' new pivot to Asia was meant to counter China's rise. The speech was followed up by an expanded military presence in the Asia-Pacific. After initially stationing 2,500 US Marines on a rotational basis in Australia, an expanded Force Posture Agreement in 2014 provided the United States with unimpeded access to a number of military facilities as well as the ability to pre-position military supplies (Department of Foreign Affairs and Trade 2014).

The Obama Administration also focused on improving relations with states in Asia, and the strengthening of traditional alliances (Shambaugh 2016). In addition, the promotion of the Trans-Pacific Partnership and the development of a new warfighting strategy known as Air-Sea Battle (later reconceptualized as the Joint Concept for Access and Maneuver in the Global Commons) were also seen to be part of the new containment strategy against China (Löfflmann 2016: 10–12).

The new US policy towards China emerged as tensions continued to escalate between the two countries. China's assertive moves in the South China Sea prompted US naval patrols including aircraft carriers to challenge its claims (Reuters 2017). In the East China Sea, China's assertion of its claims over the Senkaku islands led to high tensions with Japan in 2013, prompting the United States to shore up deterrence by reaffirming its commitment to the Mutual Defense Treaty with Japan and to clarify that the islands fell within its scope (Klingner 2014).

The strategic rivalry and tensions between China and the United States have elevated the strategic importance of Taiwan. Indeed, if China took control of Taiwan, US credibility would collapse and China would gain bases in Taiwan that would enable it to project power into the Western Pacific. As one analyst concluded, such a scenario would 'signal once and for all the end of this American-dominated era and the start of another' (Linker 2014). Employing Cold War logic, the *National Interest* thus asserted that abandoning Taiwan 'might considerably enhance China's military and geostrategic position in Asia, and severely weaken that of the United States and its allies' (Rehman 2014). Shaohua Hu concluded as well that 'without reunification, China cannot go all out on other regional and global ambitions' (2016: 161). Thus, US Secretary of State Hillary Clinton affirmed in November 2011 that Taiwan remained 'an important security and economic partner'.

There also remains support in the US Congress for Taiwan. In 2014, for instance, 52 US senators from both the Democrat and Republican parties jointly wrote to President Obama to reaffirm the importance of the Taiwan Relations Act and called for an expanded dialogue with Taiwan (Senate Committee on Foreign Relations 2014). During the presidential election in the United States in 2016 Donald Trump's adviser, Peter Navarro, called for the United States to commit more fully to the modernization of Taiwan's defence capabilities, asserting that 'maintaining Taiwan as an independent, pro-US ally is absolutely critical for strategically balancing against the rise of an increasingly militaristic China' (Navarro 2016). Following Trump's presidential victory, Navarro joined his administration as the director of the National Trade Council. The Trump Administration has also since approved a US $1.4 billion arms sale to Taiwan consisting of early warning radar, high-speed anti-radiation missiles, torpedoes and missile components. Trump also signed legislation encouraging more official visits between the two countries. In April 2018 John Bolton, who has strong pro-Taiwan leanings, became National Security Adviser (*Washington Post* 2018). The outbreak of a trade war in 2018 involving the imposition of tit-for-tat tariffs has also raised tensions once again between China and the United States (*The Guardian* 2018). In the heated and partisan domestic political atmosphere in the United States in the run-up to the mid-term congressional elections in November 2018, invective against China once again emerged, with Trump accusing China of attempting to interfere in the elections (BBC 2018). In October 2018, a near collision between a US naval warship and a Chinese navy vessel in the South China Sea raised tensions yet further between the two countries (*New York Times* 2018). The intensifying US-China tensions meant that Taiwan began to assume greater strategic significance for the United States. Indeed, the US has undertaken symbolic shows of support for Taiwan, for instance, by sailing warships through the Taiwan Strait in July and October 2018. In response, China's Minister of Defence, Lt-Gen. Wei Fenghe, declared that 'Taiwan is China's core interest' and that it is 'extremely dangerous to challenge China's bottom line repeatedly'. Furthermore, he vowed that 'if anyone tries to separate Taiwan from China, China's military will take action at all costs' (Straits Times 2018).

Conclusions

While the strategic imperative was clear, the question was what would the future be like for Taiwan-US relations following Donald Trump's ascension to the office of the president of the United States in early 2017. The Trump presidency coincided with political changes in Taiwan, where a resurgent DPP, riding on the back of an emerging sense of Taiwanese identity, won the elections in Taiwan in January 2016, capturing both the presidency and the legislature for the first time (*China Post* 2016). The election represented a turning point in Taiwanese politics, given the steady development of a separate Taiwanese identity built around its civil society and democracy. As a survey in 2014 found, 60.6 per cent of people in Taiwan identified themselves as Taiwanese, while only 3.5 per cent considered themselves to be Chinese, compared to 26.2 per cent in 1994 (*Taipei Times* 2015).

However, this drift away from China and the pro-independence DPP's ascension to political power has led to the return of Taiwan-China tensions. The problem is that the emotional nationalist imperative underlying the question of reunification within China, and the growing asymmetry in military capabilities on account of China's dramatic economic and military expansion in recent years, could well tempt China to use coercion or force to reunify Taiwan with the mainland. Indeed, a RAND study warned in 2015 that with the development of China's armed forces, particularly its anti-access capabilities that could keep US forces at bay in a regional crisis, China could be tempted to use force and overwhelm Taiwan's defences before the United States could effectively intervene (RAND Corporation 2015: 327). The growing asymmetry and imbalance on the Taiwan Strait is accentuated by Taiwan's low defence spending, which totalled US $10.4 billion in 2017 compared to $150 billion for China (IISS 2018: 249, 302). Worse, due to its failure to acquire modern weapons systems, Taiwan's armed forces are obsolete (Tan 2014: 46–49). As two Taiwanese analysts explained, Taiwan's low defence budget reflects not only the island's excessive confidence that the US will come to the rescue, but also the public's lack of confidence that any defence investment could meaningfully ward off China (Liao and Lin 2015: 151).

But will the United States come to Taiwan's aid should China use force? Taiwan's reunification with China is not in the interest of the United States, since this would boost China's power in the region and undermine the dominance of the United States in the Pacific (Hu 2016: 161). However, it is hard to envisage the United States going to war with China over Taiwan. The danger of escalation into a broader war involving nuclear weapons would be too high, given the inherent pre-emptive nature of air-sea combat (Etzioni 2013). Thus, Liao and Lin have correctly concluded that 'the inconvenient truth is that Washington is unlikely to jump to Taiwan's aid unless the costs are acceptable and Taipei could hold its ground until US troops arrive' (2015: 151).

The problem for the US government, however, has been President Trump's unpredictability. Despite accepting a telephone call from Taiwan's new President, Tsai Ing-wen, in December 2016, in a serious breach of the One China policy, Trump went on to reaffirm the United States' adherence to one China in a telephone conversation with China's President Xi Jinping in February 2017 (CNN 2017). In 2017 Trump seemingly went back on the tough anti-China stance that he adopted during the presidential campaign and sought China's assistance in dealing with a bigger threat to regional stability, namely the nuclear brinkmanship of North Korea (*Washington Post* 2017). Trump's transactional approach to foreign policy has also undermined the United States' security commitments in the region, as states in the region, including Taiwan, are unsure if their interests would be bargained away by Trump's emphasis on 'America first'. This undermines strategic stability in the Taiwan Strait as this depends on the credibility of the US commitment to Taiwan – an essential condition for the maintenance of the status quo.

While in 2019 the United States is currently demonstrating strong support for Taiwan on account of worsening China-US relations, particularly in the wake of the tit-for-tat trade tariff wars in 2018, it is clear, from this chapter's brief historical survey of US relations with Taiwan, that the United States' interest in Taiwan has waxed and waned in accordance with its own changing national interests. Despite the sympathy for Taiwan that undoubtedly still exists in the US Congress, Taiwan is in fact ultimately expendable. What has saved Taiwan since the end of the Cold War has been the growing strategic rivalry between the United States and China, and the uncertain costs to China should it attempt to use force in pursuit of reunification. Given the current strategic importance of Taiwan to the US position in Asia, it is unlikely that the United States would immediately abandon Taiwan should China actually attack the island. But this is only provided that the cost of any US intervention is acceptable. If Taiwan was overwhelmed quickly in a military strike by China, then it is likely that the United States would be forced to accept the fait accompli since the potential cost of escalation would be too high for the United States to mount a military campaign to recover Taiwan.

The bottom line is that to sustain the Taiwan-US relationship, and US support, Taiwan must not become a dangerous liability to the United States by either pushing for independence thereby sparking a serious crisis in US-China relations, or failing to invest sufficiently in its own defence to deter the use of force and also prevent any swift victory by China should conflict break out. Maintaining the status quo by bearing these two factors in mind seems to be the most realistic way forward for Taiwan.

References

Acheson, Dean (1949) 'Letter of Transmittal', *The China White Paper: United States Relations with Special Reference to the Period 1944–1949*, Washington, DC: US Department of State. Available at https://archive.org/stream/VanSlykeLymanThe ChinaWhitePaper1949/Van%20Slyke,%20Lyman%20-%20The%20China%20White %20Paper%201949_djvu.txt (accessed 16 August 2018).

BBC (2010) 'Historic Taiwan-China Trade Deal Takes Effect', 12 September. Available at www.bbc.com/news/world-asia-pacific-11275274 (accessed 18 August 2018).

BBC (2018) 'Trump Accuses China of Election "Meddling" against Him', 26 September. Available at www.bbc.com/news/world-us-canada-45656466 (accessed 26 October 2018).

Casey, Steven (2010) 'Harry S. Truman', in *Mental Maps in the Early Cold War Era, 1945–68*, Steven Casey and Jonathan Wright (eds) New York: Palgrave Macmillan.

China Post (2016) 'DPP Wins 68 Seats in Legislature for First-Ever Majority', 17 January. Available at www.chinapost.com.tw/taiwan/national/presidential-election/2016/01/17/456304/DPP-wins.htm (accessed 18 August 2018).

Clinton, Hillary (2011) 'America's Pacific Century', speech at the East-West Center, Hawaii, 10 November. Available at https://2009-2017.state.gov/secretary/20092013clinton/rm/2011/11/176999.htm (accessed 18 August 2018).

CNN (2010) 'U.S. Announces $6.4 Billion Arms Deal with Taiwan', 30 January. Available at http://edition.cnn.com/2010/WORLD/asiapcf/01/29/taiwan.arms/ (accessed 18 August 2018).

CNN (2017) 'Trump Commits to "One China" Policy in Phone Call with Xi', 10 February. Available at http://edition.cnn.com/2017/02/09/politics/trump-xi-phone-call/ (accessed 18 August 2018).

DeLisle, Jacques (2009) 'Taiwan in the World Health Assembly: A Victory, with Limits', 13 May, Washington, DC: Brookings East Asia Commentary. Available at www.brookings.edu/opinions/taiwan-in-the-world-health-assembly-a-victory-with-limits/ (accessed 18 August 2018).

Department of Foreign Affairs and Trade (DFAT) (2014) *The Force Posture Agreement between the Government of Australia and the Government of the United States of America*, 12 August. Available at www.info.dfat.gov.au/Info/Treaties/Treaties.nsf/AllDocIDs/6441A500816C2902CA257D38001DB33D (accessed 18 August 2018).

Etzioni, Amitai (2013) 'Air-Sea Battle: A Dangerous Way to Deal with China', *The Diplomat*, 3 September. Available at http://thediplomat.com/2013/09/air-sea-battle-a-dangerous-way-to-deal-with-china/ (accessed 18 August 2018).

Hickey, Dennis van Vranken (1998) 'The Taiwan Strait Crisis of 1996: Implications for US Security Policy', *Journal of Contemporary China*, 7(19).

Hu, Shaohua (2016) 'A Framework for Analysis of National Interest: United States Policy Toward Taiwan', *Contemporary Security Policy*, 37(1).

International Institute of Strategic Studies (IISS) (2018) *The Military Balance 2018*, London: IISS.

Joint Communique (1971) *Joint Communique of the United States of America and the People's Republic of China*, January 1. Available at www.taiwandocuments.org/communique02.htm (accessed 16 August 2018).

Kan, Shirley A. (2002) *Taiwan: Major U.S. Arms Sales Since 1990*, June 18, Congressional Research Service. Available at www.dtic.mil/dtic/tr/fulltext/u2/a472824.pdf (accessed 18 August 2018).

Klingner, Bruce (2014) 'Amid Chinese Aggression, Obama Affirms U.S. Defense of Japan's Senkaku Islands', *Daily Signal*, 24 April. Available at http://dailysignal.com/2014/04/24/amid-chinese-aggression-obama-affirms-u-s-defense-japans-senkaku-islands/ (accessed 18 August 2018).

Liao Nien-chung Chang and Dalton Kuen-da Lin (2015) 'Rebalancing Taiwan-US Relations', *Survival*, 57(6).

Linker, Damon (2014) 'What Would America Do If China Invaded Taiwan?' *The Week*, 21 March. Available at http://theweek.com/article/index/258467/what-would-america-do-if-china-invaded-taiwan (accessed 18 August 2018).

Löfflmann, Georg (2016) 'The Pivot between Containment, Engagement, and Restraint: President Obama's Conflicted Grand Strategy in Asia', *Asian Security*, 12(2).

Los Angeles Times (1992) 'President to Sell F-16s to Taiwan, Officials Say', 2 September. Available at http://articles.latimes.com/1992-09-02/news/mn-6340_1_united-states (accessed 17 August 2018).

Luthi, Lorenz M. (2008) *The Sino-Soviet Split: Cold War in the Communist World*, Princeton, NJ: Princeton University Press.

Mutual Defense Treaty (MDT) (1954) *Mutual Defense Treaty between the United States and the Republic of China*, 2 December. Available at http://avalon.law.yale.edu/20th_century/chin001.asp (accessed 16 August 2018).

Nathan, Andrew and Robert Ross (1997) *The Great Wall and the Empty Fortress: China's Search For Security*, New York: W. W. Norton.

National Security Council (NSC) (1949) 'NSC 48/2, The Position of the United States With Respect to Asia', A Report to the President by the National Security Council, 30 December. Available at https://history.state.gov/historicaldocuments/frus1949v07p2/d387 (accessed 18 August 2018).

Navarro, Peter (2016) 'America Can't Dump Taiwan', *National Interest*, 19 July. Available at http://nationalinterest.org/feature/america-cant-dump-taiwan-17040?page=show (accessed 18 August 2018).

NBC News (2004) 'Taiwan Calls Powell Speech Big Surprise', 26 October. Available at www.nbcnews.com/id/6337218/ns/world_news/t/taiwan-calls-powell-speech-big-surprise/#.WRztMoVOKUk (accessed 18 August 2018).

New York Times (1971) 'UN Admits Red China: Nationalists Ousted', 25 October. Available at www.archives.nd.edu/Observer/1971-10-26_v06_033.pdf (accessed 16 May 2017).

New York Times (2018) 'American and Chinese Warships Narrowly Avoid High-Seas Collision', 2 October. Available at www.nytimes.com/2018/10/02/world/asia/china-us-warships-south-china-sea.html (accessed 26 October 2018).

Obama, Barack (2011) Remarks by President Obama to the Australian Parliament, 17 November. Available at https://obamawhitehouse.archives.gov/the-press-office/2011/11/17/remarks-president-obama-australian-parliament (accessed 18 August 2018).

Office of the Historian (1982) *The August 17, 1982 U.S.-China Communiqué on Arms Sales to Taiwan*. Available at https://history.state.gov/milestones/1981-1988/china-communique (accessed 16 August 2018).
People's Daily (2005) 'Full Text of Anti-Secession Law', 14 March. Available at http://english.peopledaily.com.cn/200503/14/eng20050314_176746.html (accessed 15 August 2018).
People's Daily (n.d.) 'Major Events in Sino-US Ties'. Available at http://english.peopledaily.com.cn/features/bush/ties.htm (accessed 16 August 2018).
RAND Corporation (2015) *An Interactive Look at the U.S.-China Military Scorecard: Forces, Geography and the Evolving Balance of Power, 1996–2017*, Santa Monica, CA:RAND. Available at www.rand.org/content/dam/rand/pubs/research_reports/RR300/RR392/RAND_RR392.pdf (accessed 18 August 2018).
Rehman, Iskander (2014) 'Why Taiwan Matters: A Small Island of Great Strategic Importance', *National Interest*, 28 February. Available at http://nationalinterest.org/commentary/why-taiwan-matters-9971 (accessed 18 August 2018).
Reuters (2017) 'China Opposes U.S. Naval Patrols in South China Sea', 22 February. Available at www.reuters.com/article/us-southchinasea-china-usa-idUSKBN1600V0 (accessed 18 August 2018).
Roy, Denny (n.d.) 'Postwar Taiwan and the USA', *History Now: Journal of the Gilder Lehrman Institute*. Available at www.gilderlehrman.org/history-by-era/global-history-and-us-foreign-policy/essays/postwar-taiwan-and-usa (accessed 16 August 2018).
Scherr, Arthur (2010) 'Presidential Power, the Panay Incident, and the Defeat of the Ludlow Amendment', *International History Review*, 32(3).
Senate Committee on Foreign Relations (2014) 'Fifty-Two Senators Commemorate the 35th Anniversary of the Taiwan Relations Act in Letter to President Obama', 9 April. Available at www.foreign.senate.gov/press/chair/release/fifty-two-senators-commemorate-the-35th-anniversary-of-the-taiwan-relations-act-in-letter-to-president-obama (accessed 18 August 2018).
Shambaugh, David (2016) 'President Obama's Asia Scorecard', *Wilson Quarterly* (winter). Available at http://wilsonquarterly.com/quarterly/the-post-obama-world/president-obamas-asia-scorecard/ (accessed 18 August 2018).
Shanghai Communiqué (1972) *Joint Communique of the United States of America and the People's Republic of China*, 28 February. Available at www.taiwandocuments.org/communique01.htm (accessed 16 August 2018).
Shirk, Susan L. (2007) *China: Fragile Superpower*, New York: Oxford University. Press.
Six Assurances (1982) *The 'Six Assurances' to Taiwan*, July. Available at http://taiwandocuments.org/assurances.htm (accessed 16 August 2018).
SoongMei-ling (1943) 'Addresses to the House of Representatives and to the Senate', 18 February. Available at http://china.usc.edu/soong-mei-ling-%E2%80%9Caddresses-house-respresentatives-and-senate%E2%80%9D-february-18-1943 (accessed 16 August 2018).
Star, Marriah (2007) 'The Taiwan Lobby, Formosan Nationalism, and The K-Street Strategy: Success or Failure in Influencing U.S. Foreign Policy?' Paper presented at the annual meeting of the American Political Science Association, Hyatt Regency Chicago and the Sheraton Chicago Hotel and Towers, Chicago, 30 August. Available at http://citation.allacademic.com/meta/p209689_index.html (accessed 16 August 2018).
Straits Times (2018) 'China Calls Any Challenge on Taiwan "Extremely Dangerous"', 25 October. Available at www.straitstimes.com/asia/east-asia/chinas-defence-minister-vows-never-to-cede-any-territory-including-taiwan (accessed 26 October 2018).

Sutter, Robert (2010) *US-Chinese Relations: Perilous Past, Pragmatic Present*, Lanham, MD: Rowman and Littlefield.
Taipei Times (2008) 'Presidential Election 2008: Referendums Fail to Meet Thresholds', 23 March. Available at www.taipeitimes.com/News/taiwan/archives/2008/03/23/2003406756 (accessed 18 August 2018).
Taipei Times (2015) 'Taiwanese Identity Hits Record Level', 6 January. Available at www.taipeitimes.com/News/front/archives/2015/01/26/2003610092 (accessed 18 August 2018).
Taiwan Relations Act (1979) Taiwan Relations Act, 1 January. Available at www.ait.org.tw/en/taiwan-relations-act.html (accessed 16 August 2018).
Tan, Andrew T. H. (2014) 'The Implications of Taiwan's Declining Defence', *Asia-Pacific Review*, 21(1).
The Guardian (2018) 'China Hits Back against Latest US Tariffs; Pound Hit by Brexit Worries', 9 August. Available at www.theguardian.com/business/live/2018/aug/08/us-china-trade-war-pound-euro-brexit-oil-business-live (accessed 9 August 2018).
Tucker, Nancy Bernkopf (2009) *Strait Talk: United States–Taiwan Relations and the Crisis with China*, Cambridge, MA: Harvard University Press.
US Department of State (1943) *The Cairo Conference*. Available at https://2001-2009.state.gov/r/pa/ho/time/wwii/107184.htm (accessed 16 May 2017).
Washington Post (2017) 'Taiwan Arms Deal in Limbo as Trump Courts China', 7 May. Available at www.washingtonpost.com/opinions/global-opinions/taiwan-arms-deal-in-limbo-as-trump-courts-china/2017/05/07/37ee5654-31ba-11e7-8674-437ddb6e813e_story.html?utm_term=.fef7c7015eed (accessed 18 August 2018).
Washington Post (2018) 'Taiwan Seems to be Benefiting from Trump's Presidency: So Why Is No One Celebrating?' 29 April. Available at www.washingtonpost.com/opinions/global-opinions/taiwan-seems-to-be-benefiting-from-trumps-presidency-so-why-is-no-one-celebrating/2018/04/29/f5d38166-4966-11e8-827e-190efaf1f1ee_story.html?noredirect=on&utm_term=.558af2d8f992(accessed 9 August 2018).
White House (2003) 'President Bush and Premier Wen Jiabao Remarks to the Press', 9 December. Available at https://2001-2009.state.gov/p/eap/rls/rm/2003/27184.htm (accessed 18 August 2018).
White House (2009) 'U.S.-China Joint Statement', 17 November. Available at https://obamawhitehouse.archives.gov/realitycheck/the-press-office/us-china-joint-statement (accessed 18 August 2018).

9 New dynamics in Taiwan-Japan relations

Benjamin Schreer and Andrew T. H. Tan

Introduction

Aside from the United States, Japan is the Republic of China (ROC, or Taiwan)'s most important strategic partner in East Asia. Geographical proximity, strong historical and cultural ties, and the common challenge posed by China's increasingly assertive behaviour in the Taiwan Strait and the Sea of Japan mean that Taipei and Tokyo have to find ways to work ever more closely together, regardless of Japan's One China policy, based on the Chinese-Japanese communiqué of 1972, which stated that 'Taiwan is an inalienable part of the territory of the People's Republic of China', and that 'the Government of Japan fully understands and respects this stand' (China-Japan Joint Communique 1972). Indeed, this chapter argues that despite the remaining obstacles to much closer official Japan-Taiwan political ties due to Tokyo's concerns about Chinese reactions, both sides have intensified their interactions below the political radar screen. For strategic and sociocultural reasons, Japan has every incentive to ensure that Taiwan continues to find the necessary political and economic space it needs in order to survive.

To make its case, this chapter first briefly outlines the geostrategic and historical context of the Taiwan-Japan relationship. It then examines the cultural and personal links that have resulted in Taiwan's close relationship with Japan. The next section assesses the more recent development of closer political and economic relations, particularly since the Democratic Progressive Party's (DPP) comprehensive victory in the 2016 elections. The chapter conclude with an analysis of the future constraints and opportunities in Taiwan-Japan relations.

Geostrategic and historical context

Taiwan and Japan are inextricably bound together by geography which generally speaking has a major impact on states' strategy and policy (Gray and Sloane 1999; Grygiel 2006). They share a significant geostrategic vulnerability because of their close proximity to a rising China and the vast distance that separates them from their principle security guarantor, the United States. They are both 'frontline states' in the 'first island chain' and any major shift in US-China relations and/or in Chinese or US strategic policy towards East Asia has an impact on Taipei's and Tokyo's geostrategic position. In response, they need to adjust their respective geostrategies, and re-direct their military and diplomatic efforts towards controlling key geopolitical variables, including the stability of their borders. Failure to do so minimizes their ability to increase or maintain their relative power.

Precisely because of their geostrategic proximity, Taiwan has been essential to Japan's national security since the 1890s (Blazevic 2010; Lam 2004). Tokyo's strategy has long been informed by the recognition that it can ill afford Taipei to fall into Beijing's strategic orbit. Taiwan's geostrategic location is essential for Japan's maritime trade and the loss of the island to China would pose a direct danger to securing its long and vulnerable sea lines of communications – on which it depends for energy supplies and raw materials, as well as overseas markets – because of Beijing's ability to block sea lane traffic. Moreover, China's power through expansion in both the South China Sea and the East China Sea would be greatly enhanced, possibly leading to Chinese domination of much of these waters. Should the People's Liberation Army be able to use Taiwan as a staging ground for operations, Japanese and US forces based in the vicinity would be faced with a greatly enhanced Chinese power projection capability, utilizing the island as a gateway for China to enter the Pacific (for example using deep water ports in Taiwan's east for submarine operations), thereby further threatening Japan's security. Conversely, a de facto independent Taiwan serves as a barrier against Chinese military expansion beyond the first island chain or, in the event of a war, as a possible springboard for US-led operations against the Chinese mainland. Therefore, reflecting a widely held perception in policy circles in Japan, a Japanese defence expert observed that 'losing Taiwan (to China) … would be a game-changer for Japan' (quoted in Serchuk 2013).

Furthermore, should tensions over the Taiwan Strait lead to open conflict involving the United States, Japan would almost invariably become involved, as US military operations in the Taiwan Strait would partly depend on using US bases in Japan, and Japan is obliged to assist the United States on account of the US-Japan defence alliance (Japanese Ministry of Foreign Affairs, n.d.). Even in peacetime, however, the survival of Taiwan as a de facto independent entity serves the strategic interests of Japan since it sustains the current status quo.

For Taipei, enhanced ties with Tokyo are also essential for both strategic and military reasons. Aside from the United States, Japan is its second most important political and military lifeline given its geostrategic proximity and political-cultural congruence. Should US credibility to defend Taiwan militarily erode significantly, Japan remains the only realistic power in the region to extend informal security guarantees to Taipei. Similarly, in the context of greater US-Chinese competition practical military-operational questions of how to defend Taiwan against potential Chinese aggression will gain much greater importance in US thinking, including the operational role played by Japan's Self-Defense Forces in military contingencies involving the island.

Against this geostrategic background, Japan's involvement in Taiwan can be traced back to the Taiwan military expedition of 1874, which took place shortly after the Meiji Reformation of 1868 that initiated the modernization of Japan. This was Japan's first military expedition in over two centuries. While the expedition was aimed at seeking redress for the murder of marooned Japanese sailors, it signalled that the new Japan that emerged in the wake of the Meiji Reformation was quick to recognize that neighbouring Taiwan was part of its strategic backyard. This led to Japan's annexation and colonization of the island just two decades later, in 1895, as the spoil of the First Sino-Japanese War (Fraleigh 2010: 43; Treaty of Shimonoseki 1895). As outlined by Fraleigh, press reporting in Japan at the time was animated by the idea of an imperialist 'civilising project in Taiwan'. He also observed that 'Taiwan became configured as a part of the Japanese territory, one that held the prospect of developing in such a way as to be particularly beneficial to the metropole' (Fraleigh 2010: 56, 62).

Japan's modernization and growth as a regional power saw it expand its territorial claims to include Okinawa in the south, incorporating this into Tokyo prefecture in 1879. After acquiring Formosa (Taiwan) and the Pescadores following the conclusion of the Sino-Japanese War in 1895, Japan went on to annex islands in the South China Sea, including the Spratleys and Paracels in 1939, as Japan sought to dominate its strategic neighbourhood (Furukawa 2011: 299). Indeed, Taiwan played an important role in Japan's southward conquests during the Second World War (Cutshall 1944). Importantly, the Japanese colonization of Taiwan between 1895 and 1945 left a cultural and linguistic legacy, and in stark contrast to the negative Korean experience, has 'continued to provide a social reference point for ongoing contacts between the two people' (Thomas and Williams 2017: 116–17) today. Thousands of Japanese people lived in Taiwan before the Second World War. Japan accepted thousands of post-war political refugees, and many older generation Taiwanese were educated in Japan and married Japanese women. Around 200,000 Taiwanese fought in the Imperial Army, and the spirits of these troops also reposed at the Yasukuni Shrine in Tokyo (Lam 2004: 252).

The Japanese empire collapsed after Japan's defeat in 1945, whereupon it was forced, as a result of the San Francisco Peace Treaty in 1951, to renounce all claims to Formosa and the nearby Pescadores (Treaty of Peace with Japan 1951). Japan, however, retained the Okinotori islands, located 1,700 km south of Tokyo. Since 2004 China has disputed Japan's exclusive economic zone (EEZ) around the Okinotori Shima coral reef chain, a potentially problematic issue due to the fact that the area is an important sea corridor for US navy vessels, including submarines, in the event of military conflict over Taiwan (Furukawa 2011: 307). Japan's southern maritime border is also very close to

Taiwan, with the Yonaguni islands located just 125 km west of Taiwan. Indeed, Japan's westernmost air defense identification zone (ADIZ), a legacy of the US military before the reversion of Okinawa to Japan in 1972, passes through Yonaguni islands, with two-thirds of its air space within Taiwan's ADIZ, compelling Japanese aircraft heading for Yonaguni to seek the permission of Taiwan (ibid.: 308).

Critically for contemporary Japan-Taiwan relations, in September 1972 Japan recognized the government of the People's Republic of China (PRC, or China) as the sole legal government of China. It established diplomatic relations with Beijing and relegated Japan-Taiwan relations to a non-governmental, working-level basis. In the Japan-China Joint Communique, Tokyo stated its understanding of the PRC's stance that Taiwan is an inalienable part of the territory of the PRC, but, importantly, did not adopt that as its own position. While Japan's One China policy has placed limits on formal Japan-Taiwan relations – for instance the inability to send a Japanese ambassador to Taipei – it should be noted that its One China policy does not accept the PRC's interpretation that Taiwan is an inalienable part of China's territory, leaving the door open for the defence of Taiwan should China seek to take the island by force.

The ties that bind: Taiwan-Japan sociocultural relations

When analysing Taiwan-Japan relations, it is critical to recognize the very close cultural affinity between the peoples of the two countries and the role played by history. Japan's 'civilizing' mission in Taiwan resulted in a relatively benign colonial administration from 1895 to 1945, which modernized the island and provided access to education and other services. Taiwanese students enrolled in Japanese universities and in Japanese tertiary institutions on Taiwan itself, resulting in many Taiwanese leaders of that generation, such as Lee Teng-hui, the Kuomintang (KMT – Nationalist Party) president of Taiwan from 1988 to 2000, who retained a strong cultural affinity for Japan (Lam 2004: 251). As mentioned above, Japan's attempts to assimilate the Taiwanese culturally were so successful that some 200,000 Taiwanese served in the Imperial Japanese Army during the Second World War, some even volunteering for kamikaze missions.

In contrast, following Japan's defeat in 1945, the excesses of the KMT when its defeated forces fled to Taiwan during and after the Chinese Civil War from 1945–49 led to a strong sense of revulsion by native Taiwanese against the mainlanders. This was reflected in a new phrase adopted by native Taiwanese that 'after the dogs are gone, the pigs have arrived' (Rigger 2017: 336). Indeed, the mainlanders were perceived as an occupying force, particularly accentuated by the KMT's deep levels of corruption and an initial lack of law and order. Matters came to a head on 28 February 1947, when a trivial incident led to a full-scale revolt by native Taiwanese against the government. In response to the largely peaceful revolt, KMT forces in Taiwan engaged in shocking violence against civilian Taiwanese, killing around 28,000 people, targeting in particular the educated elite (Wang 2017). As a shocked American correspondent reported at the time:

> China put down the revolt with brutal repression, terror, and massacre. Mainland soldiers and police fired first killing thousands indiscriminately; then, more selectively, hunted down and jailed or slaughtered students, intellectuals, prominent business men, and civic leaders ... Governor General Chen Yi has turned a movement against bad government into one against any Chinese government.
>
> (Durdin 1947)

These excesses made Japanese colonialism appear benign in comparison, which partly explains the nostalgia for Japanese colonial rule among older Taiwanese. As older Taiwanese often reminisced, 'at least, the Japanese made us modern ... the Chinese made a mess' (Laskai 2014).

While the precise impact of Japanese colonialism on Taiwan's contemporary identity is subject to academic debate (Chulow 2010) and political disagreement between the DPP and the KMT (Kushner 2007), shared history and cultural ties have had an important positive impact on contemporary Japan-Taiwan relations. A (mostly) positive interpretation of colonialism, a shared bond of Asian democratic identity and mutual cultural attraction based on popular support has helped to maintain a high level of government and public support for maintaining and increasing ties. Taiwanese Japanophiles are called 'Harizu', and following the 2011 Tohoku earthquake and tsunami, Japanese civil society expressed gratitude to the Taiwanese for their donations (valued at approximately US $261 million, 90 per cent of which came from private donors) with a 'thank you Taiwan movement' and a gratitude tour (Taipei Economic and Cultural Office Miami 2012). Japan-Taiwan relations have since been described in Japan as *kizuna* – literally, an emotional bond between people. In 2016 a survey by the Interchange Association, Japan's de facto embassy in Taiwan, found that 80 per cent of Taiwanese were fond of Japan and 56 per cent considered it to be their favourite country, the highest rate of approval of Japan since the surveys began in 2009. Japan also remained the top tourist destination for Taiwanese (*Kyodo News* 2016). A 2018 Taiwan Public Opinion Foundation poll revealed that 84.6 per cent of Taiwanese had a favourable perception of Japan (Taiwanese Public Opinion Foundation 2018: 31). This affinity was reciprocated in Japan, with a survey in 2018 conducted by the same office showing that almost 65 per cent of Japanese said that they felt the most affinity towards Taiwan among all Asian countries (*Kyodo News* 2018a).

Aside from historical cultural ties, individual linkages have helped to sustain Japanese influence in Taiwan as well as Taiwan-Japan relations. Pro-Taiwan lobby groups in Japan's parliament, the Diet, include, for instance, the influential Taiwan-ROC Diet Members' Consultative Council in the ruling Liberal Democratic Party (LDP). This group plays an important role as a channel for communication for the two sides in the absence of formal diplomatic channels (Deans 2001: 156–58). The strong support for Taiwan in the Japanese Diet was best summarized in 1976 by Kaya Okinari, a key figure in the pro-Taiwan parliamentary groups in the post-war era. He provided six reasons why Japan should never abandon Taiwan:

- The long period of friendly relations since 1945;
- the ROC's membership of the 'free-world';
- the injustice of upending official recognition of a free country (ROC) in order to normalise relations with a communist regime (PRC);
- the immorality of abandoning a country that had done no wrong to Japan;
- Japan's 'four-fold indebtedness' to Taiwan;[1] and
- the absence of a crisis that would make derecognition unavoidable.

(Deans 2001: 166–67)

Moreover, under the long authoritarian reign of the KMT in post-war Taiwan, Taipei rarely criticized Japan over its colonial past, nor did it demand an apology from Japan, unlike other East Asian states such as the two Koreas and China, thus ensuring that despite prevailing anti-Japanese animosity in North-East Asia, Japan had at least one steadfast friend in the region, a fact much appreciated by Japan (Lam 2004: 251–52). Thus, the Taiwan-ROC Diet Members' Consultative Council, for instance, has always despatched a delegation to attend Taiwan's annual National Day celebrations on 10 October. Indeed, in 2018 the Council's Chairman, Keiji Furuya, and Diet Representative Seishiro Eto led two separate delegations to attend the celebrations, in addition to 223 members from goodwill ambassador associations across Japan, thereby underlining the continued depth of cultural and personal ties between the two (*Taipei Times* 2018).

In this context, it is important to note that growing support in Taiwan for de facto independence since the 1990s had the effect of strengthening the ideational dimensions of Japan's ties with Taiwan, given that both now shared a democratic political system. This development started under KMT President Lee Teng-hui (1998–2000) who reflected a Taiwanese, as opposed to Chinese, perspective on Taiwan. Indeed, Lee is emblematic of those Taiwanese who were educated in Japan and who served as officers in the Japanese Imperial Army during the Second World War. As noted by Lam:

> Lee is by far the best propagandist in the Taiwanese cause in wooing the Japanese. He skilfully played on Japanese sentiments by highlighting their common values of market capitalism, liberal democracy, and human rights, and in projecting an image that Taiwan is 'just like us' to the Japanese ... fluent in Japanese and strongly rooted in Japanese culture, Lee mesmerized the Japanese mass media with his charisma, passion and intense admiration for Japan.

(2004: 258)

Lee continued to play an influential role in sustaining Taiwan's ties with Japan long after he stepped down as president. He personally met Japanese Prime Minister Shinzo Abe on a number of occasions. In 2015 he addressed a packed Diet and had a meeting with Abe, despite Japan coming under Chinese pressure to call off the visit (*Japan News* 2015; Cole 2015). In 2018, at the age of 95, he paid a four-day trip to Okinawa, at the invitation of the Japan-Taiwan Peace Foundation, to pay tribute to Taiwanese troops killed in the battle of Okinawa in 1945 (*Japan Times* 2018).

The coming to power of the DPP in Taiwan in 2000, when Chen Shui-bian won the presidency, had a positive effect on Taiwan-Japan relations, due to the DPP's scepticism towards China and positive attitude towards Japan. As one analyst dryly observed, 'the DPP comprises mostly Taiwanese who appear to like Japan better than mainland China' (Lam 2004: 249). New personal ties were built between the DPP and Japanese politicians and other governing elites, resulting in even closer relations between Japanese and Taiwanese politicians than with the KMT (Hoppens 2018). As Thomas and Williams conclude,

> the lengths to which both sides have gone through the creation of semi-governmental and non-governmental bodies specifically designed to nurture the bilateral ties around the reality of Japan-China relations is a clear demonstration of the strength of the relationship ... Taiwan's relationship with Japan is an especially strong and enduring bilateral tie.
>
> (2017: 135)

Taiwan-Japan ties have also been sustained by the younger generation of Taiwanese who have embraced Japanese cultural influences despite not having had the experience of growing up during the Japanese colonial era. As noted by Laskai, 'Taiwanese remain voracious consumers of all things Japanese, from fashion to music, and look towards the country with admiration for its liberal values and post-industrial society' (2014). Moreover, 'the more belligerent China acts towards Taiwan, the less attractive mainland Chinese culture becomes to Taiwanese youth' (Lam 2004: 253). As mentioned above, Taiwan's support in the aftermath of the earthquake and tsunami in Japan in 2011 further strengthened cultural and bilateral ties. Despite the lack of diplomatic ties, Japan received more than 20 billion yen in donations from Taiwan, more than that offered by the United States. This fact was widely covered in Japanese media and left a deep impression on many Japanese (Kawashima 2018). A subsequent survey of Taiwanese students of the Japanese language in Taiwan also found that despite fears about the radioactive fallout following the Fukushima Daiichi nuclear catastrophe, 'their overall feelings and intentions of travelling to Japan were still positive', due to 'the affection for Japanese culture and customs' (Chen 2012). It was thus no coincidence that in 2011 three bilateral agreements covering bilateral investment, tax arrangements and open skies were signed, moves that deepened the already strong people-to-people contacts between the two countries (Kawashima 2018: 57).

That said, strong Japan-Taiwan relations are not a given despite overall close political and cultural affinity. The Ma presidency was a case in point when Taiwan-Japan political relations deteriorated significantly. This was partly due to President Ma's anti-Japanese inclinations such as criticizing the Japanese prime minister's visit to the Yasukuni Shrine; adopting China's demands for Japan to offer a 'broader view of history'; disrespectful treatment during Abe's visit to Taipei in 2010; and his decree that government documents referring to Japanese 'rule' in Taiwan be changed to 'occupation'. For its part, the Abe government failed to formally thank Taiwan for its generosity in the aftermath of the 2011 earthquake and tsunami. In 2012 coastguards on both sides fired water cannons at each other over fishery disputes concerning the Senkaku Islands (or Diaoyu Islands in Chinese) (Teufel Dreyer 2016: 599–600).

Growing Taiwan-Japan relations under the Tsai government

Under the current Tsai government, Taiwan-Japan ties have again improved and have actually strengthened even further. Tsai Ing-wen was a protégé of Lee Teng-hu and cultivated ties with Japanese leaders, meeting informally with Prime Minister Shinzo Abe in Japan in October 2015 while standing as a presidential candidate. Abe himself has strong pro-Taiwan leanings. Indeed, his maternal grandfather, Kishi Nobusuke, was a primary benefactor of the ruling LDP's pro-Taiwan faction and was the first prime minister to visit Taipei in 1957. Abe's younger brother, Kishi Nobuo, reportedly has acted as Abe's current contact with the Taiwanese leadership while Abe's mother has been active in promoting cultural exchange between the two sides (Hoppens 2018).

Shortly after Tsai was elected to the presidency, Abe and Minister of Foreign Affairs Fumio Kishida sent congratulatory messages, marking the first time that senior officials had issued such communications to a president-elect of Taiwan (Yeh 2016). This was reciprocated in October 2017 when Tsai sent a similar note to Abe on his party's victory in Japan's parliamentary elections (*China Post* 2017). This warming of ties reflected a strong consensus in Japan over the importance of strong relations with Taiwan, even though Taiwan has come under renewed political and economic pressure from China since then. The rise of an increasingly powerful and assertive China has elicited strong concerns in Japan, which sees Taiwan as a strategic partner in the region, particularly given its strategic importance to Japan and the fact that both face similar security challenges from China. Indeed, the implications of China's rise and Taiwan's increased strategic importance was noted early in the 1990s by astute Japanese officials, with then Chief Cabinet Secretary Kajiyama Seiroku, a long-time supporter of Taiwan, stating, in 1997, that the 'areas surrounding' Japan would 'naturally include the Taiwan Strait' (Deans 2001: 170).

Reflecting the high priority of relations with Japan for her administration, President Tsai appointed two high-ranking party members to oversee Taiwan-Japan relations in 2016 (Ko 2016). In January 2017 Japan reciprocated by changing the name of its de facto embassy in Taipei from the Interchange Association to the Japan-Taiwan Exchange Association, a provocative move as far as China was concerned, since it seemed to give greater recognition to Taiwan's separation from China. Furthermore, Japan's representative described bilateral relations as being at their best (Reuters 2017). This was followed by the visit of Jiro Akama, Japan's senior vice-minister of internal affairs and communications, to Taiwan in March 2017, the highest ranking Japanese official to do so in an official capacity since 1972 (*Kyodo News* 2017). In May 2017 Taiwan changed the name of the semi-official body responsible for relations with Taiwan from the Association of East Asian Relations to the Taiwan-Japan Relations Association, drawing strong protest from China (Ko 2017). The warmer relations revived interest in the prospect of a Japanese Taiwan Relations Act (similar to the US Taiwan Relations Act), an idea first broached in 2006 by Taiwan's President, Chen Shui-bian (Hoppens 2018; Tiezzi 2014), although no progress has been made to date.

Moreover, in November 2017 both sides signed a customs agreement through their respective semi-official Taiwan bodies, giving the agreement a somewhat state-to-state tone (Agreement 2017). In addition, Taiwan expressed strong interest in forging an Economic Partnership Agreement with Japan as well as eventually joining the Japan-led Comprehensive and Progressive Agreement for Trans-Pacific Partnership, both of which Japan appears keen to support (*Taipei Times* 2017; Hornung 2018). Deepening economic ties make sense for Taiwan as Japan would be an important counterweight to China should the latter resort to economic coercion against Taiwan (Chen 2016). Indeed, the current economic ties are already significant. In 2018 Japan was Taiwan's second largest trading partner while Taiwan ranked fourth for Japan. Bilateral trade between Taiwan and Japan is substantial, totalling US$67.2 billion in 2018, an increase of 7.22 per cent compared with 2017 (Bureau of Foreign Trade 2019).

Moreover, in October 2016 Taiwan and Japan held an inaugural maritime cooperation dialogue that explored opportunities for collaboration on a range of maritime issues such as fisheries, scientific research, and coastguard collaboration. At their next meeting in December 2017 they succeeded in signing a Memorandum of Understanding (MOU) on maritime search and rescue operations. The MOU enables vessels and rescue staff from either side to help in the event of a maritime emergency (*Japan Times* 2017). At their third meeting in December 2018 the two sides signed two additional MOUs: one to improve cooperation of the respective maritime security authorities to coordinate measures against smuggling and trafficking at sea, the other two promote scientific research in the areas of meteorology, geology, geophysics, ecology and environmental change (*Taiwan News* 2018).

These incremental steps are important as they demonstrate closer Taiwan-Japan cooperation in the crucial area of maritime security. They could also feed into efforts to grow security and defence ties below the official level. For instance, shortly after Tsai's election a Taiwan-Japan-US 'Track II' dialogue was resumed, having lain dormant during the Ma years. At the meeting, for instance, ideas were exchanged concerning potential multilateral military exercises and operations including ROC armed forces training alongside its Japanese and US counterparts (Teufel Dreyer 2016: 606–07). Senior officials on both sides also called for greater military cooperation in the face of China's growing assertiveness in the region (ibid. 2018). At the Indo-Pacific Security Dialogue in Taipei in August 2018, for instance, security experts from Japan and the United States openly called for greater military cooperation, starting with security dialogues and cooperation in disaster relief and humanitarian assistance (*Kyodo News* 2018b). More concrete evidence of increased military cooperation could be seen in the active assistance to Taiwan's indigenous submarine building programme provided by retired Japanese naval engineers who had previously worked at Mitsubishi and Kawasaki, the companies building Japan's submarines (Vavasseur 2018).

Limitations remain

Despite a further deepening of Taiwan-Japan relations under the current Tsai government – mostly at the non-governmental and quasi-governmental level – obstacles to further improvements remain. Most significant is the fact that the 'depths of bilateral ties remains a derivative of Tokyo's relationship with Beijing' (Hornung 2018). While strong ties with Taiwan are important for the Japanese government, at present stable and peaceful relations with China rank higher in the hierarchy of foreign policy objectives. This makes more formal and consequential support for Taiwan challenging. For instance, despite Japan lifting its self-imposed ban on exporting weapons systems in 2014, it is unlikely that Tokyo will provide Taipei with 'big ticket' items such as its Soryu-class submarines; although, as noted above, more implicit technological support for Taiwan's ship and submarine building industry is likely.

In addition, Taipei and Tokyo also need to resolve a number of bilateral issues. One of these concerns the territorial disputes over the Senkaku/Diaoyu Islands, as well as Taiwan's dispute of Japan's claim to a 400,000-square-kilometer EEZ around the Okinotori Shima coral reef chain where Taiwan seeks access to fishing around the atoll, rather than claiming sovereignty. To manage the dispute surrounding the Senkaku/Diaoyu Islands, both sides in April 2013 concluded a civil fishery agreement which excluded the territorial seas around the islands. Similarly, while President Ma had tried to politicize an incident in April 2016 when Japan's coastguard detained a Taiwanese fishing vessel that was sailing too close to the Okinotori Shima EEZ (Teufel Dreyer 2016), the Tsai government moved to de-conflict the issue through negotiations, leading to the aforementioned 2017 MOU on maritime search and rescue near the atoll.

Another source of tension is the thorny issue of the Taiwanese 'comfort women' who were forced into sexual slavery by the Imperial Japanese Army in occupied territories during the Second World War. As previously discussed, although Japan's colonial history in Taiwan has not led to lasting historical animosities as is the case of China or the Republic of Korea (South Korea), Taiwanese governments still have attempted to elicit a Japanese apology, similar to the one Abe delivered to South Korea in 2015. While under President Ma the issue was pursued very publicly, the Tsai government has sought to quieten it down by working it through semi-diplomatic channels. The government did not support the unveiling of Taiwan's first 'comfort women' statue in Tainan in August 2018, a ceremony that had the approval of both the KMT and Ma (Focus Taiwan 2018).

A final problem concerns Taiwan's ban imposed in 2011 on importing Japanese food produced in the prefectures exposed to radiation during the Fukushima Daichii nuclear power plant disaster. Japan has been incensed at Taiwan's ban and has threatened to take Taipei to the World Trade Organization, which has already ruled against South Korea in a similar case. Finding a solution to this thorny issue was not helped by the Tsai government holding a referendum on maintaining the prohibition in November 2018; the referendum came out in support for the ban, making it more complicated to find a solution since it is legally binding (*Japan Times* 2019).

Conclusion

Japan is Taiwan's second most important strategic partnership, founded on geostrategic interests as well as historical and strong sociocultural ties. Indeed, in the context of a more contested East Asian environment, it can be argued that both sides will seek to further intensify their relationship. As China ramps up the pressure on Taiwan, Japan will look for ways to assure Taiwan's strategic and economic breathing space, not least since it is vital for its own survival and well-being. And in the event of the outbreak of major hostilities between China and Taiwan, it is quite likely that Taipei can count on Tokyo's support, particularly if the United States also gets involved.

That said, it is important to keep the limitations of the relationship in mind. Despite a predisposition towards strong and friendly bilateral ties, and in the absence of a major deterioration in its relations with China, Japan is unlikely to provide much closer formal support for Taiwan. While the Tsai government has, for instance, called for a government-government dialogue on security affairs in the face of China's pressure (Focus Taiwan 2019), the Abe government has resisted such initiatives presumably owing to concerns about China's reaction. Japan can thus not substitute for Taiwan's critical relationship with the United States in terms of security. Finally, the smooth sailing in the contemporary Taiwan-Japan relationship under DPP governments – where bilateral problems exist but have never led to a derailing of ties – could end should a more China-friendly KMT and a Japan-critical president return to power in 2020.

Note

1 The four-fold indebtedness, according to Kaya, refers to the special debt that Japan owed to Taiwan on account of Chiang Kai-shek opposing the abolition of the Imperial Household after 1945; Chiang being 'strict but generous' towards Japanese soldiers and civilians after Japan's surrender; Chiang having opposed the division of Japan into zones of occupation; and Chiang having given up the right of seeking reparation payments from Japan.

References

Agreement (2017) 'Agreement between the Taiwan-Japan Relations Association and the Japan-Taiwan Exchange Association on Cooperation and Mutual Assistance in Customs Matters'. Available at www.mof.gov.tw/File/Attach/1036/File_11538.pdf (accessed 8 February 2019).

Blazevic, Jason J. (2010) 'The Taiwan Dilemma: China, Japan, and the Strait Dynamic', *Journal of Current Chinese Affairs*, 39(4).

Bureau of Foreign Trade (2019) 'Taiwan-Japan Economic Relations', Ministry of Economic Affairs (Taiwan), 22 January. Available at www.trade.gov.tw/English/Pages/Detail.aspx?nodeid=2910&pid=652139 (accessed 8 February 2019).

Chen, Farn-shing, Mei-Tzy Chen and Chao-Jen Cheng (2012) 'A Study of the Students' Travel Japan Intentions from Departments of Applied Japanese in Taiwan after 311 East Japan Earthquake', *Journal of Information and Optimization Sciences*, 33(2–3).

Chen, Yo-Jung (2016) 'Taiwan Elections: An Opportunity for Japan?' *The Diplomat*, 29 January. Available at https://thediplomat.com/2016/01/taiwan-elections-an-opportunity-for-japan/ (accessed 8 February 2019).

China-Japan Joint Communique (1972) 'Joint Communique of the Government of Japan and the Government of the People's Republic of China', 29 September. Available at www.mofa.go.jp/region/asia-paci/china/joint72.html (accessed 7 February 2019).

China Post (2017) 'Tsai Congratulates Abe on Election Victory', 23 October. Available at https://chinapost.nownews.com/20171023-158884 (accessed 23 February 2019).

Chulow, Adam (2010) 'Introduction: Statecraft and Spectacle in East Asia: Studies in Taiwan-Japan Relations', *Japanese Studies*, 30(1).

Cole, J.Michael (2015) 'Better Get Used to It, China: Taiwan and Japan Will Get Closer', *The Diplomat*, 30 July. Available at https://thediplomat.com/2015/07/better-get-used-to-it-china-taiwan-and-japan-will-get-closer/ (accessed 8 February 2019).

Cutshall, Alden (1944) 'Taiwan (Formosa): Japan's Southern Base', *Journal of Geography*, 43(7): 247–257.

Deans, Phil (2001) 'Taiwan in Japan's Foreign Relations: Informal Politics and Virtual Diplomacy', *Journal of Strategic Studies*, 24(4).

Durdin, Peggy (1947) 'Terror in Taiwan', *The Nation*, 24 May. Available at www.taiwandc.org/hst-1947.htm (accessed 7 February 2019).

Gray, Colin S. and Geoffrey Sloan (1999) *Geopolitics and Geostrategy*, London: Frank Cass.

Grygiel, Jacub J. (2006) *Great Powers and Geopolitical Change*, Baltimore, MD: Johns Hopkins University Press.

Focus Taiwan (2018) 'Taiwan Still Pushing Japan on "Comfort Women" Issue: MOFA', 15 August. Available at http://focustaiwan.tw/news/aipl/201808150011.aspx (accessed 4 March 2019).

Focus Taiwan (2019) 'Tsai Calls for Taiwan-Japan Talks on Security', 2 March. Available at http://m.focustaiwan.tw/news/aipl/201903020010.aspx (accessed 3 March 2019).

Fraleigh, Matthew (2010) 'Japan's First War Reporter: Kishida Ginko and the Taiwan Expedition', *Japanese Studies*, 30(1).

Furukawa, Koji (2011) 'Bordering Japan: Towards a Comprehensive Perspective', *Journal of Borderlands Studies*, 26(3).

Hoppens, Robert (2018) 'Understanding Contemporary Japan-Taiwan Relations', *Taiwan Insight*, 14 July. Available at https://taiwaninsight.org/2018/07/14/understanding-contemporary-japan-taiwan-relations/ (accessed 8 February 2019).

Hornung, Jeffrey W. (2018) 'Strong but Constrained Japan-Taiwan Ties', Washington, DC: Brookings Op-Ed, 13 March. Available at www.brookings.edu/opinions/strong-but-constrained-japan-taiwan-ties/ (accessed 8 February 2019).

Japan News (2015) 'Abe Met with Taiwan's Lee in Tokyo', 27 July.

Japan Times (2017) 'Japan and Taiwan Sign Memorandum of Understanding for Search and Rescue, but Fishing Dispute Remains Unresolved', 20 December. Available at www.japantimes.co.jp/news/2017/12/20/national/japan-taiwan-sign-search-rescue-memorandum-understanding-fishing-dispute-remains/#.XHYEjpMza8o (accessed 15 February 2019).

Japan Times (2018) 'Former Taiwan President Lee Teng-hui Travels to Okinawa for World War II Memorial Event', 22 June. Available at www.japantimes.co.jp/news/2018/06/22/national/former-taiwan-president-lee-teng-hui-travels-okinawa-world-war-ii-memorial-event/#.XFy7yVwzbIU (accessed 8 February 2019).

Japan Times (2019) 'Taiwan Negotiating with Japan on 'Acceptable' Solution to Food Ban', 6 January.Available at www.japantimes.co.jp/news/2019/01/06/national/politics-diplomacy/taiwan-negotiating-japan-acceptable-solution-food-ban/#.XHxomJMzZZdg (accessed 3 March 2019).

Japanese Ministry of Foreign Affairs (n.d.) 'The Guidelines for Japan-U.S. Defense Cooperation'. Available at www.mofa.go.jp/region/n-america/us/security/guideline2.html (accessed 4 March 2019).

Kawashima, Shin (2018) 'The Great East Japan Earthquake and Japan-Taiwan Relations', *The Diplomat*, 12 April. Available at https://thediplomat.com/2018/04/the-great-east-japan-earthquake-and-japan-taiwan-relations/ (accessed 8 February 2019).

Ko, Shu-ling (2016) 'Focus: Japan-Taiwan Relations to "Warm-up" under Tsai's Presidency', *Kyodo News*, 6 June.

Ko, Shu-ling (2017) 'Update: Taiwan Changes Name of Semi-Official Body Overseeing Ties with Japan', *Kyodo News*, 15 May.

Kushner, Barak (2007) 'Nationality and Nostalgia: The Manipulation of Memory in Japan, Taiwan and China Since 1990', *International History Review*, 29(4).

Kushner, Barak (2010) 'Pawns of Empire: Postwar Taiwan, Japan and the Dilemma of War Crimes', *Japanese Studies*, 30(1).

Kyodo News (2016) 'Survey Shows Japan Remains Favorite Country for Taiwanese', 22 July.

Kyodo News (2017) '*Japanese Official's Visit to Taiwan Seriously Damages Ties*', *China Daily*, 29 March.

Kyodo News (2018a) 'Majority of Japanese Have Favorable Feelings Towards Taiwan: Poll', 28 December.

Kyodo News (2018b) 'Taiwan, Japan Should Strengthen Military Relations: Experts', 30 August.

Lam, Peng-Er (2004) 'Japan-Taiwan Relations: Between Affinity and Reality', *Asian Affairs: An American Review*, 30(4).
Lam, Willy (2004) 'Beijing's Reaction to East Asia's Changing Alliances', *China Brief*, 4(15).
Laskai, Lorand C. (2014) 'History and the Possibility of Taiwan-Japan Relations', *The Diplomat*, 12 September. Available at https://thediplomat.com/2014/09/history-and-the-possibility-of-taiwan-japan-relations/ (accessed 8 February 2019).
Reuters (2017) 'Japan Representative to Taiwan Says Bilateral Ties at Their Best', 3 January.
Rigger, Shelley (2017) 'Taiwan: Margin, Center, Node,' in Michael Szonyi (ed.) *A Companion to Chinese History*, Chichester: Wiley Blackwell.
Serchuk, V. (2013) 'Obama's Silence on Taiwan Masks Its Significance in U.S. Relations with China', *Washington Post*, 23 May. Available at www.washingtonpost.com/opinions/obamas-silence-on-taiwan-masks-its-significance-in-us-relations-with-china/2013/05/23/a1b40470-c243-11e2-914f-a7aba60512a7_story.html?utm_term=.592ef680e8ea (accessed 7 February 2019).
Taipei Economic and Cultural Office Miami (2012) 'Japan to Hold Activities to Thank Taiwan for Disaster Aid', 10 March. Available at www.roc-taiwan.org/usmia_en/post/2776.html (accessed 15 February 2019).
Taipei Times (2017) 'The Nation Looks to Start EPA Talks with Japan', 20 September. Available at www.taipeitimes.com/News/taiwan/archives/2017/09/30/2003679440 (accessed 8 February 2019).
Taipei Times (2018) 'Over 400 Foreign Dignitaries Arrive', 10 October. Available at www.taipeitimes.com/News/taiwan/archives/2018/10/10/2003702083 (accessed 8 February 2019).
Taiwan News (2018) 'Successful Taiwan-Japan Maritime Cooperation Talks Conclude in Tokyo', 28 December. Available at www.taiwannews.com.tw/en/news/3606253 (accessed 19 February 2019).
Taiwanese Public Opinion Foundation (2018) 'June 2018 National Poll Summary Report: Favourite Countries of Taiwanese People', Taipei: Taiwanese Public Opinion Foundation.
Tan, Andrew T. H. (2014) 'The Implications of Taiwan's Declining Defence', *Asia-Pacific Review*, 21(1).
Teufel Dreyer, June (2016) 'Taiwan and Japan in the Tsai Era', *Orbis*, 60(4).
Teufel Dreyer, June (2018) 'Security, Defence Cooperation Puts Japan-Taiwan Relations Back on Track', Foreign Policy Research Institute, 13 July. Available at www.fpri.org/article/2018/07/security-defense-cooperation-puts-japan-taiwan-relations-back-on-track/ (accessed 8 February 2019).
Thomas, Nicholas and Brad Williams (2017) 'Taiwan's Sub-National Government Relations with Japan: Post-1979 Developments', *Journal of Contemporary Asia*, 47(1).
Tiezzi, Shannon (2014) 'To Counter Beijing, Japan Moves Closer to Taiwan', *The Diplomat*, 20 February. Available at https://thediplomat.com/2014/02/to-counter-beijing-japan-moves-closer-to-taiwan/ (accessed 8 February 2019).
Treaty of Peace with Japan (1951) Signed in San Francisco on 8 September. Available at https://treaties.un.org/doc/publication/unts/volume%20136/volume-136-i-1832-english.pdf (accessed 7 February 2019).
Treaty of Shimonoseki (1895) Signed on 17 April. Available at https://china.usc.edu/treaty-shimonoseki-1895 (accessed 7 February 2019).

Vavasseur, Xavier (2018) 'Experts from Japan to Assist Taiwan with Submarine Project', NavyRecognition.com, 18 August. Available at www.navyrecognition.com/index.php/news/defence-news/2018/august-2018-navy-naval-defense-news/6450-experts-from-japan-to-assist-taiwan-with-submarine-project.html (accessed 8 February 2019).

Wang, Amy (2017) 'For Decades, No One Spoke of Taiwan's Hidden Massacre. A New Generation Is Breaking the Silence', *Washington Post*, 28 February. Available at www.washingtonpost.com/news/worldviews/wp/2017/02/28/for-decades-no-one-spoke-of-taiwans-hidden-massacre-a-new-generation-is-breaking-the-silence/?noredirect=on&utm_term=.9bd5d41b9b78 (accessed 7 February 2019).

Yeh, Joseph (2016) 'Japanese Officials' Congrats to Tsai Signify "Cordial Ties"', *China Post*, 22 January. Available at https://chinapost.nownews.com/20160122-23222 (accessed 25 February 2019).

10 Taiwan's foreign policy

Sheryn Lee

Introduction

Taiwanese foreign policy is often characterized by some observers as changing according to its incumbent political parties. The Kuomintang (KMT – Chinese National Party) is pro-China and will push for unification with mainland China, while the Democratic Progressive Party (DPP) is incrementally pushing for de jure independence. However, such interpretations do not examine the long-term foreign policy objectives of the Republic of China (ROC, or Taiwan) and how they are intricately tied to the consolidation of its liberal democracy and increasingly Taiwanese-identifying electorate. Following the KMT's retreat to Taiwan in 1949 until today, the objective of the Taiwanese nation has been its survival with an independent political identity. The transition to developed status, constitutional reform and democratization has enabled the development of an identity that is distinct from that of mainland China. This democratic capitalist identity has evolved alongside the growing identification by ROC citizens as 'solely Taiwanese' – forming the basis of a de facto independent sovereign nation-state. Taiwan's foreign policy since the ending of martial law in 1987 has followed a pragmatic approach to ensure the survival of Taiwan's de facto independence, and by extension the maintenance of the cross-Strait status quo.

Taiwan's foreign policy objectives are guided by two principles. First, promoting the strength of its democracy and its importance as an ideological like-minded partner to major powers such as the United States and Japan. Second, and related to this, ensuring Taiwanese independence as a democratic and liberal nation has geostrategic significance for the region. The ROC administers the outer islands that lie in close proximity to the People's Republic of China (PRC, or China), including Penghu, Wuqiu, Kinmen and Matsu; it is approximately 59 nautical miles to Japan's Ryukyu island chain (Yonaguni Island); it controls the Pratas Islands, Itu Aba and Chung-Chou reef in the South China Sea; and has overlapping historical claims to the Senkaku/Diaoyu, Paracel and Spratly island chains. Taiwanese Presidents Chen Shui-Bian, Ma Ying-jeou and Tsai Ing-wen have utilized these principles to varying degrees to ensure the survival of Taiwan and the control of its territories. In particular, the current President Tsai has promoted Taiwan's value to the international community as a vibrant Asian democracy at a time when strongmen – such as Philippine President Rodrigo Roa Duterte and Thai Prime Minster and Head of National Peace and Order Maintaining Council Gen. Prayuth Chan-ocha – have become dominant in former American partner states. Tsai has actively moved away from 'chequebook diplomacy', understanding that such an approach only works on a limited scale with developing economies. Building on her predecessors' advancement of substantial yet unofficial relations, Tsai has focused on promoting Taiwan's value to the liberal order, upgrading existing ties with major powers such as the United States, India and Japan, and investing in smaller projects and people-to-people relations with South-East Asia.

This chapter examines three key dynamics. First, the domestic determinants of Taiwan's foreign policy. The Taiwanese electorate has vested issues in the survival of its political system, and the long-term resilience of Taiwan's democracy is having a significant impact on its foreign policy. Even though the current Taiwanese electorate votes substantially on local issues, such votes unwittingly have a signalling effect on the direction of Taiwanese foreign policy to its neighbours, in particular Beijing. Thus, Taiwanese foreign policy is influenced by the vested interests of three actors: the Taiwanese electorate, Washington and Beijing. Therefore, second, it examines China-US relations and the major influence that this geostrategic context has had on the development of Taiwanese foreign policy. It also examines how this has led to the greater diversification of partners, in particular Japan and South-East Asia. Finally, the chapter concludes with the implications for Taiwan's evolving foreign policy. The long-term outlook of cross-Strait relations demonstrates that Taiwanese foreign policy has been successful in strengthening its bonds with the United States and its friends and allies in Asia, thus allowing Taiwan to maintain its de facto independence. Yet this is occurring at a time of intensifying China-US strategic competition and an increasingly belligerent and authoritarian Beijing. This is incrementally altering the cross-Strait status quo, and decreasing the possibility of a 'peaceful reunification' between China and Taiwan.

The electorate's impact on Taiwanese foreign policy

As Legg and Morrison have argued, 'the most fundamental source of foreign policy objectives is perhaps the universally shared desire to ensure the survival and territorial integrity of the community and state' (1991: 62). Here foreign policy is defined as the 'sum of official external relations conducted by an independent actor', and a 'purposive action, on behalf of a single community'. For foreign policy to work well it 'needs to ensure both that diplomats, the military and domestic civil servants are pulling in the same direction, and that strategy is coordinated with "like-minded" countries' (Hill 2016: 4, 296). Thus, the making of foreign policy demonstrates the 'two-level game' between domestic and international developments, and the 'inevitability of domestic conflict about what the 'national interest' requires' (Putnam 1988: 460). 'Diplomatic tactics and strategies are constrained simultaneously by what other states will accept and what domestic constituencies will ratify' (Moravcsik 1993: 4). Particularly in the case of Taiwan, domestic actors are active participants in foreign policymaking and conversely foreign policy actively shapes the geostrategic situation that domestic actors respond to.

Many governments face political division and partisanship; however, Taiwan has the added complexity of a mixed national and ethnic identity, lasting cultural influence from Japanese colonization (1895–1945), and an unsettled sovereign status (see Lam 2004). Taiwan's de facto independence status has been supported since the 1940s – the ROC was promoted as the '"free" capitalist alternative to Communist China and supported financially and politically by the United States of America' (Dillon 2018: 187). The election of Lee Teng-hui in Taiwan's first direct, democratic presidential election in 1996 was significant – under the imposed rule of KMT martial law (1945–87), the local majority of Taiwanese people (approximately 85 per cent) felt oppressed under what they termed the 'White Terror' (Kan 2010: 1). Furthermore, during the Cold War – and especially during the Korean War – 'the PRC was the enemy, the United States was seen as the protector of Taiwan and Japan was an ally' (Dillon 2018: 187).

Taiwan's older generation have a living memory of authoritarian abuse during the period of martial law. Moreover, many Taiwanese now observe the strengthening of Communist Party of China (CPC) authoritarianism under President Xi Jinping, the dismantling of Hong Kong's democratic system, the suffocation of civil liberties in the autonomous zones of Hong Kong, Macau and Xinjiang, and Beijing's increased censorship and surveillance of its own citizens. Such an authoritarian regime has no appeal to the Taiwanese government and its citizens. Taiwan's pro-democracy reforms introduced in 1987, the creation of a stable and competitive party system, and the five successfully administered democratic elections since 1996, have led to mass public support for Taiwanese democracy and the consolidation of the country as a liberal democracy. Findings from a 2016 study demonstrated that:

- Satisfaction with democracy and feelings of external political efficacy are now almost at the same level as established democracies;
- Levels of party identification are increasing;
- Partisanship is higher among the young than in any comparable countries; and
- The relative absence of protest or anti-system parties reflects the stability of intraparty competition.

(McAllister 2016: 56–67)

Consequently, Taiwanese presidents and their administrations are beholden to an electorate with a vested interest in remaining a democracy. Both the KMT and the DPP have a mutual interest in the survival of the cross-Strait status quo which tacitly maintains the ROC's de facto independence. In 2018 polls by the Election Study Center at National Chengchi University, 47 per cent of interviewees identified as independent compared to 25 per cent for the KMT and 22 per cent for the DPP. Furthermore, 56 per cent identify as solely Taiwanese, compared to 37 per cent who identify as both Taiwanese and Chinese, and 4 per cent as solely Chinese. When considering the unification-independence stances, 33 per cent wish to maintain the status quo and decide upon it at a later date, 24 per cent wish to maintain the status quo indefinitely, and 16 per cent wish to maintain the status quo and move towards independence. Those who wish for unification represent 19 per cent of those polled, with 5 per cent wishing to push for independence as soon as possible (Election Study Center 2018). The combination of a large proportion of swing voters who identify solely as Taiwanese yet have uncertain views on independence and unification is having an effect on the formation of foreign policy, in particular relations with Washington and Beijing.

There is also a strong and vibrant civil society whose votes on local issues often affect the perception of a fluctuating Taiwanese foreign policy. Voter turnout is often high, particularly in presidential elections in which an average of 75–80 per cent of citizens vote. Of those who are eligible to vote, the turnout rate increases with age (up to 65). Furthermore, 84–86 per cent of those with a low level of political knowledge turn out to vote and 90 per cent of those with a high level of political knowledge turn out to vote . However, there are no strong differences in electoral participation between Taiwan's sub-ethnic groups who identify as either Taiwanese only or Chinese only (Wu and Li 2017: ch. 2; Berdiev and Chang 2013). Consequently, elections are considered an adequate barometer of sentiments towards the incumbent administration. For instance, despite a landslide presidential election win in 2016, in 2018 the DPP suffered heavy losses in the 'nine-in-one' local elections (83 per cent voter turnout). The majority vote share for the KMT and the loss of DPP strongholds in Kaohsiung and Taichung reflected local dissatisfaction with the DPP's central administration as opposed to an endorsement of KMT.

This was mainly due to Tsai Ing-wen's painful but necessary reform agenda to address Taiwan's worsening demographic trends and increasing economic competition with mainland China. In particular, Taiwan's birth rate has been one of the world's lowest since 2011. Taiwan's rapidly ageing demography is having a negative impact on its workforce for its technology-based economy and on the Taiwanese armed forces. According to the ROC's National Development Council (NDC), negative population growth is expected to occur by 2020 at the earliest, and by 2065 the population will have fallen to between 16 and 18.8 million, which is 68–80 per cent of the 2018 population. In 2017 the old-age (65 years and over) population exceeded the young-age population (15–64 years of age), and Taiwan will become a 'super-aged' society by 2026. This is consequential to Taiwan's ability to leverage economic advantages and military effectiveness for national power. In 2018 the dependency ratio meant that every 100 inhabitants of working age population supported 38 dependents. By 2064 that number is expected to increase to 101.4 dependents (ROC National Development Council 2018a). For instance, in June 2018 the DPP legislated unpopular but much needed pension reforms which reduced pensions to military veterans, civil servants and public school teachers. Such reforms had been discussed by Tsai Ing-wen's predecessors, Chen Shui-bian and Ma Ying-jeou, and were considered necessary to avert 'pension bankruptcy' in a super-ageing society.

Despite the negative outcome for Tsai's centrist agenda, it must be remembered that she won the general election in a landslide victory with the overwhelming popular vote in the 2016 presidential and legislative elections. The then-ruling KMT also endured a significant defeat in the 2014 'nine-in-one' elections. Such electoral changes led some observers to consider the result a litmus test for the DPP's China policy (see, for example, Hwai 2018). However, the consecutive rotations of power between rival political parties and vocal opposition and civil society are reflective of stable democratic consolidation. The outcome fits a long-term trend of the assertion of Taiwan's distinct political system in comparison to the increasingly autocratic CPC-led mainland China. Indeed, a 2018 survey demonstrated that 86 per cent of Taiwanese young people support the democratic political system, with 70 per cent saying they would fight for Taiwan if China attempted to achieve unilateral unification through military force (see results in Shih 2018).

Overall, the consolidation of Taiwan's democratic system not only affects the ability of Taiwan's citizens to express their political preferences, but it also impacts China-US relations and consequently the Asian balance of power. The successful Taiwan model has proved Chinese culture to be compatible with democracy. The principles of a free market, good governance and the rule of law have also increased American business operations in Taiwan, and in 2018 Taiwan was the 11th largest two-way trading partner with the United States (US Census Bureau 2018). In the 2018 *Soft Power 30* report, Taiwan ranks fifth in Asia – just one place behind China as it is significantly hampered with a low engagement score (McClory 2018: 90). The 2018 *World Press Freedom Index* ranked Taiwan 42nd in the world (the highest in Asia) – compared to 45th for the United States, 67th for Japan, and 176th for China. Thus, dealing with Taiwan's democracy has proved to be the most complex issue for the CPC in managing cross-Strait relations. Beijing's charm offensive of economic agreements has not achieved its objective of persuading the Taiwanese people of the benefits of unification with the mainland. Moreover, the existential threat and hostility from the Chinese communist regime towards a democratic and free Taiwan has weakened ethnic divisions and resulted in high voter turnouts in national elections to vote on the diplomatic and economic policies related to cross-Strait conciliation and conflict (McAllister 2016: 57). For the Taiwanese electorate there are compelling narratives to remain a distinct political entity from the CPC and this has had a profound effect on Taiwanese foreign policy. Consequently, any moves to alter the status quo and move towards unification needs the consent of the Taiwanese people. The living memory of martial law, generations of democratic practice, and the observation of Beijing's increasingly authoritarian practices in its autonomous provinces have raised critical concern over China's vision of 'one country, two systems' (see Table 10.1).

Table 10.1 Key concepts for Taiwan foreign policy

Term	Meaning
One China	According to the PRC, 'there is only one China in the world, Taiwan is a part of China and China's sovereignty and territorial integrity is not to be separated'. For its diplomatic partners, the PRC adds the conditions that the PRC is 'the sole legitimate government representing the whole of China', and agrees not to maintain diplomatic relations with Taiwan (State Council of the People's Republic of China 2000).
1992 Consensus	The Ma Ying-jeou administration reached tentative accommodation with the PRC on One China by agreeing to the 1992 Consensus. This refers to an informal agreement in November 1992 between the PRC's Association for Relations Across the Taiwan Strait (ARATS) and Taiwan's Straits Exchange Foundation (SEF) that 'both sides of the Taiwan Strait adhere to the one-principle' with the understanding that each side has differing interpretations of what One China means (Lawrence and Morrison 2017: 38). That is, 'both Beijing and Taipei agree that Taiwan belongs to China but they disagree on which entity is China's legitimate governing body' (Albert 2018).
One country, two systems	A term coined in 1979 by Deng Xiaoping, it proposes that mainland China continues to be governed by a 'socialist' system, whereas Taiwan can maintain its capitalist system for a longer term. It proposes that after 'reunification,' Taiwan will become a 'special administrative region'—having its 'own administration and legislative powers, an independent judiciary, and the right of adjudication of the island' (Deng 1984).
Three US-PRC joint communiqués	A set of formal statements jointly issued by the United States and China which paved the way for the establishment of diplomatic relations between America and the PRC: 1. 1972: acknowledges that there is one China and Taiwan is a part of that China. It reaffirms the US' commitment to the peaceful settlement of the Taiwan issue by 'the Chinese themselves.' 2. 1978: recognises the PRC as the sole legitimate government of China, and that US relations with Taiwan will be unofficial only. 3. 1982: states that the United States 'does not seek to carry out a long-term policy of arms sales to Taiwan ... and that it intends to gradually reduce its sale of arms to Taiwan, leading, over a period of time to a final resolution' (American Institute in Taiwan 2017a).

Term	Meaning
The Six Assurances	In explaining the 1982 communiqué to the House and the Senate, the then Assistant Secretary of State John H. Holdridge included a statement of six assurances that corresponded to then President Reagan's private assurances to Taiwan: 1. There is no agreed end date for US arms sales to Taiwan. 2. There is no mediation role for Washington between Taiwan and the PRC. 3. The United States will not exert pressure on Taiwan to enter into negotiations with the PRC. 4. There has been no change in Washington's 'long-standing position on the issue of sovereignty over Taiwan'. 5. There are no planned revisions to the Taiwan Relations Act. 6. The United States has not agreed to engage in prior consultations with Beijing on arms sales to Taiwan (US Congress 2016: 4–5).
1979 Taiwan Relations Act	The Taiwan Relations Act provides a legal basis for unofficial US-Taiwan relations and provides commitments to Taiwan's security. Washington's support is focused on arms sales to 'enable Taiwan to maintain a sufficient self-defence capability'. In 1997 it broadened to include dialogues, training, military education opportunities, and support for other 'non-hardware aspects of military capability' (American Institute in Taiwan 2017b).
Strategic ambiguity	The cornerstone US policy towards cross-Strait relations. Due to Washington's commitment to the One China policy, the three joint communiqués, the Six Assurances, and the Taiwan Relations Act, it leaves open the possibility of how and when the United States would defend Taiwan in the case of a potential Chinese attack. It is 'intended to deter the PRC from attacking Taiwan and to deter Taiwan from taking actions that might provoke a PRC attack' (Lawrence and Morrison 2017: 9).
Cross-strait status quo	For most Taiwanese, the status quo means that Taiwan maintains its de facto independence, and is neither a part of China nor an independent state. For Beijing, the status quo is understood as the 'one country, two systems' principle (Lee 2013: 80).

Facing China

Taiwan's foreign policy has to maintain a delicate balance: reassurances from Washington about its commitment to uphold a peaceful resolution to the cross-Straits issue; an increasingly belligerent Beijing that has issued threats to resolve the 'reunification' issue by force if necessary; and an electorate that has a vested interest in the continuation of Taiwanese independence and democracy. Such an approach maintains the core objective of Taiwanese survival and maintains its de facto independence.

Before proceeding, it is necessary to first clarify the key terms and policies that inform Taiwan-US-China relations:

The PRC's strategy towards Taiwan has been a formidable influence on its foreign policy since the end of the Chinese civil war (1945–49). After being defeated by Mao Zedong's CPC, Chiang Kai-shek's KMT was forced to retreat to Taiwan and established the ROC administration. It led to the realization of Taiwan's top foreign policy priority – 'Taiwan's continued survival would depend largely upon external military support' (Van Vranken Hickey 2007: 9). Both the PRC and the ROC asserted their claims as the sole legitimate authorities of China, and the competition for recognition led to active 'chequebook diplomacy' in the developing world, such as the South Pacific, Latin America and Africa (see Atkinson 2010). The ROC targeted anti-communist countries, while also directing energies to ensuring the US security guarantee.

Washington's change of recognition in 1972 to the PRC as the legitimate government of China was a great diplomatic setback for the KMT. The change in recognition – and other diplomatic setbacks such as American support for Japan's claim over the Senkaku Islands (Diaoyu Islands in Chinese) – led to Chiang Ching-kuo's period of reform and 'Taiwanization' (Rubenstein 2007: 438–41). This was a catalyst for 'innovative and creative adjustments designed to help Taiwan overcome some of the obstacles' it now had to confront as a 'unique actor' in the international system (Van Vranken Hickey 2007: 8). The loss of Washington as a diplomatic ally came at a time of isolation for Taiwan as it adhered to its own interpretation of the One China principle:

> When a country opted to recognize Beijing, Taipei would sever official relations with that country. Similarly, if an international organization chose to admit the PRC, the ROC would withdraw from it … [and] Taiwan gradually lost its international legitimacy as an independent country.
>
> (ibid.: 12).

Following Chiang's death, Taiwan pursued a more flexible approach to achieving the survival of the Taiwanese state and set Taipei on a path of pragmatism and the pursuit of 'unofficial' but substantive relations. Even though Washington signed onto the Three Joint Communiques and reaffirmed China's position on One China, it also reassured Taiwan through the Six Assurances and the Taiwan Relations Act – setting the 'strategic ambiguity' approach that continues to define Washington's cross-Strait policy (see Bernkopf Tucker 1998). The increasing domestic awareness of Taiwan's diplomatic isolation led to it seeking legitimacy through democratization –

martial law was lifted by Chiang Ching-kuo, and Taiwan entered a reform period under Lee Teng-hui. The 1995/96 Taiwan Straits Crisis proved to be a critical learning point for Beijing, as it demonstrated to the PRC that it had no tools to deter the passage of an American aircraft carrier through the Taiwan Strait (Zhao 1999: 117). This led to increased capability development by the PLA to prevent outside interference in what it considered its domestic affairs – this became the Anti-Access/Area Denial Strategy (Scobell and Nathan 2012: 141).

The first Taiwanese presidential administrations of DPP leader, Chen Shui-bian (2000–08), alarmed both Beijing and Washington as there was mutual concern lest there be a unilateral declaration of Taiwanese independence. This concern was also shared by the electorate, who rejected provocative initiatives that could have been perceived internationally as 'evoking their choice between the status quo and independence' (Hsu 2010: 693). Washington's signalling to Taipei – that it would not support Taiwan in the event of conflict if Taiwan unilaterally declared de jure independence – restrained Chen by increasing Taiwanese support for the status quo. During Chen's presidential term Beijing became aware of the two forces that influence Taiwan's independence stance – Taiwanese public opinion and the United States. This has influenced Chinese operations in Taiwan as Beijing has actively sought to garner Taiwanese popular support for unification and to use Washington as a 'lever to compel Taiwan to accept cross-Strait unification' (Tung 2005: 355, 359). Consequently, Taiwanese foreign policy moved away from formal independence to promoting the status quo as ensuring Taiwan's survival.

Under Taiwan's next President, the KMT's Ma Ying-jeou (2008–16), relations between Beijing and Taipei warmed, and consequently Washington relaxed over the prospect of cross-Strait conflict. This also coincided with a period during which the dominant belief prevailed in Washington that China could be socialized into the Western-led liberal order. However, the majority of Taiwanese citizens saw Ma's initiatives as 'selling' Taiwan to China. This sparked a series of political movements in Taiwan. In particular, the KMT's legislation of the 2010 Economic Cooperation Framework Agreement (ECFA) and the 2014 Cross-Strait Services Trade Agreement (CSSTA) were perceived by the majority of Taiwanese public opinion as making Taiwan's economy more dependent on China and severely weakening Taiwan's small and medium-sized enterprises (Lai 2018: 5). The legislation of the CSSTA sparked the Sunflower Movement – for the first time in Taiwanese history, tens of thousands of activists occupied the legislature for three weeks demanding transparency and a clause-by-clause review. The contentious agreement would have opened 80 Chinese service sectors to Taiwan, compared to 64 for Taiwan, including the telecommunications and construction sectors which are critical to the Taiwanese economy (Cole 2014). The wave of political activism blocked the CSSTA and stymied further efforts to liberalize cross-Strait trade. The Sunflower Movement also spawned new organizations emphasizing 'direct democracy, social justice, and Taiwanese identity', such as the New Power Party (Ho 2018). Like his predecessor, the KMT and Ma bore the cost of attempting to change the status quo without the consent of the Taiwanese people –the KMT lost the presidential election in 2016 to the DPP's Tsai Ing-wen.

Thus, Taiwanese foreign policy's goal of survival has transformed into maintaining the status quo. This involves a myriad of tasks: countering China's diplomatic pressure, economic inducements and military transformation; guaranteeing Washington's unofficial security commitment of the Taiwan Relations Act and the Six Assurances; and upgrading ties with partners such as Japan, South-East Asia and India. Indeed, under the Tsai administration and Xi's one-party rule, cross-Strait political dialogue is non-existent. Xi has demanded that Tsai accept the Chinese interpretation of the 1992 Consensus. The hardening of Xi's stance on Taiwan was further demonstrated at the 19th Party Congress at which he removed the last three points from the nine continuous elements of the CPC's Taiwan policy:

1. The guiding principle (*fangzhen*) of peaceful reunification of Taiwan according to the 'one country, two systems' formula and the eight-point proposal outlined by Jiang Zemin in 1995.
2. Adherence to the One China principle, the key point of which is that the territory of Taiwan is within the sovereign territory of China.
3. Strong opposition to separatism and Taiwan independence.
4. Willingness to have dialogue, exchanges, consultations, and negotiations with any political party that adheres to the One China principle.
5. Stress on the idea that the people on Taiwan and people on the mainland are 'brothers and sisters of the same blood'.
6. Establishing a connection between unification and the cause of 'the great rejuvenation of the Chinese nation'.
7. Placing hopes on the Taiwan people as a force to help bring about unification.
8. A promise that progress towards unification, and unification itself, will bring material benefits to Taiwan.
9. An expression of 'utmost sincerity' by Beijing toward the unification project.

(Quoted in Bush 2017; emphasis added)

In removing the condition of 'placing hopes on the Taiwanese people', Xi emphasizes that Beijing will place greater reliance on its own forces to achieve its unification objectives.

This has come at a time of Washington's hardening economic and security policies towards the PRC, and some positive steps forward for US-Taiwan relations. In 2017 and 2018 the White House approved two arms sales to Taiwan worth approximately US $1.7 billion. In 2018 the White House also signed the Taiwan Travel Act, which 'encourage[s] visits between US and Taiwanese officials at all levels' (US Congress 2018). Furthermore, the appointment of Randall Schriver as Assistant Secretary of Defense for Asian and Pacific Security Affairs raised the expectation of closer US-Taiwan foreign and security ties. However, intensifying China-US strategic competition has not changed Washington's overall cross-Strait policy of strategic ambiguity. When US President Donald Trump phoned Tsai on the occasion of his presidential election victory in December 2016, it broke diplomatic protocol, but just two months later, Trump affirmed the One China policy in a phone call with Xi, and Xi was later invited to Mar-a-Lago. The American Institute in Taiwan – the unofficial US embassy in Taiwan –maintains that it 'supports Taiwan's membership in international organizations that do not require statehood as a condition of membership' (American Institute in Taiwan 2018). Across Asia, Taiwan is not alone in its perception that Washington has not had credible engagement with Asia since before the Clinton Administration. This has led Taipei to increase its diversification of foreign partners with like-minded countries and to strengthen its ties to formal American allies.

Diversification

Foreign policy diversification aims to integrate Taiwan into the region to the degree that the diplomatic costs for the PRC of a unilateral 'reunification' would be too high. In President Tsai's October 2018 National Day address, she stated that

> I have consistently insisted on: Protecting the free and democratic way of life of our 23 million people; defending the sustainable development of the Republic of China; and maintaining cross-Strait peace and regional stability. These are the greatest common denominators among all the people of Taiwan, and every responsible politician and political party must defend them to the end. As the entire world is dealing with the expansion of Chinese influence, the government that I am leading will show the world Taiwan's strength and resilience. The best way to defend Taiwan is to make it indispensable and irreplaceable to the world. The people of Taiwan will never accept any attempt by external forces to unilaterally change the status quo in the Taiwan Strait. And the international community will never approve of and support the violation of universal values.
>
> (Tsai 2018)

Such a focus came at a time when diplomatic recognition of the ROC had dropped to 17 nations in 2018, down from 28 in 1990. Tsai's administration has lost São Tomé and Príncipe, Panama, the Dominican Republic, Burkina Faso and El Salvador. Furthermore, 'owing to its ambiguous sovereignty, Taipei faces unique hurdles when seeking to cultivate international partnerships' (Glaser *et al.* 2018: 61). This is mainly due to Chinese economic pressure to extract diplomatic and security concessions from developing states, which in the case of Taiwan means the switching of diplomatic recognition from the ROC to the PRC.

Due to its history of competing for international recognition, Taiwan's development assistance is a considerable instrument of its foreign policy and it is Taipei's mechanism for retaining diplomatic allies in the South Pacific, Central America and the Caribbean. However, there is growing recognition by both KMT and DPP legislators that the sums of foreign aid requested by these smaller developing nations to maintain diplomatic ties were not economically viable, especially compared to the offers from the PRC. Previous loans to Africa and South-East Asia to fund infrastructure investment faced the obstacle of Chinese pressure, meaning that such large projects and financial sums could not align with Taiwan's economic interests (Atkinson 2017: 266–67). In 2017 Taiwan contributed US $310 million in Official Development Assistance (ODA), which accounted for 0.05 per cent of its gross national income. In comparison, the PRC contributed $350 billion in development assistance between 2000 and 2014 (AidData 2018; ROC National Development Council 2018b). It is important to note that China's aid does not fit the standards of ODA as it is 'less concessional than that of other large players' and mainly consists of commercially oriented projects that seek to alleviate over-capacity in the Chinese economy. These figures consist of ODA, other official flows and vague official finance (AidData 2018). Moreover, issues of scope and scale must be taken into account. The ROC's aid is concentrated on its diplomatic partners and regional multilateral institutions, compared to the PRC's global reach of 140 countries and 4,300 projects in developing countries in Africa, Latin America, South Asia and South-East Asia.

Tsai's flagship programme is the 'New Southbound Policy' (NSP), which builds on previous initiatives by former Presidents Lee and Chen to redirect overseas investments into South-East Asia. Lee's two 'Go South' policies (1994–96 and 1997–99) and Chen's 'Go South' strategy (2002–08) also aimed to

> diversify Taiwan's outbound investment away from mainland China and into Southeast Asia. Yet the pull of Mainland China's economy, and in the case of Lee the fallout from the Asian financial crisis, left both of Tsai's predecessors achieving only limited success.
>
> (Glaser *et al.* 2018: 1)

Chen's foreign policy diversification emphasized the appeal of Taiwan's democracy and liberal norms – resonating well with developed democracies but less so in authoritarian and quasi-authoritarian regimes (Bing 2017: 120). Although Ma's administration faced criticism for decreasing expenditure on aid, its objectives remained consistent and reforms streamlined the programmes making them more efficient and less corrupt and prone to waste (Atkinson 2014: 427). Tsai's NSP focuses on long-term programme objectives in culture, education, business, science and technology with target countries of Australia, New Zealand, ten Association of Southeast Asian Nations

(ASEAN) countries, and six countries in South Asia (Bangladesh, Bhutan, India, Nepal, Pakistan and Sri Lanka), This 'people-centred' approach serves as a base for cooperative benefits with partner countries, and there already has been some initial success in increasing tourism and agricultural cooperation from NSP target countries. As of 2018, ASEAN was Taiwan's second highest trading partner (after China and before the United States, Japan and the European Union – EU).

A key partner in South-East Asia is Singapore – 29 per cent of Taiwan's ASEAN trade is with Singapore and it is the only country in Asia with a free trade agreement (FTA) with Taiwan (apart from the ECFA and an FTA with New Zealand). Singapore's founding Prime Minister, Lee Kuan Yew, had close relations to both Chiang Kai-shek and his son, Chiang Ching-kuo, and since 1975 Singapore and Taiwan have had military relations. Under an agreement known as 'Project Starlight', Singaporean armed forces train in Taiwan due to the limited land and airspace available in Singapore. In 2016 China impounded nine Singaporean troop-carrying vehicles in Hong Kong after they had been used for training exercises in Taiwan. The Chinese Ministry of Foreign Affairs demanded that Singapore should abide by the One China principle, abstain from official contact and suspend the military training exercises (quoted in Emmerson 2018: 79). In effect, China rebuked Singapore for its neutral position on Taiwan. The vehicles were eventually released to Singapore by 2017; however, the episode did not change any of Singapore's foreign policy and officials emphasized to Beijing Singapore's sovereign right to conduct military training wherever it deemed appropriate (quoted in Liu 2017).

Tsai is also consolidating Taiwan's existing relations with other major liberal democratic powers. A key partner in the region is Japan, which shares a similar geostrategic outlook on China's military transformation and the perception of US decline in Asia. Despite unofficial diplomatic ties there has been a proliferation of sub-national government agreements, and there are continually growing socio-economic relations. Japan remains Taiwan's second largest trading partner and Taiwan is Japan's fifth largest trading partner. In 2018 Japan was the fourth largest source of foreign direct investment (FDI) in Taiwan, and Japanese and Taiwanese companies actively cooperate in the manufacturing of semi-conductors, electronics and electrical products. A landmark deal was the 2013 fisheries agreement in the Senkaku Islands (Diaoyu Islands in Chinese). It established regulations in Japanese and Taiwanese fishery operations by creating an 'exemption zone' and a 'special cooperation zone' in part of the disputed exclusive economic zone covering the area between the Senkaku/Diaoyu Islands, the Yaeyama and Miyako Islands at the southern end of the Ryukyu island chain, and Taiwanese waters. As per the bilateral fisheries pact, each government regulates its fishermen in the area. In 2015 it reached another landmark amendment to expand the time available to fishermen to cast their nets and increased the required distance between fishing vessels in order to prevent collisions and conflicts over access to fish stock. This agreement has angered Beijing – it argues that Japan is utilizing Taiwan's geography to secure its own access to critical energy and transport routes and to support its naval strategy. In 2017 Japan also changed its unofficial embassy name from the Interchange Association to the Japan-Taiwan Exchange Association; and in turn Taiwan changed the name of its Japan relations agency from Association of East Asian Relations to the Association of Taiwan-Japan Relations. Beijing expressed dissatisfaction by urging Japan to uphold the One China principle.

Beyond Asia, Taiwan is also growing its economic relations and policy cooperation with the EU. The EU established its trade office in Taiwan in 2003, and the EU has a chronic trade deficit with Taiwan due to Taiwan's critical place in the global supply chain. The EU exports to Taiwan semi-finished products, machinery and equipment for Taiwan's service, manufacturing, telecommunications and transport equipment industries. In 2018 Taiwan became the EU's 15th largest trading partner – it is sixth in Asia – with total two-way trade reaching a value of US $52 billion. The EU was also the largest investor in Taiwan, with a FDI stock of $51 billion in 2017 and accounted for 43 per cent of all inbound investment into Taiwan due to Taiwan's electronic and manufacturing sector. The EU and Taiwan also have increased their policy coordination over human rights, climate change, gender equality, social welfare and poverty alleviation (see European Economic and Trade Office 2018). At the parliamentary business and social level, Taiwan's relations with the EU and its member states are growing. Moreover, the EU has become more outspoken in expressing support for the shared values that underpin Taiwan's democratic governance, and in 2018 the EU held its first human rights policy consultations with civil society organizations in Taiwan. The EU –alongside the United States, Japan and Canada – also publicly support Taiwan's participation as an observer at the World Health Assembly.

Consolidating these relations are part of Tsai's broader platform to highlight Taiwan's international value as an Asian liberal democracy. As a way to circumvent China's diplomatic isolation, Taiwan has turned to digital diplomacy to promote itself to the international community. In 2017 Tsai revived her Twitter account and posts Taiwan's foreign policies and international priorities almost exclusively in English and occasionally in Japanese. The Ministry of Education also increased the level of English teaching in schools as well as the number of bilingual schools in Taiwan. In 2019 English became an official language in Taiwan and efforts are being made to achieve a level of bilingualism similar to that found in Hong Kong and Singapore. This initiative is designed to increase Taiwan's international competitiveness as well as to improve the ease of conducting business in Taiwan. In addition, after long-standing requests, in 2018 Taiwan's department of cyber security announced that it would share data with private companies concerning Chinese state-based hacking attacks on Taiwanese computers. There are so many such attacks that Taiwan is capable of tracing malware back much further and spotting more iterations due to Chinese testing in Taiwan prior to their usage on a global scale. The measure aims to boost the training of artificial intelligence software designed to predict and prevent future cyber attacks (Hille 2018).

Implications

Taiwan's foreign policy has achieved its objectives to ensure the survival of the ROC's de facto independence, its democratic system of governance and Taiwanese identity. The democratic consolidation of Taiwan as a two-party system means that both the KMT and the DPP share a mutual interest in maintaining the cross-Strait status quo and preventing unilateral 'reunification' by the PRC. Since President Lee came to power Taiwanese foreign policy has remained consistent. Over time, however, its approach has evolved to focus on its value to the international community as a liberal democracy in Asia with geostrategic and economic significance. This has meant increasing sub-national and unofficial engagement with major extra-regional powers such as the United States, Japan, ASEAN and the EU, while streamlining its aid programme to focus on reliable diplomatic allies in the South Pacific and Central America.

There are three key implications for cross-Strait relations:

- Despite Taiwan's ambiguous standing in the international community and increasing economic, political and strategic pressure from Beijing, its foreign policy has remained consistent. Both the KMT and the DPP will continue to have a shared interest in continuing Taiwan's current foreign policy approach, maintaining American guarantees for the Six Assurances and the Taiwan Relations Act, while strengthening its sub-national and unofficial ties with major powers with common interests, such as Japan.
- The prolonging of the cross-Strait status quo advantages the maintenance of Taiwan's de facto independence and the survival of the ROC. Taiwan's democratic consolidation and the Taiwanese electorate complicates the PRC's interpretation of the One China principle and its chances for a 'peaceful reunification'. The authoritarian consolidation of control by President Xi and the lack of success from its financial diplomacy could result in the PRC taking more coercive measures towards Taiwan to accept 'one country, two systems'.
- Increasing Taiwan's integration into the region and expanding its relations to countries and organizations with similar democratic values and ideologies raises the diplomatic cost for China to achieve unilateral 'reunification'. However, such long-term objectives are subject to Taiwan's electoral cycle. Votes for either the DPP or the KMT have an unwitting signalling effect on the status of cross-Strait relations and could potentially disrupt successful foreign policy initiatives that ensure Taiwan's survival.

References

AidData (2018) *By the Number's China's Global Development Footprint*. Available at www.aiddata.org/china-official-finance (accessed 3 December 2018).

Albert, E. (2018) 'China-Taiwan Relations', Council on Foreign Relations, 15 June. Available at www.cfr.org/backgrounder/china-taiwan-relations#chapter-title-0-2 (accessed 3 December 2018).

American Institute in Taiwan (2017a) *Key US Foreign Policy Documents for the Region: US-PRC Joint Communique on Arms Sales (the 1982 Communique); US-PRC Joint Communique on the Establishment of Diplomatic Relations (Normalization Communique); and US-PRC Joint Communique*. Available at https://web-archive-2017.ait.org.tw/en/key-documents.html (accessed 7 December 2018).

American Institute in Taiwan (2017b) *Key US Foreign Policy Documents for the Region: Taiwan Relations Act (PL 96–8)*. Available at https://web-archive-2017.ait.org.tw/en/key-documents.html (accessed 7 December 2018).

American Institute of Taiwan (2018) 'Current Issues', *AIT: Policy and History*. Available at www.ait.org.tw/our-relationship/policy-history/ (accessed 7 December 2018).

Atkinson, J. (2010) 'China-Taiwan Diplomatic Competition and Pacific Islands', *Pacific Review*, 4(23): 407–427.

Atkinson, J. (2014) 'Aid in Taiwan's Foreign Policy: Putting Ma Ying-Jeou's Aid Reforms in Historical Perspective', *Pacific Review*, 27(3): 409–431.

Atkinson, J. (2017) 'Comparing Taiwan's Foreign Aid to Japan, South Korea and DAC', *Journal of the Asia Pacific Economy*, 22(2): 253–272.

Berdiev, A. N. and C. P. Chang (2013) 'Explaining Vote Turnout in Taiwanese Legislative Elections', *International Economic Journal*, 27(4): 645–661.

Bernkopf Tucker, N. (1998) 'China-Taiwan: US Debates and Policy Choices', *Survival*, 4(40): 150–167.

Bing, N. C. (2017) 'Taiwan's Go South Policy: Déjà Vu All Over Again?' *Contemporary Southeast Asia*, 39(1): 96–126.

Bush, R. C. (2017) 'What Xi Jinping Said About Taiwan at the 19th Party Congress', Washington, DC: Brookings Institution, 9 October. Available at www.brookings.edu/blog/order-from-chaos/2017/10/19/what-xi-jinping-said-about-taiwan-at-the-19th-party-congress/ (accessed 3 December 2018).

Cabestan, J. P. (2011) 'European Views on EU-Taiwan Relations and Taiwan's Economic and Geostrategic Importance', paper presented at *Taiwan's Future in the Asian Century: Toward a Strong, Prosperous and Enduring Democracy Conference*, Washington, DC: American Enterprise Institute, 10 November.

Cole, J. M. (2014) 'Sunflowers in Springtime: Taiwan's Crisis and the End of an Era in Cross-Strait Cooperation', *China Brief*, 14(7), April. Available at https://jamestown.org/program/sunflowers-in-springtime-taiwans-crisis-and-the-end-of-an-era-in-cross-strait-cooperation/ (accessed 3 December 2018).

Deng, X. (1984) 'One Country, Two Systems', 22–23 June. Available at http://en.people.cn/dengxp/vol3/text/c1210.html (accessed 7 December 2018).

Dillon, M. (2018) *Lesser Dragons: Minority Peoples of China*, Reaktion Books, London.

Election Study Centre (2018) 'Important Political Attitude Trend Distribution', National Chengchi University, August. Available at https://esc.nccu.edu.tw/course/news.php?class=203 (accessed 3 December 2018).

Emmerson, D. K. (2018) 'China in Xi's "New Era": Singapore and Goliath?', *Journal of Democracy*, 29(2).

European Economic and Trade Office (2018) *EU-Taiwan Relations in 2018*, Taipei: European Economic and Trade Office.

Glaser, B. S., Kennedy, D. Mitchell and F. P. Funaiole (2018) *The New Southbound Policy: Deepening Taiwan's Regional Integration*, Washington, DC: CSIS China Power Project and Rowman & Littlefield.

Hill, C. (2016) *Foreign Policy in the Twenty-First Century*, 2nd edn, New York: Palgrave Macmillan.

Hille, K. (2018) 'Taiwan to Share Chinese Hacks Data with Private Companies', *Financial Times*, 23 October. Available at www.ft.com/content/e3e39f54-d5fc-11e8-a b8e-6be0dcf18713 (accessed 24 January 2019).

Ho, M. (2018) 'The Activist Legacy of Taiwan's Sunflower Movement', *Carnegie: Civic Research Network*, 2 August. Available at https://carnegieendowment.org/ 2018/08/02/activist-legacy-of-taiwan-s-sunflower-movement-pub-76966 (accessed 3 December 2018).

Hsu, S. P. (2010) 'Between Identity Quest and Risk Aversion: Lessons from the Chen Shui-bian Presidency for Maintaining Cross-Strait Stability', *Journal of Contemporary China*, 19(66): 693–717.

Hwai, L. S. (2018) 'Taiwan Awaits Results of Key Election Test for Pro-Independence Ruling Party', *Straits Times*, 24 November. Available at www.straitstimes.com/asia/ea st-asia/taiwan-votes-in-test-for-pro-independence-ruling-party-as-china-watches (accessed 12 May 2019).

Kan, S. A. (2010) *Democratic Reforms in Taiwan: Issues for Congress*, Congressional Research Service Report, R41263 (May).

Kuo, M. S. and Chen, H. W. (2017) 'The Brown Movement in Taiwan: Making Sense of the Law and Politics of the Taiwanese Same-Sex Marriage Case in a Comparative Light', *Columbia Journal of Asian Law*, 31(1), Fall, 72–149.

Lam, P. E. (2004) 'Japan-Taiwan Relations: Between Affinity and Reality', *Asian Affairs*, 30(4): 249–267.

Lee, S. H. (2018) 'Taiwan Awaits Results of Key Election Test for Pro-Independence Ruling Party', *Straits Times*, 24 November. Available at www.straitstimes.com/asia/ east-asia/taiwan-votes-in-test-for-pro-independence-ruling-party-as-china-watches (accessed 7 December 2018).

Lai, C. (2018) 'Dancing with the Wolf: Securitizing China-Taiwan Trade in the ECFA Debate and Beyond', *Asian Security* (February): 1–19.

Lawrence, S. V. and W. M. Morrison (2017) *Taiwan: Issues for Congress*, Congressional Research Service Report, R44996 (30 October).

Lee, S. (2013) 'China and Taiwan Relations: Challenges and Prospects', in Andrew T. H. Tan (ed.) *East and South-East Asia: International Relations and Security Perspectives*, Abingdon: Routledge.

Legg K. and J. Morrison (1991) 'The Formulation of Foreign Policy Objectives', in R. Little and M. Smith (eds) *Perspectives on World Politics*, London: Routledge.

Liu Z. (2017) 'Singapore-Taiwan Military Agreement to Stay in Place Despite Pressure from Beijing', *South China Morning Post*, 5 October. Available at https://www.scmp. com/news/china/diplomacy-defence/article/2114170/no-reason-singapore-cut-militar y-ties-taiwan-sources (accessed 24 January 2019).

McAllister I. (2016) 'Democratic Consolidation in Taiwan in Comparative Perspective', *Asian Journal of Comparative Politics*, 1(1): 44–61.

McClory, J. (2018) *The Soft Power 30: A Global Ranking of Soft Power 2018*, Los Angeles, CA: Portland and the USC Center on Public Diplomacy.

Moravcsik, A. (1993) 'Introduction: Integrating International and Domestic Theories of International Bargaining', in P. B. Evans, H. K. Jacobson and R. D. Putnam (eds) *Double-Edged Diplomacy: International Bargaining and Domestic Politics*, Berkeley: University of California Press.

Putnam, R. D. (1988) 'Diplomacy and Domestic Politics: The Logic of Two-Level Games', *International Organization*, 42(3), Summer, 427–460.

ROC National Development Council (2018a) 'Population Projections for the Republic of China (Taiwan): 2018–2065', Taipei: Department of Human Resources Development, September. Available at www.ndc.gov.tw/en/cp.aspx?n=2E5DCB04C64512CC&s=002ABF0E676F4DB5 (accessed 7 December 2018).

ROC National Development Council (2018b) *Taiwan Statistical Data Book 2018*, Taipei: National Development Council.

Rubenstein, M. A. (2007) *Taiwan: A New History*, 2nd edn, Armonk, NY and London: M. E. Sharpe.

Scobell, A. and A. J. Nathan (2012) 'China's Overstretched Military', *Washington Quarterly*, 25(4): 135–148.

Shih, H. (2018) 'Taiwanese People Willing to Fight for Democracy: Surveys', Focus Taiwan News Channel, 19 April. Available at http://focustaiwan.tw/news/aipl/201804190036.aspx (accessed 7 December 2018).

State Council of the People's Republic of China (2000) 'The One-China Principle and the Taiwan Issue', White Paper, Beijing.

Tsai, I. (2018) '2018 National Day Address', Taipei: Office of the President, ROC. Available at https://english.president.gov.tw/News/5548 (accessed 7 December 2018).

Tung, C. (2005) 'An Assessment of China's Taiwan Policy under the Third Generation Leadership', *Asian Survey*, 45(3): 343–361.

US Census Bureau (2018) 'Top Trading Partners – August 2018: Year-to-Date Total Trade', *Foreign Trade*, July. Available at www.census.gov/foreign-trade/statistics/highlights/top/top1808yr.html (accessed 7 December 2018).

US Congress (2016) 'Reaffirming the Taiwan Relations Act and the Six Assurances as Cornerstones of United States-Taiwan Relations', 114th Congress, Second Session, S. Con. Res. 28, 19 May, Washington, DC: Government Publishing Office.

US Congress (2018) 'H.R.535 – Taiwan Travel Act', 115th Congress (2017–2018). Available at www.congress.gov/bill/115th-congress/house-bill/535 (accessed 7 December 2018).

Van Vranken Hickey, D. (2007) *Foreign Policy Making in Taiwan: From Principle to Pragmatism*, London and New York: Routledge.

Wu, C. L. and Li T. P. (2017) 'Political Participation in Taiwan ', in C. H. Achen and T. Y. Wang (eds) *The Taiwan Voter*, Ann Arbor: University of Michigan Press. Available at https://quod.lib.umich.edu/u/ump/mpub9375036/1:12/--taiwan-voter?rgn=div1;view=fulltext.

Zhan, B. (2018) 'In Taiwan, the DPP's Loss Is China's Gain and a Setback for the US', CNN, 26 November. Available at https://edition.cnn.com/2018/11/25/opinions/taiwan-election-us-china-intl/index.html (accessed 7 December 2018).

Zhao, S. (1999) 'Changing Leadership Perceptions: The Adoption of a Coercive Strategy', in S. Zhao (ed.) *Across the Taiwan Strait: Mainland China, Taiwan, and the 1995–1996 Crisis*, New York and London: Routledge.

11 Taiwan's armed forces: development and prospects

Shang-Su Wu

Introduction

Taiwan's armed forces possess considerable capabilities that are superior to those of some its regional counterparts, and they also enjoy the advantage of geographic obstacles that can help to impede an external invasion, such as one by China. However, the modernization and expansion of the Chinese People's Liberation Army (PLA) have been formidable, and Taipei's response has not been adequate. This chapter examines whether Taiwan's armed forces are capable of defending the island in the face of China's rising military capability and the volatile political conditions on the island. Since the Republic of China (ROC, or Taiwan) is still the official name of the regime in Taiwan, the official names of its armed forces will be used in this chapter.

The current situation

The capabilities and structure of the ROC armed forces have been shaped in terms of the need to defend the island in the event of an invasion from across the Taiwan Strait, namely from China. After decades of evolution, Taipei's defence strategy has gradually developed into a three-dimensional defence strategy that includes air dominance, sea dominance and counter-landing, in contrast to the 'retaking the mainland' strategy of the Cold War. Although the Ministry of National Defense has carried out structural reforms since the 1990s, this three-dimensional strategy has determined the development of the three services since the Cold War, especially after Taiwan became internationally isolated in the 1970s. The ROC Air Force (ROCAF)'s aim is air superiority at least in its air defence by its fighter fleets and surface-to-air missile (SAM) units. The ROC Navy (ROCN) aims to protect Taiwan's sea lines of communication (SLOCs) and to prevent an invasion from the sea. The ROC Army aims to defend the country using anti-landing operations, along with other potential forms of further resistance in case of the failure to stop a foreign landing operation (Ministry of National Defense 2006: 99). In the 2017 edition of the government defence report, a similar strategy still prevails, expressed in a more refined term, namely layered defence (ibid. 2017c: 66–67). The report determines and guides the strategies and structures of the three services of the ROC armed forces.

The ROCAF is centred on fighters and surface-to-air missiles (SAMs) of varying size and capability. The fighter aircraft arm comprises 143 F-16A/B MLUs, 127 Indigenous Defence Fighters (IDFs), 55 Mirage 2000–05s and dozens of ageing F-5E/Fs, making a total of more than 350 aircraft. Taiwan's air force thus has more fourth-generation combat aircraft than its regional counterparts, including the Republic of Korea (South Korea), Japan, Australia and South-East Asian states, such as Singapore, Vietnam and Thailand (see Table 11.1) (IISS 2019: 250, 279, 286, 304, 309–10, 313, 316). These combat aircraft are also supported by six E-2T airborne warning and command aircraft (AWAC). In terms of SAMs, Taiwan has acquired more than 500 Patriot Advance Capability (PAC)-3 missiles, in addition to its indigenous Tien-Kung ('Sky Bow') I, II, III SAMs and other short-range models (Lostumbo et al. 2016: 4; Ministry of National Defense 2017c: 83–84). Aside from air defence, the ROCAF also possesses 12 P-3C anti-submarine warfare aircraft for supporting naval operations, 19 C-130H transporters for airlift operations, 19 H225 and S-70C utility helicopters for search and rescue missions, plus other assets for training and logistics, such as T-34 trainers and Beech-1900 aircraft (IISS 2018: 305). The current structure of the ROCAF has been maintained since the Cold War era, with minor improvements, such as anti-submarine warfare capabilities added in the late 1960s by the use of S-2A/E aircraft (SIPRI 2018).

Table 11.1 Comparison of combat aircraft owned by the ROCAF and those of its regional counterparts

Service	Aircraft	Notes
ROC Air Force (ROCAF)	143 F-16A/B, 127 IDF, 55 M-2000, ? F-5E/F. Total: about 350.	ROCAF possesses 87 F-5E/Fs, but some are in storage
Republic of Korea Air Force (ROKAF)	4 F-35A, 174 F-5E/F, 60 F-4E, 59 F-15K, 163 KF-16, 50 FA-50. Total: 510.	F-35 is joining the service
Japan Air Self-Defense Force (JASDF)	189 F-15J, 88 F-2A/B, 51 F-4EJ, 9 F-35. Total: 337.	F-35 will replace F-4
Royal Australian Air Force (RAAF)	71 F/A-18A/B, 24 F/A-18F, 10 F-35. Total: 105.	F/A-18A/B are being decommissioned
Republic of Singapore Air Force (RSAF)	60 F-16C/D, 40 F-15SG. Total: 100	
Vietnam People's Air Force (VPAF)	35 Su-30MK2, 11 Su-27SK/UBK, 27 Su-22M. Total: 73	
Royal Thai Air Force (RTAF)	24 F-5E/F, 53 F-16A/B, 11 JAS-39C/D. Total: 88.	

Source: IISS (2019: 250, 279, 286, 304, 309–310, 313, 316).

The ROCN is predominantly made up of surface vessels including major surface combatants, fast attack craft (FAC) and corvettes, amphibious ships, mine warfare vessels, as well as a small underwater flotilla and a Marine Corps. The submarine flotilla contains two Hai Lung (Zwaardvis)-class, and two Hai Shih (Guppy II)-class diesel-electric submarines. Four Keelung (Kidd)-class destroyers, ten Cheng Kung (Oliver Hazard Perry)-class, six Kang Ding (Lafayette)-class, and six Chin Yang (Knox)-class frigates are the major multi-purpose surface combatants for air defence, anti-submarine warfare and anti-ship missions. There are 31 Kwang Hua (KW)-class FACs, 11 larger Jin Chiang (JC)-class and one Tuo Jiang (TJ)-class corvette in service with more stealth TJ-class vessels expected to be commissioned. The nine mine warfare vessels were procured from Germany and the United States. The amphibious fleet is made up of one landing ship dock, eight landing ship tanks and 12 utility landing craft. Apart from the landing ships, the ROCN Marine Corps (ROCNMC) also has up to 90 AAV-7 amphibious vehicles for transporting troops to beachheads and to destinations further inland (IISS 2019: 308–09; SIPRI 2018). In addition to its regular naval assets, Taiwan also has a sizable coastguard with a dozen patrol ships having displacements of more than 1,000 metric tons, and numerous other small patrol boats (Coastguard Administration 2018).

The structure of the ROCN reflects various historical factors. Following the country's defeat by the communists during the Chinese civil war, the amphibious fleet and the ROCNMC represented offensive icons with which the ROC regime would 'retake the mainland'. Despite the offensive plan lacking feasibility, amphibious assets remain important for Taipei to supply its positions in the South China Sea and some offshore islands close to the Chinese coastline. By the same token, large surface combatants are required to escort supplies to those locations away from Taiwan, in addition to the need for them to operate in rough seas during the winter months (Sui 1994: 138). The major surface combatants are also expected to protect the SLOCs from China's sea denial capabilities during wartime. There is a need for larger and newer submarine units, but Taiwan's international isolation has constrained the likelihood of purchasing additional boats since its last deal with the Netherlands in 1982, as the domestic political deadlock in the 2000s ruined a rare opportunity to acquire submarines from the United States (Kan 2011: 33–47).

The structure of the ROCA reflects its concerns over island defence: six regular infantry brigades and 21 reserved brigades are in place for static defence, with four armoured, three mechanic infantry and two airborne brigades, including helicopters, in place for strikes on confirmed invasion locations (IISS 2019: 308). Some of these assets, such as attack helicopters, are formidable. The ROCA possesses a total of 90 attack helicopters, consisting of US-made AH-1Ws and AH-64Es, second only to the South Korean Army and more than Japan or any other South-East Asian counterpart (see Table 11.2). Other assets are mixed with some new acquisitions, such as indigenous CM-32 armoured personnel carriers (APC) and RT-2000 multiple-launch rocket systems (MLRS),

Table 11.2 Comparison of attack helicopters owned by the ROCA and its regional counterparts

Service	Attack helicopters	Notes
ROCA	61 AH-1W, 29 AH-64E. Total: 90.	
ROKA	60 AH-1F/J, 36 AH-64E. Total: 96.	
JGSDF	59 AH-1S, 11 AH-64D. Total: 71	OH-1 cannot be used for ground attack.
RAA	22 Tiger	
RSAF (Singapore)	19 AH-64D	
VPAF (Vietnam)	26 (?) Mi-24	
RTA (Thailand)	7 AH-1F	

Source: IISS (2018: 311, ibid. 2019: 249, 277, 284, 305, 311, 316).

However, legacy weapons systems from the Cold War, such as M60A3 and M48H main battle tanks (MBTs), M-113 APCs and even some from the Second World War, such as M-114 155mm howitzers, are still in service (IISS 2019: 249, 277, 284, 305, 311, 316, ibid. 2018, 311).

Despite their scale and capabilities, Taiwan's armed forces are not perceived to be comparable to their counterparts in China, a view that also reflects the public perception of the situation (Myers and Horton 2017). The negative perception of Taiwan's armed forces can be attributed to factors which are China-based and others which are not. The former refers to the PLA's rising capabilities which have significantly undermined Taiwan's defence capabilities, while the latter refers mostly to domestic factors within Taiwan.

The pale sky

During the past two decades it has been observed that the ROCAF has become incapable of dealing with both conventional and unconventional threats from the PLA. In the 1990s Taipei acquired three new types of combat fighter aircraft with beyond visual range (BVR) capability comprising mid-range air-to-air missiles (AAMs). These combat aircraft are supported by six E-2T AWACs that were acquired in the 1990s and 2000s. With such assets, Taipei temporarily created a certain qualitative and quantitative superiority over its counterparts across the Taiwan Strait. The PLA Air Force (PLAAF) and the PLA Naval Air Force (PLANAF) only had Flanker combat aircraft with BVR capabilities when the indigenous PL-12 AAM went into service in 2004, and they did not have AWACs until the mid-2000s (Shlapak 2013: 200; IISS 2003: 155, ibid. 2004: 172).

The trend shifted from the mid-2000s. Political deadlock in Taiwan impeded further modernization, such as the failed procurement of 66 F-16 C/Ds (Wolf 2010). Meanwhile, Beijing caught up with the large-scale production of its J-10s,

J-11s and J-16s, in addition to purchasing Russian Su-30MKs and Su-35s. By 2018 Beijing's total complement of fourth-generation fighters numbered 852. The PLANAF has also obtained an aircraft carrier that can launch air strikes from a mobile location, and there are plans for more carriers in the coming years. In the meantime, the number of Chinese AWACs and aerial refuelling aircraft has risen as well (IISS 2019: 238, 260–61).

China's unconventional tactics, which are aimed at neutralizing the ROCAF's capabilities, pose a more serious challenge to the ROCAF than the expansion of the PLAAF and PLANAF conventional capabilities. Despite the fact that Beijing has gradually established superiority in terms of the number of fighters and supportive capabilities that it possesses, it would take some time to annihilate Taipei's 300-plus fighters supported by an intensive SAM network. In contrast, disruption or even paralysis of ROCAF bases could facilitate immediate air superiority for China's air forces. Taiwan's SAM network is supposed to provide alternative air defence, but that too might fall prey to such unconventional tactics on the part of China (Lostumbo et al. 2016: 12–13). Once Beijing achieves air superiority, the ROCN and the ROCA would be vulnerable when conducting their missions.

Unconventional means for China to use against Taiwan's air power include the projection of firepower and sabotage. Since the early 1990s the PLA has deployed ballistic missiles succeeded by cruise missiles in the 2000s that can be aimed at ROCAF bases (Kagan 2007: 122; Center for Strategic and International Studies 2016; Office of the Secretary of Defense 2018: 101). Due to the width of the Taiwan Strait, many Chinese tactical projectiles with a range of 180 km and above are capable of striking Taiwanese airbases to the west of the Strait, whereas other bases to the east would be exposed to submarine-launched missiles and other kinds of munitions, such as air-to-surface missiles (ASMs) (Executive Yuan 2019). If the PLA adopts the concept of Russian container missiles and launches attacks from cargo ships offshore or even from Taiwanese ports, the warning time would be further shortened (Stott 2010). The use of such stand-off weapons with conventional warheads may not completely destroy airbases, but the disruption or paralysis caused by the initial salvos would considerably decrease or pause the ROCAF's capacity for launching interception sorties (Lostumbo et al. 2016: 5–6, 16–17; Office of the Secretary of Defense 2018: 29).

Beijing may also send special forces for sabotage purposes. Recent urbanization trends mean that most ROCAF bases are gradually being surrounded by civilian buildings which provide good cover for observation, sniping and other attacks using rockets, anti-tank missiles, improvized explosive devices (IEDs) and drones. Furthermore, appropriate espionage operations could lead to the successful penetration of bases and more effective sabotage. An even broader impact in terms of paralysis would be achieved if Chinese special forces were also to attack surveillance facilities and the chain of command (Lavender 2013: 14–15).

The impact from the ROCAF's loss of air superiority would be widespread. Taipei would have to make cautious use of its remaining fighters due to their vulnerability and inferiority vis-à-vis China's combat fighters, while the SAMs would also face conventional and unconventional attacks. Under such serious threats and without air superiority, other aspects of defence, such as protecting SLOCs and anti-landing operations, would prove more challenging for Taiwan. The ROCN's vessels would face airborne attacks and the ROCA's field air defence units would face serious challenges. The strategic consequence of the ROCAF's failure would therefore be devastating.

The ROCAF has responded to the challenges by developing offensive capabilities and modernizing its assets. The IDF fighters are armed with indigenous Wan Chien ('Ten Thousand Arrows') ASMs with a range of about 200 km, and the US-made AGM-154C and AGM-88B ASMs have a range of more than 100 km when fired from the air force's newly upgraded F-16Vs (Defence Update 2014; Defense Security Cooperation Agency 2017; Raytheon 2019a, 2019b). The air force also possesses other ground attack weapons, such as AGM-65G missiles and Paveway guided bombs, but their relatively short ranges would prove unsuitable for offensive missions and increase exposure of their aircraft to PLA countermeasures (IISS 2019: 310). Apart from airborne munitions, Taiwan also has land-attack cruise missiles, with the deployment of Hsiung Feng (HF)-IIE and the possibility of Yun Feng surface-to-surface missiles (SSMs) in the future (CSIS Missile Threat 2018). If Taipei is able to project firepower to the adjacent Chinese provinces, particularly airbases and other key military facilities, Beijing could either lose some of its forces during pre-emptive attacks or would have to use assembly locations further away from Taiwan. Either outcome would give Taiwan more time in which to respond, and present China with more challenges to achieve its strategic goals. Taiwan's offensive capabilities could also extend warfare to the Chinese territory, particularly to major cities such as Shanghai, thus having an economic as well as a psychological impact. Indeed, the recent shifting of the missile command to the ROCAF has made for improved integration of offensive capabilities (Ministry of National Defense 2017c: 72).

The ROCAF has also been modernizing both its fighter wings and the SAM network. The air force is upgrading its F-16A/Bs to F-16Vs, the IDFs have been modified from F-CK-1 A/B to C/D, and the Mirage-2000s have been overhauled (Chen 2018; Phipps 2018; Chin and Lo 2018). Furthermore, the planned procurement of 66 F-16Vs would enlarge the size of the fighter fleet (Yeo 2019). Such upgrades and purchases can be seen as short or medium-term measures, as Taipei has expressed interest in the new US-made F-35B vertical or short take-off and landing (V/STOL) combat aircraft (Ministry of National Defense 2017a: 44; Gady 2018). The ageing F-5E/Fs are expected to be replaced by a new indigenous advanced training aircraft, which is based on the IDF (Pocock 2017). The National Chung-Shan Institute of Science and Technology has also developed a range of SAMs, from the short-ranged Antelope, the mid-range Tienchien (Sky Arrow)–II, to the long-range Tienkung (Sky Bow) III. These are in addition to the US PAC-3 SAMs (Ministry of National Defense 2017c: 75, 79, 83–84).

Although Taiwanese defence planners have taken action to counter PLA threats to the ROCAF, their efforts may be inadequate. Upgrading three kinds of combat fighter aircraft through the acquisition of additional ones will indeed improve the air force's readiness and capability vis-à-vis its PLA counterpart; nonetheless, the acquisition of fifth-generation combat fighter aircraft will remain essential. Following previous deals with Australia, South Korea and Japan, selling F-35s to Taipei would be more acceptable to the United States and its regional allies. However, there are several obstacles that could prevent the ROCAF from obtaining the F-35s: first, the high unit cost which stands at around US $115.5 million for the B model with V/STOL capability, would discourage Taipei, which has an annual defence budget of less than $11 billion (Lockheed Martin 2018; IISS 2018: 302). Despite continued promises to increase the defence budget to 3 per cent of gross domestic product (GDP), in 2019 this goal remained far from reality (Teng 2018). Taiwanese decision makers could arrange a special budget for the acquisition F-35s, but opposition to this is likely in a volatile democracy. An incoming new administration in 2020 could push through the procurement order, while an opposition party with a majority of seats in the legislature or congress could reject such an expensive procurement. Ultimately, however, a key determining factor in the issue is whether Washington offers the F-35s and when that might occur. A major concern for Washington would be the frequent cases of espionage in the ROC armed forces leading to a high risk that classified information about the F-35 might be leaked to China (Mattis 2017). Even if a deal were to be struck, a decade for delivery and commission would be the likely timeframe (Lostumbo et al. 2016: 86). The ROCAF's continued inability to purchase fifth-generation F-35s would see it fall technologically even further behind its PLA counterpart.

In the case of non-conventional threats from China, the ROCAF's efforts would be of little use. Despite Taiwan's gradual acquisition of specific missiles for offensive purposes, their limited numbers and payloads would make their use unwise for striking the PLA's numerous ballistic missiles, cruise missiles and other stand-off weapons that are mobile and concealed. Furthermore, to launch pre-emptive strikes requires strong and decisive leadership, because Taipei could be perceived internationally as a troublemaker for disrupting the status quo. Taiwan's defensive PAC-3 and TK-III SAMs would still be outnumbered if used to intercept approaching Chinese missiles and other projectiles, leaving their locations exposed to attack. Unless SAM units are properly preserved, they may be neutralized too early to provide crucial air cover for the ROCN or the ROCA during critical moments, such as striking invading amphibious fleets or anti-landing attacks (Lostumbo et al. 2016: 12, 20–21). Since both Taipei's offensive and defensive means are unlikely to neutralize Beijing's firepower projection, the ROCAF bases would remain vulnerable and likely to suffer deterioration. Similarly, the ROCAF's measures do not cover base security. Without significant improvements to internal security in Taiwan, efforts to deal with threats of sabotage would be ineffective. With airbases remaining vulnerable, the effect of modernizing existing fighters would be reduced or even invalidated. In other words, survivability becomes the most critical factor and challenge for the ROCAF.

The troubled waters

The ROCN has not achieved a major strategic transformation from sea control to sea denial in the face of China's rising sea power. Taiwan's trade-oriented economy and lack of natural resources, particularly energy, make maintaining sea control for SLOCs strategically important. This goal has, however, gradually become unfeasible in the face of the PLA Navy (PLAN)'s anti-access and area denial (A2/AD) strategy and capabilities. As a result, sea denial against the PLAN, especially against amphibious invasion, presents an asymmetrical means for the weak to deter the strong. Taipei has indeed strengthened its denial capabilities, such as building up stealth fast attack craft (FACs), but the lack of new submarines makes this plan incomplete (Petrucelli 2018). Furthermore, the ROCN still needs to retain certain sea control capabilities for various peacetime missions, such as supporting and supplying ROC controlled islands, and patrolling large territorial waters, especially during winter. As such, major surface vessels and other fleets with specific functions, such as minesweepers and amphibious vessels, are required for these purposes. This, however, compromises their roles during wartime.

Under the status quo, each major capability of the ROCN corresponds to its respective strategic predicament. Submarines have always been the focal point of Taiwan's defence because of their impact in deterring the PLAN. They are the most independent element of defence and deterrence for Taipei to rely on, as they do not require air superiority or other direct support. However, the ROCN underwater flotilla is too old and too small, comprising two boats dating from the 1940s and the two more from the 1980s (SIPRI 2018). This implies uncertain issues regarding safety and readiness, a lack of advanced technology, and periods of unavailability due to routine maintenance. After decades of failed procurements, the ongoing indigenous submarine project is meant to provide a fundamental solution, with sub-launched missiles to be used to supplement offensive capabilities. However, the timeframe for delivery and various quality issues pose significant challenges. Based on the Australian example, a decade is an unavoidable timeframe with potential quality flaws likely to occur for any new submarine design (Australian Submarine Corporation 2019; Watt 2013). The South Korean example is more positive, but it takes more than a decade to build up a fleet (Naval Technology 2019). Before the project reaches a credible outcome, the defects of the ROCN's underwater force will remain and may even get worse due to its reliance on its four ageing submarines.

Major surface combatants are the most salient targets for China's A2/AD firepower during wartime, thus suggesting a 'fleet-in-being' strategy. Given that all of Taiwan's naval bases are exposed to China's firepower, the ROCN's fleet-in-being strategy would be to place these destroyers and frigates in a position adjacent to Taiwan, probably in the Pacific, to deter or contain the PLAN main force, in particular its amphibious fleet (Corbett 2004: 167). However, this strategy is gradually losing feasibility, as the transit to and from its staging location could expose them to China's A2/AD firepower. Although the ROCN's major surface combatants have a certain capacity for countering A2/AD firepower from the air, land and sea, they may eventually be overwhelmed in saturated attacks. If the PLAN's A2/AD firepower continues and no third party intervenes (e.g. from the United States), the ROCN's major surface combatants may face serious annihilation before any strategic impact is achieved (Chen and Edmonds 2006: 71). However, if destroyers and frigates were assigned to protect SLOCs, their dispersed force may mean that their loss would be even faster. Undeniably, the new models of destroyers and frigates listed in indigenous shipbuilding projects would have better survivability under A2/AD threats, but China's A2/AD capabilities are also improving. Unless revolutionary technologies, such as laser or electromagnetic weapons, are applied, the new ROCN major surface combatants would continue to be vulnerable.

The ROCN's FAC units, the mainstay of Taiwan's A2/AD force, are relatively modern, but the operational environment may not be favourable for them. Taipei has been developing its FAC force since the late 1970s, with such assets already moving into the second generation of indigenous design, whereby the KW class has replaced the Israeli-origin Hai-Ou (Seagull) class (Cole 2012). Armed with HF-II or HF-III anti-ship cruise missiles, these FACs would be lethal in thwarting a seaward invasion, especially amphibious operations (RT 2016). The stealth designs of the KW-class and the TJ-class would have better survivability. However, they lack suitable hideouts along the straight and flat coastline of western Taiwan where landings are most likely to occur. The many bays of the northern and eastern coastlines offer suitable places to conceal the FACs, but they have to move to strike and risk exposure to PLA surveillance (Ministry of the Interior 2015). If China achieves air superiority, the FACs would be vulnerable to China's aerial platforms. Furthermore, suitable hideouts along coastlines can easily confirmed by Chinese spies. The cross-Strait integration mechanisms present Beijing with opportunities to deploy operatives in various channels such as tourism to inspect possible locations and even carry out continuous monitoring (Wu 2015).

The minesweeping units of the ROCN are used to protect SLOCs, and mines have been laid to counter invasion, as well as for search and rescue operations during peacetime. From the 1990s they have been modernized, and new vessels, both sweepers and fast minelayers with smart mines, are expected to join the services (SIPRI 2018) (Ministry of National Defense 2017c: 87). The most salient challenge to them is the unavoidable delay in receiving new vessels due to the Ching Fu scandal, concerning a contractor with financial problems (Agence France-Presse 2018). Operationally, minesweepers with weak air defence capabilities are unlikely to operate without air cover from combat fighter-aircraft, SAMs or major surface combatants, but even so each of the latter could be suppressed if not neutralised by PLA firepower. Similarly, in the future, fast minelayers could face serious aerial threats.

The amphibious fleet is struggling to retain a role in Taiwan's strategic picture. As a legacy of the 'retaking the mainland' policy, the fleet has been considerably reduced in size as the potential for an amphibious invasion of China is clearly unfeasible. Its role during wartime under A2/AD firepower would be even more problematic. Although the need to supply offshore positions during peacetime remains, the fleet's military deployment in Kinmen, Matsu and other offshore islands close to China has been massively reduced (Hsieh and Tsai 2017: 260). The remaining military deployment in the Pescadores Islands and the South China Sea has led to a reduced demand for amphibious capacity. Additionally, the ROCN has also listed humanitarian aid and disaster relief as a reason for an indigenous project for landing platform docks (Yeo 2017). Likewise, the amphibious vehicles of the ROCNMC have played an outstanding role in humanitarian aid and disaster relief operations during some recent disasters, mostly due to flooding (Ministry of National Defense 2017b). However, the amphibious fleet would not play a significant role in countering an attack from China.

If air cover were more secure, most of Taiwan's surface fleet would be able to serve its function. If not, it is evident that a large portion of the ROCN would make little contribution to defence during wartime. The consequence of ineffective sea denial by the ROCN would be an increase in the probability of a PLA amphibious invasion.

The land of multiple fronts

The expanding capabilities of the PLA poses a sophisticated set of threats to the ROCA and the ROCNMC. China could launch airborne and amphibious invasions after securing air superiority and sea control. ROC ground troops might have difficulty in defending Taiwan because of certain structural defects, such as mobilization issues and inferior investment in capabilities. Given the limited size of its regular units, Taipei does not have enough troops to hold the entire coastline, making mobilized units the essential first line of coastal defence. In the event of a major invasion, the regular units, particularly the artillery, armoured and helicopter units, would launch counter-attacks against the invader's beachhead. The same strategy would apply to an airborne invasion (Easton *et al.* 2016: 6, 16).

Two fundamental issues arise from this strategy: the quality of mobilized troops and the timing of mobilization. A crossing of the Taiwan Strait would require a longer and more obvious preparation by the PLA than in normal land campaigns, thus providing Taiwan with a longer response time. However, it is uncertain as to whether the Ministry of National Defense's Armed Forces Reserve Command (AFRC) would be able to assemble and deploy sufficient numbers of quality mobilized reserves and equipment in assigned locations on time. Aside from the official high reporting rates during exercises, it is evident from some reports that the AFRC usually only calls up some reserves rather than entire units, and many reserve soldiers in fact go overseas to avoid being re-called for drills (Chen 2018; Chong 2018; Chu and Chou 2016). Taipei also implemented an all-volunteer force (AVF) policy in 2018 whereby conscripts receive only four months of basic and specialized training, followed by five to eight days of drills every two years according to rank, thus making the quality of reserves doubtful (Easton et al. 2016: 21–22). Strategically, political leaders would need a very strong case to call for the mobilization of reserves. Such action would cause serious disruption to the economy and daily routines as well as signal the escalation of a crisis. The situation would be more difficult if the PLA remained confrontational rather than carrying out an invasion that was expected, because Taiwan's economy would be severely affected during a state of mobilization. Such a potential impact might mean that political leaders might shy away from announcing mobilisation, with postponement likely to result in incomplete defence fronts. If China were to achieve air superiority before such a decision were made, mobilization would also be disrupted. While the Ministry of National Defense has introduced integrated mobile messages and modified regulations to enhance the reporting of reserves to drills, it presents no solution to the challenging decision of when to mobilize (Chou 2018).

Carrying out anti-landing campaigns under aerial threat from an adversary would be hazardous without air cover. The ROCA attack helicopters have the swiftest strike capability in an invasion, and their low-fly nature makes them difficult targets for Chinese combat aircraft (Peck 2018). Moreover, utility and transport helicopters can carry soldiers to deploy on land to retake positions or to reinforce the defence. However, their sustainability could be disrupted by the logistical facilities, and bases and alternative sites for operations being located and attacked by PLA firepower. MBTs, other armed vehicles and artillery systems could benefit from certain topographical features and buildings used for shelter and camouflage, but their mobility would be slow in Taiwan's terrain of rivers and ridges, and movement would expose units to air strikes. As a result, the ROCA has procured several batches of FIM-92 SAMs since the late 1990s for the M1097 Avenger air defence system and portable use, in addition to older M48 Chaparral SAMs, 20 mm and 40 mm anti-aircraft guns (SIPRI 2018; IISS 2019: 308). Such air defence assets may inflict certain costs on the PLA, but their ranges would be too short to threaten aerial platforms equipped with newer longer-ranged ASMs and other munitions. Thus, the survival of the ROCAF's mid- and long-range SAMs are essential for the ROCA and the ROCNMC to be able to conduct anti-landing operations.

The most likely threat for ROC ground troops may not come from the sea or the air, but rather from inland. As previously mentioned, there are many channels for PLA special forces to infiltrate Taiwan openly (Chin and Chung 2017). Although ROC troops would still enjoy numerical superiority, attrition in the number of ground troops along with the poor recruitment of volunteer soldiers would constrain the capacity to respond to acts of sabotage (Morgan 2018). Furthermore, the PLA's brigade-sized special forces would not be concentrated in certain locations but spread out in order to maximize their individual effect, as they can initially choose where, when and how to attack. One potential tactic is to disguise themselves as ROC armed forces to create confusion, with the resulting chaos paving the way for larger operations, such as the decapitation of the chain of command. It remains uncertain as to what China's special forces might achieve strategically, but it could be critical given that Taiwan has a low land defence capacity.

Taiwan also invests less in its military land systems in contrast to its aerial and naval ones, thus leaving various ageing or even obsolete assets vulnerable. Despite the important role of being the spearhead in any counterattack, the ROCA's armour units have not acquired any new MBT since the 1990s (SIPRI 2018). Furthermore, Taiwan's M48H and M60A3 MBTs with their original steel armour and no advanced technology are vulnerable to most anti-tank weapons (Ministry of National Defense 2017c: 74; IISS 2019: 308; *China Post* 2016). As such, they will be inadequate in counterattack operations. Reported upgrades to M60A3 or the procurement of M1A2 MBTs would take time, which means continued reliance on currently obsolete armour units (Au 2017; Keck 2018). The artillery units appear to have the oldest assets in the armed forces, with several types of towed howitzers dating from the Second World War. Their short range would constrain deployment for anti-landing and poor mobility may render them more like decoys rather than weapons with sustainable firepower (Haskew 2008, 67–68). Despite the acquisition of some new artillery systems, the overall modernization of the land force is still clearly inadequate (IISS 2019: 308).

The non-China factors

The four major non-China factors having an overall effect on Taiwan's armed forces are uncertain alliances; domestic politics; insufficient budget; and an AVF. External alliances are usually crucial for small states, especially for those under strategic pressure such as Taiwan. For Taipei, the United States is its only available ally for military supply and external support purposes, given the United States' military deployments in the region, such as on nearby Okinawa. The severance of official ties since Washington's normalization of relations with China in the 1970s, however, has prevented both sides from returning to the situation before 1979, when the bilateral defence treaty was in effect (Defense Security Cooperation Agency 2017). Without any clear guidance regarding joint operations, the ROC armed forces are forced to plan for self-sufficient defence, and shoulder the resulting heavier strategic pressure, unlike other regional countries which have formed external alliances, such as South Korea and Japan. On an operational level, the uncertain military ties form an obstacle to possible joint operations between the armed forces of Taiwan and the United States. Undeniably, bilateral ties have been improved, especially during the Trump Administration, but remain some way from a bilateral alliance (Moriarty 2018).

Since the democratization in Taiwan began in the 1990s, volatile domestic politics have determined all public issues in Taiwan, including military issues. The strategies of the last four administrations have varied between emphasizing offence, namely by the Democratic Progressive Party (DPP), and defence, by the Kuomintang (KMT – Nationalist Party). The lack of consistency has resulted in differing military plans, such as the development of the HF-IIE SSMs which began during the first DPP administration in 2001 (CSIS Missile Threat 2017). This was followed by an opposite emphasis by the KMT's Ma Ying-jeou administration on stiffened defence to absorb attacks from China rather than deterrence through offensive capability (Ministry of National Defense 2009: 6–9, ibid. 2013: 30–34). The long period of time needed to develop defence capabilities means that Taiwan struggles to implement long-term plans or grand strategies due to frequent political changes and diverse views on sovereignty and other fundamental political issues. Low or medium levels of policy changes are common in democratic countries, but excessive debate and division in this area can exacerbate the maintenance of a consistent and practical defence policy.

Budget has been a clear indicator of the restrictions placed on Taiwan's armed forces. Since 2000 the defence budget has dropped to less than 3 per cent of GDP, sometimes even lower than 2 per cent, an extremely low amount for a small state under a clear threat to its existence from the second strongest military power in the world (SIPRI 2019). Although defence expenditure still occupies the largest portion of the total governmental budget, only about 26 per cent of the defence budget goes on investment, indicating a limited commitment to modernization (Ministry of National Defense 2017c: 134–36). A series of ongoing high-cost indigenous defence projects may force an increase in defence budgets, but vocal and divisive domestic politics may disrupt the funding of such projects.

The pursuit of an AVF directly influences manpower supply to the ROC armed forces, particularly to the ROCA. Professional soldiers have the advantage of longer and more comprehensive training, and their recruitment has been a common policy goal for the DPP and KMT administrations, probably due to its popularity (Speck 2008; Ministry of National Defense 2017c: 128). However, poor recruitment levels have undercut the manpower supply, with the shortage reaching to the level of officers and non-commissioned officers. Officially, there is a shortage of more than 30,000 troops, despite the relaxation of physical and intellectual requirements (Morgan 2018; Hung 2017). Therefore, the combat readiness of units has suffered both quantitatively and qualitatively (McCauley 2016). The gap in recruitment is attributed to the lack of young people voluntarily joining the military, due to issues such as salary and internal management, and this is exacerbated by the shrinking youth demographic due to low birth rates (McNamara 2018: 48–50).

Besides the financial burden and recruitment issues, the main concern for the AVF is the lack of popular commitment to defence. Given the country's proximity to China, the public should be aware that no one in Taiwan would be out of the range of China's firepower and any outbreak of war would affect the whole population. Popular participation in defence through conscription will strengthen Taipei's deterrence against Beijing, because a large military-trained population can continue resistance, even when the three layers of defence have been defeated. However, the current short training period for conscripts would not be sufficient for either regular or irregular warfare. Undeniably, Taiwan's conscription system is problematic, but fixing it would be more effective for defence and deterrence than the current policy of marginalizing it (Wu 2018: 722–23).

Conclusion

Despite certain strengths and advantages, the ROC's armed forces are surpassed by the improving capabilities of the PLA and undermined by a number of largely domestic factors. Taiwan's current military capabilities rest on either previous legacies, such as combat fighter fleets acquired in the 1990s, or recently acquired weapons systems with limited strategic impact, such attack helicopters. The layered defence strategy is under significant threat stemming from the lack of air superiority and insufficient sea denial capability, leaving ground troops in an inferior position facing various challenges. The potential for resistance beyond conventional warfare in the form of guerrilla warfare is also undermined by the downgrading of conscription. As the issues confronting the military also reflect political developments, non-China-related factors, such as weaknesses within Taiwan's armed forces in terms of strategy, funding and conscription will not be sufficiently addressed until a firm and consistent political consensus is achieved, or unless a Cold War-like confrontation causes the island to unite to address current defence issues. Before such a situation arises, Taipei ought to endeavour to strengthen its military, but it is less likely that structural constraints could be overcome. Taiwan is on a trajectory of increasing inferiority vis-à-vis China in this regard unless further efforts are made on many levels.

References

Agence France-Presse (2018) 'Ching Fu Chairman Chen Ching-Nan and Four Others, Including His Wife and Son, Formally Accused of Falsifying Documents to Secure Loans', *South China Morning Post*, 13 February. Available at https://www.scmp.com/news/china/policies-politics/article/2133177/boss-taiwanese-shipbuilding-company-charged-fraud-over (accessed 11 January 2019).

Au, Charles (2017) 'Taiwan Initiates M60A3 Upgrade Plan', *Shephard*, 6 October. Available at www.shephardmedia.com/news/landwarfareintl/taiwan-initiates-m60a3-upgrade-plan/ (accessed 13 January 2019).

Australian Submarine Corporation (2019) 'Collins Class Submarines'. Available at www.asc.com.au/submarines/collins-class-submarines/ (accessed 11 January 2019).

Center for Strategic and International Studies (CSIS), Missile Threat (2016) 'Hong Niao Series (HN-1/-2/-3)', 12 August, available at https://missilethreat.csis.org/missile/hong-niao/ (accessed 25 October 2018).

Center for Strategic and International Studies (CSIS), Missile Threat (2017) 'Hsiung Feng IIE', 13 July. Available at https://missilethreat.csis.org/missile/hsiung-feng-iie/ (accessed 1 January 2019).

Center for Strategic and International Studies (CSIS), Missile Threat (2018) 'Yun Feng', 15 June. Available at https://missilethreat.csis.org/missile/yun-feng/ (accessed 9 January 2019).

Chen, Chuanren (2018) 'Taiwan's Ching-kuo Upgrade Complete, SEAD Role Next', *Aviation International News*, 20 March. Available at www.ainonline.com/aviation-news/defense/2018-03-20/taiwans-ching-kuo-upgrade-complete-sead-role-next# (accessed 15 January 2019).

Chen, Ya-Fan (2018) 'Reserves Reported to Mobilised Brigade in Chenghua County', *Now News*, 6 August. Available at www.nownews.com/news/20180806/2797747/ (accessed 13 January 2019).

Chen, York W. and Martin Edmonds (2006) *Taiwan's Defense Reform*, ed. Martin Edmonds and Michael M. Tsai, London: Routledge.

Chin, Jonathan and Chung, Li-Hua (2017) '5,000 Chinese Spies in Taiwan: Source', *Taipei Times*, 13 March. Available at www.taipeitimes.com/News/front/archives/2017/03/13/2003666661 (accessed 31 October 2018).

Chin, Jonathan and Lo, Tien-pin (2018) 'Deals Inked for Mirage Parts, Training', *Taipei Times*, 26 September. Available at www.defenseworld.net/news/17883/Taiwan_To_Locally_Upgrade_MICA_Missiles_in_ITS_Mirage_2000_Jets#.W9VQAORReh0 (accessed 28 October 2018).

China Post (2016) 'Taiwan Army Suspends All CM-11 Main Battle Tanks after Cannon Explodes During Drill, Injuring Soldier', *Strait Times*, 1 September. Available at www.straitstimes.com/asia/east-asia/taiwan-army-suspends-all-cm-11-main-battle-tanks-after-cannon-explodes-during-drill (accessed 12 January 2019).

Chong, Li-Hua (2018) 'Problematic Reserve Force: 1642 Reserved Charged for Dodging Retraining in Three Years', *Liberty Times*, 3 August. Available at https://news.ltn.com.tw/news/politics/breakingnews/2507909 (accessed 13 January 2019).

Chou, Li-Shing (2018) 'Three New Measures for Reserves', *Military News Agency*, 27 December. Available at http://mna.gpwb.gov.tw/post.php?id=13&message=92348 (accessed 13 January 2019).

Chu, Jen-Kai and Chou Sai-Yu (2016) 'MND Unfairly Calling for Drills: The Same Reserves Called Four Times', *China Times*, 8 May. Available at http://www.chinatimes.com/newspapers/20160508000280260102 (accessed 13 November 2016).

Coast Guard Administration (2018) *Vessels*, Taipei: Ocean Affairs Council. Available at www.cga.gov.tw/GipOpen/wSite/lp?ctNode=1561&mp=999 (accessed 5 December 2018).

Cole, J. Michael (2012) 'China Plans Navy's New Attack Boat', *Taipei Times*, 12 January. Available at www.taipeitimes.com/News/taiwan/archives/2012/01/12/2003523049 (accessed 11 January 2019).

Corbett, Julian S. (2004) *Principles of Maritime Strategy*, New York: Dover.

Defense Security Cooperation Agency (2017) 'Taipei Economic and Cultural Representative Office (TECRO) in the United States', 29 June. Available at www.dsca.mil/tags/taipei-economic-and-cultural-representative-office-tecro-united-states (accessed 9 January 2019).

Defense Update (2014) 'Taiwan Unveils "Wan Chien" Air-to-Ground Stand-Off Weapon', 20 January. Available at https://defense-update.com/20140120_taiwan-unveils-wan-chien-air-ground-cruise-missile.html (accessed 5 October 2018).

Easton, Ian, Mark Stokes, Cortez A. Cooper and Arthur Chan (2016) *Transformation of Taiwan's Reserve Force*, Santa Monica, CA: RAND Corporation.
Executive Yuan (2019) 'Geography', 8 January. Available at https://english.ey.gov.tw/cp.aspx?n=1082F2A7077508A4 (accessed 8 January 2019).
Gady, Franz-Stefan (2018) 'Defense Minister: Taiwan Is Seeking F-35 Stealth Fighter', *The Diplomat*, 15 May. Available at https://thediplomat.com/2018/05/defense-minister-taiwan-is-seeking-f-35-stealth-fighter/ (accessed 28 October 2018).
Haskew, Michael E. (2008) *Artillery: Compared and Contrasted*, Heatherton: Hinkler.
Hsieh, Pasha L. and TsaiPei-Lun (2017) *Chinese (Taiwan) Yearbook of International Law and Affairs*, vol. 33, ed. MaYing-Jeou, Leiden: Koninklijke Brill.
HungJer-Cheng (2017) 'Still a Gap of 15000 Troops for Volunteer Soldiers, How Would the Military Do?' *United Daily*, 31 December. Available at https://udn.com/news/story/10930/2904417 (accessed 18 March 2018).
International Institute for Strategic Studies (IISS) (2003) *Military Balance 2003*, London; IISS.
International Institute for Strategic Studies (IISS) (2004) *Military Balance 2004*, London: IISS.
International Institute for Strategic Studies (IISS) (2018) *Military Balance 2018*, London: IISS.
International Institute for Strategic Studies (IISS) (2019) *Military Balance 2019*, London: IISS.
Kagan, Richard C. (2007) *Taiwan's Statesman: Lee Teng-hui and Democracy in Asia*, Annapolis, MD: Naval Institute Press.
Kan, Shirley A. (2011) *Taiwan: Major U.S. Arms Sales Since 1990*, Washington, DC: Congressional Research Service.
Keck, Zachary (2018) 'Taiwan Wants American M1 Abrams Tanks. And the Reason Is China', *National Interest*, 5 May. Available at https://nationalinterest.org/blog/the-buzz/taiwan-wants-american-m1-abrams-tanks-the-reason-china-25692 (accessed 13 January 2019).
Lavender, Darryl J. (2013) *China's Special Operations Forces Modernization, Professionalization and Regional Implications*, Carlisle Barracks, PA: US Army War College.
Lockheed Martin (2018) 'Pentagon and Lockheed Martin Agree to Reduced F-35 Price in New Production Contract', 28 September. Available at www.f35.com/news/detail/pentagon-and-lockheed-martin-agree-to-reduced-f-35-price-in-new-production (accessed 5 October 2018).
Lostumbo, Michael J., David R. Frelinger, James Williams and Barry Wilson (2016) *Air Defense Options for Taiwan*, Santa Monica, CA: RAND Corporation.
Mattis, Peter (2017) 'Counterintelligence Remains Weakness in Taiwan's Defence', *China Brief*, 17 August. Available at https://jamestown.org/program/counterintelligence-remains-weakness-in-taiwans-defence/ (accessed 29 October 2018).
McCauley, Kevin (2016) 'Taiwan's Military Reforms and Strategy: Reset Required', *The Jamestown Foundation*, 22 August. Available at https://jamestown.org/program/taiwans-military-reforms-and-strategy-reset-required/ (accessed 13 January 2019).
McNamara, Whitney (2018) 'Challenges to Taiwan's Shift to All Volunteer Force', in Bonnie S. Glaser and Matthew P. Funaiole (eds) *Perspectives on Taiwan: Insights from the 2017 Taiwan-U.S. Policy Program*, Washington, DC: Center for Strategic and International Studies.
Ministry of National Defense, ROC (2006) *2006 National Defense Report*, Taipei: Ministry of National Defense.

Ministry of National Defense, ROC (2009) *Quadrennial Defence Review 2009*, Taipei: Ministry of National Defense.

Ministry of National Defense, ROC (2017a) *2017 Quadrennial Defense Review*, Taipei: Ministry of National Defense.

Ministry of National Defense, ROC (2017b) 'Defense News', 24 October. Available at www.mnd.gov.tw/English/Publish.aspx?title=Defense%20News&p=75461 (accessed 3 January 2019).

Ministry of National Defense, ROC (2017c) *National Defense Report 2017*, Taipei: Ministry of National Defense.

Ministry of the Interior, ROC (2015) *Maps of Coastal Areas*, Taipei: Ministry of the Interior.

Morgan, Scott (2018) 'Taiwan Military Working Towards 169,000 Active Personnel Goal', *Taiwan News*, 6 November. Available at www.taiwannews.com.tw/en/news/3569018 (accessed 13 January 2019).

Moriarty, James (2018) 'Remarks by AIT Chairman James Moriarty at U.S.-Taiwan Defense Industry Conference', American Institute in Taiwan, 29 October. Available at www.ait.org.tw/remarks-by-ait-chairman-james-moriarty-at-u-s-taiwan-defense-industry-conference/ (accessed 16 January 2019).

Myers, Steven Lee and Chris Horton (2017) 'Once Formidable, Taiwan's Military Now Overshadowed by China's', *New York Times*, 4 November. Available at www.nytimes.com/2017/11/04/world/asia/china-taiwan-military.html (accessed 30 December 2018).

Naval Technology (2019) 'ROKN Chang Bogo Class Submarines'. Available at www.naval-technology.com/projects/chang-bogo-class-submarine-south-korea-rokn/ (accessed 11 January 2019).

Office of the Secretary of Defense (2018) *Annual Report to Congress: Military and Security Developments Involving the People's Republic of China 2018*, Washington, DC: Office of the Secretary of Defense.

Peck, Michael (2018) 'Why Taiwan's New Apache Helicopter Brigade Won't Stop China', *National Interest*, 16 August. Available at https://nationalinterest.org/blog/buzz/why-taiwans-new-apache-helicopter-brigade-wont-stop-china-28887 (accessed 13 January 2019).

Petrucelli, Joe (2018) 'A Question of Time: Improving Taiwan's Maritime Deterrence Posture', Center for International Maritime Security, 15 November. Available at http://cimsec.org/a-question-of-time-enhancing-taiwans-maritime-deterrence-posture/38830 (accessed 11 January 2019).

Phipps, Gavin (2018) 'Taiwan Takes Delivery of First F-16V Aircraft', *Jane's 360*, 22 October. Available at www.janes.com/article/83947/taiwan-takes-delivery-of-first-f-16v-aircraft (accessed 28 October 2018).

Pocock, Chris (2017) 'Taiwan Confirms Indigenous Jet Trainer Development', *Aviation International News Online*, 16 February. Available at www.ainonline.com/aviation-news/defense/2017-02-16/taiwan-confirms-indigenous-jet-trainer-development (accessed 12 November 2018).

Raytheon (2019a) 'High-Speed Anti-Radiation Missile'. Available at https://www.raytheon.com/capabilities/products/harm (accessed 9 January 2019).

Raytheon (2019b) 'JSOW Weapon System'. Available at https://www.raytheon.com/capabilities/products/jsow (accessed 9 January 2019).

RT (2016) 'Taiwan Misfires Supersonic Missile in China's Direction, Kills Own Fisherman', 1 July. Available at www.rt.com/news/349138-taiwan-misfires-supersonic-missile/ accessed (11 January 2019).

Shlapak, David (2013) *The Chinese Air Force: Evolving Concepts, Roles and Capabilities*, ed. Richard P. Hallion, Roger Cliff and Philip C. Saunders, Washington, DC: National Defense University Press.
Speck, Andreas (2008) 'Taiwan to Shorten Conscription Term to One Year', *Taiwan News*, 3 December. Available at www.etaiwannews.com/etn/news_content.php?id= 802676&lang=eng_news (accessed 26 October 2016).
Stockholm International Peace Research Institute (SIPRI) (2018) 'Trade Registers'. Available at http://armstrade.sipri.org/armstrade/page/trade_register.php (accessed 4 December 2018).
Stockholm International Peace Research Institute (SIPRI) (2019) 'SIPRI Military Expenditure Database'. Available at www.sipri.org/databases/milex (accessed 15 January 2019).
Stott, Michael (2010) 'Deadly New Russian Weapon Hides in Shipping Container', Reuters, 26 April. Available at www.reuters.com/article/us-russia-weapon/deadly-new-russian-weapon-hides-in-shipping-container-idUSTRE63P2XB20100426 accessed 31 October 2018).
Sui Shi-Feng (1994) 'Waves in South China Sea', in ZhouDi, LiangYan-Bo and ZengCheng-Kui (eds) *Oceanology of China Seas*, vols 1–2, Dordrecht: Kluwer Academic, pp. 134–140.
Taipei Economic and Cultural Representative Office in the United States (2017) 'Taiwan-U.S. Relations', 30 September. Available at www.roc-taiwan.org/us_en/post/ 24.html (accessed 16 January 2019).
Teng, Pei-ju (2018) 'Defence Budget to Increase by NT$18.3 Billion in 2019: Taiwan Premier', *Taiwan News*, 27 July. Available at www.taiwannews.com.tw/en/news/ 3492793 (accessed 9 January 2019).
Watt, David (2013) 'More Problems with the Collins Class Submarines', Parliament of Australia, 27 September. Available at www.aph.gov.au/About_Parliament/Parliamentary_Departments/Parliamentary_Library/FlagPost/2013/September/More_problems_ with_the_Collins_Class_submarines (accessed 12 November 2018).
Wolf, Jim (2010) 'Taiwan Overdue for F-16 Jets, Ex U.S. Official Say', Reuters, 7 July. Available at www.reuters.com/article/us-taiwan-usa-fighters-interview/taiwan-overdue-for-f-16-jets-ex-u-s-official-say-idUSTRE6655BL20100706 (accessed 27 October 2018).
Wu, Shang-su (2015) 'Commentary: The Gradual Undermining of Taiwan', *Defense News*, 9 February. Available at www.defensenews.com/story/defense/commentary/ 2015/02/09/commentarygradualunderminingtaiwan/ (accessed 25 October 2018).
Wu, Shang-su (2018) 'Taiwan's Defense under the Tsai Administration', *Asian Survey*, 58(4).
Yeo, Mike (2017) 'Taiwan's Navy Seeks First Indigenous Landing Platform Dock', *Defense News*, 19 April. Available at www.defensenews.com/naval/2017/04/19/taiwans-navy-seeks-first-indigenous-landing-platform-dock/ (accessed 11 January 2019).
Yeo, Mike (2019) 'Taiwan Requests Fighter Jets from the US, but with an Unusual Twist', *Defense News*, 11 March. Available at www.defensenews.com/air/2019/03/11/taiwan-requests-fighter-jets-from-the-us-but-with-an-unusual-twist/ (accessed 12 March 2019).

12 Defending Taiwan against China

Yves-Heng Lim

For observers of cross-Strait relations, the dawn of 2019 offered a stark reminder of the fragility of the status quo between the People's Republic of China (PRC, or China) and the Republic of China (ROC, or Taiwan). On 1 January 2019 Chinese President Xi Jinping celebrated the 40th anniversary of the National People's Congress's 'Message to Compatriots in Taiwan' by reminding his audience that, for Beijing, '[t]he difference of systems is not an obstacle to unification and is even less an excuse for separation' and that

> [China] will not promise to renounce the use of military force. The choice to retain all necessary means is aimed at the interference of foreign parties and the very few 'pro-independence' elements and their splitist activities, and not at our Taiwan compatriots.
>
> (Xi 2019)

Xi's vision was promptly rebuked by the Taiwanese President Tsai Ing-wen, who reiterated her non-acceptance of the '1992 Consensus' and protested against Beijing's arm-twisting strategies. There was little new in Xi's reformulation of Beijing's mantra or in Tsai's response, but the verbal skirmish between the two leaders immediately prompted comments about the heightened risk of war (Huang 2019). Xi's remarks per se do not tell us a lot about a possible increase in the likelihood of military conflict. But, in a context whereby China's military has grown much more powerful, Beijing's enduring assertion of its right to use military force presents Taipei with daunting challenges. The growing power imbalance has prompted Taipei to revisit its defence strategy and to reconsider the type of forces it will need in a future confrontation with its Goliath-like neighbour. This chapter explores Taiwan's options to defend itself against China, highlighting recent changes in Taiwan's posture but also the limitations of Taiwan's change of defence posture.

The chapter must start with three caveats about what it does not discuss. First, the question of the defence of Taiwan is considered in a bilateral context. This is admittedly a huge simplification of the cross-Strait equation as the Taiwan Relations Act continues to make the United States the ultimate guarantor of the security of the island – although this guarantee is conditional as reflected in the notion of 'strategic ambiguity'. The question of the US guarantee is discussed at length elsewhere in this volume and the chapter is premised on the almost tautological idea that a discussion of Taiwan's defence must start with an assessment of what Taiwan can do to defend itself. Second, the chapter focuses on what can be done to prevent China from successfully crossing the Strait – a sort of area denial strategy 'with Taiwanese characteristics'– and leaves unexplored the question of what Taiwan could do should the battle for control of the air and sea in the Strait be lost. Several studies have emerged to discuss Taiwan's options, suggesting the possibility for Taipei to opt for deeply asymmetric strategies that could impose costs on the invading force and deter China from invading Taiwan (Thomas et al. 2014; Easton 2017; Hunzeker and Lanoszka 2018). Making a Chinese invasion as costly and painful as possible constitutes a potentially potent deterrent, but should China take full control of the air and sea and in the absence of a US intervention, it is difficult to see how such an option could do more than delay a final People's Liberation Army (PLA) victory – although with the possible satisfaction of turning it into a pyrrhic one. Third, this chapter focuses on the threat of a Chinese attempt to cross the Strait, leaving aside the question of a Chinese attempt to coerce the island through blockade operations. Although the possibility of a blockade has been the source of constant speculation (Glosny 2004; Goldstein and Murray 2004; Grubb 2007), blockades are likely to be less attractive than they seem. The purpose of a blockade would be to inflict economic pain in order to force Taipei to accept Beijing's terms. But the interruption of cross-Strait trade – on which almost half of Taiwanese exports depend (Mainland Affairs Council 2018; World Trade Organization 2018) – and the seizure of Taiwanese assets on the mainland – worth more than US $170 billion in 2017 (Mainland Affairs Council, 2018) – although technically challenging (Tanner 2007), would probably be sufficient to create economic chaos in Taiwan. In addition, Chinese sources suggest that a blockade would present high risks of escalation. According to *Campaign Theory Study Guide*, a textbook published by the National Defense University, a blocked country is likely to

> face intense enemy resistance. Therefore, it is not sufficient to simply carry out the blockade; it is also indispensable to support [the blockade] by proceeding to required attacks. This requires using elite forces to destroy incoming enemy forces or to proceed actively to attacks on its bases, ports and airports and to destroy its vital forces.
>
> (Xue, 2001: 331)

This escalatory logic makes the imposition of a blockade less attractive because it erodes the 'limited' use of force logic that is one of the principal advantage of a blockade over larger-scale operations.

Because the present and future of Taiwan's national defence is most likely to be determined by what Taiwanese forces can achieve at sea and in the air, this chapter is divided into two sections. The first section examines how the evolution of the air balance has an impact on Taiwan's security, how Taiwan has responded to the challenge, and what are the island's options to consolidate its capacity to deny Beijing control of the air. The second section does the same for the naval domain.

Contesting air superiority

The changing air imbalance

The first pillar of Taiwan's security lies in its ability to prevent China from achieving a sufficient level of air superiority in the Taiwan Strait. As repeatedly emphasized in any scenario of a Chinese invasion of Taiwan (O'Hanlon 2000; Wood and Ferguson 2001; Hunzeker and Lanoszka 2018), a crossing of the Strait by the PLA is simply unimaginable without the PLA Air Force gaining and maintaining a high degree of air superiority throughout the campaign.

China's rapid military modernization has dramatically altered the air equation in the Taiwan Strait over the last two decades. At the turn of the millennium, Michael O'Hanlon could still conclude that the PLA had little chance of gaining any degree of air superiority in a cross-Strait confrontation. Beijing could only rely on a couple of hundred ballistic missiles whose lack of accuracy was illustrated in the 1995–96 crisis when they were used to target Taiwanese runways. Among the 4,000 fighters listed in the PLA Air Force order of battle, fewer than 100 – all imported from the Russian Federation – were of modern design (IISS 2000).[1] In any conceivable scenario, the PLA Air Force would have suffered crippling losses in a confrontation against its more modern and capable Taiwanese counterpart (O'Hanlon 2000), preventing it from gaining any degree of air superiority in the Taiwan Strait.

In less than 20 years, the balance has changed dramatically. As of 2018 China can count on more than 700 fourth-generation aircraft (IISS 2018) – a two-to-one advantage over its Taiwanese counterpart in this sector. The mainstay of the Chinese air force is constituted of various versions of the indigenously developed J-10 of which approximately 350 units have been produced to date and which have been widely considered as a rough equivalent to the F-16. China has also successfully built on its experience with the Su-27/J-11 and has produced a series of highly capable variants, including the aircraft carrier-based J-15 and the 'strike-optimized' J-16 (Caffrey 2015). The PLA Air Force is moving beyond a fourth-generation force as the J-20s has reportedly entered active service – although its exact performances are shrouded by secrecy (Dominguez 2018; Chan 2018) – while the J-31 is likely to become operational before the end of the decade (Office of the Secretary of Defense 2018). A large proportion of the Chinese air force could be brought to bear in the Taiwan Strait in any invasion scenario. A recent RAND report indicates that existing infrastructures in the regions within range of Taiwan could allow China to 'allocate as many as 35 fighter and 5 bomber regiments to offensive operations' (Heginbotham *et al.* 2015: 73) in the Taiwan Strait.

Moreover, an air battle in the Taiwan Strait would be dramatically affected by Chinese land-based capabilities. Chinese sources have long suggested that 'in the initial phase of an amphibious campaign' the PLA would 'use missile forces and air power to achieve surprise ... and conduct comprehensive strike operations against key targets such as enemy C2 infrastructures naval and air bases and missile bases' (Zhang 2006: 318). In the Taiwan Strait, the PLA Rocket Forces – formerly the Second Artillery Corps – now has the means to fulfil its ambitions. Estimates by the US Department of Defense suggest that the PLA operates between 1,000 and 1,200 short-range ballistic missiles (SRBM) within striking range of Taiwan (Office of the Secretary of Defense 2018). The accuracy of at least part of this arsenal has improved tremendously over the past 20 years. The warheads of the new DF-15B and DF-16 (medium-range ballistic missiles) have a reported Circular Error Probable (CEP) as low as 5–10 metres compared with 300 metres for the earliest version of the DF-15 (Dominguez and Gibson, 2017). Simulation tests run by the RAND Corporation in the early 2010s showed that a first salvo of 200 relatively inaccurate SRBM – with a notional CEP of 40 metres – would have 'a greater than 90 percent chance of cutting all runways' (Shlapak et al. 2009: 43). With more advanced missiles, China could now use an even smaller portion of its arsenal to shut down Taiwanese air bases and thereby end the air battle before it had even begun.

Taiwanese aircraft surviving a first salvo would continue to face land-based challenges. China has dedicated considerable efforts to the development of long-range air defence systems. Beijing purchased its first batteries of S-300PMU (with a range of 150 km) from Russia in 1992 (SIPRI 2018) and launched its own HQ-9 air defence system (with a range of 200 km) five years later – possibly after some reverse engineering of the imported S-300. In 2015 China purchased the brand-new Russian S-400, although it is not entirely clear whether Russia agreed to sell the 400 km-range system or a shorter-range version (ibid.; Gady 2018a). Meanwhile, China has developed longer-range systems dubbed HQ-9B or HQ-19 with an expected range of between 250 and 300 km (Gao 2018). In combination with the advance of China's airborne early warning and control programmes, the maturation of these long-range air defence systems implies that Taiwanese aircraft operating in the air column above the island will soon be vulnerable to Chinese land-based air defences (Thomas et al. 2014: 15–17; Johnson 2015).

Taiwan's asymmetric option

In sharp contrast with the accelerated modernization of the PLA Air Force, the Taiwanese air force (ROC Air Force, or ROCAF) has essentially failed to develop since the turn of the millennium. Taiwan operates today a little more than 300 fourth-generation fighter aircraft including the F-16, the Mirage 200-V and the F-CK1. Taiwan's 144 F-16s are expected to benefit from significant upgrades over the next few years (Jennings 2017), but its 55 Mirage 2000-Vs and

127 F-CK-1s will become obsolescent during the next decade. Taiwan has faced daunting challenges in its attempts to modernize its air force. The last three US administrations have requested the sale of additional F-16s or F-35Bs for the Tsai administration (Gady 2018b) – but Washington has, to date, been unwilling to comply. For Taipei, the modernization problem is, however, becoming increasingly salient as some analysts have warned that Taipei could be just a decade away from a fighter aircraft 'shortage' (Jennings 2017). In the absence of an American solution, Taipei might be tempted to develop a domestic alternative. The decision, taken by the Tsai administration, to develop a new jet trainer – 66 of which are expected to be delivered during the next decade – fulfil, from this perspective, the dual goal of replacing the ageing AT-3s and F-5s and of preserving the industrial know-how necessary for the development of a successor to the F-CK-1 (Reuters 2017; Focus Taiwan 2018).

For obvious budgetary reasons, neither the sale of additional F-16s nor the development of a new generation of indigenous fighters will allow Taiwan to re-establish any degree of equilibrium in the Strait. In this unfavourable context, Taipei has progressively revisited its air strategy and moved towards an increased emphasis on 'asymmetric' solutions. At a broad level, the 2013 *National Defense Report* emphasized the need for Taiwan to adopt 'innovative/asymmetric operational concepts' (Ministry of National Defense 2013: 122) to support the development of a 'Hard ROC' strategy. The shift appears to be even more noticeable under Tsai Ing-wen as part of the doctrinal shift to 'resolute defense, multi-domain deterrence' (ibid. 2017; An 2018). The 2017 *National Defense Report* makes asymmetry the keystone of Taiwan's new defence strategy, stating that 'The ROC will not engage in an arms race with the PRC in the face of its huge military threat, but will apply asymmetric capability to achieve relative advantage for our Armed Forces' (Ministry of National Defense 2017: 86). In the air, the asymmetric logic of Taiwan's strategy has translated into the guideline: 'early reconnaissance and warning, flexible command and control, long-distance precision engagement and joint multi-layered interception' (ibid.: 88).

From a theoretical perspective, however, a hiatus continues to exist between the advertised shift towards asymmetry and the primary objective assigned to the Taiwanese air force. In line with the previous iterations of the *National Defense Report*, the 2017 edition emphasized the need for the Taiwanese air force to 'gain air superiority … to facilitate joint operations missions with the Army and Navy' (Ministry of National Defense 2017: 58).[2] This emphasis on air superiority and control appears at odds with the more modest – but much more realistic – aim that should, in theory, characterize an asymmetric air doctrine, namely to deny the opponent control of the skies without seeking control for one's self (Hallion 1997).

This relative ambiguity at the heart of Taiwan's air strategy is reflected in the direction taken by the modernization of Taiwan's air defence capabilities. Multiple studies have identified the logic behind asymmetric alternatives

(Murray 2008, 2014; Thomas *et al.* 2014; Lostumbo *et al.* 2017; Hunzeker and Lanoszka 2018) and offered blueprints for what an asymmetric air force would look like. On the one hand, Taiwan appears to have followed at least part of these blueprints. In September 2017, for instance, the ROCAF inaugurated a new Air Defense and Missile Command, tying together the former Air Defense Artillery and Air Defense Missile commands and allowing Taiwan to 'achieve the objective of unified command and control' for its air defence (Shen Yi-ming, cited in Broadcasting Corporation of China 2017).

On the other hand, some choices appear to be at odds with the logic of an asymmetric air defence. This is most notably the case of Taipei's push for the acquisition of F-35B (Gady 2018b).[3] A recent RAND report projects that Taiwan is expected to spend approximately US $25 billion over the next two decades, a sum that would allow Taipei to acquire and operate between 50 and 60 F-35Bs if Taipei was to retire *all* the F-16, Mirage and IDF models it currently operates (Lostumbo *et al.* 2017; Gady 2017). Moreover, the F-35 would enjoy higher survivability in an increasingly challenging environment, 'with only 57 JSF STOVLs, the PRC would always have many more aircraft and UAVs in the air, and some aircraft would likely be able to follow the JSF STOVL to its landing strip and direct a strike' (Lostumbo *et al.* 2017: 51). Preserving the current number of fourth-generation aircraft constitutes an equally problematic alternative as it is conceivable that Beijing could destroy all of Taiwan's runways in a first SRBM salvo. Even hypothesizing a failure of this 'first strike', the quantitative and qualitative gap in fourth- and fifth-generation aircraft will continue to evolve in China's favour, making a the current force structure – even with the possible addition of 66 F-16s – a less than ideal solution for Taiwan.

This dilemma has led many analysts to argue that the best option for the Taiwanese air force is to move away from a fighter-centric paradigm. In the air, the core logic behind the argument for a radical shift to asymmetric is summarized by a 2014 Center for Strategic and Budgetary Assessments report that emphasizes that 'although maintaining ROC control over its airspace and the airspace over the Strait may not be a realistic goal, substantially delaying or degrading the PLA's ability to gain control of ROC airspace remains feasible' (Thomas *et al.* 2014: 44).

The forces that Taiwan would need to conduct a 'guerrilla air defense campaign' (Thomas *et al.* 2014: 44) would, however, look radically different from the existing force structure. Rather than investing heavily in maintaining a relatively large or high-end fleet of air superiority fighters, Taiwan could capitalize on the asymmetric advantage – and the lower price – offered by land-based defence systems. Recent simulations run by the RAND Corporation emphasize that '[i]n high-intensity coercion or invasion scenarios, the survivability of the SAMs makes them a clearly preferred option to contest Taiwan's airspace' (Lostumbo *et al.* 2017: 82). The same RAND report concludes that the only force capable of facing high-intensity scenarios would have to be built around a small fleet of 85 F-16Vs that would allow for the addition of 12 PAC-3 batteries and the creation of 21 air defence platoons developed around Sentinel radars and AIM-9X and AIM-120 ground-launched missiles (ibid.). Various combinations of long- and short-range systems – including PAC-3, PAC-2, Tien-Kung 3, I-Hawk, ground-based Sidewinder, or systems inspired by the Russian Gauntlet SA-15 – have been envisioned (ibid.; Thomas *et al.* 2014; Hunzeker and Lanoszka 2018; Murray 2014), but the core logic remains the same: a force structured around land-based air defence systems constitutes the cheaper, most efficient, most survivable and therefore preferable alternative for a Taiwanese air denial campaign.

Beyond these major shifts in Taiwan's force structure, an air denial/'guerrilla air defence' stance would require a redefinition of Taiwan's air defence tactics. Both the aforementioned CSBA report and William Murray suggest that Taiwan could seek inspiration in tactics employed by Serbia in the 1999 Kosovo conflict (Murray 2014; Thomas *et al.* 2014). Serbia's emphasis on survivability and mobility drastically limited the success of the North Atlantic Treaty Organization (NATO)'s Suppression of Enemy Air Defenses campaign as the 700-plus anti-radiation missiles fired by NATO forces resulted in the destruction of only three out of the 25 Serbian SA-6 SAM batteries. The adoption of such tactics by Taiwan – as opposed to tactics seeking the destruction of a maximum number of incoming Chinese aircraft – would have the advantage of preventing the PLA Air Force from operating at optimal altitudes for strike operations (Murray 2014). At the same time, they would extend the time window within which Chinese aircraft could be placed at risk as the CSBA model suggests that 80 per cent of Taiwanese air defence systems could still be active after 60 days of conflict (Thomas *et al.* 2014). This stance would 'complicate, disrupt, and slow PLA air operations' (ibid.: 47), making certain that China could not secure the degree of air superiority it needs to mount an amphibious assault against the island.

Contesting sea control

The changing naval balance

A 'working' degree of sea control (Till 2018) is an obvious *sine qua non* to any Chinese amphibious operation across the Taiwan Strait. For the essential part of the PLA Navy's history, however, gaining and preserving sea control in the Strait constituted a daunting task. At the turn of the millennium, the PLA Navy was still hardly in a position to guarantee the safety of a hypothetical invasion force. Aside from its vulnerability from the air, 'the Chinese navy [was] qualitatively outmatched in most categories of warships' (Wood and Ferguson 2001: 60). The PLA Navy operated around 60 major surface combatants, but around two-thirds of this force was composed of Luda destroyers and Jianghu frigates of obsolete design and dubious war-fighting capabilities (Cole 2010). Overall, the PLA Navy operated only one destroyer that could be considered on a par with the Western platform, the first of the four Sovremmeny that it had purchased from Russia. The PLA Navy did possess a large conventional submarine fleet of around 55 boats, but more than 85 per cent remained of the obsolescent Romeo and Ming design which lacked the ability to carry anti-ship missiles (ASM) (IISS 2000).

The situation has radically changed over the past decade. China boasts today the second largest navy worldwide in terms of surface combatants and the largest fleet of modern diesel-electric submarines. A large proportion of its cruisers, destroyers, frigates and submarines appears to be on a rough qualitative par with Western platforms (Cole 2010; O'Rourke 2018) which has led analysts to warn against the possible 'overtaking' of the US Navy by the PLA Navy (Fanell and Cheney-Peters 2017; Ross 2018). China has devoted significant resources to the development of air defence and anti-submarine capabilities (O'Rourke, 2018) but as pointed out by the last Office of Naval Intelligence report: '[t]he PLA(N) continues to emphasize ASUW as a core strength, with continued development of advanced ASCMs [anti-ship cruise missiles] and OTH-T [over-the-horizon targeting] systems' (Office of Naval Intelligence 2015: 16).

As of 2018 China has operated a slightly larger number of major combatants than it did 20 years ago, but the large majority of these platforms are on a relative par with their Western counterparts. The PLA Navy possesses 29 modern destroyers – a number that has doubled over the past six years – and 43 frigates (O'Rourke 2018). China launched its first three Renhai/Type-055 large destroyers/cruisers, 'the most capable surface combatant ever commissioned by the PLAN' (Tate 2017) rivalling with the Ticonderoga, in 2017 and 2018. Serial production begun almost immediately after the first unit was launched and analysts expect a class of at least ten units. All these major combatants carry potent long-range ASM including the Russian Sunburn, the YJ-83, the YJ-62 or the brand-new YJ-18 – widely reported to be a derivative of the formidable Russian Klub but with a range of 500 km – that is expected to progressively replace older ASCMs on most of the major combatants (Pilger 2015). China has finally developed a fleet of around 40 modern, quiet diesel-electric submarines – i.e. Kilo, Song and Yuan classes – that carry a range of ASM and would probably form the first line of attack against the Taiwanese Navy.

For China, however, control of the sea is important only to the extent that it guarantees the safety of invasion forces crossing the Strait. A puzzling evolution of the PLA Navy, considering the oft-mentioned centrality of Taiwan in China's strategic thinking, is that Beijing has devoted only modest efforts to the expansion of its amphibious fleet. The number of amphibious platforms has grown at roughly the same pace as China's fleet of surface combatants (O'Rourke 2018), and the PLA Navy's capacity to transport Chinese troops across the Strait remains largely limited. As stated in the 2018 Department of Defense report,

> China's amphibious ship fleet ... has in recent years focused on acquiring a small number of LPDs [landing platform docks], indicating a near-term focus on smaller scale expeditionary missions rather than a large number of LSTs [tank landing ships] and medium landing craft that would be necessary for a large-scale direct beach assault.
> (Office of the Secretary of Defense 2018)

This, however, might be the only positive development for Taipei in a context where the naval balance is rapidly and irreversibly tilting in China's favour.

Taiwan's asymmetric option

When contrasted with its highly dynamic Chinese counterpart, the Taiwanese navy has undergone much more modest changes over the past decade. Taiwan now operates 24 major surface combatants – Kidd-class destroyers, Lafayette-, Knox- and Cheng Kung-class frigates – as well as more than 40 patrol and missile boats and four submarines (IISS 2018). The list of major combatants has remained almost unchanged since the mid-2000s when the four Kidd-class destroyers were commissioned. Two Cheng-Kung/Perry-class frigates were commissioned in 2018 after the United States agreed to transfer the two warships to Taiwan in 2012. Taipei's unsuccessful quest to acquire modern submarines (Wang and Tan 2015) has meant that the Taiwanese Navy continues to operate two ageing Zwaardis it acquired from the Netherlands in the mid-1980s and two venerable Guppy IIs built by the United States more than half a century ago. By contrast, Taiwan has almost renewed a large part of its fleet of patrol and missile boats over the last ten years. Thirty-one Kwang Hua-class patrol boats –which carry four Hsiung-Feng II ASMs – have joined the 12 larger Jing Chiang-class patrol combatants launched in the 1990s (Wertheim 2014). In 2014 the first 'carrier-killer' Tuo Jiang-class corvette joined the Taiwanese Navy, as the result of an increased effort to build 'effective asymmetrical counter against an adversary's larger warships' (Wong 2016).

To a certain extent, the pattern described above can be explained by Taipei's adaptation to the unfavourable evolution of the cross-Strait naval balance. A shift was perceptible under Ma Ying-jeou's 'hard ROC' strategy' (Ministry of National Defense 2011: 2013), which advocated for the development of 'asymmetric/innovative' solutions and put a stronger emphasis on sea denial capabilities (Turner 2016). The principles of asymmetry and innovation have continued to guide Taipei's naval thinking under Tsai Ing-wen (Ministry of National Defense 2017). Taipei's new motto – 'resist the enemy on the other shore, attack the enemy on the sea, destroy the enemy in the littoral area, and annihilate the enemy on the beachhead' (Ministry of National Defense 2017, 39) – clearly identify the sea and the littoral as the key domain for Taiwan's defence, while the developing 'overall defense concept' puts a clear emphasis on asymmetric defence capabilities at sea (Thompson 2018; US-China Economic and Security Review Commission 2018).

In this context of increased emphasis on asymmetry, Taipei's naval modernization plan, unveiled by the Tsai administration in 2016 (Minnick 2016), is somewhat puzzling. In simple terms, Taipei's US $15 billion effort seeks to create a more advanced navy but appears to preserve the idea of a *balanced* navy rather than a force focused on asymmetry and sea denial. Some of the platforms included in the modernization plan will clearly contribute to a denial strategy – i.e. advanced submarines, Tuo Jiang-class corvettes and high-speed minelayers (*Taipei Times* 2016). At the same time, however, the plan has ambitions to renew a large part of Taiwan's fleet of major combatants, advocating for the development of a new generation of Aegis-type destroyers and missile frigates as well as amphibious ships, including a large landing helicopter dock.

While Taipei's reluctance to see the most visible assets of its fleet dwindle is understandable, the priority given to a balanced force is problematic for at least two reasons. First, large combatant and amphibious platforms create enormous opportunity costs. Australia's recent experience reveals that modern destroyers, frigates and landing helicopter docks command a staggering high unitary price – between US $1.1 and $2.5 billion. A unit-for-unit replacement of the ageing Kidd-class destroyers and Knox-class frigates would leave Taiwan with little, and almost likely nothing, left to spend on other, and arguably more useful, platforms and weapons. Second, and more importantly, studies dating back at least to the last decade have repeatedly emphasized the vulnerability of Taiwan's major combatant to an array of Chinese threats (Murray 2008, 2014; Thomas *et al.* 2014; Holmes 2016). William Murray emphasizes that 'a surprise attack by a few dozen SRBMs could destroy the majority of Taiwan's large warships' (2014: 65) that are moored at pier, while China's extensive arsenal of accurate, long-range land-, ship-, submarine- and air-launched ASMs makes it difficult to envision the survival of these platforms in the Strait, making them potentially entirely irrelevant to a direct cross-Strait confrontation.

As opposed to an across-the-board modernization programme, James Holmes observes that an asymmetric, denial strategy would be best served by 'dispers[ing] firepower among many stealthy combatants rather than concentrate[ing] it in a few large, easy-to-target hulls' (2016). Correspondingly, William Murray somewhat provocatively argues that Taiwan could 'learn from Iran' (2014) and its sea denial strategy that relies on swarms of small, fast patrol boats equipped with a few potent ASMs. Taiwan has taken significant steps in that direction. The last decade has seen the introduction of 30 Kwang Hua-class patrol boats carrying four Hsiung-Feng IIs and, under the current modernization programme, the Taiwanese Navy should ultimately operate 12 new wave-piercing, stealthy Tuo-Jiang corvettes, which carry 16 ASMs (Thim and Liao 2016). There are nonetheless limiting factors to a further shift towards a 'guerrilla sea denial' navy (Thomas *et al.* 2014: 36). As mentioned above, Taipei's ambitions in terms of major surface combatants will create severe opportunity costs. The Tuo-Jiang comes with a modest US $73 million unitary price tag, which means that at least a dozen units could be acquired for the price of one new destroyer or frigate (*Taipei Times* 2014). Recent debates have also proven that domestic infighting could be a limiting factor. In December 2018 the Legislative Yuan slashed half of the funding for the development of the type of very small, fast missile boats that William Murray sees as pivotal to the development of a Taiwanese sea denial force (*Asia Times* 2018).

Below the surface, Taiwan has multiple options to support a sea denial strategy. Taipei has been hoping to acquire modern submarines since at least 2001, when George W. Bush approved the sale of eight diesel-electric submarines (Wang and Tan 2015). The absence of an international solution to the acquisition of modern submarines in the subsequent years has pushed the Tsai administration to announce the launch of an indigenous defence submarine programme in 2017. In many ways, the acquisition of a submarine force makes perfect sense for Taipei as submarines have been historically 'the weapon of choice for weaker naval powers that wish to contest a dominant power's control of the seas or its ability to project power ashore from the sea' (Cote 2003: 1). Taiwanese submarines could be used to threaten an invading force in the Strait or alternatively be used in a more an offensive way to mine Chinese ports at the outset of a conflict – although this option would be likely to provoke escalatory action (Murray 2008, 2014).

Analysts have, however, suggested that the relatively large type of submarine (1,200–3,000 metric tons) (Phipps 2016) that Taipei has committed to develop might not best fit Taipei's needs. William Murray (2014) argues that Taiwan could hardly hope to have more than half of its eight submarines at sea at any time making the underwater defensive line very thin. These submarines could be further threatened by Chinese plans to develop a sound surveillance system-like system in the near seas, which could degrade their stealth and usefulness in the Taiwan Strait (Fisher 2016). Rather than building large, 'traditional' submarines, CSBA analysts have advocated for the development of an extensive fleet of midget submarines and autonomous underwater vehicles (Thomas *et al.* 2014). Multiple models of midget submarines have recently emerged in addition to the Iranian *Ghadir* or the North Korean counterpart *Yono* – one of which was probably responsible for the sinking of the South Korean *Cheonan* corvette in 2010 (Bermudez and Dewey 2016). Indonesia and Thailand have forged ahead with their own programmes, while the Chinese MS200 – carrying two heavyweight torpedoes and with a submerged range of 120 nautical miles – has been advertised for export (Wong 2017). For the same sum spent on eight high-end submarines, CSBA analysts estimate that the Taiwanese navy could afford as many as 42 midget submarines that could form a dangerous picket against Chinese surface forces (Thomas *et al.* 2014).

Sea mines would constitute a potent force multiplier in any attempt to thwart a Chinese invasion (Murray 2008; Thomas *et al.* 2014; Murray 2014; Hunzeker and Lanoszka 2018). Taiwan possesses an array of old MK-6 mines and indigenously developed Wanxiang mines – a second version of which was launched in the 2000s (Liu 2018). Mine warfare seems to have gained a degree of salience in Taiwanese defence strategy (Thompson 2018). One of the prominent items on Taipei's naval modernization list is a high-speed mine layer and the Ministry of National Defense has called for the development of a new generation of smart sea mines. An article published in the journal of the Taiwanese Navy further concludes that 'in order to foster our asymmetric combat capabilities, Taiwan needs to develop more actively its mine warfare capabilities, and strengthen its preparation for the use of sea mines (Liu 2018: 94).

Taiwan could finally turn the tables on China by 'using the land to (deny) control (of) the sea' to the PLA Navy (Erickson and Yang 2009: 79). A pivotal part of William Murray's 'porcupine Republic' concept lay in the acquisition of 'mobile coastal-defense cruise missiles (CDCMs), such as truck-mounted Harpoons' which could 'devastate China's armor-carrying amphibious shipping' (2008: 27). The alternative of a land-based sea denial capability is attractive for at least two reasons. On the one hand, it is highly affordable. The 2014 CSBA report notes that '[t]o hold a putative invasion fleet at risk, which could consist of roughly 32 amphibious transport ships and 60 naval combatant escorts, the ROC would require just over 1,200 ASCMs' (Thomas et al. 2014: iii), and calculates that Taiwan could probably build such a force for less than US $2 billion. Taiwan could arguably opt for an even larger force to ensure some degree of redundancy. On the other hand, a force of 300 or more mobile missile batteries is highly survivable, because it disperses firepower among small targets that are hard to identify and track. One last advantage is that Taiwan already possesses the technological expertise to build such a force – i.e. Hsiung Feng II and III – which makes it a very low-risk option in comparison with the development of a new generation of submarines or surface combatants.

Conclusion

As the military balance in the Taiwan Strait continues to shift rapidly in Beijing's favour, Taiwan is facing increased pressure to adapt its strategy and force structure. Responding to the degradation of its security environment, Taipei's strategic thinking – as reflected in official documents – has evolved significantly over the last decades. The notions of 'innovation' and 'asymmetry' have gained an increasingly central position in Taiwan's discourse on its own defence under both Ma and Tsai. At the same time, however, the restructuring of Taiwan's naval and air forces around an asymmetric, denial strategy has suffered from a degree of inertia. While Taipei has taken steps to acquire the kind of platforms and weapons that would support such a strategy, it is also devoting considerable resources to items that would arguably be suboptimal in the event of a cross-Strait confrontation.

In many ways, Taipei finds itself at a crossroads. Choices that are currently made by Taipei in terms of military modernization will shape Taiwan's force structure for the decades to come. In a context where Beijing shows signs of impatience, adopting a suboptimal strategy and/or pushing the force structure in an inadequate direction could have a very serious impact on Taipei's chances of ensuring its survival. Ironically, Robert Ross (2009: 65) pointed out a decade ago that China ran the risk of falling victim to the 'prestige' trap, as its naval modernization process appeared to include platforms of little strategic value for China. In a way, Taiwan now appears to face a prestige trap of its own. William Murray (2014) observed that 'Taiwan's current air force and much of its navy have symbolical and operational value in peacetime, but their utility in wartime is at best suspect, and quite possibly approaches nil', and the current comprehensive naval modernization programme runs the risk of perpetuating, in large part, this state of affairs. A retrospective look at China's naval – and more generally military – modernization programme suggests that Beijing was able to successfully overcome the prestige trap. Whether Taiwan will be able to do so too and consolidate its ability to defend itself against a possible Chinese attack remains an open question.

Notes

1 The *Military Balance* reported that the PLA Air Force was then operating 65 Su-27s, while its 40 Su-30MKK had not yet entered service.
2 For a previous statement, see for instance Ministry of National Defense (2015, 121).
3 As the sale of the F-35 appears to be increasingly unlikely, Taiwan's interest seems to have recently reverted back to requesting the sale of additional F-16Vs (Chung 2018).

References

An, D. (2018) *Reconstructing Taiwan's Military Strategy: Achieving Forward Defense through Multi-Domain Deterrence*, Seattle, WA: National Bureau of Asian Research.
Asia Times (2018) 'Taiwan's Small Missile Boat Program Hamstrung by Budget Cuts', *Asia Times*, 13 December. Available at www.atimes.com/article/taiwans-small-missile-boat-program-hamstrung-by-budget-cuts/ (accessed 29 January 2019).
Bermudez, J. S. Jr and K. Dewey (2016) 'North Korea Modernises Submarine Fleet', *Jane's Intelligence Review*, 9 February. Available at www.janes.com/images/assets/463/57463/North_Korea_modernises_submarine_fleet1.pdf (accessed 21 December 2019).
Broadcasting Corporation of China (2017) 'Kongjun Fangkongbu Fubian' ('Reorganization of the ROCAF Air Defense Department'), 1 September. Available at www.bcc.com.tw (accessed 4 December 2018).
Caffrey, C. (2015) 'Closing the Gaps: Air Force Modernisation in China', *Jane's Defence Weekly*, 2 October. Available at https://janes.ihs.com (accessed 4 December 2018).
Chan, M. (2018) 'China 'Nearing Mass Production' of J-20 Stealth Fighter after Engine Problems Ironed Out', *South China Morning Post*, 5 September. Available at www.scmp.com/news/china/military/article/2162765/china-nearing-mass-production-j-20-stealth-fighter-after-engine (accessed 4 December 2018).
Chung, L. (2018) 'Taiwan Hints F-16V Fighter Jets Are Back on Its Defence Shopping List', *South China Morning Post*, 29 November. Available at www.scmp.com/news/china/military/article/2175614/taiwan-hints-f-16v-fighter-jets-are-back-its-defence-shopping (accessed 7 December 2018).
Cole, B. D. (2010) *The Great Wall at Sea: China's Navy in the Twenty-First Century*, Annapolis, MD: Naval Institute Press.
Cote, O. R. Jr (2003) *The Third Battle: Innovation in the U.S. Navy's Silent Cold War Struggle with Soviet Submarines*, Newport, RI: Naval War College.
Dominguez, G. (2018) 'PLAAF Inducts J-20 into Combat Units', *Jane's Defence Weekly*, 12 February. Available at www.janes.com/article/77794/plaaf-inducts-j-20-into-combat-units (accessed 4 December 2018).

Dominguez, G. and N. Gibson (2017) 'PLA Rocket Force Trains Deployment of Dong Feng Ballistic Missiles', *Jane's Defence Weekly*, 6 February. Available at https://janes.ihs.com (accessed 5 December 2018).

Easton, I. (2017) *The Chinese Invasion Threat: Taiwan's Defense and American Strategy in Asia*, Arlington, VA: The Project 2049 Institute.

Erickson, A. S. and D. D. Yang (2009) 'Using the Land to Control the Sea: Chinese Analysts Consider the Anti-ship Ballistic Missile', *Naval War College Review*, 62(4): 53–86.

Fanell, J. E. and S. Cheney-Peters (2017) 'Defending against a Chinese Navy of 500 Ships', *Wall Street Journal*, 19 January. Available at www.wsj.com/articles/defending-against-a-chinese-navy-of-500-ships-1484848417 (accessed 17 December 2018).

Fisher, R. D.Jr. (2016) 'China Proposes "Underwater Great Wall" That Could Erode US, Russian Submarine Advantages', *Jane's Defence Weekly*, 17 May. Available at http://defensenews-alert.blogspot.com/2016/05/china-proposes-underwater-great-wall.html (accessed 14 December 2018).

Focus Taiwan (2018) 'AIDC to Deliver 66 Advanced Jet Trainers by 2026', 31 August. Available at http://focustaiwan.tw/news/aipl/201808310009.aspx (accessed 8 December 2018).

Gady, F. S. (2017) 'Why Selling F-35s to Taiwan Is a Terrible Idea', *The Diplomat*, 7 April. Available at https://thediplomat.com/2017/04/why-selling-f-35s-to-taiwan-is-a-terrible-idea/ (accessed 7 December 2018).

Gady, F. S. (2018a) 'China's Military Accepts First S-400 Missile Air Defense Regiment from Russia', *The Diplomat*, 26 July. Available at https://thediplomat.com/2018/07/chinas-military-accepts-first-s-400-missile-air-defense-regiment-from-russia/ (accessed 14 December 2018).

Gady, F. S. (2018b) 'Taiwan Wants the F-35 Stealth Fighter', *The Diplomat*, 21 March. Available at https://thediplomat.com/2018/03/taiwan-wants-the-f-35-stealth-fighter/ (accessed 7 December 2018).

Gao, C. (2018) 'China's HQ-9 vs. Russia's S-300 Air Defense System: What's the Difference?' *National Interest*, 10 November. Available at https://nationalinterest.org/blog/buzz/chinas-hq-9-vs-russias-s-300-air-defense-system-whats-difference-35777 (accessed 7 December 2018).

Glosny, M. A. (2004) 'Strangulation from the Sea? A PRC Submarine Blockade of Taiwan', *International Security*, 28(4): 125–160.

Goldstein, L. J. and W. S. Murray (2004) 'Undersea Dragons: China's Maturing Submarine Force', *International Security*, 28(4): 161–196.

Grubb, M. C. (2007) 'Merchant Shipping in a Chinese Blockade of Taiwan', *Naval War College Review*, 60(1): 81–102.

Hallion, R. P. (1997) 'Airpower Past, Present and Future', in R. P. Hallion (ed.) *Airpower Confronts an Unstable World*, London: Brassey's, pp. 1–12.

Heginbotham, E. M., Nixon, F. E., Morgan, J. L., Heim, J., Hagen, S. Li, J. Engstrom, M. C. Libicki, P. DeLuca, D. A. Shlapak, D. R. Frelinger, B. Laird, K. Brady and L. J. Morris (2015) *The U.S.-China Military Scorecard: Forces, Geography, and the Evolving Balance of Power, 1996–2017*, Santa Monica, CA: RAND Corporation.

Holmes, J. (2016) 'Securing Taiwan Starts with Overhauling Its Navy', *National Interest*, 5 February. Available at https://nationalinterest.org/feature/securing-taiwan-starts-overhauling-the-navy-15122 (accessed 2 December 2018).

Huang, C. (2019) 'China's Xi Jinping Has Opened the Door to War with Taiwan', *South China Morning Post*, 13 January. Available at www.scmp.com/week-asia/op

inion/article/2181403/chinas-xi-jinping-has-opened-door-war-taiwan (accessed 24 January 2019).

Hunzeker, M. A. and A. Lanoszka (2018) *A Question of Time: Enhancing Taiwan's Conventional Deterrence Posture*, Arlington, VA: Center for Security Policy Studies/ George Mason University.

International Institute for Strategic Studies (IISS) (2000) *The Military Balance 2000*, London: IISS.

International Institute for Strategic Studies (IISS) (2018) *The Military Balance 2018*, London: IISS.

Jennings, G. (2017) 'Taiwan Begins F-16V Modernisation Effort', *Jane's Defence Weekly*, 17 January. Available at https://janes.ihs.com (accessed 7 December 2018).

Johnson, R. F. (2015) 'Russian Official Confirms S-400 Sale to China', *Jane's Defence Weekly*, 15 April. Available at https://janes.ihs.com (accessed 7 December 2018).

Liu, B. (2018) 'Haijun Bulei Zuozhan Yunyong' ('The Operational Use of Mines by the Navy'), *Haijun Xueshu*, 52(4): 81–94.

Lostumbo, M. J., D. R. Frelinger, J. Williams and B. Wilson (2017) *Air Defense Options for Taiwan: An Assessment of Relative Costs and Operational Benefits*, Santa Monica, CA: RAND.

Mainland Affairs Council, ROC (2018) 'Cross-Strait Economic Statistics Monthly', 298. Available at www.mac.gov.tw (accessed 2 December 2018).

Martin, L. (1967) *The Sea in Modern Strategy*, New York: Praeger.

Ministry of National Defense, ROC (2011) *National Defense Report, 100th Anniversary*, Taipei: Ministry of National Defense.

Ministry of National Defense, ROC (2013) *National Defense Report 2013*, Taipei: Ministry of National Defense.

Ministry of National Defense, ROC (2015) *National Defense Report 2015*, Taipei: Ministry of National Defense.

Ministry of National Defense, ROC (2017) *National Defense Report 2017*, Taipei: Ministry of National Defense.

Minnick, W. (2016) 'Taiwan Moves on $14.7B Indigenous Shipbuilding, Upgrade Projects', *Defense News*, 23 June. Available at www.defensenews.com/naval/2016/06/23/taiwan-moves-on-14-7b-indigenous-shipbuilding-upgrade-projects/ (accessed 2 December 2018).

Murray, W. S. (2008) 'Revisiting Taiwan's Defense Strategy', *Naval War College Review*, 63(1): 13–38.

Murray, W. S. (2014) 'Asymmetric Options for Taiwan's Deterrence and Defense', in M. C. M. Chu and S. L. Kastner (eds) *Globalization and Security Relations across the Taiwan Strait: In the Shadow of China*, London: Routledge, pp. 61–79.

O'Hanlon, M. (2000) 'Why China Cannot Conquer Taiwan', *International Security*, 25 (2): 51–86.

O'Rourke, R. (2018) *China Naval Modernization: Implications for U.S. Navy Capabilities –Background and Issues for Congress*, Washington, DC:Congressional Research Office. Available at www.everycrsreport.com/reports/RL33153.html (accessed 21 November 2018).

Office of Naval Intelligence (2015) *The PLA Navy New Capabilities and Missions for the 21st Century*, Washington, DC: Office of Naval Intelligence.

Office of the Secretary of Defense (2018) *Annual Report to Congress: Military and Security Developments Involving the People's Republic of China 2018*, 16 May.

Available at https://media.defense.gov/2018/Aug/16/2001955282/-1/-1/1/2018-CHINA-MILITARY-POWER-REPORT.PDF (accessed 28 November 2018).

Phipps, G. (2010) 'Taiwan Commissions First Kwang Hua 6 Squadron', *Jane's Defence Weekly*, 19 May. Available at https://janes.ihs.com (accessed 4 December 2018).

Phipps, G. (2016) 'Island Endeavour: Taiwan Country Briefing', *Jane's Defence Weekly*, 22 March. Available at www.janes.com/images/assets/307/59307/Island_endeavour_Taiwan_country_briefing.pdf (accessed 14 December 2018).

Pilger, P. (2015) *China's New YJ-18 Antiship Cruise Missile: Capabilities and Implications for U.S. Forces in the Western Pacific*, Washington, DC: US-China Economic and Security Review Commission. Available at https://www.uscc.gov/sites/default/files/Research/China%E2%80%99s%20New%20YJ-18%20Antiship%20Cruise%20Missile.pdf (accessed 1 December 2018).

Reuters (2017) 'Taiwan to Build 66 Jet Trainer Aircraft by 2026 to Bolster Defenses', 7 February. Available at www.reuters.com/article/us-taiwan-defence/taiwan-to-build-66-jet-trainer-aircraft-by-2026-to-bolster-defenses-idUSKBN15M0KB (accessed 8 December 2018).

Ross, R. (2009) 'China's Naval Nationalism: Sources, Prospects, and the U.S. Response', *International Security*, 34(2).

Ross, R. S. (2018) 'Keeping Up with China's PLAN', *National Interest*, 15 April. Available at https://nationalinterest.org/feature/keeping-chinas-plan-25383 (accessed 17 December 2018).

Shlapak, D. A., D. T. Orletsky, T. I. Reid, M. S. Tanner and B. Wilson (2009) *A Question of Balance Political Context and Military Aspects of the China-Taiwan Dispute*, Santa Monica: RAND Corporation.

South China Morning Post (2017) 'Taiwan Grounds All Mirage Jets after Pilot Goes Missing during Exercise', 8 November. Available at www.scmp.com/news/china/policies-politics/article/2118912/taiwan-grounds-all-mirage-jets-after-pilot-goes-missing (accessed 8 December 2018).

Stockholm International Peace Research Institute (SIPRI) (2018) *Arms Transfer Database*. Available at http://armstrade.sipri.org (accessed 2 December 2018).

Taipei Times (2014) 'Carrier-Killer Starts Trials', 28 October. Available at www.taipeitimes.com/News/taiwan/archives/2014/10/28/2003603112 (accessed 5 December 2018).

Taipei Times (2016) 'Navy to Spend NT$470bn on 12 Shipbuilding Projects', 21 June. Available at www.taipeitimes.com/News/taiwan/archives/2016/06/21/20036491272016 (accessed 2 December 2018).

Tanner M. S. (2007) *Chinese Economic Coercion against Taiwan a Tricky Weapon to Use*, Santa Monica, CA: RAND Corporation.

Tate, A. (2017) 'Assessing the Capabilities of China's Type 055 Destroyer', *Jane's Defence Weekly*, 7 July. Available at https://janes.ihs.com (accessed 1 December 2018).

Thim, M. and Y. Liao (2016) 'Taiwan Navy Emphasizing Domestic Shipbuilding Program in Ongoing Maritime Restructure', *USNI News*, 25 March. Available at https://news.usni.org/2016/03/25/taiwan-navy-emphasizing-domestic-shipbuilding-program-in-ongoing-maritime-restructure (accessed 4 December 2018).

Thomas, J., J. Stillion and I. Rehman (2014) *Hard ROC 2.0: Taiwan and Deterrence Through Protraction*, Washington, DC: CSBA.

Thompson, D. (2018) 'Hope on the Horizon: Taiwan's Radical New Defense Concept', *War on the Rocks*, 2 October. Available at https://warontherocks.com/2018/10/hope-on-the-horizon-taiwans-radical-new-defense-concept/ (accessed 2 December 2018).

Till, G. (2018) *Seapower: A Guide for the Twenty-First Century*, London: Routledge.

Tsai, I. (2019) 'President Tsai Issues Statement on China's President Xi's "Message to Compatriots in Taiwan"', Taipei: Office of the President, ROC, 2 February. Available at https://english.president.gov.tw/News/5621 (accessed 21 January 2019).

Turner, J. M. (2016) 'The Cost of Credible Deterrence in Taiwan', *War on the Rocks*, 13 January. Available at https://warontherocks.com/2016/01/the-cost-of-credible-deterrence-in-taiwan/ (accessed 15 December 2018).

US-China Economic and Security Review Commission (2018) *2018 Annual Report*, 14 November. Available at www.uscc.gov/Annual_Reports/2018-annual-report (accessed 20 January 2019).

Wang, J. and Tan, C. (2015) 'Taiwan's Submarine Saga', *The Diplomat*, 11 May. Available at https://thediplomat.com/2015/05/taiwans-submarine-saga/ (accessed 6 December 2018).

Wertheim, E. (2014) *The Naval Institute Guide to Combat Fleets of the World*, Annapolis, MD: Naval Institute Press.

Wong, K. (2016) 'Carrier Killer: Taiwan's Tuo Jiang-Class Missile Corvette', *Jane's International Defence Review*, 8 December. Available at www.janes.com/images/assets/163/66163/Carrier_killer_Taiwans_Tuo_Jiang-class_missile_corvette.pdf (accessed 9 December 2018).

Wong, K. (2017) 'China Targets Export Market with Latest Submarine Designs', *Jane's International Defence Review*, 11 December. Available at https://janes.ihs.com (accessed 8 December 2018).

Wood, P. M. and C. D. Ferguson (2001) 'How China Might Invade Taiwan', *Naval War College Review*, 54(4): 55–68.

World Trade Organization (2018) 'Time Series: Total Merchandise Trade [Taiwan]'. Available at http://stat.wto.org (accessed 2 December 2018).

Xi, J. (2019) 'Xi Jinping: Wei Shixian Minzu Weida Fuxing, Tuijin Zuguo Heping Tongyi er Gongtong Fendou. Zai Gao "TaiwanTongbao Shu Fabiao" 40 Zhounian Jinianhui shang de Jianghua' ('Xi Jinping: Striving Together for the Great Rejuvenation of the Nation and the Promotion the Peaceful Reunification of the Motherland: Speech at the 40th Anniversary of the "Message to Compatriots in Taiwan"'), Xinhua, 2 January. Available at http://www.xinhuanet.com (accessed 21 January 2019).

Xue, X. (2001) *Zhanyi Lilun Xuexi Zhinan* (*Campaign Theory Study Guide*), Beijing: National Defense University Press.

Zhang, Y. (2006) *Zhanyi Xue* (*The Science of Military Campaigns*), Beijing: National Defense University.

13 Thinking about how to forge lasting peace in the Taiwan Strait

Derek Grossman[1]

On 7 November 2015 Taiwanese President Ma Ying-jeou and Chinese President Xi Jinping met at a summit of sorts in Singapore. In preparation for the historic event, both sides hammered out in excruciating detail all the ins and outs of the encounter in order to avoid political traps. Ma and Xi addressed each other not as leaders but as gentlemen citizens, or *xiansheng*, of their respective countries. That way Xi did not have to recognize 'President' Ma of the 'renegade province' of Taiwan. After exchanging pleasantries and sipping *maotai* together, it appeared that a formal declaration of peace between the bitter adversaries was finally within reach. But the lasting image of Ma and Xi shaking hands paradoxically revealed the true limitations of cross-Strait negotiation on the sovereignty issue.

Significantly, nothing even close to a 'peace accord' was agreed to at the Xi-Ma summit following seven years of cross-Strait warming under Ma, underscoring just how difficult it is to achieve an official end to the decades-long state of hostilities across the Strait – even in the most favourable of circumstances.[2] This is because mutual suspicions and strategic calculating for an uncertain future prevented any genuine breakthroughs. For one thing, Xi clearly had ulterior motives in meeting with Ma at that particular juncture. In late 2015 Tsai Ing-wen of the opposition and Taiwan-centric Democratic Progressive Party (DPP) was considered Ma's near-certain successor. Beijing surely assessed that by engaging Ma, it could in turn undercut Tsai's future administration. The hope was that the Xi-Ma summit might lock Tsai into agreeing to the so-called 1992 Consensus – China's preferred sovereignty formulation emphasizing One China – since Ma had already done so. Additionally, the Chinese did not engage in any confidence-building measures, such as removing short-range ballistic missiles pointed at Taiwan. Instead, Chinese military modernization, with an emphasis on conducting amphibious landing and other operations against the island, continued apace. For its part, Taiwan did not pledge to forego future independence activities that Beijing commonly labels as 'separatist'. In other words, the summit was the best albeit missed opportunity to forge real and lasting peace in the Strait.

Regrettably, the current situation is a world apart from the heady times of the Ma-Xi summit. In the first week of 2019 Xi and Tsai gave rousing speeches on the sovereignty dispute. In her annual New Year's Day address, Tsai unveiled her 'four musts', saying that Beijing must recognize the island's existence; must respect Taiwan's freedom and democracy; deal with the island peacefully and on equal terms; and only communicate through government-authorized channels (Office of the President, ROC, 2019a). The following day, Xi commemorated the 40th anniversary of China's 'Message to Compatriots in Taiwan' by dispensing with the notion that the 1992 Consensus implicitly allows for 'different interpretations' of One China and instead equating it *exclusively* with the One China principle' (*Economic Daily* 2019). He also emphasized 'one country, two systems' – envisioning one China, but with different governments – as the future cross-Strait political framework. Tsai then responded by saying that 'we have never accepted the 1992 Consensus' and Taiwan 'will absolutely not accept "one country, two systems"' (Office of the President, ROC, 2019b). Indeed, the 'cold peace' that has prevailed in the Strait since Tsai's election in January 2016 is getting even frostier, making a peace deal seem increasingly remote (Grossman 2016).

Despite the long odds, this chapter takes a fresh look at what might be required for Beijing and Taipei to sign a formal and sustainable peace accord – or, at a minimum, to find ways to forge constructive dialogue on the political question. The stakes are simply too high – and chance for armed conflict too real – to be complacent about the future. Disappointingly, my research strongly suggests that Xi's decision to 'move the goalposts' on cross-Strait relations makes it highly unlikely that any sort of peace accord or even confidence-building measures (CBMs) towards initiating political negotiations are possible in the Strait. Xi's decision to discard or at least downplay former Chinese President Hu Jintao's emphasis on preventing Taiwanese independence and deferring reunification into the indefinite future, and instead to emphasize Deng Xiaoping's 'one country, two systems' framework that envisions only one China, but with different governments, is simply a non-starter with Taiwan. And likewise, Tsai's refusal to recognize the 1992 Consensus in the exact wording and with the exact meaning that Xi desires will only prolong the political stand-off. Nevertheless, there are elements of a peace deal that could significantly bolster the peaceful status quo and avoid potential calamity. However, maintaining the peace will probably require a bit of compromise on both sides and the use of CBMs to work up to political talks deferred to another day.

The rest of this chapter proceeds as follows. First, I assess Beijing versus Taipei's preferences for a peace deal and explain their underlying motivations to achieve these end states. Second, I describe the contours of past proposals for cross-Strait peace agreements – including Chinese, Taiwanese and Western-inspired ideas – and identify ways in which the current state of cross-Strait relations could benefit (or not) from these proposed pacts. Finally, I offer several concluding thoughts based on my analysis.

Differing preferences in the Strait

What China wants

Beijing has consistently held that Taiwan's peaceful unification – or, in its words, 'reunification' – with the mainland is the preferred option for resolving the 'Taiwan issue'.[3] However, the degree to which Chinese leaders over time have focused on reunification has varied. Although Mao Zedong, Deng and Jiang Zemin argued strongly for reunification (whether through war or peacefully), Hu took a decidedly less confrontational approach, deferring discussions on reunification indefinitely and instead focusing on preventing Taiwanese independence (People's Republic of China White Paper 2000; Jiang 1995; Xinhua 2008). Xi has tied reunification with Taiwan to his 'China dream' of national rejuvenation (Bloomberg 2019). His approach to Taiwan policy has built upon the past in the sense that the One China principle and the prevention of Taiwanese secession remain key priorities. But Xi, unlike Jiang and Hu, has used Taiwan's concurrence with the 1992 Consensus as the exclusive litmus test for whether Taipei's intentions can be trusted in cross-Strait relations (Huang 2017: 239–48). For example, in his 19th Party Congress speech in October 2017, Xi urged Taiwan to 'recognize the historical fact of the 1992 Consensus and that the two sides both belong to one China, *and then* our two sides can conduct dialogue to address through discussion the concerns of the people of both sides, and no political party or group in Taiwan will have any difficulty conducting exchanges with the mainland' (Xinhua 2017a, emphasis added). This is in stark contrast to Hu's complete omission of the 1992 Consensus from the 17th Party Congress speech, and his mention of it in his 18th Party Congress speech merely in passing and not as a prerequisite for further cross-Strait exchanges (Hu 2007, 2012).[4]

Xi has also emphasized the 'one country, two systems' framework for future relations with Taiwan. During his 19th Party Congress speech Xi stated that 'we must uphold the principles of "peaceful reunification" and "one country, two systems", work for the peaceful development of cross-Straits relations, and advance the process toward the peaceful reunification of China' (Cheung 2017). Xi's re-inclusion of 'one country, two systems' to describe the desired end state of China-Taiwan relations is significant (ibid.). Paramount leader Deng created the expression in the 1980s, but not since his time has it been elevated by the leadership to characterize the preferred means for Taiwan's integration with the mainland (Huang and Li 2010: 310).[5] Xi has touted the success of the 'one country, two systems' framework in special administrative regions Hong Kong and Macau, suggesting that the arrangement would work similarly well for Taiwan if only the opportunity presented itself. This is worrisome as Beijing has increasingly interfered in the politics and elections in these ostensibly autonomous regions. Taiwan has watched the implementation of this system in these places and it has only bolstered the public's belief that the 'one country, two systems' framework would be bad for democracy and the rule of law on the island (Tan 2017). In early January 2019 Tsai flatly rejected the notion of 'one country, two systems' in response to Xi's speech, and even the opposition and more China-friendly Kuomintang (KMT – Nationalist Party) in Taiwan came out against Beijing's plan (Hsu 2019; *Straits Times* 2019).

With the election of Tsai in January 2016 as president of Taiwan, Chinese leaders including Xi himself have been greatly dissatisfied by Tsai's refusal to agree to the 1992 Consensus. She has attempted to mend fences with Beijing, but to no avail. Shortly after her election victory, for instance, Tsai gave an interview in which she referred for the first time ever to the 'existing political foundation' across the Strait. She further stated for the first time that the Straits Exchange Foundation (SEF)-Association for Relations Across the Taiwan Strait (ARATS) –known as SEF-ARATS, a Track 2.0 dialogue – meeting establishing the 1992 Consensus was a 'historical fact' (Tsou 2016; *Focus Taiwan* 2016; *People's Daily* 2016). In March 2016, however, Xi mandated that Taiwan should recognize 'the core connotation of the 1992 Consensus', implying that only a clear public statement of commitment to the 1992 Consensus would suffice (Bush 2016). Indeed, analysts had wondered if Xi had set the rhetorical bar even higher for Tsai – that is, she would have to explicitly accept that One China includes both mainland China and Taiwan *without* differing interpretations – and Xi's speech in January 2019 essentially confirmed this hypothesis (Cole 2015). Xi's rhetoric overall has become increasingly hostile towards Taiwan. In March, during the National People's Congress, for example, he railed against Taiwan's 'acts and ploys', saying that such activities 'will be condemned by the Chinese people and punished by history' (Lim 2018).

In Chinese eyes, Tsai's affiliation with the DPP automatically makes her motives suspicious. Beijing has neither forgotten nor forgiven Tsai's work in the late 1990s on Taiwanese President Lee Teng-hui's 'special state-to-state' formulation of cross-Strait relations, implying two separate and sovereign states on either side of the Strait. Furthermore, they have neither forgotten nor forgiven Tsai's rejection of the 1992 Consensus during her failed campaign to become president in 2012, or her response to Hu's request that the DPP 'change' its pro-independence stance. As DPP chairwoman, Tsai argued that Hu's 'demand that a political party must first abandon its main principles as a precondition for interaction is not in accord with democratic principles' (Hu 2008; *Liberty Times* 2009).[6] In her role as President, Tsai has also been attacked personally, with a senior Chinese military official criticizing her for being 'extreme' and 'emotional' because she is unmarried. Although he was quickly dismissed from his post and his words roundly condemned in China, the fact that the article ever appeared in the first place in the *International Herald Leader* – a newspaper affiliated with the state-run Xinhua news agency – speaks to the depths of vitriol mustered against Tsai (Hernandez and Piao 2016).

China is also suspicious of the DPP (and implicitly Tsai's) role in the Taiwanese youth-led protests in 2014 against the cross-Strait Trade-in-Services Agreement, culminating in the Sunflower Movement (Chung 2016a). It is likely that Beijing interpreted the protest as being anti-China (even though it mostly pertained to domestic socio-economic issues) and is almost certainly concerned about activist exchanges between Sunflower and Umbrella Movement members who have protested against the political order in Hong Kong (Cheung 2016).

But distrust of Tsai is not the only force shaping the mainland's thinking. Beijing sees two further, perhaps more sinister, trends developing in Taiwanese politics. The first is Tsai's decision in September 2017 to appoint Lai Ching-te, or William Lai, to the premiership. Lai is the former mayor of Tainan, which is located in the deep south and is considered a DPP stronghold. In late September 2017, during an open session of the legislature, he unambiguously advocated Taiwanese independence (*Taipei Times* 2018). Tsai appropriately distanced herself from Lai's remarks, but the damage had clearly been done. In April the Chinese communist party mouthpiece, the *Global Times*, attributed People's Liberation Army (PLA) drills held in the Strait to Lai's 'high profile advocacy for independence' (Zhang 2018). Lai resigned following the DPP's losses in local elections in November 2018, and now has jumped into the 2020 presidential race against Tsai (Lin 2018). And second, two former presidents – Lee Tung-hui and Chen Shui-bian – joined forces in a grassroots effort to push for a referendum on using the name 'Taiwan' instead of 'Chinese Taipei' at the Winter Olympics in 2022. The resolution failed in November 2018, although pro-independence groups within Taiwan have continued to call for a national sovereignty referendum (Horton 2018a).

From Beijing's perspective, Tsai's obstinance regarding the 1992 Consensus and her alleged untrustworthiness, coupled with other gathering ominous trends on the island, have convinced China of the need to pressurize the island into submission. Beijing has deployed diplomatic, economic and military means to accomplish its objective. China, for example, has broken the long-standing diplomatic truce that was intact under President Ma and is now actively poaching Taiwan's remaining official diplomatic allies. Most recently, in August 2018, El Salvador switched its recognition from Taipei to Beijing, thereby becoming the fifth country to be lost since the start of the Tsai administration (others include The Gambia, São Tomé and Príncipe, Panama and the Dominican Republic) and bringing Taiwan's total down to just 17 partners (Horton 2018b). Other key partners, such as the Holy See and Eswatini, could follow, which would signify the end of Taiwan's diplomatic presence in Europe and on the African continent, respectively (Sands 2018; Gao 2018).

On the economic front, while Beijing has reportedly kept in place the 23 agreements signed with President Ma in 2010 known collectively as the Economic Cooperation Framework Agreement (ECFA), it is likely that Chinese officials have slowed the implementation of some agreements and baulked at going any further in negotiations until Tsai recognizes the 1992 Consensus.[7] Beijing has also sought to weaponize Chinese tourism to the island – a significant source of income for Taiwan – against the Tsai administration (Xinhua 2018). Perhaps as early as 2016 Beijing began limiting the number of travellers and was rumoured to be doing the same on a larger scale in 2018.

Finally, Xi has instructed the PLA to ramp up its threats against Taiwan. China's new and only aircraft carrier, the *Liaoning*, for instance, has transited the Strait on multiple occasions over the last two years. Xi has also promoted H-6K bomber flights to encircle the island, and these flights have been on the rise, particularly since the end of 2017 (Grossman *et al.* 2018).

China probably assesses that the DPP's landslide electoral defeat to the KMT in November 2018 has dampened the prospect that Tsai might act radically in the remainder of her term. It has yet to be seen, however, whether such an assessment will translate into less Chinese pressure on Tsai going forward. To be sure, Chinese leaders may just as easily persuade themselves that their pressure tactics are working and that they need to proceed to ensure that Tsai does not get re-elected in 2020.

What Taiwan wants

Besides Ma's decision to recognize the 1992 Consensus, which is significant, it is actually an outlier in Taiwanese politics. Indeed, Taiwan's overarching approach to China policy has consistently reflected the widely held belief that maintaining the peaceful, albeit ambiguous, cross-Strait status quo is the top preference of the Taiwanese people.[8] Of course, there is some measure of debate on how precisely to do that, and whether Tsai's refusal to acknowledge the 1992 Consensus is a wise decision over the long term.[9] Nevertheless, Tsai has been consistent in her message that her top priorities are to (1) protect the free and democratic way of life in Taiwan; (2) to defend the island's sustainable development; and (3) to maintain cross-Strait peace and regional stability (Tsai 2018). She has also made numerous overtures to Beijing for peace during her presidency of Taiwan (ibid). Press reporting in 2018 indicated that Taiwan's Mainland Affairs Council (MAC) would like to facilitate a Tsai-Xi summit – based on Taipei's traditional approach of no political preconditions – but given the high tensions, this seems unlikely (Focus Taiwan 2018a). Regardless, China has never publicly or positively reciprocated to Tsai's overtures.

This is unfortunate because, and despite Beijing's perceptions, Tsai has proven herself to be quite a pragmatic and credible partner for China across the Strait. Although Chinese leaders view her as a potential secessionist, Tsai has steadfastly adhered to the One China principle, if only in spirit. Tsai has distanced herself from elements within Taiwan that seek to elevate the issue of Taiwanese sovereignty. For instance, when confronted with Premier Lai's comments that he was a 'political worker for Taiwanese independence', Tsai responded that Lai knows 'what the limits are' (Focus Taiwan 2018b; *Taipei Times* 2017). She has refused to endorse national referenda on Taiwanese sovereignty. Tsai has also made the point that she would never unilaterally attempt to change the status quo, unlike her DPP predecessor, Chen Shui-bian who attempted to do so. During her last National Day speech Tsai said: 'As president, I want to assure everyone that we will neither act rashly to escalate confrontation, nor will we give in … Instead, we will respond by seeking stability, adaptability, and making progress' (Tsai 2018a).

Even on the sensitive issue of growing Taiwanese relations with the United States, Tsai has been particularly cognizant of the need to avoid unnecessarily antagonizing Beijing. Although she did call Donald Trump in December 2016 to congratulate him on winning the presidency, the call was treated with the utmost care by Tsai's government, both in its execution and aftermath. According to the official Taiwanese readout of the meeting, the two leaders discussed 'domestic economic development and national defense' as well as 'views on conditions in the Asian region' (Office of the President, ROC, 2016). There was no discussion of Taiwan's status vis-à-vis China, which certainly would have alarmed leaders in Beijing. Tsai later informed visiting US journalists that the call was 'not a policy shift of the United States' in order to downplay the significance of the call (Chung 2016b). It is also important to note that Tsai astutely contacted Trump while he retained the status of President-*elect*, knowing full well that Chinese leaders would interpret a call to a sitting US president – which has never happened – as being far more provocative. The Tsai administration was also especially cautious after Trump noted on 11 December 2016, in a *Fox News* interview, that the One China policy might be up for renegotiation (Hsu 2016). Declining to directly address Trump's comments, Tsai's spokesman, Alex Huang, stated that Taiwan is only seeking enhanced freedom and international space through its relationship with the United States (Yeh and Chang 2016). Huang further stated that Taiwan seeks to maintain positive and stable cross-Strait relations (Lu and Wu 2016).

More recently, spiralling US-China bilateral relations, coupled with strengthening US-Taiwan ties, has put Tsai in the at times uncomfortable and delicate position of having to balance major power concerns about Taiwan. And she has done so extremely admirably. The US Congress, on a bipartisan basis (a rarity these days indeed), has passed legislation that Trump later signed authorizing senior-level leadership exchanges between the United States and Taiwan as well as encouraging US navy ship visits to Taiwanese ports and closer military-to-military relations broadly, including in the sensitive area of joint wargaming (H.R. 535 Taiwan Travel Act 2018; H.R. 2810 National Defense Authorization Act 2018: section 1259; H.R. 5515 John S. McCain National Defense Authorization Act 2019: sections 1257, 1258). Some in Congress have also proposed a bill called the 'TAIPEI Act' – which stands for Taiwan Allies International Protection and Enhancement Initiative – that is designed to punish Taiwan diplomatic allies that switch relations to China (Taipei Act 2018: section 3406). Meanwhile, the Trump Administration has unilaterally instructed the State Department to lift the long-standing ban on US defence contractors being allowed to discuss technologies for Taiwan's indigenous defensive submarine program. The Administration has also publicly highlighted

Taiwan's key role in the its Indo-Pacific Strategy to maintain the region as 'free and open' (US Department of Defense 2019). In addition, Taiwan, for the first time, is mentioned by name in the National Security Strategy (NSS) of the United States. The NSS reads: 'we will maintain our strong ties with Taiwan in accordance with our 'One China' policy, including our commitments under the Taiwan Relations Act to provide for Taiwan's legitimate defense needs and deter coercion' (White House 2017). Trump has also seemingly emphasized the importance of regularizing arms sales to Taiwan, which always irritates Beijing (Chung and Zhen 2018). In light of all these US actions to defend Taiwan from growing Chinese threats, Tsai has neither gloated nor become emboldened. Rather, she has maintained a reserved and measured position, neither overly encouraging nor discouraging US support.

Differing visions of cross-Strait peace

The search for a viable and long-lasting cross-Strait peace agreement includes proposals from Chinese, Taiwanese and Western sources. It is noteworthy that, since the election of Tsai in January 2016, there seems to have been a decline in the number of proposals put forward, on all sides, suggesting that actors involved in and observers of cross-Strait policy believe that the hardened positions of both Tsai and Xi on the 1992 Consensus greatly reduces the prospects for peace at this time. This is in stark contrast to the late 1990s that features a greater sense of urgency to forge peace following the 1995–96 cross-Strait missile crisis. There was another proliferation of ideas from 2008 to 2016, corresponding to Ma's tenure, as peace seemed to be within reach after he recognized the 1992 Consensus and met with Xi in Singapore. Here I cover key thoughts from each body of literature, which are comprised of official statements, proposals by former leaders, and scholarly or think tank analyses.

Chinese peace ideas

Any examination of Chinese proposals must begin with two key documents: the 'Anti-Separatism Law' (or more commonly known as 'Anti-Secession Law' in the West) and the State Council Information Office's 'Taiwan Issue and China's Unification' (Anti-Secession Law 2005; State Council 1993). Each document lays out visions for how Taiwan would be properly integrated into Beijing's 'one country, two systems' arrangement after Taipei acknowledges the 1992 Consensus or the One China principle. Passed in 2005, the Anti-Secession Law primarily serves as a dire warning to Taiwan about the fact that declaring independence (Taiwanese President Chen looked to be moving in that direction at the time) would trigger Chinese military intervention. But in Item 7 of the law, which is often overlooked, Beijing also calls for officially ending the antagonistic state of cross-Strait relations and the development of plans for the promotion and cultivation of cross-Strait ties once Taipei recognizes the One

China principle. It also leaves open the possibility of international activity space for Taiwan that corresponds to its status, typically meaning in the areas of people-to-people and economic exchanges.

The State Council statement offers a much more detailed vision of the nature of future relations between China and Taiwan under the 'one country, two systems' framework. Issued in August 1993, it emphasizes the need to take care of 'Taiwan compatriots' by looking out for their interests.[10] Following reunification with the mainland, Taiwan's current social and economic system, lifestyle, and cultural and economic exchanges would remain unchanged. After reunification, Taiwan would continue to benefit from a high degree of political autonomy – including in administrative, legislative and judicial powers – and enjoy certain foreign affairs rights. Beijing would not send troops or administrative personnel to the island and Taiwanese politicians could play a role in national-level state institutions. Regarding participation in international organizations, Taiwan would be required to identify itself as 'Chinese Taipei' or 'Taiwan, China' in order to maintain the perception that there is and only ever will be one China.

Party Congress reports suggest a subtle evolution in Beijing's approach to Taiwan. For instance, the 15th Party Congress in 1997 under Jiang was the first to propose a staged negotiation of peace proposal (Jiang 1997). By the 16th Party Congress in 2002, Jiang for the first time mentioned that the two sides could set aside their political disputes temporarily if Taiwan would agree to One China. He stated that

> We may discuss how to end the cross-Straits hostility formally. We may also discuss the international space in which the Taiwan region may conduct economic, cultural and social activities compatible with its status, or discuss the political status of the Taiwan authorities or other issues. We are willing to exchange views with all political parties and personages of all circles in Taiwan on the development of cross-Straits relations and the promotion of peaceful reunification.
>
> (Jiang 2002)

The last points clearly expand the possibility of political negotiation. During the 17th Party Congress Hu proposed that both sides sign a peace agreement and construct a cross-Strait peace and development framework (Hu 2007). Finally, Xi has integrated these thoughts into his Taiwan approach, but overlaid them with his China Dream of National Rejuvenation, of which reunification with Taiwan is an integral part. Additionally, and as mentioned above, Xi emphasizes Tsai's recitation of the 1992 Consensus using the exact wording and with Beijing's preferred meaning. He has also re-elevated the importance of the 'one country, two systems' framework as the future model for cross-Strait relations (Xi 2016).

Chinese academic and think tank commentary has focused mainly on how to strengthen the 'one country, two systems' framework or to convince Taiwan of its value. According to a recent article, Xi needs to bolster cross-

Strait economic and military connections in order to cultivate good communication and people-to-people dialogues because it will eventually help to bridge the political divergence (*DW News* 2018). Sun Yafu, deputy director of ARATS, argues that the 'one country, two systems' framework has a bad reputation in Taiwan and actually has worked out quite well in Hong Kong and Macau. Under the arrangement, Beijing would be very attentive to Taiwan's preferences and offer it maximum flexibility (*China News* 2018). A separate piece suggests that the framework would empower Taiwan more than the average resident state in a federalistic structure, and another recent analysis from a professor at Renmin University in 2018 directly states that the 'one country, two systems' framework would *not* be tantamount to federalism at all (Li 2001; Wang 2018). Instead, it would feature one central government, but a second, quasi-central, government in Taiwan, suggesting some level of co-equal status for the island.

Taiwanese peace ideas

Taiwan's core objective has entailed maintaining the well-being and functioning of democratic governance on the island. In an interview in June 2018, Tsai noted that in dealing with China, 'our free and democratic way of life cannot be infringed on' (Office of the President, ROC, 2018). The president's website related to cross-Strait affairs quotes Tsai as saying 'we will work to maintain the existing mechanism for dialogue and communication across the Taiwan Strait' (Tsai n.d.). And in an interview in November 2017, the director of her MAC, Chang Hsiao-yueh, said that '"one country, two systems" has no value whatsoever in Taiwan. The Taiwanese people, however, appreciate Xi's plan of "respecting Taiwan's existing social institutions and lifestyles"' (Zaobao 2017). In the main, these official statements reinforce Taiwan's position that maintaining the cross-Strait status quo is preferable. Meanwhile, former KMT President Ma recently proposed a 'three noes' policy for dealing with Beijing, including not ruling out the possibility of unification with China (a shift from no unification with the mainland during the period when he was president), no support for Taiwan independence, and no use of force. Tsai responded that Ma's 'three noes' were counterproductive because the proposal undermines the peoples' right to choose their fate (Yeh and Wang 2018).

As Taiwan is a democracy, there has also been a proliferation of views on cross-Strait relations from the political parties and academic and observer communities. Following major victories in Taiwan's recent local elections, for example, KMT mayors have since called on recognizing the 1992 Consensus so that their cities – particularly Kaohsiung and Taichung – may engage with the mainland on a city-to-city level (Cole 2018). The KMT's National Policy Foundation think tank has traditionally argued for the merits of Taipei recognizing the 1992 Consensus, which has been reflected in the KMT party platform (National Policy Foundation n.d.; KMT 2017). Their argument is that the consensus is actually not an agreement, but a verbal expression of a common view to uphold 'one China, separately expressed [一中各表]', with an emphasis on the latter point (although Beijing disagrees and Xi's speech in January 2019 gives the KMT serious pause, as mentioned above). Agreeing to the 1992 Consensus would resurrect ECFA negotiations and support Taiwan's long-term growth. Of course, the DPP is more fixated on the One China part and the implications for Taiwan's democratic system to be compromised as well as potentially precluding the people from voting for independence if, later on, they choose to declare it.

Academic and commentary pieces are numerous. In one particularly insightful academic analysis, Nien-Chung Chang Liao argues that Beijing would have to offer most of the reassurances to Taiwan because of its 'intrinsic credibility problem'. Liao further assesses that China's superior power to control cross-Strait security dynamics, however, will mitigate the risks it faces in doing so (Nien-Chung 2012: 105–45). Most commentaries seem to criticize Tsai for deciding against accepting the 1992 Consensus. One argued that common cross-Strait cultural beliefs were sufficient to forge a common national identity, and that the socio-economic environments are already synched and should be expanded (*Business Today* 2018).

Western peace ideas

Finally, Western observers have weighed in on possible ways to forge cross-Strait peace as well. In a comprehensive analysis from 2009, Phillip Saunders and Scott Kastner noted that 'functional cooperation' in the Strait could be enhanced if 'a core bargain of no Taiwan independence and no PRC use of force' is established (2009). They also provide a review of the literature in their article demonstrating that this fundamental trade-off has been a common theme throughout past Western analyses (Lieberthal 2005: 53–63; Manning and Montaperto 1997; Nye 1998; White 2006) Long-time observer of cross-Strait dynamics, Richard Bush, proposed in 2005 that perhaps the key to peace lies in each side finding what they like about the 1992 Consensus and sticking to these ideas, rather than focusing on what they dislike (2005: 286–87). Others, such as Linda Jakobson, have discussed the possibility of Beijing reaching out to the DPP, instead of spurning it, as the best way to achieve its objectives (2005: 27–39).

Concluding thoughts

My analysis strongly suggests that without some measure of compromise – primarily though not necessarily exclusively from the Chinese side – the prospects for achieving cross-Strait peace remain very low. Xi's dug-in position on the 1992 Consensus and the 'one country, two systems' framework hold Tsai to an incompatibly high standard given her priorities of defending democratic governance on the island. In addition, cross-Strait proposals from both China and Taiwan are unfortunately underdeveloped and only fragmentary in nature.

The best possible scenario for peace or, at the very least, to initiate cross-Strait political dialogue, is that Xi decides to compromise on the 1992 Consensus so that he and Tsai can move beyond the roadblock. Tsai then might be able to express it in her own way. Alternatively, she could choose to recognize the consensus as Xi wishes, but while also emphasizing the 'differing interpretations' component as the key to her adherence. Indeed, as Richard Bush has described, the two sides have picked and chosen their points of emphasis in the 1992 Consensus in the past and it has been effective in keeping dialogue going. Tsai could use the reinstatement of ECFA to demonstrate much needed domestic economic progress. Discarding independence language could also bolster Tsai's standing on the world stage and enable Taiwan to rejoin the World Health Assembly and other international organizations. It could also stem the tide of Taipei's diplomatic partners switching recognition to China. Perhaps most importantly, a peace deal would unfreeze government-to-government discussions and shed further light on how Beijing is considering the sovereignty issue going forward.

Although falling far short of starting political negotiations, China and Taiwan could engage in CBMs that might, one day, get them to the negotiating table. In this sense, Western analyses probably hold some value. If Beijing were to agree to renounce the use of military force, then Taipei should probably renounce the threat of declaring independence in the future – meaning the elimination of the independence clause from the DPP's charter. Such an accord would stop well short of the 1992 Consensus, but it could nevertheless give each side a major victory. Xi could credibly claim that Tsai's decision to reject independence represented a de facto, albeit implicit, acknowledgement of the One China principle. And he would be correct. Now that Tsai has resigned as DPP chairwoman following her party's landslide electoral losses in November 2018, she would have to pressure the new chairperson, Cho Jung-tai, to remove the independence language. Given Cho's policy alignment with Tsai, it probably would not be too onerous a task (Huang 2019). Doing so would go against her own party's interests, but could satiate Beijing for the remainder of Tsai's first term and could give both sides positive momentum if she were to win re-election in 2020. Tsai could benefit from the general lack of knowledge the average Taiwanese has for the implications of endorsing the 1992 Consensus (Wang *et al.* 2018). Tsai could likewise claim that the China military threat had diminished on her watch, and hold Bejing's feet to the fire if it renaged..

To be sure, the downsides could be quite significant as well. Signing such a pact would probably lock Taiwan into eventually fully agreeing with the 1992 Consensus under Tsai or her successor. Taiwan would also struggle to determine whether China was actually reducing the military threat to the island. For example, Beijing could publicly remove hundreds of short-range ballistic missiles aimed at Taiwan, but could compensate for the loss in this capability by shifting to other capabilities. Notably, the PLA Air Force is becoming increasingly capable of conducting air assault missions over Taiwan. China might also regret signing a peace agreement. Doing so with Tsai could provoke a DPP backlash that leads to a more extreme DPP president who is less amenable to the 1992 Consensus in the future.

Either way, between now and Taiwan's next presidential election in January 2020, the prospects of forging a sustainable peace are exceptionally low. Both Xi and Tsai are dug into their respective positions. And Xi's new 1992 Consensus and prioritization of the 'one country, two systems' framework is likely to make the situation unnecessarily even tenser. Indeed, it is quite telling that, following Xi's January 2019 'Message to Compatriots in Taiwan' speech, even the KMT rejected his demands. If the DPP and KMT positions coalesce in opposition to China going into 2020, then this would be a nightmare scenario for Beijing. Hopefully, Xi will reassess his position to stem such an outcome, but his recent doubling-down suggests – at least for the time being – that China believes that it has the upper hand.

Notes

1 The author would like to express his deep appreciation to Macquarie University and his home organization of the RAND Corporation for their generous support of this research. He greatly appreciates the research support of RAND colleagues Christian Curriden and Keren Zhu.
2 In 2010, under Ma, China and Taiwan signed the Economic Cooperation Framework Agreement (ECFA) comprising over 20 cross-Strait trade pacts. The two sides in 2009 also established regularly scheduled direct flights between mainland China and Taiwan to enhance people-to-people ties. See ECFA (2010) and *Xinhua News* (2009).
3 Beijing almost certainly prefers reunification to entail Taiwan becoming a fully fledged province under Chinese control. However, no Chinese leader believes this to be a real possibility, and instead the leadership has set its sights on more achievable goals such as integrating Taiwan under the 'one country, two systems' framework, described here.
4 Hu's 18th Party Congress speech is softer on the importance of the 1992 Consensus: 'The two sides of the Taiwan Straits *should* uphold the common stand of opposing Taiwan independence and of following the 1992 Consensus. Both sides *should* increase their common commitment to upholding the one China framework and, on this basis, expand common ground and set aside differences' (emphasis added).
5 Also, conversation with senior-level Taiwanese interlocutor, 26 November 2018.
6 Hu's Six Proposals (or 'Points') included (1) firm adherence to the One China principle; (2) strengthening commercial ties, including negotiating an economic cooperation agreement; (3) promoting personnel exchanges; (4) stressing common cultural links between the two sides; (5) allowing Taiwan's 'reasonable' participation in global organizations; and (6) negotiating a peace agreement. For an analysis of Hu's Six Proposals, see Hsiao (2009).
7 In good faith, China has apparently retained the ECFA and has even made adjustments to ECFA-related pacts after Ma's presidency to the benefit of Taiwan. See, for example, Xinhua (2017b), which states that 'more products will enjoy zero tariffs' under the ECFA. See also Focus Taiwan (2016b). However, without Tsai's recognition of the 1992 Consensus, Taiwan should not expect progress on the ECFA. See also the *China Times* (2016).
8 In the last such poll, the results of which were published in November 2018, nearly 80 per cent of respondents blamed China for threatening the peaceful status quo. See *Taiwan Today* (2018).

9 For example, former KMT President Ma himself has been an outspoken critic of Tsai's China policy. He has recently publicized his own thoughts on how to achieve peace in the strait, which I discuss in greater detail in the next section.
10 Use of 'Taiwan compatriots' mirrors China's 'National People's Congress Standing Committee Letter to Taiwan Compatriots, 1978', State Council (1978).

References

Anti-Secession Law (2005) *Anti-Secession Law*. Available at www.gwytb.gov.cn/gjstfg/xfl/201101/t20110123_1724057.htm (accessed 29 January 2019).

Bloomberg (2019) 'China's Xi Seeks Talks to Unify Taiwan with China', 1 January. Available at www.bloomberg.com/news/articles/2019-01-02/china-s-xi-says-taiwan-must-be-unified-with-mainland (accessed 29 January 2019).

Bush, Richard C. (2005) *Untying the Knot: Making Peace in the Taiwan Strait*, Washington, DC: Brookings Institution Press.

Bush, Richard C. (2016) 'Decoding Xi Jinping's Latest Remarks on Taiwan', Washington, DC: Brookings Institution, 17 March. Available at www.brookings.edu/blog/order-from-chaos/2016/03/17/decoding-xi-jinpings-latest-remarks-on-taiwan/ (accessed 29 January 2019).

Business Today (2018) 'Recognizing the 1992 Consensus: Is It World Peace?' 28 May. Available at www.businesstoday.com.tw/article/category/80392/post/201805280004/%E6%89%BF%E8%AA%8D92%E5%85%B1%E8%AD%98%EF%BC%8C%E5%B0%B1%E5%A4%A9%E4%B8%8B%E5%A4%AA%E5%B9%B3%EF%BC%9F (accessed 29 January 2019).

Cheung, Tony (2016) 'The Sunflower and the Umbrella: Hong Kong Activists Travel to Taiwan, Call for Closer Ties, New Policies from Incoming Government', *South China Morning Post*, 18 January. Available at www.scmp.com/news/hong-kong/politics/article/1901985/sunflower-and-umbrella-hong-kong-activists-travel-taiwan (accessed 29 January 2019).

Cheung, Tony (2017) 'Beijing Official Says Xi Jinping Has Given "One Country, Two Systems" a Status Boost', *South China Morning Post*, 31 October. Available at https://www.scmp.com/news/hong-kong/politics/article/2117827/beijing-official-says-xi-jinping-has-given-one-country-two (accessed 29 January 2019).

China News (2018) 'Sun Yafu: One Country, Two Systems Will be Re-Recognized by the Taiwanese People', 23 January. Available at www.chinanews.com/tw/2018/01-23/8430816.shtml (accessed 29 January 2019).

China Times (2016) 'ECFA Follow-Up Consultations to Be Suspended without 1992 Consensus', 16 May. Available at www.chinatimes.com/newspapers/20160516000595-260301 (accessed 29 January 2019).

Chung, Lawrence (2016a) 'Taiwan's President-Elect Tsai Ing-wen Faces Anti-Beijing Challenge from Radical Party', *South China Morning Post*, 20 March. Available at www.scmp.com/news/china/diplomacy-defence/article/1927600/taiwans-president-tsai-ing-wen-faces-anti-beijing (accessed 29 January 2019).

Chung, Lawrence (2016b) 'What Does Taiwan Hope for Following Tsai-Trump Call?' *South China Morning Post*, 11 December. Available at www.scmp.com/news/china/article/2053580/what-does-taiwan-hope-following-tsai-trump-phone-call (accessed 29 January 2019).

Chung, Lawrence and Liu Zhen (2018) 'Beijing Tells U.S. to Cancel $330 Million Taiwan Arms Deal', *South China Morning Post*, 25 September. Available at www.

scmp.com/news/china/diplomacy/article/2165609/us-announces-new-taiwan-arms-deal-worth-us330-million (accessed 29 January 2019).
Cole, J. Michael (2015) 'China Demolishes the Taiwan Consensus', *National Interest*, 11 March. Available at https://nationalinterest.org/feature/china-demolishes-the-taiwan-consensus-12396 (accessed 29 January 2019).
Cole, J. Michael (2018) 'What Comes Next after Taiwan's Elections?' *National Interest*, 29 November. Available at https://nationalinterest.org/feature/what-comes-next-after-taiwans-elections-37382 (accessed 29 January 2019).
DW News (2018) 'Can Xi Jinping "Solve the Taiwan Issue" in His Tenure?' 8 September. Available at http://news.dwnews.com/taiwan/news/2018-09-07/60083321_all.html (accessed 29 January 2019).
ECFA (2010) 'Cross Straits Economic Cooperation Framework Agreement'. Available at www.ecfa.org.tw/EcfaAttachment/ECFADoc/ECFA.pdf (accessed 29 January 2019).
Economic Daily (2019) 'Full Text: Xi Jinping's First Five Principles Exploring the One Country, Two Systems Taiwan Plan', 2 January. Available at https://money.udn.com/money/story/5603/3569712 (accessed 29 January 2019).
Focus Taiwan (2016a) 'Full Text of President Tsai's Inaugural Address', 20 May. Available at http://focustaiwan.tw/news/aipl/201605200008.aspx (accessed 29 January 2019).
Focus Taiwan (2016b) 'Existing Cross-Strait Pacts to Continue: Chinese Official', 18 August. Available at http://focustaiwan.tw/news/acs/201608180007.aspx (accessed 29 January 2019).
Focus Taiwan (2018a) 'MAC Pushing for Tsai-Xi Meeting', 2 July. Available at http://focustaiwan.tw/news/aipl/201807020006.aspx (accessed 29 January 2019).
Focus Taiwan (2018b) 'Tsai Wants Reciprocity, No Preconditions for a Meeting with Xi', 14 May. Available at http://focustaiwan.tw/news/aipl/201805140017.aspx (accessed 29 January 2019).
Gao, Charlotte (2018) 'Is eSwatini on the Brink of Cutting Ties with Taiwan?' *The Diplomat*, 4 September. Available at https://thediplomat.com/2018/09/is-eswatini-on-the-brink-of-cutting-ties-with-taiwan/ (accessed 29 January 2019).
Grossman, Derek (2016) 'A Bumpy Road ahead for China-Taiwan Relations', *Defense Dossier*, 22 September. Available at www.rand.org/blog/2016/09/a-bumpy-road-ahead-for-china-taiwan-relations.html (accessed 29 January 2019).
Grossman, Derek, Nathan Beauchamp-Mustafaga, Logan Ma and Michael S. Chase (2018) *China's Long-Range Bomber Flights: Drivers and Implications*, Santa Monica, CA: RAND Corporation. Available at www.rand.org/pubs/research_reports/RR2567.html (accessed 29 January 2019).
Hernandez, Javier C. and Vanessa Piao (2016) 'Tsai Ing-wen, Taiwan's First Female Leader, Is Assailed in China as Being Too "Emotional"', *New York Times*, 25 May. Available at www.nytimes.com/2016/05/26/world/asia/china-taiwan-tsai-unmarried-single.html?mtrref=undefined (accessed 29 January 2019).
Horton, Chris (2018a) 'As China Rattles Its Sword, Taiwanese Push for a Separate Identity', *New York Times*, 26 October. Available at www.nytimes.com/2018/10/26/world/asia/taiwan-name-republic-of-china.html (accessed 29 January 2019).
Horton, Chris (2018b) 'El Salvador Recognizes China in Blow to Taiwan', *New York Times*, 21 August. Available www.nytimes.com/2018/08/21/world/asia/taiwan-el-salvador-diplomatic-ties.html (accessed 29 January 2019).
Hsiao, Russell (2009) 'Hu Jintao's "Six Points" Proposition to Taiwan', *China Brief*, Jamestown Foundation, 12 January. Available at https://jamestown.org/program/hu-jintaos-six-points-proposition-to-taiwan/ (accessed 29 January 2019).

Hsu, Stacy (2016) 'Taipei Mum on Trump's Remarks', *Taipei Times*, 13 December. Available at www.taipeitimes.com/News/front/archives/2016/12/13/2003661105 (accessed 29 January 2019).

Hsu, Stacy (2019) 'Tsai Blasts "One Country, Two Systems"', *Taipei Times*, 3 January. Available at www.taipeitimes.com/News/front/archives/2019/01/03/2003707244 (accessed 29 January 2019).

Hu Jintao (2007) 'Hu Jintao's Report at the 17th Party Congress: Hold High the Great Banner of Socialism with Chinese Characteristics and Strive for New Victories in Building a Moderately Prosperous Society in All', 15 October. Available at www.china.org.cn/english/congress/229611.htm (accessed 29 January 2019).

Hu Jintao (2008) 'Hu Jintao's Speech at the Symposium to Mark the 30th Anniversary of the Publication of the Taiwan Compatriots: Work Together to Promote the Peaceful Development of Cross-Strait Relations and Realize the Great Rejuvenation of the Chinese Nation', 31 December. Available at http://politics.people.com.cn/GB/1024/8610403.html (accessed 29 January 2019).

Hu Jintao (2012) *Full Text of Hu Jintao's Report at 18th Party Congress*, 27 November. Available at www.china-embassy.org/eng/zt/18th_CPC_National_Congress_Eng/t992917.htm (accessed 29 January 2019).

Huang Jing (2017) 'Xi Jinping's Taiwan Policy: Boxing Taiwan in with the One-China Framework', in Lowell Dittmer (ed.) *Taiwan and China: Fitful Embrace*, Oakland: University of California Press. Available at www.jstor.org/stable/pdf/10.1525/j.ctt1w76wpm.16.pdf?refreqid=excelsior%3Afd7890d369bb55b1a67e9d0c46aec8c6 (accessed 29 January 2019).

Huang Jing and Xiaoting Li (2010) *Inseparable Separation: The Making of China's Taiwan Policy*, Singapore: World Scientific Publishing Company.

Huang Tzu-ti (2019) 'Pro-Tsai Candidate Claims Victory as New Leader of Taiwan's DPP', *Taiwan News*, 6 January. Available at www.taiwannews.com.tw/en/news/3611382 (accessed 29 January 2019).

Jakobson, Linda (2005) 'A Greater Chinese Union', *Washington Quarterly*, 28(3), Summer.

Jiang Zemin (1995) 'The 8-Point Proposition Made by Jiang Zemin on China's Reunification', Embassy of the People's Republic of China in the United States of America. Available at www.china-embassy.org/eng/zt/twwt/t36736.htm (accessed 29 January 2019).

Jiang, Zemin (1997) 'Hold High the Great Banner of Deng Xiaoping Theory for an All-Around Advancement of the Cause of Building Socialism with Chinese Characteristics into the 21st Century', report delivered at the 15th National Congress of the Communist Party of China, 12 September. Available at www.bjreview.com.cn/document/txt/2011-03/25/content_363499.htm (accessed 29 January 2019).

Jiang Zemin (2002) *Full Text of Jiang Zemin's Report at the 16th Party Congress*, 8 November. Available at www.fmprc.gov.cn/mfa_eng/topics_665678/3698_665962/t18872.shtml (accessed 29 January 2019).

Kuomingtang (KMT) (2017) 'Chinese KMT Policy Program Innovation, Unity, Return to Power', 20 August. Available at www.kmt.org.tw/p/blog-page_3.html (accessed 29 January 2019).

Li Jiaquan (2001) 'Creating a Taiwanese Model of "One Country, Two Systems," on Both Sides of the Taiwan Strait'. Available at www.china.com.cn/chinese/TCC/haixia/31791.htm (accessed 29 January 2019).

Liberty Times (2009) 'China Urges Full Response to Hu's Six Points', 8 January. Available at http://news.ltn.com.tw/news/politics/paper/271714 (accessed 29 January 2019).

Lieberthal, Kenneth (2005) 'Preventing a War over Taiwan', *Foreign Affairs*, 84(2): March/April.

Lim Yan Liang (2018) 'NPC 2018: Chinese President Xi Jinping Warns Taiwan Will Face 'Punishment of History' for Separatism', *Straits Times*, 20 March. Available at www.straitstimes.com/asia/east-asia/npc-2018-china-president-xi-jinping-vows-to-continue-to-serve-as-peoples-servant (accessed 29 January 2018).

Lin, Sean (2018) 'Su to Replace Lai, Report Says', *Taipei Times*, 28 December. Available at www.taipeitimes.com/News/taiwan/archives/2018/12/28/2003706917 (accessed 29 January 2019).

Lu Hsin-hui and Lilian Wu (2016) 'Taiwan Wants Good Relations with U.S., Stable Cross-Strait Ties', *Focus Taiwan*, 13 December. Available at http://focustaiwan.tw/news/aipl/201612130016.aspx (accessed 29 January 2019).

Manning, Robert A. and Ronald N. Montaperto (1997) 'The People's Republic and Taiwan: Time for a New Cross-Strait Bargain', *INSS Strategic Forum*, 103, February.

National Policy Foundation (n.d.) '1992 Consensus Q&A'. Available at www.npf.org.tw/13/8642 (accessed 29 January 2019).

Nien-Chung, Chang Liao (2012) 'Building Trust across the Taiwan Strait: A Strategy of Reassurance', *Issues and Studies*, 48(3), September.

Nye, Joseph S. Jr (1998) 'A Taiwan Deal', *Washington Post*, 8 March.

Office of the President, ROC (2016) 'President Tsai and U.S. President-elect Donald J. Trump Engage in Phone Conversation', 3 December. Available at http://english.president.gov.tw/Default.aspx?tabid=491&itemid=38406&rmid=2355 (accessed 29 January 2019).

Office of the President, ROC (2018) 'President Accepts an Interview with AFP', 25 June. Available at www.president.gov.tw/News/23447 (accessed 29 January 2019).

Office of the President, ROC (2019a) 'President Tsai's New Year's Talk for 2019', 1 January. Available at https://english.president.gov.tw/NEWS/5618 (accessed 29 January 2019).

Office of the President, ROC (2019b) 'President Tsai Issues Statement on China's President Xi's 'Message to Compatriots in Taiwan', 2 January. Available at https://english.president.gov.tw/NEWS/5621 (accessed 29 January 2019).

People's Daily (2016) 'Mainland Says Tsai's Speech on Cross-Strait Ties an Incomplete Test Answer', 21 May. Available at http://en.people.cn/n3/2016/0521/c90000-9061066.html (accessed 29 January 2019).

People's Republic of China, White Paper (2000) 'The One China Principle and the Taiwan Question'. Available at www.china.com.cn/ch-book/taiwan/itaiwan.htm (accessed 29 January 2019).

Sands, Gary (2018) 'What the China-Vatican Deal Means for Taiwan', *The Diplomat*, 21 September. Available at https://thediplomat.com/2018/09/what-the-china-vatican-deal-means-for-taiwan/ (accessed 29 January 2019).

Saunders, Phillip C. and Scott L. Kastner (2009) 'Bridge over Troubled Water?: Envisioning a China-Taiwan Peace Agreement', *International Security*, 33(4).

State Council, PRC (1978) 'National People's Congress Standing Committee Letter to Taiwan Compatriots'. Available at www.gwytb.gov.cn/gjstfg/xfl/201101/t20110123_1723995.htm (accessed on 29 January 2019).

State Council, PRC (1993) 'The Taiwan Issue and China's Unification', August, Beijing: State Council Information Office. Available at www.scio.gov.cn/zfbps/ndhf/1993/Document/308013/308013.htm (accessed 29 January 2019).

Straits Times (2019) 'KMT Rejects Xi's Plan for HK-Style Union with Taiwan', 5 January. Available at www.straitstimes.com/asia/east-asia/kmt-rejects-xis-plan-for-hk-style-union-with-taiwan (accessed 29 January 2019).

Taipei Times (2017) 'Tsai Renews Call for New Model on Cross-Strait Ties', 4 October. Available at www.taipeitimes.com/News/front/archives/2017/10/04/2003679676/1 (accessed 29 January 2019).

Taipei Times (2018) 'Lai Explains Approach to Independence', 16 April. Available at www.taipeitimes.com/News/front/archives/2018/04/16/2003691399 (accessed 29 January 2019).

Taiwan Today (2018) 'Regular MAC Poll Finds Majority in Taiwan Disapprove of China's Threats', 2 November. Available at https://taiwantoday.tw/news.php?unit=2&post=144615 (accessed 29 January 2019).

Tan, Huileng (2017) 'Taiwan Watches as China Closes in on Hong Kong', CNBC, 19 July. Available at www.cnbc.com/2017/07/19/taiwan-watches-as-china-closes-in-on-hong-kong.html (accessed 29 January 2019).

Tsai, Ing-wen (2018) 'Full Text of President Tsai Ing-wen's National Day Address', *Focus Taiwan*, 10 October. Available at http://focustaiwan.tw/news/aipl/201810100006.aspx (accessed 29 January 2019).

Tsai, Ing-wen (n.d.) 'Cross-Strait Issues', Office of the President, ROC. Available at https://english.president.gov.tw/Issue/145 (accessed 29 January 2019).

Tsou Ching-wen (2016) 'Tsai Ing-wen: 1992 Is an Historical Fact, Promoting Cross-Strait Relations', *Liberty Times*, 21 January. Available at http://news.ltn.com.tw/news/focus/paper/951154 (accessed 29 January 2019).

US Department of Defense (2019) 'Indo-Pacific Strategy Report: Preparedness, Partnerships, and Promoting a Networked Region', June. Available at https://media.defense.gov/2019/May/31/2002139210/-1/-1/1/1/DOD_INDO_PACIFIC_STRATEGY_REPORT_JUNE_2019.PDF (accessed 6 June 2019).

US Congress (2018) Taipei Act of 2018. Available at www.congress.gov/bill/115th-congress/senate-bill/3406/text?q=%7B%22search%22%3A%5B%22taiwan%22%5D%7D&r=1 (accessed 29 January 2019).

US House of Representatives (H.R.) (2018a) 2810 National Defense Authorization Act Fiscal Year 2018. Available at www.congress.gov/bill/115th-congress/house-bill/2810/text (accessed 29 January 2019).

US House of Representatives (H.R.) (2018b) 535 Taiwan Travel Act Available at www.congress.gov/bill/115th-congress/house-bill/535 (accessed 29 January 2019).

US House of Representatives (H.R.) (2019) 5515 John S. McCain National Defense Authorization Act Fiscal Year 2019. Available at www.congress.gov/bill/115th-congress/house-bill/5515/text (accessed 29 January 2019).

Wang, Austin, Charles K. S. Wu, Yeh Yao-Yuan and Fang Yu-Chen (2018) 'What Does the 1992 Consensus Mean to Citizens in Taiwan?' *The Diplomat*, 10 November. Available at https://thediplomat.com/2018/11/what-does-the-1992-consensus-mean-to-citizens-in-taiwan/ (accessed 29 January 2019).

Wang, Yingjin (2018) 'On the Composite "One Country, Two Systems" Taiwan Model', Renmin University, 27 June. Available at http://m.chinaelections.net/wap/article.aspx?id=249101 (accessed 29 January 2019).

White House (2017) *National Security Strategy of the United States of America*, December. Available at www.whitehouse.gov/wp-content/uploads/2017/12/NSS-Final-12-18-2017-0905.pdf (accessed 29 January 2019).

White, Lynn T. (2006) 'PRC, ROC, and U.S. Interests: Can They Be Harmonized?' in Shiping Hua (ed.) *Reflections on the Triangular Relations of Beijing-Taipei-Washington Since 1995: Status Quo at the Taiwan Straits?* New York: Palgrave Macmillan.

Xi Jinping (2016) 'Safeguard and Promote the Peaceful Development of Cross-Strait Relations and the Great Rejuvenation of the Chinese Nation', Taiwan Affairs Office of the State Council, 15 October. Available at www.gwytb.gov.cn/wyly/201610/t20161016_11593556.htm (accessed 29 January 2019).

Xinhua (2008) 'Six Proposals Offered for Cross-Strait Relations', 31 December. Available at www.chinadaily.com.cn/china/2008-12/31/content_7357490.htm (accessed 29 January 2019).

Xinhua (2009) 'Chinese Mainland, Taiwan Increase Regular Direct Flights', 31 August. Available at www.china.org.cn/travel/news/2009-08/31/content_18434525.htm (accessed 29 January 2019).

Xinhua (2017a) 'Full Text of Xi Jinping's Report at 19th CPC National Congress', 3 November. Available at www.xinhuanet.com/english/special/2017-11/03/c_136725942.htm (accessed 29 January 2019).

Xinhua (2017b) 'China Announces Tariff Adjustment for 2018', 5 December. Available at www.xinhuanet.com/english/2017-12/15/c_136829160.htm (accessed 29 January 2019).

Xinhua (2018) 'China Focus: Taiwan's Lackluster Mainland Tourist Market', 26 June. Available at www.xinhuanet.com/english/2018-06/26/c_137282312.htm (accessed 29 January 2019).

Yeh, Sophia and S. C. Chang (2016) 'Taiwan Not to Become a "Chip" in Geopolitical Game: Official', *Focus Taiwan*, 12 December. Available at http://focustaiwan.tw/news/acs/201612120032.aspx (accessed 29 January 2019).

Yeh Su-ping and Flor Wang (2018) 'Tsai: Ma's "Three Noes" Proposal Hurts Taiwan Sovereignty', *Focus Taiwan*, 9 November. Available at http://focustaiwan.tw/news/aipl/201811090014.aspx (accessed 29 January 2019).

Yeo, Mike (2018) 'State Department OKs License for Submarine Tech Sales to Taiwan', *Defense News*, 9 April. Available at www.defensenews.com/naval/2018/04/09/us-state-department-oks-license-for-submarine-tech-sales-to-taiwan/ (accessed 29 January 2019).

Zaobao (2017) 'Taiwan Affairs Council: "One Country, Two Systems," Has No Market Value at All in Taiwan', 15 November. Available at www.zaobao.com.sg/realtime/china/story20171115-811215 (accessed 29 January 2019).

Zhang, Hua (2018) 'PLA Drills in the Taiwan Straits Send Clear Warning', *Global Times*, 22 April. Available at www.globaltimes.cn/content/1099162.shtml (accessed 29 January 2019).

14 Reassessing Taiwan's strategic future

Benjamin Schreer

Introduction

After vanishing from the international agenda for a couple of years, the Taiwan issue is back in full swing, disappointing scholarly expectations that the cross-Strait political and economic 'rapprochement' during the previous Taiwanese government of President Ma Ying-jeou would lead to a peaceful resolution of the conflict through ever closer cooperation between Taipei and Beijing (Gilley 2010; Saunders and Kastner 2009). While these arguments were already problematic during the Ma administration (Lee and Schreer 2013; Roy 2015), cross-Strait relations deteriorated significantly after President Tsai Ing-wen took office in 2016. The People's Republic of China (PRC, or China) responded to her election victory by freezing official political dialogues, imposing implicit economic sanctions, exacerbating Taiwan's diplomatic isolation, and engaging in frequent military sabre-rattling. Beijing also made Taipei's acceptance of the 1992 Consensus the *sine qua non* for the resumption of political dialogue, despite the fact that President Tsai repeatedly signalled her willingness to cooperate in the broader framework of that concept.

In addition, the Tsai government faced greater uncertainty over the credibility of the United States' security commitments. Not a formal military ally, the Republic of China (ROC, or Taiwan) relies on the 1979 Taiwan Relations Act and Washington's long-standing position of 'strategic ambiguity' – a position that seems less and less effective in maintaining cross-Strait stability as Beijing changes the strategic balance vis-à-vis Washington and has worked relentlessly to erode the US Congress' commitment to Taiwan and the Taiwan Relations Act (Mitchell 2017; Armitage *et al.* 2018: 6). Under the previous US Administration of Barack Obama it became less clear from Taipei's perspective whether Washington would indeed defend the island nation against Chinese aggression (Lao and Lin 2015). Current President Donald Trump's conflicting signals on Taiwan have not helped to alleviate these concerns, because they have wavered between publicly questioning America's One China policy and signalling greater willingness to support Taiwan militarily on the one hand, but implying a Chinese veto over closer US-Taiwan relations on the other.

As a result, Taiwan's future looks more uncertain amid the major power shifts in East Asia. Indeed, some scholars and statesmen have long predicted that its fate is sealed. For instance, John Mearsheimer (2014) concluded that 'if China continues its impressive rise, Taiwan appears destined to become part of China'. For Robert Sutter (2011: 4), Taiwan has no other choice than to 'follow a path leading to accommodation of and eventual reunification with China'. Others (for instance Glaser 2011; Gomez 2016) have argued that the United States should abandon its security commitment towards Taiwan because it is simply too costly in the context of the new US-China power balance. And for the late Singaporean Prime Minister Lee Kuan Ye (2000) Taiwan's unification with China is all but 'inevitable'.

In sum, what is at stake is whether Taiwan will cease to exist as a de facto independent nation and one of East Asia's most vibrant democracies. The case against Taiwan is based on assumptions about Beijing's growing ability to coerce Taipei into accepting unification with the mainland. To be sure, the Chinese Communist Party (CCP) could resort to brute force and attempt to militarily invade Taiwan. However, as Michael O'Hanlon has pointed out, for China '[c]oercive uses of force are more likely than an invasion – both because their costs to Beijing would be lower, and because their prospects of success would be greater' (2000: 53). Similarly, Denny Roy (2017, 1138) concluded that 'Beijing is actually highly averse to attempting unification through military force except as a last resort'. China's authoritarian model is hardly acceptable for most Taiwanese who show no political support for peaceful unification on China's terms. Consequently, consideration of coercion, defined as 'the threat of damage, or of more damage to come, that can make someone yield or comply' (Schelling 2008: 3), is the most realistic policy option for Beijing in dealing with Taipei.

To be sure, China's coercive leverage over Taiwan could grow insurmountably owing to three interrelated factors. First, Beijing's political, economic and military power could simply overmatch Taiwan, not least since the CCP has made unification with the 'renegade province' a question of national survival and therefore invests significant resources into achieving this 'core interest'. Second, Taiwan's domestic resilience against Chinese pressure could falter because political, economic and demographic issues obstruct effective countermeasures. Finally, the United States could ultimately renege on its commitment to defend the island nation since the costs of trading 'Los Angeles for Taipei' are deemed too high now that the People's Liberation Army (PLA) can directly target US forces across all military domains.

Nevertheless, this chapter argues that China's ability to translate its growing power into greater coercive leverage over Taiwan to a point where Taipei has to concede its national sovereignty is likely to remain limited. Indeed, contrary to predictions about Taiwan's eventual downfall and emergence as another Chinese province, such outcomes are neither inevitable nor likely; neither are assumptions about Chinese domination, Taiwan's lack of resilience and US abandonment. Precisely because the strategic environment becomes more conflicted Taiwan also has a major opportunity to enhance its position as a secure, viable and prosperous democracy in the region. While this will require operating in a more contested East Asia and taking greater foreign policy risks, the country is well positioned to exploit a series of advantages, while minimizing its weaknesses. There is no compelling case that the ROC will cease to exist as a democratic bulwark in East Asia in the face of China's authoritarian coercion.

The limits of Chinese power

At first glance, China's political, economic and military power appears simply too great for Taiwan to resist. China is now a great power and, by some predictions (Kennedy 2018), could overtake the United States as the world's largest economic power by 2030 when comparing their respective gross domestic product (GDP). It is the most important trading partner for almost all countries in the Indo-Pacific region and has become a major trading partner for the United States as well as many other countries around the world. In contrast, in 2018 Taiwan ranked 23rd globally and its economy continued to face uncertainties owing to global economic trends, the US-China 'trade war', and a high economic integration with mainland China (Reuters 2018; Stratfor 2018). Moreover, under President Xi China has ramped up the diplomatic pressure on Taiwan to narrow its strategic breathing space. It used its political leverage to prevent Taipei from joining multilateral fora such as the International Civil Aviation Organization, the United Nations Framework Convention on Climate Change, INTERPOL and the World Health Assembly. China also persuaded Gambia, São Tomé and Príncipe, Panama, Burkina Faso, El Salvador and the Dominican Republic to end their diplomatic recognition of Taiwan, reducing Taipei's formal diplomatic allies in early 2019 to 16 states, plus the Vatican.

Moreover, China has worked to change the military balance across the Taiwan Strait in its favour. Fuelled by its economic growth, it has invested significantly in increasing the PLA's capability, with a major focus on Taiwan Strait contingencies and on deterring a potential US intervention to assist Taiwan in the event of military conflict. This has included the deployment of large arsenals of ground-launched land-attack cruise missiles to target Taiwan's air combat capability, command and communications centres, and airfields. The PLA has also significantly enhanced its air combat and naval strike assets, dwarfing the ROC's capabilities in these areas. A 2018 Pentagon assessment concluded that the PLA 'continued to develop and deploy increasingly advanced military capabilities intended to coerce Taiwan, signal Chinese resolve, and gradually improve capabilities for an invasion' (US Department of Defense 2018: 93). It also noted that 'Taiwan's advantages continue to decline as China's modernization efforts continue' (ibid.: 101). Similarly, the 2018 annual report by the US-China Economic and Security Review Commission emphasized that the 'threat to Taiwan from China's military posture and modernization continues to grow, and Beijing has increased coercive military activities to intimidate Taipei' (2018: 340).

Furthermore, not only has China significantly enhanced its military capability to threaten the ROC and its military forces, it has also strengthened its ability to inflict major military damage on US forces in order to deter US intervention. As the US-China Economic and Security Review Commission report concluded:

> Beijing is currently capable of contesting U.S. operations in the ground, air, maritime, and information domains within the second island chain, presenting challenges to the U.S. military's longstanding assumption of supremacy in these domains in the post-Cold War era. By 2035, if not before, China will likely be able to contest U.S. operations throughout the entire Indo-Pacific region.
>
> (2018: 205)

Finally, Taiwan's 2017 Quadrennial Defense Review (QDR) report also stressed the growth of China's military threat towards Taiwan and expressed greater uncertainty over the future role of the United States in the region (Republic of China 2017). In tandem with President Xi's repeated claims that Taiwan's unification with the mainland was inevitable and that Beijing would use military force to resist the island's independence (Kuo 2019), these trends appear to turn the pages in China's favour.

Nevertheless, the assumption that China will be able to translate its growing power into coercing Taiwan to move towards unification on its own terms is problematic for several reasons. The first has to do with assumptions about the nature of Chinese power. Scholarly analysis predominantly focuses on the increase in GDP and military hardware as evidence of China's 'inevitable rise' (see, for example, Jacques 2009; Kiernan 2012; Allison 2017). However, these gross indicators for measuring national power generally suffer from significant shortfalls which has implications for thinking about China's power. As Michael Beckley notes,

> Obviously China is not as weak today as it was in the nineteenth century, but neither is it as powerful as its gross resources suggest. China may have the world's biggest economy and military, but it also leads the world in debt; resource consumption; pollution; useless infrastructure and wasted industrial capacity.
>
> (2018: 42–43)

Beckley also raises issues such as alleged scientific fraud, spending on internal security, border disputes and an ageing population. Meanwhile, a 2018 Economic Freedom Index found that China's economy remained 'mostly unfree', ranking the country 110th globally (Heritage Foundation 2018). Even more problematic for Beijing, however, is the fact that its economy has faced increasing problems and at the end of 2018 showed structural challenges to sustain the growth trajectory of recent years (Stephens 2018; *Wall Street Journal* 2018). China's 'inevitable' rise is thus much less certain than is often assumed and it might face serious economic and political difficulties in the years ahead (Chang 2016).

This not only leaves question marks over China's ability to dominate East Asia's future – particularly if met with resistance from powerful nations such as the United States, Japan and India – but also its potential to exert compelling pressure on Taiwan. To be sure, China could, for example, further reduce the number of Taiwan's formal diplomatic allies by essentially buying them off. However, a good argument can be made that losing even more formal allies, while not desirable, would not spell disaster for Taiwan (Greer 2018). In fact, most of these remaining diplomatic partners are relatively weak, foreign aid-dependent countries, and Taiwanese financial resources spent on supporting these nations in return for diplomatic recognition could be better invested elsewhere (Chung 2018). Arguably, for Taiwan it is much more important to secure political support from major powers such as the United States, Japan and, in the future, India. As will be argued below, both the United States and Japan are likely to intensify their political, economic and military support to Taiwan should Chinese pressure in the islands increase. For both, safeguarding the strategic future of Taiwan remains an important political objective. And India-Taiwan ties also show signs of gradual improvement.

In addition, China's ability to put economic pressure on Taiwan to a breaking point is limited, too. To be sure, Taiwan's economy is now deeply integrated with that of the mainland and its highly advanced and important information technology sector now depends on production facilities in China. In 2018 over 40 per cent of its exports went to China and Hong Kong (Taiwan Ministry of Finance 2018) and up to 20 per cent of Taiwan's GDP is derived from its economic relationship with China. Chinese leaders have in the past openly stressed the objective to use Taiwan's economic dependency as leverage to reduce the island's political autonomy (Lee 2015: 115). Nevertheless, economic coercion as a strategy 'historically, has rarely been effective in compelling target governments to undertake major changes in policy, nor has it often been effective in deterring target countries from undertaking major policies that the initiating country considers offensive (Tanner 2007: 24).

Owing to the high stakes involved for Taiwan, i.e. its sovereignty and way of life, its leaders and population are unlikely to yield to Chinese economic coercion. Indeed, not only would Taiwan have options to circumvent China's economic pressure but attempts to coerce Taiwan would also significantly hurt China. As Denny Roy points out,

> the dislocation caused by a disruption of China-Taiwan economic cooperation would be most acute in some of the geographic areas and sectors that are the most important to China's economic development. Taiwan supplies one-quarter of the foreign direct investment in Jiangsu Province and Shanghai.
>
> (2017: 1150)

Putting major economic pressure on Taipei in times of economic fragility could be a counterproductive strategy for China. In fact, since the China-Taiwan economic relationship has shifted from a complementary to a competitive one, Taiwanese businesses have already become more reluctant to invest in mainland China and Beijing's 'economic card' appears to have waned as an instrument to win the 'hearts and minds' of Taiwanese voters (Iharu 2018a), let alone coerce them. Moreover, Taiwanese voters are acutely sensitive of possible attempts by their government to 'sell out' Taiwan's autonomy for economic gain, which partly led to the major electoral defeat of the Kuomintang (KMT – Nationalist Party) in the 2016 general elections. Taiwanese society can thus be expected to accept significant economic hardship if the prize is to maintain the country's sovereignty.

Finally, despite China's military build-up across the Taiwan Strait its options to 'conquer' Taiwan continue to face significant hurdles. For instance, a naval blockade against Taiwan would amount to a declaration of war and could trigger undesired escalatory consequences for China, such as the involvement of the United States and Japan, aside from Taiwan's ability to endure such an embargo and re-route its shipping and China's operational challenges to conduct such complex operations (Roy 2003). Alternatively, China could seek to compel Taiwan through aerial bombardment with precision strikes against military and civilian targets as part of a fait accompli strategy. Yet, aside from the Taiwan military's ability to recover (for example, through enhanced runway repair capabilities) and to launch counter-strikes against Chinese targets, if the history of such aerial bombardment is any guide, strategic bombing campaigns more often than not fail to collapse the adversary's will to resist (Gentile 2001; Biddle 2009). It stands to reason that such operations would not only harden Taiwanese resistance but could also negatively affect domestic support within China since many Chinese citizens are also likely to oppose the killing of their 'brothers and sisters' in Taiwan; indeed, the issue of unification seems not as high on the agenda of most Chinese citizens, contrary to CPC propaganda (Chang 2016).

The last military option for China to enforce unification would be to invade Taiwan. However, while the PLA has focused on developing the capability to unify Taiwan with the mainland by force if necessary, a decision to invade would carry enormous risks for China. The PLA still has only limited amphibious assault capabilities and it is doubtful that it could sustain such operations given Taiwan's difficult terrain, its ability to resist an invasion, and the likelihood of third party intervention. As the Pentagon's 2018 report on China's capability concludes,

> [l]arge-scale amphibious invasion is one of the most complicated and difficult military operations. Success depends upon air and sea superiority, the rapid buildup and sustainment of supplies onshore, and uninterrupted support. An attempt to invade Taiwan would likely strain China's armed forces and invite international intervention. These stresses, combined with

China's combat force attrition and the complexity of urban warfare and counterinsurgency (assuming a successful landing and breakout), make an amphibious invasion of Taiwan a significant political and military risk.
(US Department of Defense 2018: 95)

Moreover, even if the PLA were able to occupy Taiwan it would be likely to face a sustained guerrilla warfare campaign, aside from the enormous political costs internationally. Moreover, should the United States and/or Japan become involved in the military conflict, the political, economic and military costs would be devastating for China. As a result, it has been very difficult for Beijing to define practical red lines which Taiwan would have to cross to trigger a military attack on the island (Roy 2017: 1137). Unless Taiwan declares formal independence, Beijing's ability to compel Taipei to move towards unification is likely to remain much more limited than is often assumed (Schreer 2017a).

Taiwan's resilience

Directly related to China's limited potential to compel Taiwan into accepting a path to unification on its terms is Taiwan's high degree of political-societal, economic and military resilience. The key to understanding the recent deterioration in cross-Strait relations since President Tsai came to power in 2016 is not the DPP's traditional 'pro-independence' stance, which still informs its 'deep green' faction, and China's strong opposition to it. Rather, it is the general incongruence of two very different political systems: China's move towards ever greater authoritarianism under President Xi on the one hand and Taiwan's emergence as a consolidated democracy on the other.

This divergence greatly reduces China's attractiveness for Taiwanese voters and its ability to persuade or coerce them into accepting unification. A majority of Taiwanese now identify as 'solely Taiwanese' and prefer to maintain the status quo, i.e. Taiwan's de facto independence. For instance, in 2018 55.8 per cent of Taiwanese identified as 'Taiwanese' and only 3.5 per cent as 'Chinese' (Election Study Centre 2018a). Moreover, 33.4 per cent preferred to 'maintain the status quo, decide at a later stage', 25.7 per cent wanted to 'maintain the status quo indefinitely', and 15.5 per cent opted for 'maintain the status quo, move towards independence'. Meanwhile, only 12.5 per cent supported 'unification as soon as possible' and even fewer, 4.8 per cent, wanted 'independence as soon as possible' (ibid. 2018b).

In essence, voters overwhelmingly prefer the status quo of Taiwan as a de facto sovereign, democratic country. They also do not support a push towards de jure independence, knowing full well that this would trigger a major Chinese response. But it also means that there is not much political support for moving closer to China. Consequently, President Tsai's approach ever since she came to power to reject Beijing's 'one country, two systems' formula as the precondition for improved political relations has met with full approval from a majority of Taiwanese. Indeed, Tsai's 'four musts' formulated in her 2019 New Year's Address (Office of the President, ROC, 2019) – Beijing must recognize the island's existence; must respect Taiwan's freedom and democracy; deal with Taiwan peacefully and on equal terms; and communicate through government-authorized channels – reflected the understanding of Taiwan as a fully fledged democracy. In an opinion poll in early January 2019, more than 80 per cent of Taiwanese opposed unification under President Xi's 'one country, two systems' framework currently on display in Macau and Hong Kong, and supported Tsai's 'four musts' (Radio Free Asia 2019).

Importantly, the opposition KMT also rejected 'one country, two systems' as a framework for the bilateral relationship (*Focus Taiwan* 2019), demonstrating awareness of Taiwanese voters' preferences. The incompatibility of political systems between China and Taiwan thus not only renders progress towards unification on Beijing's terms highly unlikely. The bilateral relationship is also bound to become even more conflicted (Grossman 2019). However, greater Chinese pressure on Taiwan is likely to backfire given the stakes for the Taiwanese people. If anything, increased 'menacing by China, to include the actual use of force, is not likely to reduce Taiwan's determination to maintain its autonomy, but might strengthen it' (Roy 2017: 1142).

Moreover, Taiwan's economic resilience should not be underestimated. As mentioned above, the country's exports remain significantly dependent on China/Hong Kong. That said, China's economy also benefits from economic integration with the ROC. But more importantly, Taiwan's economy has key strengths that its leaders can utilize in a strategy of economic diversification. For a start, its economy remains open, agile and highly competitive. Indeed, the 2018 Economic Freedom Index ranked Taiwan's 'mostly free' economy at an impressive 13th position worldwide (Heritage Foundation 2018). Moreover, according to the International Monetary Fund (IMF), its GDP in 2018 was the 19th highest in the world on a purchasing-power parity basis, whereas China only ranked 79th (Everington 2018). During the second quarter of 2018 Taiwan's GDP grew by 3.29 per cent, its fastest pace since 2015 (Reuters 2018), and this was partly attributable to some economic and labour market reforms initiated by the Tsai government.

Its 'New Southbound Policy' (NSP) policy, designed to reduce economic over-reliance on China by diversifying trade and investment particularly with South-East Asia, has also made progress. This has involved increased Taiwanese exports to Association of Southeast Asian Nations (ASEAN) countries, growing people-to-people ties, and a bilateral investment agreement with the Philippines in December 2017, which could pave the way for similar arrangements with Thailand, Malaysia, Indonesia, Vietnam and India (Marston and Bush 2018). While the NSP still faces challenges and at present can only complement Taiwan's economic relationship with China, over time it could well lead to its increased economic integration not just with South-East Asia but also with other Indo-Pacific economies. In this context, trade relations with the

United States and Japan are worth emphasizing. The United States is Taiwan's third most important trading partner, accounting for 11.8 per cent of all exports in 2018, an increase of 7.5 per cent compared with the previous year. Exports to Japan grew by 11.1 per cent, making it Taiwan's fourth largest trading partner (Taiwan Ministry of Finance 2018). Importantly, Taiwan was the United States' 11th biggest trading partner in 2018, ranked by total exchange of goods (Gray 2018), while Taiwan was Japan's fourth most important trading partner in 2017, with whom it had a significant trade surplus (Japan External Trade Organization 2018).

Moreover, a rarely noticed development is the increased investment of the European Union (EU) into Taiwan. For instance, in 2017 the EU was the largest investor in Taiwan with foreign direct investment (FDI) of €44.67 billion, accounting for 28 per cent of foreign FDI (European Economic and Trade Office 2018: 5). For the EU, Taiwan is an increasingly important economic partner, particularly in regard to the global supply chain of high-quality manufacturing. Furthermore, the commonality of values such as human rights, democracy and the rule of law has led to improved EU-Taiwan ties. Indeed, it is quite likely that the EU would react very strongly and negatively to Chinese use of force against Taiwan, adding yet another complicating factor to China's cost calculation.

Taiwan, therefore, retains significant economic options in the face of Chinese pressure, challenges notwithstanding. And its resilience extends into the diplomatic arena, supported by Taiwan's 'soft power' and 'geostrategic importance'. Its soft power works in at least two ways. First, Taiwan has arguably managed to positively influence Chinese citizens' image of the islands through popular culture and tourism, despite the tight control of the CPC over China's 'Taiwan narrative' (Tsang 2017). Second, Taiwan's evolution as a consolidated democracy provides an additional incentive for the United States, Japan and other liberal democracies to support its autonomy. While America's approach towards Taiwan will be dealt with in more detail below, Japan's close cultural and strategic relationship with Taiwan is worth pointing out at this juncture.

The Japanese colonization of Taiwan between 1895 and 1945 left a cultural and linguistic legacy and 'continued to provide a [positive] social reference point for ongoing contacts between the two people' (Thomas and Williams 2017: 116–17). President Tsai's strategy to promote Taiwan's democracy in the face of growing Chinese authoritarianism and increasing attempts to isolate Taiwan from the international community has further contributed to its bond with Japan. The positive interpretation of colonialism, a shared bond of Asian democratic identity and mutual cultural attraction based on popular support has helped to maintain a high level of government and public support for maintaining and strengthening ties.

Moreover, owing to its close geostrategic proximity, Taiwan has been essential to Japan's national security since the 1890s (Blazevic 2010: 153). Tokyo's strategy has long been informed by the recognition that it can ill afford for Taipei to fall into Beijing's strategic orbit. Taiwan's geostrategic location is essential for Japan's maritime trade and a loss of the island to China would pose a direct danger to its economic lifeline because of Beijing's ability to block sea lane traffic. Moreover, China's power through expansion in both the South China Sea and the East China Sea would be greatly enhanced, possibly leading to Chinese domination of much of these regions. Should the PLA be able to use Taiwan as a staging ground for operations, Japanese forces would be faced with a greatly enhanced Chinese power projection capability, utilizing the island as a 'gateway' for China to enter the Pacific, thereby further threatening Japan's security. Conversely, a de facto independent Taiwan serves as a barrier against Chinese military expansion beyond the 'first island chain' or, in the event of a war, as a possible 'springboard' for US-led operations against the Chinese mainland to which Japanese forces are likely to contribute given the high stakes involved. Consequently, both sides have looked to increase their security ties, for instance through closer informal intelligence sharing (Ihara 2018b) and the signing of a Memorandum of Understanding on maritime search and rescue operations in 2017. While Japan is unlikely to formalize its political and security ties with Taiwan as long as China does not severely threaten Taiwan's autonomy (Hornung 2018), it is equally unlikely that Tokyo will not support Taipei in a major cross-Strait crisis (Chang 2016).

Finally, Taiwan's military options are not as dire as is often assumed. True, as several studies have shown, Taiwan's defence policy faces some significant challenges, including low levels of spending; problems of moving towards an all-volunteer force (AFV), recruitment and retention; and a focus on major weapons platforms (see, for example, Schreer 2015). In this context, the Tsai government's 2017 QDR set the objective to develop a 'resolute defense, multi-domain deterrence' (Republic of China 2017: 5). Overall, the document displayed a 'remarkable amount of thematic consistency in areas such as defense strategy, reform of the military service system, and defense budget constraints with earlier versions' (Grossman *et al.* 2017). However, the government has also supported a more robust defence posture, focused on disruptive capabilities. Taiwan's 2017 National Defense Report outlined initiatives for a 'layered deterrence' based on 'innovative and asymmetrical warfare (Ministry for National Defense 2017). And the government has provided strong support for an indigenous submarine programme, further investments in road-mobile, supersonic anti-ship missiles, upgrades to air defence and air combat systems, hardening command and control centres, and cyber warfare assets to make Taiwan 'indigestible' for advancing Chinese forces (*The Economist* 2019).

In fact, given the islands' difficult terrain and the major challenges for the PLA to conduct large-scale amphibious operations, the ROC armed forces should be in a good position to employ an 'anti-access/area denial' (A2/AD) approach towards the PLA, i.e. to hold at risk and target advancing Chinese forces by multi-layered offensive and defensive capabilities (on A2/AD options by the United States and its allies, including Taiwan, see Biddle and Oehlrich 2016). Taiwan has invested for years in military and civil capabilities designed to frustrate and defeat a Chinese invasion (Easton 2017). Therefore, despite China's growing military build-up, there is a distinct possibility that the ROC armed forces could defeat a PLA attempt to invade the islands through an amphibious landing even without support from the United States (Roy 2017: 1152–55; Greer 2018). Should US and Japanese forces become involved, the PLA's operational challenges would be compounded even further.

America's role in Taiwan's defence

The final factor influencing Taiwan's strategic future is America's role in the defence of the island. Of course, there are no absolute guarantees that Washington would come to the aid of Taipei in the event of a major escalation with Beijing. The Taiwan Relations Act does not constitute a formal military alliance and does not obligate the United States to defend Taiwan. However, there is a good case for optimism that Washington's informal security guarantees for Taiwan will remain firm and in fact will be strengthened over the coming years. The main driver for this scenario is the growing US-China strategic competition. China's continued assertiveness has triggered a bipartisan consensus in Washington about the need to push back (Shambaugh 2018; Campbell and Ratner 2018). Consequently, the Trump Administration's 2017 National Security Strategy (NSS) identified China as a 'revisionist power' (White House 2017: 25), while its 2018 National Defense Strategy labelled it a 'strategic competitor' (US Department of Defense 2018b: 1).

A prolonged period of US pushback against China in multiple policy areas is thus very likely (Sutter 2018). Geostrategically, the United States will seek to retain its position as the pre-eminent sea power in the Western Pacific and Taiwan remains a central element in this strategy as a 'barrier' against greater Chinese military power projection into the Pacific and as a 'springboard' for potential US operations against the Chinese mainland (Schreer 2017b). Moreover, the defence of Taiwan as a consolidated democracy and an important trading partner could take on a strategic dimension for the United States. Therefore, 'any PRC attempt to gain control of Taiwan would almost certainly be regarded as an attack on the vital interests of the United States, and therefore repelled by any means necessary, including military force' (Easton 2016: 4).

The recent evolution in US-Taiwan strategic affairs provides evidence of growing American support in the face of China's pressure. For instance, the US Congress has assumed stronger oversight to ensure that the provisions of the Taiwan Relations Act are adhered to, including a push towards normalization of US arms sales for Taiwan in the 2018 National Defense Authorization Act (NDAA). The NDAA not only contained a proposal for port calls by the US navy to Taiwan but also mandated the Secretary of Defense to report to the

Congress on progress to normalize arms sales to the islands; overall the US Congress has shored up support for Taiwan's self-defence (Kan 2018).

Analysts also noted that the 2017 NSS explicitly embraced Taiwan by name and vowed to adhere to the Taiwan Relations Act commitments. In the context of a greater US pushback against China, the Trump Administration has given greater importance to shoring up Taiwan's future (Cronin 2018:17–18). Practical steps included:

- a major arms sale to Taiwan in 2017 and general agreement for a second deal in 2018;
- the opening in June 2018 of a new de facto US embassy building in Taipei as an important symbolic gesture of support (Tan 2018);
- Trump's signing of the Taiwan Travel Act in March 2018, allowing for high-level US officials to visit Taiwan and vice versa;
- US State Department approval in 2018 for US defence companies to market submarine technology to Taiwan to support its indigenous submarine programme (Yeo 2018);
- Trump's signature of the Asia Reassurance Initiative Act in January 2019 which calls on the president to support the regular transfer of military equipment for Taiwan (Panda 2019);
- the appointment of pro-Taiwan Assistant Secretary of Defense for Asian and Pacific Security Affairs Randy Schriver;
- and increased transits of US warships through the Taiwan Strait in 2018.

As of early 2019 there were no signs of US abandonment of Taiwan. On the contrary, in the context of growing US-China competition it is quite likely that Taiwan is becoming more, not less, important to America politically and strategically. It is prudent to expect that the more China seeks to pressure Taiwan, the more the United States will increase its direct and indirect support for the embattled island. For Chinese political and military planners, the decision to resort to maximum pressure on Taiwan, including the use of military force, remains fraught with a very high risk that the United States would become involved, thus raising the stakes enormously.

Conclusion

In a more uncertain East Asia, Taiwan's strategic future does not look as dire as is commonly assumed. Indeed, precisely because the region has become more contested Taiwan has more options to maintain its status as a de facto independent nation. Its political and geostrategic value for the United States, Japan and other regional powers has increased. Growing US-China strategic competition has produced a bipartisan consensus in the United States to preserve Taiwan's current status, and this appears to be supported by the basic instincts of the current presidency. There is little evidence that other external powers have 'given up on Taiwan'. This development further complicates China's ability to exert coercive pressure on Taiwanese leaders to accept steps towards unification on Beijing's terms. Indeed, Taiwan is a remarkable case study of a small power resisting the coercive pressures of a much larger neighbour and evidence of the real limitations of China's power. Taiwan's political, societal, economic and military resilience, while not without challenges, remains remarkably strong.

As a result, neither peaceful unification on China's term nor 'bandwaggoning' with mainland China is a realistic prospect for Taiwan's strategic future. Instead, Taiwan faces two other stark options: the positive scenario is its continuation as a de facto independent, democratic country, supported by mostly informal political and security mechanism by the United States, Japan and other important players. This chapter has demonstrated that this option is quite likely for the foreseeable future, barring unforeseen domestic developments in Taiwan. The negative scenario would be a Chinese attempt to 'unite' the island by force, having run out of other options to compel Taiwan to accept unification as an inevitable process. While such a step would, as mentioned above, be highly risky and success far from guaranteed, it is also not impossible to conceive of a situation whereby China's political and military leaders, (over-) confident in their country's military capabilities, might seek to 'solve' the Taiwan issue through military measures. Indeed, a 2019 report entitled 'China's Military Power' by the US Defense Intelligence Agency warned that PLA leaders might become increasingly confident in their capabilities to invade the island as its weaponry becomes more sophisticated (US Defense Intelligence Agency 2019). While it is far from certain that China would win a war in the Taiwan Straits, the consequences of such a conflict would be grave for all parties involved. Barring such a worst-case scenario, however, Taiwan has every prospect to retain its status as a de facto independent, democratic nation in East Asia.

References

Allison, G. (2017) *Destined for War: Can America and China Escape Thucydides Trap?* Boston, MA: Houghton Mifflin Harcourt.
Armitage, R. L., I. Easton, and M. Stokes (2018) *U.S.-Taiwan Relations in a Sea of Change: Navigating Toward a Brighter Future*, Arlington, VA: Project 2049 Institute.
Beckley, M. C. (2018) 'The Power of Nations: Measuring What Matters', *International Security*, 43(2).
Biddle, S. and I. Oelrich (2016) 'Future Warfare in the Western Pacific: Chinese Anti-access/ Area Denial, U.S. AirSea Battle, and Command of the Commons in East Asia', *International Security*, 41(1).
Biddle, T. D. (2009) *Rhetoric and Reality in Air Warfare: The Evolution of British and American Ideas about Strategic Bombing, 1914–1945*, Princeton, NJ: University Press.
Blazevic, J. J. (2010) 'The Taiwan Dilemma: China, Japan, and the Strait Dynamic', *Journal of Current Chinese Affairs*, 39(4).
Campbell, K. M. and E. Ratner (2018) 'The China Reckoning: How Beijing Defied American Expectations', *Foreign Affairs*, March/April. Available at www.foreignaffairs.com/articles/china/2018-02-13/china-reckoning (accessed 13 January 2019).

Chang, G. G. (2016) 'Say Hello to Taiwan', *National Interest*, 18 October. Available at https://nationalinterest.org/feature/say-hello-taiwan-18092 (accessed 10 January 2019).

Chung, L. (2018) 'Should Taiwan Be Worried If It Loses all Its Allies?' *South China Sea Morning Post*, 1 September.

Cronin, P. (2018) 'The Trump Administration's Policy Toward Taiwan', *National Bureau for Asian Research (NBR), Strengthening U.S.-Taiwan Defense Relations*, Seattle, WA: NBR.

Easton, I. (2016) *Strategic Standoff: The U.S.-China Rivalry and Taiwan*, Washington, DC: Project 2049 Institute.

Easton, I. (2017) *The Chinese Invasion Threat: Taiwan's Defense and American Strategy in Asia*, Manchester: Eastbridge.

Election Study Centre (2018a) *Changes in the Taiwanese/Chinese Identity of Taiwanese as Tracked in Surveys by the Election Study Centre, NCUU (1992~2018.06)*, National Chengchi University, 2 August. Available at https://esc.nccu.edu.tw/course/news.php?Sn=166 (accessed 12 January 2019).

Election Study Centre (2018b) *Taiwan Independence vs. Unification with the Mainland (1992/06~2018/06)*, National Chengchi University, 2 August. Available at https://esc.nccu.edu.tw/course/news.php?Sn=167 (accessed 12 January 2019).

European Economic and Trade Office (2018) *EU-Taiwan Relations 2018*, Taipei: European Economic and Trade Office.

Everington, K. (2018) 'Taiwan Ranked 19th Highest GDP in World Based on PPP', *Taiwan News*, 28 May. Available at www.taiwannews.com.tw/en/news/3442183 (accessed 11 January 2019).

Focus Taiwan (2019) 'KMT Chief Clarifies Contents of "1992 Consensus"', 4 January. Available at http://focustaiwan.tw/news/aipl/201901040026.aspx (accessed 10 January 2019).

Gentile, G. P. (2001) *How Effective Is Strategic Bombing? Lessons Learned from World War II To Kosovo*, New York: New York University Press.

Gilley, B. (2010) 'Not So Dire Straits', *Foreign Affairs*, 89(1).

Glaser, C. (2011) 'Will China's Rise Inevitably Lead to War?' *Foreign Affairs*, 90(1).

Gomez, E. (2016) 'A Costly Commitment: Options for the Future of the U.S.-Taiwan Defense Relationship', *Policy Analysis 800*, CATO Institute, 28 September.

Greer, T. (2018) 'Taiwan Can Win a War with China', *Foreign Policy*, 25 September. Available at https://foreignpolicy.com/2018/09/25/taiwan-can-win-a-war-with-china/ (accessed 13 January 2019).

Gray, S. (2018) 'These Are the Biggest U.S. Trading Partners', *Fortune*, 2 April. Available at http://fortune.com/2018/03/07/biggest-us-trade-partners/ (accessed 11 January 2019).

Grossman, D. (2019) 'Is a Sustainable Peace Possible in the Taiwan Strait?' *RAND Commentary*, 7 January. Available at www.rand.org/blog/2019/01/is-a-sustainable-peace-possible-in-the-taiwan-strait.html (accessed 10 January 2019).

Grossman, D., M. S. Chase and L. Ma (2017) 'Taiwan's 2017 Quadrennial Defense Review in Context', *Rand Blog*, 14 June. Available at www.rand.org/blog/2017/06/taiwans-2017-quadrennial-defense-review-in-context.html (accessed 10 January 2019).

Heritage Foundation (2018) *2018 Index of Economic Freedom*, Washington, DC: Heritage Foundation. Available at www.heritage.org/index/ (accessed 10 January 2019).

Hornung, J. W. (2018) 'Strong but Constrained Japan-Taiwan Ties', *Brookings Op-ed*, 13 March. Available at www.brookings.edu/opinions/strong-but-constrained-japan-taiwan-ties/ (accessed 13 January 2019).

Iharu, K. (2018a) 'With Economic Allure Fading, Taiwan Keeps Its Distance from China', *Nikkei Asian Review*, 21 May.

Iharu, K. (2018b) 'Taiwan Wants Intelligence-Sharing Arrangement with Japan', *Nikkei Asian Review*, 26 January.

Jacques, M. (2009) *When China Rules the World: The End of the Western World and the Birth of a New World Order*, New York: Penguin.

Japan External Trade Organization (2018) *Japanese Trade and Investment Statistics*. Available at www.jetro.go.jp/en/reports/statistics/ (accessed 14 January 2019).

Kan, S. (2018) 'Congressional Support for Taiwan's Defense through the National Defense Authorization Act', *Strengthening U.S.-Taiwan Defense Relations*, Seattle, WA: National Bureau for Asian Research.

Kennedy, S. (2018) 'China Will Overtake the U.S. Economy in Less than 15 Years, Says HSBC, Challenging Trump's Claim', *Bloomberg*, 25 September.

Kiernan, P. D. (2012) *Becoming China's Bitch: And Nine Catastrophes We Must Avoid Right Now*, New York: Turner.

Kuo, L. (2019) 'All Necessary Means: Xi Jinping Reserves Right to Use Force against Taiwan', *The Guardian*, 2 January.

Lao, C. and D. Lin (2015) 'Rebalancing Taiwan-US Relations', *Survival*, 57(6).

Lee, K. Y. (2000) 'The Cruel Game', *Far Eastern Economic Review*, 8 June.

Lee, S. (2015) 'China's Strategy Towards Taiwan', in Andrew T. H. Tan (ed.) *Security and Conflict in East Asia*, Abingdon: Routledge.

Lee, S. and B. Schreer (2013) 'The Taiwan Strait: Still Dangerous', *Survival*, 55(3).

Marston, H. and R. C. Bush (2018) 'Taiwan's Engagement with Southeast Asia Is Making Progress under the New Southbound Policy', *Brookings Institution Op-ed*, 30 July. Available at www.brookings.edu/opinions/taiwans-engagement-with-southeast-asia-is-making-progress-under-the-new-southbound-policy/ (accessed 12 January 2019).

Mearsheimer, J. J. (2014) 'Say Goodbye to Taiwan', *National Interest*, March-April. Available at https://nationalinterest.org/article/say-goodbye-taiwan-9931 (accessed 2 December 2018).

Ministry of Finance, ROC (2018) 'Trade Figures for December 2018'. Available at www.mof.gov.tw/File/Attach/82516/File_18462.pdf (accessed 11 January 2019).

Ministry of National Defense, ROC (2017) *2017 Quadrennial Defense Review*, Taipei: Ministry of National Defense, March.

Mitchell, M. (2017) 'Taiwan and China: A Geostrategic Reassessment of U.S. Policy', *Comparative Strategy*, 36(5): 383–391.

Office of the President, ROC (2019) 'President Tsai's New Year's Talk For 2019', 1 January. Available at https://english.president.gov.tw/NEWS/5618 (accessed 10 January 2019).

O'Hanlon, M. (2000) 'Why China Cannot Conquer Taiwan', *International Security*, 25(2).

Panda, A. (2019) 'What ARIA Will and Won't Do for the US in Asia', *The Diplomat*, 14 January. Available at https://thediplomat.com/2019/01/what-aria-will-and-wont-do-for-the-us-in-asia/ (accessed 15 January 2019).

Radio Free Asia (2018) 'More Than 80 Percent of Taiwanese Reject China's "Unification Plan"', 9 January. Available at www.rfa.org/english/news/china/more-than-80-percent-of-taiwanese-01092019115150.html (accessed 11 January 2019).

Reuters (2018) 'Update 1-Strong Exports Lift Taiwan's Q2 Growth, but Economy Faces Headwinds', 31 July.

Roy, D. (2003) 'PLA Capabilities in the Next Decade', in M. Edmonds and M. M. Tsai (eds) *Defending Taiwan: The Future Vision of Taiwan's Defence Policy*, Abingdon: Routledge.

Roy, D. (2015) 'Collision Course: The Looming U.S.-China Showdown Over Taiwan', *National Interest*, 21 February.

Roy, D. (2017) 'Prospects for Taiwan Maintaining its Autonomy under Chinese Pressure', *Asian Survey*, 57(6): 1135–1158.

Saunders, P. C. and S. L. Kastner (2009) 'Bridge over Troubled Water? Envisioning a China-Peace Agreement', *International Security*, 33(4).

Schelling, T. C. (2008) *Arms and Influence*, New Haven, CT: Yale University Press

Schreer, B. (2015) 'Taiwan's Defence Options', in Andrew T. H. Tan (ed.) *Security and Conflict in East Asia*, London: Routledge.

Schreer, B. (2017a) 'The Double-Edged Sword of Coercion: Cross-Strait Relations after the 2016 Taiwan Elections', *Asian Politics & Policy*, 9(1).

Schreer, B. (2017b) 'Towards Contested "Spheres of Influence" in the Western Pacific: Rising China, Classical Geopolitics, and Asia-Pacific Stability', *Geopolitics*. Available at www.tandfonline.com/doi/full/10.1080/14650045.2017.1364237.

Shambaugh, D. (2018) 'The New American Bipartisan Consensus on China Policy', *China-US Focus*, 21 September. Available at www.chinausfocus.com/foreign-policy/the-new-american-bipartisan-consensus-on-china-policy (accessed 13 January 2019).

Stephens, B. (2018) 'The Real China Challenge: Managing Its Decline', *New York Times*, 29 October.

Stratfor (2018) 'Taiwan Confronts the Costs of Economic Integration with Mainland China', *Assessments*, 2 October.

Sutter, R. (2011) 'Taiwan's Future: Narrowing Straits', *NBR Analysis*, No. 96, Seattle, WA: National Bureau of Asian Research.

Sutter, Robert (2018), "Pushback: America's New China Strategy," *The Diplomat*, 2 November, available at https://thediplomat.com/2018/11/pushback-americas-new-china-strategy/ accessed 12 January 2019.

Tan, R. (2018) 'The U.S. Government Has Opened a Huge New Facility in Taiwan, and China Isn't Happy', *Washington Post*, 18 June. Available at www.washingtonpost.com/news/worldviews/wp/2018/06/18/the-u-s-government-has-opened-a-huge-new-facility-in-taiwan-and-china-isnt-happy/?noredirect=on&utm_term=.694522c10396 (accessed 12 January 2019).

Tanner, M. S. (2007) *Chinese Economic Coercion against Taiwan: A Tricky Weapon to Use*, Santa Monica, CA: RAND Corporation.

The Economist (2019) 'Dire Strait', 26 January.

Thomas, N. and B. Williams (2017) 'Taiwan's Sub-national Government Relations with Japan: Post-1979 Developments', *Journal of Contemporary Asia*, 47(1).

Tsang, S. (ed.) (2017) *Taiwan's Impact on China: Why Soft Power Matters more than Economic or Political Inputs*, London: Palgrave Macmillan.

US-China Economic and Security Review Commission (2018) *2018 Report to Congress, US-China Economic and Security Review Commission*, Washington, DC: US-China Economic and Security Review Commission.

US Defense Intelligence Agency (2019) *China Military Power: Modernizing a Force to Fight and Win, US Defense Intelligence Agency*. Available at www.dia.mil/Portals/27/Documents/News/Military%20Power%20Publications/China_Military_Power_FINAL_5MB_20190103.pdf (accessed 20 January 2019).

US Department of Defense (2018a) *Annual Report to Congress: Military and Security Developments Involving the People's Republic of China 2018*, Washington, DC: Office of the Secretary of Defense.

US Department of Defense (2018b) *Summary of the 2018 National Defense Strategy of the United States of America: Sharpening the American Military's Competitive Edge*, Washington, DC:Office of the Secretary of Defense.

Wall Street Journal (2018) 'China's Economy Flashes New Warning Signs', 14 December.

White House (2017) *National Security Strategy of the United States of America*, Washington, DC: White House.

Yeo, M. (2018) 'US State Department OKs License for Submarine Tech Sales to Taiwan', *Defense News*, 9 April. Available at www.defensenews.com/naval/2018/04/09/us-state-department-oks-license-for-submarine-tech-sales-to-taiwan/ (accessed 10 January 2019).

Index

Page numbers in bold refer to tables. Page numbers followed by "n" refer to notes.

A2AD (anti-access, area denial) capabilities 22, 219–20
Abe, Shinzo 129, 130, 133
Acheson, Dean 44, 108
Afghanistan 33, 92, 114
AFRC *see* Armed Forces Reserve Command (AFRC)
air imbalance, changing 176–7
Air-Sea Battle 116
air superiority, contesting 176–7
Akama, Jiro 131
all-volunteer force (AVF) policy 166–8, 219
America *see* United States (USA, US)
American Institute in Taiwan 112, 148
Anti-Access/Area Denial Strategy 146
Anti-Secession Law of 2005 62–4, 80, 92, 113, 198; Article 2 13; Article 3 17; Article 4 13; Article 8 13
Anti-Separatism Law *see* Anti-Secession Law of 2005
ARATS *see* Association for Relations Across the Taiwan Straits (ARATS)
armed forces of Taiwan 156–69; current situation 156–9; land of multiple fronts 165–7; pale sky 159–62; troubled waters 163–5
Armed Forces Reserve Command (AFRC) 165
ASEAN *see* Association of Southeast Asian Nations (ASEAN)
Asia Reassurance Initiative Act of 2018 221; Section 209 68
Asian Financial Crisis of 1997–98 33
Association for Relations Across the Taiwan Straits (ARATS) 61, 63, 65, 67, 90, 92, 194

Association of East Asian Relations 131, 151
Association of Southeast Asian Nations (ASEAN) 4, 149–50, 152, 217
Association of Taiwan-Japan Relations 151
Attlee, Clement 44
Australia 38, 50, 115, 149
AVF *see* all-volunteer force (AVF) policy
Azerbaijan 22

Beckley, Michael 213
Beijing 1, 3, 5, 91, 102, 139, 174; bombardment of Taiwan's offshore islands 76; bullying tactics 53; changing social attitudes and 36; China–US rapprochement and 111; and cross-Strait destabilization 81; cross-Strait military balance and US–Taiwan policy 97; and cross-Strait rapprochement 66; and cross-Strait relations 92, 96; economic growth 2; ideological rivalry and peaceful unification era 77; Innenpolitik and 78; and Japan–Taiwan relations 126; lasting peace in Taiwan Strain and 191, 197, 198, 200; neo-functionalist approach 82; 'One-China Principle and the Taiwan Issue' 77; and reunification 203n3; small state survival and 22; structural weakness and 32–4; support for revolutionary movements 43; Taiwan's foreign policy and 37, 39, 139; and Taiwan's relationship with great powers 47, 49, 50, 54, 55; Taiwan's strategic future and 211, 216, 217, 220, 222; and

tragedy of asymmetric trust 86; and Trump Administration 100; unification agenda 93, 94
Belt and Road Initiative 96, 202
Benvenuti, Andrea 6
beyond visual range (BVR) capability 159
Bolton, John 116
Britain 44
Burkina Faso 96, 212
Burma: relations with United States 46
Busby, Scott 38
Bush Administration 113, 114
Bush, George W. 113, 184
Bush, Richard 201
BVR *see* beyond visual range (BVR) capability

Cambodia 49
Campaign Theory Study Guide (National Defense University) 175
Canada 50, 151
Caribbean, the 149
Carter Administration 50, 111
Carter, Jimmy 51, 55n3
CBMs *see* confidence-building measures (CBMs)
CEFC *see* China Energy Fund Committee (CEFC)
Center for Strategic and Budgetary Assessments (CSBA) 179, 180, 184, 185
Center for Strategic and International Studies 84
Central America 96, 149
CEP *see* Circular Error Probable (CEP)
Chan-ocha, Prayuth 139
Chen, Mark 80
Chen Mintong 84
Chen Shui-bian 3, 19, 31, 33, 37, 54, 77, 84, 86, 92, 113, 114, 131, 138, 146; cross-Strait destabilization 81, 82; and cross-Strait relations 95; era, Anti-Secession Law of 2005 and 62–4; and 'Go South' strategy 149; Innenpolitik, primacy of 78–9; re-election, missed opportunity following 80; visit to Latin America 53; visit to United States 53; waning electoral fortunes 81
Chen Yi 127
chequebook diplomacy 139, 145
Chiang Ching-kuo 30, 31, 52, 60, 81, 145, 146; and Taiwan–China relationship 61–2

Chiang Kai-shek 28, 30, 44, 46, 47, 49, 59, 60, 107, 108, 134n1, 145, 150; and Taiwan–China relationship 61–2
China: Anti-Secession Law of 2005 13; Belt and Road Initiative 96, 202; defence budget in 2017 2; economic growth 2; military power of 14–15; preferences in the Strait 193–6; State Council 40n4, 199, 204n10; Taiwan Affairs Office 39, 40n4; and United States, rivalry between 1, 4, 7, 21; *see also individual entries*
China Dream of National Rejuvenation 199
China Energy Fund Committee (CEFC) 40n1
China–Japan Joint Communique (1972) 123, 126
China Times 203n7
China Unification Promotion Party (CUPP) 35, 40n3, 41n6
China–US Mutual Defense Treaty 75, 110, 111
China–US rapprochement 110–13
Chinese Civil War (1945–49) 126
Chinese Ministry of Foreign Affairs 150
Chinese Nationalists 43; cross-border guerrilla operations 46
Chinese power, limits of 212–16
Chinese–Soviet alignment, formation of 75
Chinese–Soviet split 110
Cho Jung-tai 202
Chou Enlai 60
Chou Tzu-yu 20
Chu, Eric 66
Churchill, Winston 108
Circular Error Probable (CEP) 177
civic nationalism 35
Civil Aviation Agency 4
Clinton Administration 53, 97, 148
Clinton, Bill 113
Clinton, Hillary 116
Cole, J. Michael 6, 28
Commonwealth Secretariat 21
Communist Party of China (CPC) 1, 3, 59, 90; Anti-Secession Law and 62; and asymmetric trust in Taiwan–China relations 73, 75, 76, 87; and cross-Strait relations 94; and détente during the Ma Ying-jeou era 65, 66; domestic dynamics and foreign policy 29, 32; small state and 16, 17; and Taiwan's foreign policy 140, 142,

145, 147; and Taiwan's relationship with great powers 46, 48, 52; and Taiwan's strategic future 211, 218; and Taiwan–US relations 108–9
Comprehensive and Progressive Agreement for Trans-Pacific Partnership 131
confidence-building measures (CBMs) 192, 202
Cornell University 18
CPC *see* Communist Party of China (CPC)
Cross-Strait Agreement on Joint Crime-fighting and Judicial Mutual Assistance (2009) 65
cross-Strait destabilization 81
cross-Strait military balance, and US–Taiwan policy 96–101
cross-Strait peace, differing visions of: Chinese peace ideas 198–200; Taiwanese peace ideas 200–1; Western peace ideas 201
cross-Strait relations 1, 7–9, 58, 174; Anti-Session Law and 64; asymmetric trust in Taiwan–China relations 73–5, 77, 79, 84, 85, 87; Chinese perspective on Taiwan and 90, 91, 98, 101; détente during the Ma Ying-jeou era and 65; key implications for 152; lasting peace in 192–4, 197–200; Ma Ying-jeou and Obama 115; Taiwanese problem or issue and 19; Taiwan's foreign policy and 139, 142; during the Ma and Tsai eras 92–6; Tsai administration and 1992 Consensus 69
Cross-Strait Service Trade Agreement (CSSTA) 34, 66, 67, 83, 146
cross-strait status quo 8, 78, 84, 138, 139, **144**, 152, 196, 200
CSBA *see* Center for Strategic and Budgetary Assessments (CSBA)
CSSTA *see* Cross-Strait Service Trade Agreement (CSSTA)
Cultural Revolution 50, 60, 76
CUPP *see* China Unification Promotion Party (CUPP)
Curriden, Christian 203n1

dangwai ('outside') movement 30
de Gaulle, Charles 48
de-Sinicification 90
Democratic Progressive Party (DPP) 1, 3, 7; and Chinese perspectives on Taiwan 95, 101; lasting peace in Taiwan Strait and 191, 194, 195, 196, 201–3; and Taiwan–China relations 60, 62, 64, 67–9, 73, 74, 79, 85–8; Taiwanese problem of issue and 19, 20; and Taiwan–Japan relations 123, 127, 129, 133; Taiwan's armed forces and 168; Taiwan's domestic dynamics and foreign policy 30–7; Taiwan's foreign policy and 138, 140–2, 147, 149, 152; and Taiwan's relationship with great powers 53; and Taiwan–US relations 107, 117
democratization 7, 28, 30, 31, 35, 38, 52, 73, 74, 113, 138, 145, 168
Deng Xiaoping 9, 60, 76, 87, 192, 193
Department of Defense 38; Quadrennial Defense Review 95
Department of State 38
Dittmer, Lowell 19
Dominican Republic 66, 96, 195, 212
DPP *see* Democratic Progressive Party (DPP)
Duterte, Rodrigo Roa 139

East Asian Youth Games 68
East China Sea 115, 116, 124, 219
ECFA *see* Economic Cooperation Framework Agreement (ECFA)
Economic Cooperation Framework Agreement (ECFA) 3, 19, 34, 83, 91, 93, 115, 146, 150, 195, 201, 202, 203n2,n7
Economic Freedom Index 213
Economic Partnership Agreement 131
Eisenhower Administration 47
Eisenhower, Dwight 46, 47
El Salvador 96, 195, 212
11 September 2001 terrorist attacks 32, 114
Eswatini 195
EU *see* European Union (EU)
European Economic Community 48
European Union (EU) 151, 152, 218

FDI *see* foreign direct investment (FDI)
First Sino-Japanese War 125
Force Posture Agreement of 2014 115
foreign direct investment (FDI) 150, 218
Formosa Alliance 37
Formosan Association for Public Affairs 32, 81
Fraleigh, Matthew 59, 125
'Free and Open Indo-Pacific' strategy 101

230 Index

free trade agreement (FTA) 150
French recognition of the PRC (1964) 48
FTA *see* free trade agreement (FTA)
Fukushima Daiichi nuclear catastrophe 129
Furuya, Keiji 128

Gambia 65, 96, 195, 212
GCTF *see* Global Cooperation and Training Framework (GCTF)
GDP *see* gross domestic product (GDP)
Germany 108, 158
Global Cooperation and Training Framework (GCTF) 38
Global Financial Crisis of 2008 115
Greece 52
gross domestic product (GDP) 2, 14, 95, 98, 162, 168, 212–14, 217
Grossman, Derek 9, 191

Han Kuang war games 66
Handel, Michael 6, 12, 22, 23
'Hard ROC' strategy 178
Harizu 127
Hashimoto, Ryutaro 53
Hasluck, Paul 49
Hickey, Dennis van Vranken 113
Ho, Patrick 40n1
Hobbesian international system 22
Holmes, James 183
Holy See 195
Hong Kong 1, 3, 39, 61, 63, 100–1, 150, 151, 193, 195, 200, 214, 217
Hsiao, Russell 203n7
Hu Jintao 9, 58, 64, 79, 81, 82, 92, 192, 199; Six Proposals 203n6
Hu, Shaohua 116
huadu movement 35
Huang, Alex 197
Huang, Roger Lee 7, 58
Hung Hsiu-chu 34
Huong Le Thu 68

ICAO *see* International Civil Aviation Organization (ICAO)
ideological rivalry 76–7
IMF *see* International Monetary Fund (IMF)
Inbar, Efraim 6
independence movement (*taidu*) 35
India 4, 214
Indo-Pacific Security Dialogue 132
Indo-Pacific Strategy 198
Innenpolitik 78–9

Interchange Association 127, 131
International Civil Aviation Organization (ICAO) 4, 37, 66, 68, 82, 212
International Economic Cooperation Development Fund 51
International Herald Leader (newspaper) 194
International Labour Conference 4
International Monetary Fund (IMF) 2, 217
Interpol 37, 212
Iraq 33

Japan 4, 6, 8, 22, 29–30, 38, 50, 53, 151, 167, 214, 215, 218, 219; alliance with Nazi Germany 108; defeat in Second World War 59; exclusive economic zone (EEZ) 125; relationship with Taiwan *see* Taiwan–Japan relationship; Self-Defense Forces 125; westernmost air defense identification zone (ADIZ) 126
Japan-Taiwan Exchange Association 131, 151
Japan-Taiwan Peace Foundation 129
Japanese Diet 128
Japanese Imperial Army 128, 132
Japanese Taiwan Relations Act 131
Jiang Zemin 62, 193, 199
Johnson, Lyndon 49
Joint Concept for Access and Maneuver in the Global Commons 116
Jones, Matthew 55n1

Kastner, Scott 201
Kawasaki 132
Khrushchev, Nikita 110
Kim, Samuel S. 55, 55n2
Kinman 110
Kishida, Fumio 130
Kissinger, Henry 76
KMT-CPC forum 64
KMT *see* Kuomintang (KMT—Nationalist Party)
Ko Wen-je 85
Korean War 17, 59, 75, 109
Kuomintang (KMT—Nationalist Party) 1, 3, 8; and asymmetric trust in Taiwan–China relations 79; and Chinese perspectives on Taiwan 91, 94, 96; and domestic dynamics 29–35; 'Guoguang Project' ('National Recovery Project') Office 76; lasting peace in Taiwan Strait and 194,

199–201, 203; and Ma Ying-jeou rapprochement 81; National Policy Foundation 200; and Taiwan–China relationship 59, 61–3, 65–7, 73–6; Taiwanese problem or issue and 16–17, 20; and Taiwan–Japan relationship 126, 127, 129, 133; Taiwan's armed forces and 168; Taiwan's foreign policy and 39, 138, 140–2, 145–7, 149, 152; and Taiwan's relationship with great powers 43–5, 47, 52, 54; Taiwan's strategic future and 215; and Taiwan–US relationship 107–10

Lai Ching-te, William 95, 195
Lai, William 195
LDP *see* Liberal Democratic Party (LDP)
Lee Kuan Yew 150, 211
Lee Ming-che 40n4
Lee, Sheryn 8, 138
Lee Teng-hui 18, 31, 51, 53, 61–3, 81, 82, 113, 128–30, 140, 146, 195; 'special state-to-state relations' doctrine 62, 77–9, 194
Legislative Yuan 31
Liao, Nien-chung Chang 118
Liberal Democratic Party (LDP) 127
Lien Chan 64
Life (magazine) 108
Lim, Yves-Heng 8–9, 174
Lin, Dalton Kuen-da 118
Lon Nol 49
Lowe, Will 63
Luce, Henry 108

Ma Ying-jeou 1, 203n2, 204n9; administration 114–17; anti-Japanese inclinations 130; Anti-Secession Law and 63; and asymmetric trust in Taiwan–China relations 86; and China's perspective on Taiwan 91, 98; and cross-Strain relations 92–6; era, détente during 64–7; lasting peace in Taiwan Strait and 191, 198, 200; One China principle 82; pro-Beijing' policies 34; rapprochement (2008–14) 81–3; Taiwanese nationalism and 77; Taiwanese problem or issue and 20; Taiwan–Japan relations and 132, 133; Taiwan's armed forces and 168; Taiwan's domestic dynamics and 29, 33, 37; Taiwan's foreign policy and 29, 33, 37, 138, 146; Taiwan's strategic future and 210
MAC *see* Mainland Affairs Council (MAC)
Macau 1, 3, 193, 200, 217
Mainland Affairs Council (MAC) 40n4, 196, 200
Manchuria 108
Maniruzzaman, Talukder 22
Mao Zedong 30, 47, 48, 50. 76 87, 110, 145, 193
Marshall Islands 14
Matsu 110
Meiji Reformation of 1868 59, 125
Memorandum of Understanding (MOU) 131, 132
military liberation era (1949–66) 74, 75
Ministry of Education 30
Ministry of Foreign Affairs 30
Ministry of National Defence 30
Mitsubishi 132
MOU *see* Memorandum of Understanding (MOU)
Murray, William 183–6

Nathan, Andrew 110
National Defense Authorization Act of 2018 (NDAA) 100, 220
National Defense Authorization Act for Fiscal Year 2019 38
National Defense Report (2013 and 2017) 178, 219
National Development Council (NDC) 141
National Intelligence Estimate (NIE) 46, 47
National People's Congress (NPC): 'Message to Compatriots in Taiwan' 60
National Reunification Council 64
National Reunification Guidelines 64
National Security Council 109
National Unification Council 78, 81, 114
National Unification Guidelines 78, 81
NATO *see* North Atlantic Treaty Organization (NATO)
Nauru 14
naval balance, changing 180–2
Navarro, Peter 116
NDAA *see* National Defense Authorization Act of 2018 (NDAA)
NDC *see* National Development Council (NDC)

Netherlands, the 182
New Power Party 146
New Southbound Policy (NSP) 37, 149, 217
New Zealand 50, 93, 149
Ngo Dinh Diem 49
NIE *see* National Intelligence Estimate (NIE)
Nien-Chung Chang Liao 201
1992 Consensus **143**, 174; Anti-Secession Law and 62, 63; Chinese perspective on Taiwan and 90–2, 95, 96, 101, 102; lasting peace in Taiwan Strait and 191–3, 195, 196, 198, 201, 202, 203n4; Ma Ying-jeou rapprochement 82; Sunflower Movement and 84; Taiwan's foreign policy and 37, 40n4; Taiwan's strategic future and 210; Tsai administration under the curse of 67–9
Nixon Administration 76, 110
Nixon, Richard 50, 110–11; visit to China 18
Nobuo, Kishi 130
Nobusuke, Kishi 130
North Atlantic Treaty Organization (NATO) 44; Suppression of Enemy Air Defenses campaign 180
North Korea 118; attack on the South (1950) 44
NPC *see* National People's Congress (NPC)
NSP *see* New Southbound Policy (NSP)

Obama Administration 114–17, 210
ODA *see* Official Development Assistance (ODA)
Office of Naval Intelligence 181
Official Development Assistance (ODA) 149
O'Hanlon, Michael 176, 211
Okinari, Kaya 128
Okinotori Shima EEZ 132
One China principle 5, **143**, 210; Chinese perspectives on Taiwan and 92, 101; lasting peace in Taiwan Strait and 191, 193, 194, 196, 198–9, 202; Ma Ying-jeou rapprochement and 82; military liberation era 75; primacy of Innerpolitik and 78; small state survival and 16; Taiwan–China relations and 59, 61–3, 67, 126; Taiwan's foreign policy and 145, 151, 152; Taiwan's relationship with great powers and 52, 54; Taiwan–US relationship and 115, 118
'one country, two systems' principle 1, 3, 39, 52, 53, 60, 90, **143**, 193–4, 198, 201, 216

Pacific Pact of 1949 44
Palau 14
Panama 66, 96, 195, 212
Paraguay 66
'peaceful reunification' strategy 60, 64, 90, 139, 147, 152, 193, 199
'peaceful unification' strategy 3, 67, 73, 74, 76–7, 87, 93, 193, 211, 222
People's Liberation Army (PLA) 2, 4, 8, 9, 102; cross-Strait military balance and US–Taiwan policy 96–8, 100; defending Taiwan against China 175, 180; small state survival and 21; and Taiwan–Japan relations 66; Taiwan's armed forces and 156, 162, 166, 169; Taiwan's foreign policy and 146; Taiwan's strategic future and 211, 212, 215, 216, 219, 220, 222
People's Republic of China (PRC) *see* China
Pescadores 108
Philippines, the 48
PLA *see* People's Liberation Army (PLA)
PLA Air Force (PLAAF) 159, 176, 177, 202
PLA Naval Air Force (PLANAF) 159, 160
PLA Navy (PLAN) 181, 185; anti-access and area denial (A2/AD) strategy and capabilities 163–5
PLA Rocket Forces (PLARF) 177
PLAAF *see* PLA Air Force (PLAAF)
PLAN *see* PLA Navy (PLAN)
PLANAF *see* PLA Naval Air Force (PLANAF)
Portugal 52
Powell, Colin 80, 114
PPP *see* purchasing power parity (PPP)
PRC *see* People's Republic of China (PRC)
pro-unification 32, 33, 35, 41n6, 93
purchasing power parity (PPP) 2

QDR *see* Quadrennial Defense Review (QDR)
Quadrennial Defense Review (QDR) 95, 213, 219

Index 233

RAND Corporation 2, 117, 176, 177, 179, 203n1
Reagan Administration 16, 99, 112, 113
Republic of China (ROC) *see* Taiwan
resilience 5
ROC Air Force (ROCAF) 156, 157, **157**, 160–2, 177; Air Defense and Missile Command 179; Air Defense Artillery command 179; Air Defense Missile command 179
ROC Army (ROCA) 156, 158, **159**, 160–2, 165–8
ROC Navy (ROCN) 156, 158, 160–5
ROCN Marine Corps (ROCNMC) 158, 165, 166
Roosevelt, Theodore 108
Ross, Robert 110
Rothstein, Robert 12
Roy, Denny 110, 211, 214

São Tomé and Príncipe 96, 195
Saunders, Phillip 201
Schreer, Benjamin 1, 8, 9, 123, 210
Schriver, Randall 148
sea control, contesting 180–2
sea lines of communication (SLOCs) 156, 158
Second Artillery Corps *see* PLA Rocket Forces (PLARF)
Second Taiwan Strait Crisis 60
Second World War 16
SEF *see* Straits Exchange Foundation (SEF)
Seiroku, Kajiyama 130
Senkaku/Diaoyu Islands 150
Shang Su-wu 8, 21–4, 156
Shanghai Communiqué 18
Sheffer, Gabriel 6
Sihanouk, Norodom 49
Singapore 22, 23, 61, 93, 150, 151, 191
SIPRI 98
Six Assurances 8, 16, 99, 112, **144**, 145, 147, 152
SLOCs *see* sea lines of communication (SLOCs)
small state: characteristics of 15; Taiwan as 13–16
small state survival: challenges of 21–4; in international system 12–13
societal attitudes, changing 34–7
Soong May-ling 108
South America 96

South China Sea 116, 117, 124, 125, 138, 158, 165, 219
South-East Asia 150
South Korea 48, 133, 167
South Vietnam 48–50
Soviet Union 14
'special state-to-state relations' doctrine 62, 77–9, 194
State Council Information Office: 'Taiwan Issue and China's Unification' 198
State Department 44
Straits Exchange Foundation (SEF) 61, 63, 65, 67, 90, 92, 194
strategic ambiguity 4, 18, 54, 84, 85, 91, 99, 112, 113, **144**, 145, 148, 175, 210
Su Chi 85
Sullivan, John 63
Sun Yafu 200
Sunflower Movement (2014–18) 3, 20, 34, 35, 66, 83–5, 94, 146, 195
Sutter, Robert G. 51, 108, 211

TAIPEI (Taiwan Allies International Protection and Enhancement Initiative) Act 38, 197
Taipei 3, 8, 9, 41n4, 110, 133, 148, 202; Chinese perspective on Taiwan and 91, 96, 100; Cross-Strait Services Trade Agreement 34; defending Taiwan against China 174, 183, 184; great powers–Taiwan relationship and 46, 48, 50, 52; structural weakness and 30; Taiwan's strategic future and 210, 215; ties with Tokyo 124
Taipei Economic and Cultural Representative Office (TECRO) 32
taishang 32
Taiwan: asymmetric option 177–80, 182–5; against China, defending 174–86; Chinese perspectives on 90–102; Congress 38, 51; Cross-Strait Services Trade Agreement 34; defence budget in 2017 2; domestic dynamics 28–41; economic growth 2; independence movement (*taidu*) 35; military power of 14–15; Ministry of Education 151; Ministry of National Defense 156, 165, 166, 184, 186n2; preferences in the Strait 196–8; as problem or issue 16–21; as small state 13–16; *see also individual entries*

Index

Taiwan-Japan Relations Association 131
Taiwan-Japan-US 'Track II' dialogue 131–2
Taiwan Public Opinion Foundation 127
"Taiwan Question and Reunification of China, the" 17–19
Taiwan Relations Act of 1979 (TRA) 4, 8, 68–9, 91, 116, **144**; China–US rapprochement and 112; defending Taiwan against China 174; foreign policy 147, 152; lasting peace in Taiwan Strait 198; small state survival and 16, 18; strategic future 210, 220, 221; structural weakness and 33; Taiwan–China relations under Tsai government 131; US arms sales to the ROC 51, 99
Taiwan-ROC Diet Members' Consultative Council 127, 128
Taiwan Solidarity Union 31
Taiwan Strait 1, 2, 5–9, 58, 91; armed forces and 156; defending Taiwan against Taiwan 177; differing preferences in 193–8; domestic dynamics and foreign policy 28, 32, 33, 36, 39, 40; Japan–Taiwan relationship and 124; lasting peace, forging 191–204; Ma Ying-jeou rapprochement 82; military balance and US–Taiwan policy 96, 98, 101; periodic shifts between status quo policy and nationalism 79; relationship with great powers 44, 53; small state survival and 14, 16, 18, 19, 21; US–Taiwan relationship and 114, 115, 117
Taiwan Strait Crisis 46, 146
Taiwan Travel Act of 2018 5, 38, 69, 100, 147, 221
Taiwan–China relationship 58–69; Anti-Secession Law and Chen Shui-bian era 62–4; asymmetric trust 73–88; détente during the Ma Ying-jeou era 64–7; early antecedents 59; after the Chiang's 61–2; during the Cold War 59–61; Tsai administration under the curse of 1992 Consensus 67–9; 2020 presidential elections and beyond 69
Taiwanese foreign policy 6, 37–9, 138–52; diversification 148–52; electorate's impact on 139–43; facing China 144–8; implications of 152; key concepts for **143–4**
Taiwanese Japanophiles 127
Taiwanese nationalism: rise of 77–8; and status quo policy, periodic shifts between 79
Taiwan–great powers relationship 6–7, 43–55; during the early Cold War (1949–69) 44–50; after the end of the Cold War 52–4; during the late Cold War (1969–89) 50–2
Taiwan–Japan relationship 48, 123–34; geostrategic and historical context 123–6; limitations of 132–3; sociocultural relations 126–30; under Tsai government 130–2
Taiwan's strategic future, reassessment of 210–22; Chinese power, limits of 212–16; resilience 216–20
Taiwan–US relationship 5, 107–19; China–US rapprochement and 110–13; end of the Cold War 113–14; historical antecedents 107–10; Ma Ying-jeou and Obama administration 114–17
Tan, Andrew T. H. 1, 6, 7, 58, 107, 123
TECRO *see* Taipei Economic and Cultural Representative Office (TECRO)
Thailand 48
Third Plenum of the 11th CPC Central Committee (1978) 76
Third Taiwan Strait Crisis 61
'Third Wave' of democratization 31
Thomas, Nicholas 129
Three Joint Communiques **143**, 145
Tiananmen Square massacre (1989) 28, 113
Tibet 58
Time (magazine) 108
Tito, Josip Broz 44
TRA *see* Taiwan Relations Act of 1979 (TRA)
Trans-Pacific Partnership 115
Truman Administration 44–6, 99, 109
Trump Administration 4, 5, 92, 100, 102, 167, 197–8, 201
Trump, Donald 21, 68, 116–18, 148, 197, 210; Asia 'strategy' 5
Tsai Ing-wen 1, 3, 5, 9; administration under the curse of 1992 Consensus 67–9; and asymmetric trust between

Taiwan–China relationship 86; and Chinese perspectives on Taiwan 90, 91; and cross-Strain relations 92–6; defending Taiwan against China 182; domestic dynamics and foreign policy 29, 36, 37; foreign policy under 37–9, 148; and lasting peace in Taiwan Strait 191–2, 197, 198, 201–3; and New Southbound Policy 149; and Sunflower Movement 83, 84; and Taiwan–Japan relationship 130–2; and Taiwan's foreign policy 138, 139, 147; and Taiwan's relationship with great powers 53, 54; and Taiwan's strategic future 210, 216–18
Tung-hui 195
228 Massacre 30
two state theory 62, 63

UFWD *see* United Front Work Department (UFWD)
Umbrella Movement 195
UN *see* United Nations (UN)
UN Charter: Article 51 15
United Front Work Department (UFWD) 68
United Nations (UN) 13, 16, 22, 28, 40, 50, 58, 110, 114; Framework Convention on Climate Change 212; Security Council 14, 48, 111
United States (USA, US) 5, 6, 13, 16, 29, 40, 43, 45, 124, 151, 211; and China, rivalry between 1, 4, 7, 21, 38; Congress 4, 5, 18, 23, 92, 107, 112, 113, 116, 118, 197, 210; Defense Intelligence Agency 222; Department of Defense 177; Department of State 16; economic growth 2; 11 September 2001 terrorist attacks 32; 'Free and Open Indo-Pacific' strategy 101; Marine Corps 99, 100; Military Assistance Advisory Group 110; National Security Strategy (NSS) 198, 220, 221; relations with Burma 46; relationship with Taiwan 5, 107–19; role in maintaining cross-Strait stability 91; role in Taiwan's defence 220–1; Seventh Fleet 44; State Department 197
US-PRC joint communiqués **143**
USA/US *see* United States (USA, US)
US–China Communiqué on Arms Sales to Taiwan (1982) 112

US–China Economic and Security Review Commission emphasized 212–13
US–China Shanghai Communiqué (1972) 111
US–China 'trade war' 212
USS *Panay* 107
USSR 45, 49, 51
US–Taiwan Mutual Defence Treaty 17, 18, 47, 50, 59–60
US–Taiwan policy, cross-Strait military balance and 96–101

Vatican 3, 212
vote buying 34–5

Wang, Jianwei 81
Wang Yang 87
Washington 34, 44, 46–8, 50, 51, 78, 91–2, 98, 99, 110, 139, 145, 146, 210; containment policy 43; Western European allies 48
Washington–Beijing–Taipei trilateral relations 74, 80
weak states 12, 22–3
Weak States in the International System (Handel) 6
Weber, Max 15
Wei Fenghe 2, 13, 101, 117
Wen Jiabao 114
Sung Wen-ti 7, 73
Western Europe 48
WHA *see* World Health Assembly (WHA)
White Terror 30, 140
Wild Strawberries Movement (2008) 66
Williams, Brad 129
World Health Assembly (WHA) 4, 37, 66, 68, 82, 91, 115, 202, 212
World Press Freedom Index 142
Wright, Martin 12
Wu, Joseph 84, 85

Xi Jinping 1, 7, 9, 118; and Chinese perspectives on Taiwan 90–4; defending Taiwan against China 174; and lasting peace in Taiwan Strait 191–4, 196, 198–200, 202, 203; and small state survival 21; and Taiwan–China relationship 58, 65, 67, 85, 87; and Taiwan's domestic dynamics 29, 34, 38; and Taiwan's foreign policy 29,

34, 38, 140, 147; and Taiwan's strategic future 216, 217
Xinhua News 203n2
Xinjiang 58

Yang, Alan H. 68

Ye Jianying 60
Yoshida, Shigeru 48
Yuan Jingdong 7, 90

Zhu, Keren 203n1

Printed in the United States
by Baker & Taylor Publisher Services